Anaïs Nin

ANAÏS NIN

An Introduction

Benjamin Franklin V and Duane Schneider

Ohio University Press
Athens, Ohio

80-31631

Library of Congress Cataloging in Publication Data

Franklin, Benjamin, 1939–
    Anaïs Nin.

    Bibliography: p.
    Includes index.
    1.   Nin, Anaïs, 1903-1977—Criticism and interpreta-
tion.   I.   Schneider, Duane, joint author.
PS3527.I865Z64   818'.5'209   79-10635
ISBN 0-8214-0395-8
ISBN 0-8214-0432-6 pbk.

For Jo and JoAnne

Contents

Acknowledgments

We are grateful to the Swallow Press, to Harcourt Brace Jovanovich, and to Macmillan Publishing Co. for permission to quote from the works of Anaïs Nin.

Quotations from Nin's fiction and her study of D. H. Lawrence are from the editions published by the Swallow Press.

Children of the Albatross (© 1959)
Collages (© 1964)
D. H. Lawrence: An Unprofessional Study (© 1964)
The Four-Chambered Heart (© 1959)
House of Incest (© 1958)
Ladders to Fire (© 1959)
Seduction of the Minotaur (© 1961)
A Spy in the House of Love (© 1959)
Under a Glass Bell (© 1948)
Winter of Artifice (© 1945, 1946, 1948)

Quotations from *The Diary of Anaïs Nin* are taken from the following volumes: By permission of Harcourt Brace Jovanovich, Inc.; copyright © 1966, 1967, 1969, 1971, 1974, 1976 by Anaïs Nin.

The Diary of Anaïs Nin 1931-1934. Edited and with an Introduction by Gunther Stuhlmann. (Swallow/Harcourt, Brace & World, 1966)
The Diary of Anaïs Nin 1934-1939. Edited and with an Introduction by Gunther Stuhlmann. (Swallow/Harcourt, Brace & World, 1967)
The Diary of Anaïs Nin 1939-1944. Edited and with an Introduction by Gunther Stuhlmann. (Harcourt, Brace & World, 1969)
The Diary of Anaïs Nin 1944-1947. Edited and with an Introduction by Gunther Stuhlmann. (Harcourt Brace Jovanovich, 1971)
The Diary of Anaïs Nin 1947-1955. Edited and with an Introduction by Gunther Stuhlmann. (Harcourt Brace Jovanovich, 1974)
The Diary of Anaïs Nin 1955-1966. Edited and with an Introduction by Gunther Stuhlmann. (Harcourt Brace Jovanovich, 1976)

Quotations from *The Novel of the Future* by permission of the Macmillan Publishing Co. (1968; copyright © 1968 by Anaïs Nin).

A portion of the conclusion appeared in slightly different form in *Dictionary of Literary Biography: American Novelists Since World War II,* ed. Jeffrey Helterman and Richard Layman (Detroit: Bruccoli Clark/Gale Research, 1978).

Preface

Anaïs Nin's fiction is among the most neglected substantial literature of this century. It is not always successful, but in what it attempts and occasionally accomplishes it stands as modern work of the first order in its plumbing of characters' subconscious states. There are two primary reasons for its neglect: first, it appeared at a time that was unpropitious for psychological fiction; second, the popularity of the long-heralded *Diary* elevated Nin (who shares the name of the *Diary*'s persona) above the role of author to that of a celebrity, possibly a cult figure, and certainly to that of one who spoke for thousands of women who saw their own lives reflected and eloquently related in the *Diary*. For these and other reasons Nin the novelist and story writer never received due recognition, even though she regularly made her most honest and profound comments in her fiction, not in her *Diary*, impressive as it is.

The critics have not been kind to Nin. They ignored her for thirty years and then praised her excessively for the *Diary*. Neither response did justice to her work. The early commentators found it generally inpenetrable because of its lack of surface reality, and those who praised her after the publication of the first *Diary* tended to do so for nonliterary reasons. Serious Nin scholarship began with Oliver Evans' study of her work in 1968. It remains valuable. In the 1970s Evelyn Hinz and Sharon Spencer have written perceptive critical books on her *oeuvres*, and Robert Zaller has edited a collection of essays that provides various approaches to and interpretations of Nin's literature.

This volume is an introduction to Nin's various works published during her lifetime. It is for other studies to place her fully in the context of contemporary literature; to define the coterie that she, Henry Miller, Lawrence Durrell, and others formed in Paris during the 1930s; to locate her position as a feminist; to pursue her elusive biography (which is quite different from, or at least much more complex than, the life she portrays in the published *Diary*); and to examine her work using the tools of textual criticism. We hope that we have provided readings of the works that both new and experienced readers of Nin will find useful, but above all we hope that this book will encourage further *serious* study of Anaïs Nin.

Benjamin Franklin V
Duane Schneider

PART 1

Fiction

1

House of Incest

Anaïs Nin's work, particularly her fiction, has never received a wide readership. The reasons for this neglect may reflect not so much on the quality of her work as on the tastes of the reading public, who required chiefly realistic fiction during most of this century. Not one of her thirteen books published prior to 1966 (the date of the first volume of her *Diary*) was widely acclaimed, and only the three-hundred-copy edition of *Under a Glass Bell*, which had been reviewed by Edmund Wilson, reached a second edition in the United States. But with the publication of the long-heralded diaries, and with the advent of the women's liberation movement during the early 1970s, Nin's popularity increased significantly, so much so that the Swallow Press has kept ten of her books in print for a decade. Moreover, she became much in demand as a lecturer, she became a regular contributor of short pieces to magazines, and the prices of her first editions rose more quickly during the 1960s and early 1970s than those of possibly any other author's in recent times.[1]

One must examine why Nin's fiction, which, with the exception of *Collages*, became relatively and increasingly traditional, met with a continuing cool response from American readers. Nin confronts this problem herself in *The Novel of the Future* (1968), where she suggests that all American writers who have dealt with the surreal, "unreal," or the psychological in fiction have met resistance in this country. The reason seems fairly obvious: from the Puritans, to the frontier, to William

3

James, and to this century, Americans have had a pragmatic or realistic philosophic outlook. Yet, despite the dominance of such thought, many American writers have not been cowed by it, and their temperament and artistry have led them to produce fiction that directly opposes it. No American writer has dealt more successfully with the psychological, for example, than Henry James, the great American realist. Nin offers Djuna Barnes, William Goyen, John Hawkes, Nathanael West, Marguerite Young, and others as authors who have presented this alternative literature to a basically hostile environment; but the author in *The Novel of the Future* who receives the greatest attention is Nin herself. She dedicates her book "to sensitive Americans" and adds, "May they create a sensitive America." Possibly she is asking Americans to provide an environment in which the authors mentioned above, and others as well, might flourish; possibly she is upbraiding a culture for failing to recognize her own work that she struggled to produce in a fashion that was honest and grounded in her artistic integrity.

Her first, best, and most challenging volume of prose fiction was all but unknown in America until the late 1950s. *House of Incest*, usually designated a prose poem, is a book of dreams, fantasies, half-realities, visions, interior monologues, and journeys; an esoteric description of a progress through experiences and relationships that actually represent the unnamed narrator dealing with her own multifaceted self.[2] The device employed by the author to reveal the narrator's character is psychological revelation; the world described consists frequently of nebulous images surfacing in the universe of the subconscious. The uninitiated reader of Nin will find this work particularly perplexing, for at first glance there appears to be no context and frame of reference in which to base the action. And yet the reader will surely encounter a voyage through the subconsciousness of the chief character, a journey that depicts and dramatizes a relationship similar to the one designated in Nin's book on Lawrence as showing the "deep, subterranean connection between . . . the 'dark gods' in us."[3] In succinct form, *House of Incest* contains the basic ideas, themes, and images that Nin develops more fully (and yet less satisfactorily) in the five volumes that make up her continuous novel (1946–61). The work is unmatched as her finest example of a fusion of language, tone, poetic style, and diction. The dream, or nightmare, that the narrator recounts is superbly enhanced, as we shall see, by a style that is not simply appropriate to the content, but organically related to it.

One of the overriding questions here, as in all of Nin's work, concerns the nature of reality: what it is, what its benefits and disadvantages may be, and what one's attitude toward it ought to be. This concern permeates *House of Incest*, although the narrator is infrequently in a state of reality (that is, awake). Two such occasions are described in two brief prologues where she relates her conception of the story that is to follow. The first of these prefatory passages is emblematic of the whole work.

ALL THAT I KNOW IS CONTAINED
IN THIS BOOK WRITTEN WITHOUT
WITNESS, AN EDIFICE WITHOUT
DIMENSION, A CITY HANGING IN
THE SKY.

[*Incest*, p. 9]

The suggestion of independent achievement inherent in the images of the amorphous "edifice" and the city suspended from an expanse of sky points to the creation of some sort of structure, an independent and self-sufficient organism that exists in space and yet is unrelated to the environment. It is not a free-flowing figure in the middle of a rigid setting, but a constructed body of material in the context of something approaching a void. This is foremost a statement of a creation. The claim that the author makes here may seem casual or arbitrary, even though one senses a kind of enthusiasm behind it, but one finds that her later work is made up of the themes that are presented in *Incest*, although they are varied and restated. In this way, she is saying more than she intends when she states that "all that I know is contained in this book." She goes on, however, to move from the confines of a book to an "edifice" without dimension and a "city" hanging in the sky. The effect of this movement is to take the reader from the reality of the printed page to the unlimited realm of the narrator's dream and the story that follows (the creation). Boundaries between night and day fade; the conscious and the subconscious merge; all things are possible in the structures of the edifice (house), the city (incestuous community).

An intensity similar to that of the first prologue is present also in the second one, which is a single introductory page describing the morning when the narrator began the book: "The morning I got up to begin this book I coughed. Something was coming out of my throat: it was strangling me" (*Incest*, p. 11). It is her heart (or the book that she is about to present) that has been welling up inside her until she is choked by it. She breaks the thread that holds it, and yanks the heart out: "I went back to bed and said: 'I have just spat out my heart'" (ibid.). The depth of the narrator's feeling is even more intensely conveyed when it is compared to the flute an Indian makes of his dead mistress's bones. Nin strives to combine the two images. The heart, being the seat of the emotions and the symbol of love and passion (and compassion), represents the core of the narrator; it (the heart, the book) must come out, and she will suffer greatly if she does not emit it. The *quena* (an instrument made of human bones) makes a haunting sound, brought on not so much by its actual substance as by the haunting memories associated with it. The narrator combines these two key images in the conclusion to the prologue:

> Those who write know the process. I thought of it as I was spitting out my heart.
> Only I do not wait for my love to die. [Ibid.]

The process that Nin describes is both significant and representative. In her own writing, and especially in the keeping of the diary, one senses the value she placed upon immediacy, taking incidents and experiences and putting them to paper while they were still alive and close. In her essay "On Writing," she describes the process briefly.

> It was while writing a Diary that I discovered how to capture the living moments.
> Keeping a Diary all my life helped me to discover some basic elements essential to the vitality of writing.
> . . . .
> The Diary dealing always with the immediate present, the warm, the near, being written at white heat, developed a love of the living moment, of the immediate emotional reaction to experience, which revealed the power of recreation to lie in the sensibilities rather than in memory or critical intellectual perception.[4]

It is this notion Nin used in the narration of *House of Incest*; events, experiences, and emotions are not so much recalled or remembered by the narrator as they are relived and reexperienced; and those things are internal rather than external to her. Much of the hallucinatory effect is achieved through surrealistic writing in the present tense, which is exactly what is needed to give the effect of living in the dream or the nightmare.

After these prologues the reader is no longer the addressee of the narrator's thoughts, because all seven of the next sections present her dreams, and only infrequently is her consciousness present in the book.

A few more introductory words may be said about the problem of reality in *House of Incest*, as well as its thematic importance in other works. Nin took the view that it is surely necessary to recognize the existence of so-called objective reality, but too great a reliance upon it stifles its opposite, the dream, which is equally as important to the emotional welfare of human beings. In *House of Incest*, however, as nowhere else in her fiction, she employs Jung's dictum to "proceed from the dream outward," although one may question how far out from the dream she progresses. While there are dangers in living too much in reality, there are also dangers in living too exclusively in the dream state. In *House of Incest* the narrator is seldom in a "real" or awakened state after the prologues, and her dream, which is the book, is a nightmare in which she is entrapped. The image of expectorating the heart takes on added significance, then, when one realizes that it is the nightmare (or her season in hell, as Nin sometimes alluded to *House of Incest*) that the narrator produces after the spitting out is completed. Symbolically it might be taken on a dualistic basis: that she must die (spit out the heart) in order to live immortally (in art, in the book). Perhaps there is a narcissistic quality or at least loving of sameness implied in this process; certainly the idea of duality and of the twin is a basic concern in the remainder of the book.

In the first section of *House of Incest* the narrator looks back yearningly on her first vision of the earth.

> My first vision of earth was water veiled. I am of the race of men and women who see all things through this curtain of sea, and my eyes are the color of water.
> . . . .
> I remember my first birth in water. All round me a sulphurous transparency and my bones move as if made of rubber. I sway and float, stand on boneless toes listening for distant sounds, sounds beyond the reach of human ears, see things beyond the reach of human eyes. [*Incest*, p. 15]

For her, this floating and moist existence is clearly a positive one because it is painless; she listens for inaudible sounds, is filled with memories of the lost Atlantide (Atlantis), and is standing forever on the threshold of intimacy. She views this as a "paradise of soundlessness," and once she is ejected from it she may regain it only at night through the dream. Here and throughout the book it is possible to see the physical representing the psychological, for although the narrator is enumerating the pleasant easiness of the dream state, and she finds the surfacing into consciousness undesirable ("a monster brought me up on the surface" [ibid., p. 16]), she reveals that total existence in the dream world is untenable. In dreams she is totally passive; experiencing such painlessness is "like yawning" (ibid). Here there are "no currents of thoughts, only the caress of flow and desire mingling, touching, travelling, withdrawing, wandering—the endless bottoms of peace" (ibid., p. 17). Caresses and other explicit sexual imagery prefigure the psychosexual association that is developed in the next chapter and seems to serve as a bridge to it. But in the first chapter, the dream is always there, "there was always the water to rest on, and the water transmitted the lives and the loves, the words and the thoughts" (ibid., pp. 16–17). But no effort is exerted; there are no feelings, no hunger, no warmth or cold, no fecundity, no passion, no commitment.

The short first section closes with a paragraph of one sentence, however, that casts a new light on what has gone before: "I awoke at dawn, thrown up on a rock, the skeleton of a ship choked in its own sails" (Incest, p. 17). The very means of movement, the sails, paradoxically choke the skeleton of the ship; movement stops, fluidity and rhythm cease as the ship leaves the water; the advancement of the narrator from the world of dreams and painlessness into the world of rock-hard reality is symbolically accomplished. It is an interesting and complex image, because it implies that there are aspects of itself that preclude movement and mobility. Thus in this final passage the narrator is clearly caught in a dilemma: reality is painful, but painlessness and protection are offered only in dreams. Nin herself proposes throughout her work that one must achieve a balance between the two states and that to dwell exclusively in one or the other is to court great danger. And because the narrator does choose to inhabit only the realm of the dream, it is bound soon to become a nightmare.

The narrator slips back into the dream state as the second and longest section begins. "The day and night unglued, and I falling in between not knowing on which layer I was resting, whether it was the cold grey upper leaf of dawn, or the dark layer of night" (Incest, p. 18). As she falls, she encounters Sabina's face suspended in the darkness of the garden, where Sabina's passion, energy, age, weight, and rhythm pervert its natural quality. Here the narrator's focus shifts from herself chiefly to Sabina, who is described in steel imagery to illustrate that in her rigidity and domination of those she meets she is inhuman.

The steel necklace on her throat flashed like summer lightning and the sound of the steel was like the clashing of swords . . . Le pas d'acier . . . The steel of New York's skeleton buried in granite, buried standing up. Le pas d'acier . . . notes hammered on the steel-stringed guitars of the gypsies, on the steel arms of chairs dulled with her breath; steel mail curtains falling like the flail of hail, steel bars and steel barrage cracking. Her necklace thrown around the world's neck, unmeltable. She carried it like a trophy wrung of groaning machinery, to match the inhuman rhythm of her march. [Ibid., p. 21]

Sabina and the narrator turn their "harlot eyes" into each other; Sabina's talk—half-talk, phrases, legends of the men and women she has embraced—resonates in the narrator's memory, and ultimately Sabina becomes part of the narrator: "One woman within another eternally, in a far-reaching procession, shattering my [the narrator's] mind into fragments, into quarter tones which no orchestral baton can ever make whole again" (ibid., p. 22). Here again Nin is arguing that the fusion of similarities (two women in this instance) is untenable and unproductive; in the end the relationship is sterile and can produce nothing. All this, it must be remembered, is played against the backdrop of the opening paragraph in which the narrator finds herself in a kind of limbo between night and day. Further, this woman who at first appears to be distinct from but who becomes a part of the narrator is not a "real" woman with her own identity. Sabina is rather a portion of the narrator's own psychological being that she has been unable to acknowledge, and her interaction with Sabina is part of her subconscious effort to accept herself.

The two women are different in obvious ways: Sabina is dominant and is "an idol in Byzance, an idol dancing with legs parted" (*Incest*, p. 22), while the narrator has gone through life unnoticed, is compelled to ask in a later passage, "DOES ANYONE KNOW WHO I AM?" (ibid., p. 26), and is an author who writes with "pollen and honey" (ibid., p. 22). One is dominant, the other is passive; one is a dynamic dancing idol, the other a writer. An orgiastic trip follows, and one of the most remarkable and evocative passages in the book grows in intensity as the two women walk together. They swallow the asphalt road, the telegraph poles, stray cats (omnivorousness to be outdone only by the ensuing): "Sabina's labyrinthian smile on the keyhole. The door moaning, opening. Her smile closed. A nightingale disleafing melliferous honeysuckle. Honey-suckled. Fluted fingers. The house opened its green gate mouth and swallowed us. The bed was floating" (ibid., pp. 23-24). But the narrator sees ashes beneath Sabina's skin, and almost simultaneously she is aware that Sabina is losing her power of fusion and integration. Even though the narrator realizes that there is no mockery between women, she cannot avoid sensing limitations in Sabina's character and behavior. The reader is hardly aware of this increased awareness on the part of the narrator, but she puts into effect her newfound wisdom by attempting to persuade Sabina to visit her island where there are "ploughmen, trilling, swearing, trilling and cursing, dropping perspiration on the earth with the seeds" (ibid., p. 25). Such an island is only reported and is never seen, because it is only an ideal, a place where there is life and where Sabina and the narrator therefore cannot as yet reside.

At the same time that she evinces awareness of Sabina's short-comings, the narrator also recognizes the strength of Sabina's fantasy. The narrator even goes so far as to announce her intention of helping Sabina destroy reality, but not, we are told, without the narrator dropping behind her "Adriadne's golden thread—for the greatest of all joys is to be able to retrace one's lies" (*Incest,* p. 26). This statement could as easily be made by Nin about the realm of the dream: it is not only good and fertile land to visit, but it is also mandatory to do so in order to give balance and fruitfulness to one's life. Yet, as stated above and throughout *House of Incest,* there is a considerable danger in cultivating the dream exclusively, and one is wise to leave a trail in order to be able to retrace one's steps to reality from the journey into the dream.

Sabina is absent from the last few pages of the second section and from most of the rest of the book, but her relationship with the narrator is somewhat resolved when the narrator urges her to become for only an hour her other self (the softness and love that she has discarded) by embracing the other half of herself in the narrator. The narrator states at the same time that it was only because she adopted some of Sabina's characteristics such as hardness and passion that she was able to write her book, and large, capital letters appear:

I AM THE OTHER FACE OF YOU
....
THIS IS THE BOOK YOU WROTE
AND YOU ARE THE WOMAN
I AM
[*Incest,* p. 28]

That is, the narrator has been able to reveal her inner self by fusing her own being with its missing parts in Sabina; the result (the book) is, she hopes, fertility, fecundity, productivity, and creativity. These are values that Nin must have acquired partly from D. H. Lawrence and his insistence upon wholeness, organicism, and livingness in life. But despite to what degree the narrator in *House of Incest* has become whole, her final words to Sabina suggest that the lesson she has learned is ephemeral: "Only our faces must shine twofold—like day and night—always separated by space and the evolutions of time" (ibid., p. 29). Through a mixture of verb tenses, a complex narrative technique employed here, Nin moves the reader smoothly from the experience of fusion (noted above), to a recollection (the "smoke sent my head to the ceiling"), to a new present tense ("if I only imagined her one night"), and to still a new awareness of reality ("I am freezing and my head falls down through a thin film of smoke. I am searching for Sabina again with deep anguish through the faceless crowd" [ibid.]). The narrator apparently is compelled to continue seeking Sabina in order to reach fulfillment and wholeness, and the search is not for a woman alien to herself but for a part of herself that she cannot acknowledge or assimilate into her conscious self.

The narrator is agitated by the warring factions of anger and love, passion and pity, dancer and writer, Sabina and herself, that struggle within her. They tear and slash at each other as they try to grow separately, and it is a great effort for her to keep them unified. Her only aid is music, a bar of which acts as a panacea and calms the conflicting elements. But even music cannot fuse the narrator with the other face of herself (Sabina), because "the two of us have leaped beyond cohesion" (*Incest*, p. 30). Music functions in Nin's work as a healing and unifying force, but it is not always employed successfully, and often it is with the more dramatic absence or disappearance of music, symbolized by snapped guitar strings, that she is effectively able to suggest the fragmentation of the character under examination.

The second section of *House of Incest* ends with the distintegration of the narrator as she is at home with neither night nor day and crumbles in "a room with a ceiling threatening me like a pair of open scissors" (*Incest,* p. 31). All her connections break, her house becomes empty, and her desire to fuse disparate elements of herself diminishes altogether. So she turns within herself, which is now no longer the pollen and honey as it was with Sabina but is, rather, acidic and self-defeating. She suffers anguish at her divided love: "I writhed within my own life, seeking a free avenue to carry the molten cries, to melt the pain into a cauldron of words for everyone to dip into, everyone who sought words for their own pain. What an enormous cauldron I stir now; enormous mouthfuls of acid I feed the others now, words bitter enough to burn all bitterness" (ibid., p. 32). This "too clear pain of love divided" (ibid., p. 33) seems to spur the narrator on her way, searching, until she comes upon a white path that "sprouted from the heart of the white house" (ibid., p. 34). The house is egg-shaped, which is a significant symbol in Nin's fiction, for eggs, though holding the promise of life, appear as consistently and paradoxically sterile. The cotton carpeting and windowless walls shut out the narrator from the music that might possibly unite her with love, and she becomes inundated with images that render her mind useless: "reality was drowned and fantasies choked each hour of the day" (ibid., p. 34).

The basic unity of structure visible in the second section is more orthodox than it might first appear. For although the section is permeated by a high degree of unity and intensity, beginning with the face of Sabina, the narrator takes the reader on a journey that includes recognition, fusion, fiery climax, opposition, falling off, disintegration, and finally a death: "Nothing seems true today except the death of the goldfish who used to make love at ninety kilometers an hour in the pool. The maid has given him a Christian burial. To the worms! To the worms!" (*Incest*, p. 34). The parallel to the experiences detailed in the second section is explicit.

The short third section, really an interchapter, is one in which the narrator reflects upon herself in a semidream state and ponders how she is affected by dreams and reality: "I am floating again. All the facts and all the words, all images, all presages are sweeping over me, mocking each other. The dream! The dream! . . . I always rise after the crucifixion, and I am in terror of my ascensions. THE FISSURE IN REALITY. The divine departure. I fall. I fall into darkness after the collision with pain, and after pain the divine departure" (*Incest,* p. 37). While elevated in the dream, the only sense she possesses is hearing, and the sounds she hears are primal ones emitted from areas outside normal human experience, though they are "overtones only, or undertones" (ibid., p. 38). For her the dream state contains no essence; instead, all that she hears is filtered through distance (which, in reality, might cure her injuries), and she is discontented with diluted sensation. She compares the distance to a church in which weddings and funerals traditionally occur, both of which are ceremonies characterized by passion, genuine feeling, and some pain as well. But, she states, "I never attended the wedding or the burial. Everything for me took place either in the belfry where I was alone with the deafening sound of bells calling in iron voices, or in the cellar where I nibbled at the candles and the incense stored away with the mice" (ibid., p. 39). She is unable to participate in the human condition. Her plight is similar to that of Henry James's John Marcher who goes through life afraid to experience the love of May Bartram because of some beast in the jungle that he imagines will do something drastic to him. Only when he visits May's grave and sees another man nearby demonstrating grief at the loss of a loved one does Marcher realize, too late, that he has missed life because he refused to participate in it. The narrator's plight in *House of Incest* is even more pathetic than Marcher's, because she is aware all along that she is missing life, but she is unable to bear the pain that is required to experience it. Yet, all is not hopeless for her; although she admits that "there is a fissure in my vision and madness will always rush through," at the same time she is able to call out to humanity at large for assistance, "Lean over me, at the bedside of my madness, and let me stand without crutches" (ibid.). Her plea is of the anguished kind that the modern reader senses so poignantly in the characters of Samuel Beckett. She desires desperately to attain wholeness; her humanity is made manifest by her cry for help from other human beings. She concludes the third section with some hopefulness: "I walk ahead of myself in perpetual expectancy of miracles" (ibid., p. 40), but she feels enmeshed in her lies; the truth would be "death-dealing." She thinks it better to prefer fairy tales and the dream when the pain of reality becomes too intense.

Sabina is replaced in the fourth section by Jeanne as the woman with whom the narrator is concerned. Unlike the vibrant Sabina, Jeanne, as part of the narrator's psychological makeup, is another woman who is frightened by reality and its painfulness: she is unable to consummate a sexual relationship with her fiancé. When the bells ring to announce their wedding, the sounds are so harsh that she backs away from that pain and, by extension, from the possibility of pain with the man, and she isolates herself in the love of her brother. Jeanne represents the narrator's fear of reality, and neither is able to find a satisfactory refuge from it. Jeanne's physical makeup is a key to her psychological state. Her eyes are above the usual level of human eyes, but she is forever tied to the earth (reality) quite literally by her crippled leg that drags behind her everywhere she goes. She is a narcissistic woman painfully aware of her defects. Through music she attempts to establish a rhythm to unify her disparaties. But as she tunes the guitar strings, one of them breaks; music and rhythm are impossible for her, and she becomes aware of her plight as "her eyes were terror-stricken as by the snapping of her universe" (*Incest*, p. 44). And as her more-or-less normal world is destroyed, she reveals that she loves her brother and then looks lovingly at herself in a mirror. Incest and narcissism, then, are two of the insular results of her incompleteness that might have been avoided had she not been prevented from finding sustenance in the dream. Her life becomes nonproductive as she loves herself within another, her brother, just as the narrator does with Sabina. Nothing fruitful can be produced by a wedding of similarities. The reader will infer from Nin's comments on Lawrence that tension, polarity, and flux can have positive values and, as Blake says, lead to progression. Jeanne is aware of her condition and considers it ambivalently: "I have such a fear of finding another like myself, and such a desire to find one! I am so utterly lonely, but I also have such a fear that my isolation be broken through, and I no longer be the head and ruler of my universe. I am in great terror of your understanding by which you penetrate into my world; and then I stand revealed and I have to share my kingdom with you" (ibid., pp. 46-47). Despite this fear of being known by the narrator, she nonetheless performs her new role of adviser to herself (Jeanne) and states one of the key themes that Nin is trying to emphasize in this work: insularity leads to madness, and it is only the fear of madness that may lead one to leave solitude, to "burn down the walls of our secret house and send us out into the world seeking warm contact. Worlds self-made and self-nourished are so full of ghosts and monsters" (ibid., p. 47). This belief in man, this attitude that appears to be complete faith, ultimately, in the human condition, is what the characters in this and all Nin's works must learn, but here the narrator is unable to convince herself of this verity. Instead, as this section ends, Jeanne attempts to kiss her brother but instead kisses his shadow. Not only does she fail to consummate the incestuous relationship, but her new paramour is her brother's shadow.

One problem in narration that develops in this section is an aspect of *House of Incest* that may be especially perplexing to the reader. Often the speakers of the various passages (cast into alternating dialogue) are difficult to identify, and when Jeanne is speaking, her voice is occasionally indistinguishable from the narrator's. But such confusion may be understandable when one recognizes that the dialogue is all

taking place in the narrator's mind. There are twenty-two paragraphs
in this section (if one counts "I LOVE MY BROTHER!" as part of the
fifteenth), and the speakers of each of them may be identified by the
following chart. In every instance in this section, the first person is
Jeanne.

Paragraph	Speaker
1	Narrator
2	Narrator
3	Narrator
4	Narrator
5	Narrator and Jeanne
6	Jeanne
7	Narrator
8	Jeanne
9	Narrator
10	Narrator
11	Jeanne
12	Narrator
13	Jeanne
14	Narrator
15	Jeanne
16	Narrator
17	Jeanne
18	Narrator
19	Jeanne
20	Jeanne
21	Narrator
22	Jeanne

After giving advice to Jeanne that she cannot herself heed in the
fourth section, the narrator follows her to the house of incest, which is a
difficult edifice to locate because it is "the only house which was not
included in the twelve houses of the zodiac" (*Incest*, p. 51). The house
itself is static, lacking, as it does, any sense of flow or fertility. Each
room is on a different level, and the windows function as spyglasses, but
ironically they permit no visual contact between individuals: "little
spying-eyed windows, so that one might talk in the dark from room to
room, without seeing the other's face" (ibid.). A rhythm in the rooms
comes not from the sea but from many seashells: "Everything had been

made to stand still in the house of incest, because they all had such a fear of movement and warmth, such a fear that all love and all life should flow out of reach and be lost!" (ibid., p. 52). Even the narrator is appalled at this stasis and sterility. She had advised Jeanne against such a life before, and the conditions she views in the house of incest help to substantiate her earlier belief. As she gains an awareness of the part of herself that is Jeanne, she is able to accept and deal with it maturely and critically, although she as a whole woman who is at ease with all parts of herself remains an unattainable state.

The house of incest and its inhabitants are doomed if only because the physical surroundings are as deadly as the house itself. Outside the house is a "forest of decapitated trees, women carved out of bamboo, flesh slatted like that of slaves in joyless slavery" (*Incest*, p. 55), and faces that are separated by a fissure, as Sabina's and the narrator's were, and that shall never become whole. But beyond the forest is yet another of white plaster eggs that are "an elegy to birth" (ibid., p. 56). So even though the decapitated trees of the other forest are a perversion of nature and fecundity, they can nonetheless reproduce branches endlessly and so stand in contrast to the forest of white plaster eggs as well as to the inhabitants of the house of incest. The fate of Jeanne and her brother is clear; not only is their perverse house surrounded by two rings of perverse forests, but the room Jeanne and her brother occupy is a fortress that, like the house itself, cannot be found because it has no window, a room "where the mind and blood coalesced in a union without orgasm. . . . The promiscuity of glances, of phrases, like sparks marrying in space. The collision between their resemblances, shedding the odor of tamarisk and sand, of rotted shells and dying sea-weeds, their love like the ink of squids, a banquet of poisons" (ibid., p. 52).

The brother has disappeared, and in the sixth section Jeanne searches for him. As she examines the exterior of the house for the one window that will lead to him, she hastens to the house's garden of dried semen, dead trees, and minerals. It is a silent, painless scene that is attractive to her. She finds her brother as she notices "one window with the blind shut tight and rusty, one window without light like a dead eye, choked by the hairy long arm of old ivy" (*Incest*, p. 60). She trembles; even she is appalled by her own lack of outrage at this cryptlike existence that she and others have chosen: "She struggled with her death coming: I do not love anyone; I love no one, not even my brother. I love nothing but this absence of pain, this cold neutral absence of pain" (ibid.). Being enamored of the painlessness of life in the house of incest, she cannot exert herself to save her life. When she finally reaches her brother, he is asleep before a portrait of her; he tells her that he fell asleep among the paintings where he could worship her unchanging portrait. He would not have to accommodate those changes that would occur as she aged:

> They bowed to one part of themselves only—their likeness.
> Good night, my brother!
> Good night, Jeanne!
> With her walked distended shadows, stigmatized by fear. They carried their compact like a jewel on their breast; they wore it proudly like their coat of arms. [Ibid., p. 61]

There appears to be little hope for them, or for the narrator whose psychic parts they are.

The final section begins with the narrator's recapitulation of what has gone before. She began the book (entered her dream) to find peace, but she has found that total existence there is as dangerous and as unpleasant as a life lived entirely in reality without the dream as a place of refuge. She begins to feel that she has been repeating herself, and indeed the theme is one which the book insists upon many times; but she tries for one final time to summarize her basic notion: "LIES CREATE SOLITUDE" (*Incest*, p. 67). What she means is now explicit: incest, narcissism, sterility, and other similar qualities that are associated with these characters are lies because they are out of balance with the basic nature of things, they upset the natural order of the human condition, and they lead to a self-defeating insularity. The logic of this is tautological, because it is difficult to discern whether lies create solitude or solitude creates lies, but in the end it does not matter because the result is the same. After this comment the narrator visits, as a spectator, three other inhabitants of the house of incest, all of whom, like Sabina and Jeanne, represent different parts of herself, although one senses that they are now diminished parts.

The first of these is an unfeeling paralytic with transparent skin; he wishes most to capture his elusive thoughts so that he will be able to tell what he thinks is "the whole truth." But in order to tell the truth he would have to write four pages at once, a symbolic way of suggesting that truth is a composite of multiple views rather than one single perspective. He is not a developed character; he functions primarily as a forerunner of the modern Christ "who is crucified by his own nerves, for all our neurotic sins!" (*Incest*, p. 68). The paralytic, whom one assumes to be paralyzed by his own neurosis, bows and introduces the modern Christ to Sabina, Jeanne, and the narrator. Sitting in an agony of drug-torture, the modern Christ is addressed by the narrator, who indicates that in their writings they are brothers, both using the "language of nerves" and having "arrived at the same place at the same moment" (ibid.), namely, in the house of incest. The modern Christ is in the house of incest for a number of reasons, but chiefly because he feels everything and is hurt by contact with other people. He is there for protection against life; the paralytic is there because he cannot feel life. Ironically, the modern Christ is unable to save himself or others from the house of incest and its dangers, but he is able to perceive, at last, that life there is not life at all: "If only," he says, "we could all escape from this house of incest, where we only love ourselves in the other, if only I could save you all from yourselves" (ibid., p. 70). But, he goes on to say, none of them could be moved to pass through the tunnel leading from the house into the world; fear, hopelessness, and despair prevent them from believing in what is, after all, the only true remedy for their ills. He is speaking here for the narrator's emerging mature consciousness.

The last character to be introduced is the only one in the entire book who is able to escape from the house of incest and find wholeness in life. Identified only as a dancer, this woman is in the house of incest because of her formerly selfish and possessive nature; her inability to relinquish her hold on people and things she has loved led her, figuratively, to lose her arms and to dance in hope of regaining them. Her dancing is futile, though, because she is dancing to a rhythm that is unheard by the others. But finally, in the grand climax to the book, the dancer regains her arms.

> She looked at her hands tightly closed and opened them slowly, opened them completely like Christ; she opened them in a gesture of abandon and giving; she relinquished and forgave, opening her arms and her hands, permitting all things to flow away and beyond her.
> I could not bear the passing of things. All flowing, all passing, all movement choked me with anguish.
> And she danced; she danced *with* the music and *with* the rhythm of earth's circles; she turned *with* the earth turning, like a disk, turning all faces to light and to darkness evenly, dancing towards daylight. [*Incest*, pp. 71–72, italics added]

It is difficult to discern whether the speaker in the penultimate paragraph is the narrator or the dancer, but it matters little because it indicates the fusion of the two and suggests that the condition that led them to the house of incest has been remedied: the dancer finds a natural rhythm which she now dances to; she is able to give to others; and she is now a part of the flow of life, dancing toward daylight, promise, and life. And inasmuch as all of the other characters are part of the narrator's true self, so too is the dancer. When she regains her arms and dances *with* the music, the narrator recognizes her complete self and her relationship to life and is able to end her nightmare of fragmentation, narcissism, incest, and isolation, becoming a woman at ease with her complete self. The dream that is the book has been of great benefit, because it has permitted her to acknowledge her true self; but had she continued to reside there the results would have been quite different. It is a crucial point that as she finds herself she leaves her nightmare. She will obviously dream subsequently, but those dreams will be of a shorter duration than this one and will be a source of stimulation and life for her.

House of Incest is a strange and challenging work that demands the full attention of the reader. It is not so much a story of people (although it certainly is that) as it is a visit into the hellish nightmare of the narrator's experience from which she emerges satisfactorily. But however one approaches the work, *House of Incest* is Nin's best piece of fiction and one that contains most of the basic themes, images, and patterns that she would use in her later work.

2

Winter of Artifice

An author's second book has traditionally been the most difficult to write because something approaching all that he knows has been spent in his first effort. Nin states as much at the outset of *House of Incest,* and she was never able to match the artistry of that first work of fiction. Her second, *The Winter of Artifice* (1939), contains many of the themes of the prose-poem, but this collection of novelettes is not as tightly or convincingly written as its predecessor. Of all of her works she seems to have had the most difficulty with this one: she signed a contract for it as early as 1935, she decided upon its final contents only after two decades and five editions, she permanently cast aside one novelette and completely rewrote two others after the 1939 edition, and she evidently felt so strongly that the contents of the first edition were inadequate that a revised *Winter of Artifice* was the first volume she published under the imprint of her own Gemor Press in New York in 1942. Further, in 1939, the year of the first edition, World War II was beginning, Nin misplaced numerous copies of what must have been a small press run, copies sent to America were impounded by the postal authorities (this according to Nin, without documentation), and she and her friends were in the process of fleeing Paris and Europe for New York and America.[1] With this turmoil surrounding its writing and publication it is surprising that *Winter of Artifice* is as good as it is.

As originally published, *The Winter of Artifice* contained three sections. The first, "Djuna," has never been reprinted, although there are analogues and parallel episodes in the first volume of the *Diary*. "Lilith," the second section, eventually became entitled "Winter of Artifice." The third part, "The Voice," has always been retained in later editions, although it, like "Lilith," went through a number of substantial alterations in text, stylistics, and tone.

The collection has been designated as *Winter of Artifice,* with no definite article, in every edition after the first. "Stella," now placed first in the volume as it is constituted, was never a part of the collection of novelettes prior to 1961. It originally appeared in *This Hunger* (1945), another collection of Nin's novelettes that was never reprinted and whose contents were used later in other books. "Stella" appeared for the second time in *Harper's Bazaar* (August 1946), and also in that year it became the first section of Nin's first novel, *Ladders to Fire,* but it has not appeared again in that work.[2] Although such changes might lead one to question the organic integrity of *Ladders to Fire* and, to a lesser degree, *Winter of Artifice,* her work, as has been suggested, is mostly of one piece and a repositioning of one part of the tapestry does not necessarily violate or corrupt its texture.

"Stella"

Stella is a movie star (this is implicit in her name) who is unable to reconcile her image on the screen with her real self. On the screen she is glamorous, larger than life, graceful, and perfectly able to satisfy the fantasies of the audience; in the reality of existence off the screen she is, to her own way of thinking, a small, mousy individual who is filled with doubt and insecurity. In her attempt to overcome the disparity between the two Stellas, she surrounds herself with glamorous accoutrements: a "Movie Star bed of white satin" (*Artifice,* p. 10), rows of shoes, a closet full of hats, and a room of mirrors. All of these, of course, are ineffectual because it is Stella herself who impedes her growth into wholeness. The real Stella is, in fact, jealous of her image on film and so imitates that; it is the screen Stella who earns the love and responses of the people; it is the screen Stella whom the people come near and touch and love. More importantly, it is the screen Stella who is free; it is this woman whom the people court. The neurosis of the real-life Stella exists partly because of this disparity between the reality and the image, but it is also nurtured by her own inner obstacles that keep her stature small in her own eyes. The irony of her situation becomes clear: she is not so limited as she thinks she is; also, it is her image on the screen that is able to bring happiness (love) to the movie audience, whose limitations are her own; and, finally, the ideal to which she actually aspires (the fantasy life of glamour) is not only unattainable but also undesirable. Every one of Nin's women is haunted to one degree or another by this problem of incompleteness.

What Stella wants is joy, especially joy as love, for this is what she had taken away from her in her youth. Yet, instead of explaining fully the circumstances of Stella's painful childhood, Nin takes the reader to the time when, later in life, she has as a lover Bruno, who is a married man with whom she is destined to be unhappy. His qualities oppose her own. Although it is the yoking together of opposites rather than similarities that is consistently encouraged in Nin's work, here it produces nothing because of Stella's jealousy and her inability to function maturely. When she does move in rhythm with Bruno, she immediately moves into a vast world where the joy she attains is so intense that Bruno is unable to share in it. Consequently, what she thereby achieves is a split between reality (human love) and an unattainable ideal (her exuberance), which is a dichotomy similar to the separation of the real self and her screen image. This is one of the themes that is basic to Nin's work.

The love of Stella and Bruno is doomed when Stella goes outside the realm of humanity (always a dangerous direction in Nin's fiction), but it is also doomed by her inability to love Bruno on a human level. She is possessive; she needs continual assurance of his love (as she tries to reassure herself by gathering luxurious objects about her). But when she suspects him of neglecting her (as when he arrives at the hotel without his valise) she feels betrayed and withdraws from him. The love she offers is a love of doubt and suspicion, a love that is unsatisfactory because it is less than an absolute, ideal love. Neither Bruno nor anyone else can meet her demands.

Bruno's own life with his wife and children has become routine; certainly he has found a new vitality in his relationship with Stella, but, unlike her, he will not take his love outside human bounds because he cannot give all to love. Bruno needs moorings (contacts with reality, one might call them) in order for his love to be sincere and to survive. If he were to lose himself in love, as Stella does, it would be counterfeit because it would be rootless. So when Stella finds his love limited, she feels a sense of frustration that is understandable but that stands as a more important symptom of the deeper frustration that has been hers since childhood. No man can fulfill her needs.

After this focus on Stella's involvement with him, Bruno appears only once more in the story, but their relationship is summarized symbolically in the sixth of the twelve sections that comprise the novelette. Immediately prior to this section Stella has fled from him and has experienced real human emotion (exemplified in the tangibility of the tears she shed). Soon thereafter Bruno calls her on the telephone at a pre-arranged time, but instead of answering it, she plays a recording of a concerto and ascends the small stairway leading to her bedroom. She is unable to answer his call because she has lost the feeling that she felt when she cried, and she has now thrown her vision "back into seclusion again, into the wall of the self" as she enters "the solitary cell of the neurotic" (*Artifice*, p. 25). Throughout this section Stella is confused, altering the natural qualities of music and the telephone. Music, which usually serves as a unifying device in Nin's work, is used here by Stella to move her toward isolation. The telephone, being mechanical and cold, yet bearing the warm voice of Bruno, is disregarded, though it ought to function as a medium for connecting the two lovers. Stella further simplifies and distorts the nature of the music she hears when she perceives in the trombone a caricature of men and in the flutes the essence of women, so that she takes great pride in hearing the flutes (of Stella) emerge victorious over the trombones (of Bruno): "And as for the flute, it was so easily victimized and overpowered. But it triumphed ultimately because it left an echo. Long after the trombone had had its say, the flute continued its mischievous, insistent tremolos" (ibid., p. 26). When the telephone rings again, Stella moves farther up the stairs, away from the caller: "Fortunate for her that the trombone was a caricature of masculinity, that it was an inflated trombone, drowning the sound of the telephone. So she smiled one of her eerie smiles, pixen and vixen too, at the masculine pretensions. Fortunate for her that the flute persisted in its delicate undulations, and that not once in the concerto did they marry but played in constant opposition to each other throughout" (ibid.). Aloft in her solitary cell, the music that helped her gain that isolated height is "without the power to suck her back into the life with Bruno and into the undertows of suffering" (ibid.). Here, as elsewhere, the ideal is untenable; isolation is self-defeating; and in order to experience love and life, one must accept pain and imperfection. In this way, Stella's performance not on the screen, but in real life with

Bruno (especially in the sixth section), serves symbolically as a vivid example of this recurring truth in Nin's fiction. It is an idea similar to the one that Hawthorne wrote about so persistently. When Aylmer eradicates his wife Georgiana's birthmark so that she will be perfect, she can only die. Perfection is not of this world, and to approach attaining it is a kind of imperfection because one is necessarily dehumanized. Conversely, to accept imperfection is a form of perfection because it is accepting the realities of the human condition. Hawthorne's narrator states this position effectively; Georgiana's birthmark is "the fatal flaw of humanity, which Nature, in one shape or another, stamps ineffaceably on all her productions, either to imply that they are temporary and finite, or that their perfection must be wrought by toil and pain. The Crimson Hand [the birthmark] expressed the ineludible gripe, in which mortality clutches the highest and purest of earthly mould, degrading them into kindred with the lowest, and even with the very brutes, like whom their visible frames return to dust."[3]

The sixth section is a symbolic portrait of Stella's relationship with Bruno; the next symbolizes the origin of her trouble. After the concerto scene, Stella goes to her bedroom in which she keeps her movie-star accoutrements, the objects that nurture her own false view of herself. Although she is feeling lighthearted from having ascended the staircase, she is also feeling considerable pain. The irony is clear. She is suffering from having cut herself off from a human relationship, but the relationship itself brought her anguish. She frightens herself by discovering that she has been seeking pain all along; she brands herself a masochist. This kind of self-analysis is, in Stella's case, neither whimsical nor casual, for she is attempting to learn the source of the suffering that has been hers for so long. But she is unable to discover the true cause of her psychological difficulty. Shortly after this point in the narrative, Stella views a movie about Atlantis that is accompanied by Stravinsky's music. On the screen she sees images that take her back to the painless and rhythmic prebirth of Atlantis and the world (her own prenatal life); she dissolves into the "paradise of water and softness" (*Artifice,* p. 29), just as the narrator does at the beginning of *House of Incest.* The peace of the prebirth is short-lived, however, for an explosion causes a new continent to be born above the old, submerged one. Atlantis and Stella disappear; earth reforms itself after multiple explosions; and in the new world that develops, Stella views a small and insignificant figure that is obviously herself. She has now arrived, in her own subconsciousness, at the cause of her years of suffering: as the world began with an explosion, so did her own life, but the result was the fragmentation of herself into many separate parts and lives that did not cohere, that were not linked, that did not form a whole. She recalls several incidents from her childhood that caused her considerable pain and embarrassment. A child is normally at one with himself, but as she reflects upon her past, she realizes that by the time she was eleven no image of herself had evolved; but more importantly, perhaps, she recognizes that by the time she was fourteen she had begun to disguise herself as an "actress multiplied into many personages" (ibid., p. 31). More astonishing is her conviction that she could possibly regain her lost vision of herself only by *acting* herself, thus recreating herself into a whole and single being. This self-prescribed remedy will not do, however. Although one "can look back upon a certain scene of life and see only a part of the truth," later

> a deeper insight, a deeper experience will add the missing aspects to the past scene, to the lost character only partially seen and felt. Still later another will appear. So that with time, and with time and awareness only, the scene and the person become complete, fully heard and fully seen.
> Inside of the being there is a defective mirror, a mirror distorted by the fog of solitude, of shyness, by the climate inside of this particular being. It is a personal mirror, lodged in every subjective, interiorized form of life. [Ibid., p. 33]

As unsatisfactory as Stella's state is, she is in a better condition than the narrator at the outset of *House of Incest* who yearns for the state of prebirth and nonlife of the Atlantide and finally becomes entrapped in an incestuous house. Stella laments the loss of a painless life, but she is able to function, though less than totally, in reality and in society.

Most of the remainder of the novelette concerns her father, who was the real culprit in her life. He is an actor who left his family and destroyed their ability to love. This man, who is central to most of *Winter of Artifice,* is now married to a girl-woman named Laura who is described in terms similar to those used to characterize the titular figure in "The Mouse." The father's treatment of Laura parallels his behavior with Stella's mother; in all relationships he seems to function as one who is detached, not as a person with human sympathies. He wears sterile clothes; he keeps people at a distance and considers them to be intruders in his life. It was he, of course, who caused Stella's suffering. When she had been twelve years old and living in a state of want and need, her father would occasionally entertain her in a grand and opulent fashion, but then he would return her to a life of poverty with her mother. This recurring disparity between the real and the ideal evolved into her psychological problem and explains why she—functioning, actually, in a manner similar to her father—is unable to sustain a relationship with Bruno. There is a key difference, however, between the father and the daughter: he pretends to be something he is not (an ideal), while she aspires to regain a reality that truly exists within her. Her father functions as a cold and impersonal human being who is directly responsible for the unhappy plight of his daughter, but he also kills the love of his former wife (Stella's mother) and of Laura. When he suffers a heart attack, he is acting out in reality a physical death that mirrors the psychological distance he has maintained from mankind. When his heart falters he must die, for he draws his sustenance from women; and yet he kills the love of the three women closest to him. At what must be his death, only Stella of the three is there to comfort him, not because she loves him, but because she feels a closeness to him as a fellow human being. His death then, is, in a sense, a suicide.

The remainder of the story unwinds quickly as Stella becomes enamored of Philip, a Don Juan who represents joy and happiness to her. One day he asks her to wait for him in his apartment, and while she is there she examines the articles in his bedroom and discovers a set of silver toilet articles similar to those of her father. Her father thus reappears in Philip so that she concludes her story with a future resembling her past: she anticipates that once his glamorous appeal has subsided, he will treat her as her father has treated her. She recalls, simultaneously, the past and future loss of love and recognizes that the "people who fall in love with the performers are like those who fall in love with magicians; they are the ones who cannot create the illusion or magic with the love—the mise-en-scene, the producer, the music, the role, which surrounds the personage with all that desire requires" (*Artifice*, p. 52). At the end Stella has no one, not Bruno, Philip, her father, nor any other human being. She was strangled in her childhood and youth by her father, and she has not yet learned to breathe again: "How could joy have vanished with the father?" (ibid., p. 53), she asks. The answer is inexplicable, but it happened, and part of the answer may lie in the fact that "human beings have a million little doorways of communication. When they feel threatened they close them, barricade themselves. Stella closed them all. Suffocation set in. Asphyxiation of the feelings" (ibid., p. 54). Her image, "the outer shell of Stella," continues to appear on the screen. But she recognizes that the rare bouquets sent by her fans are more appropriately to be labeled as flowers for the dead, for Stella is as close to life-in-death as any person can be.

"Winter of Artifice"

"Winter of Artifice" was published originally in the 1939 collection under the title "Lilith," though the text came to be greatly altered. For example, in its earlier version Lilith narrates the story, but later Nin recast it into the third-person point of view. One cannot help but recognize that in some ways the first-person point of view is strikingly more effective in a story that recounts the events of a daughter's reunion with her father after twenty years' absence. One might consider, for example, the different effects of the two following passages, the first from the 1939 version, the second from the revised text.

> I am waiting for him. I have waited for him for twenty years. He is coming to-day.
> She is waiting for him. She was waiting for him for twenty years. He is coming today.[4]

The first passage is immediate and engaging; the second is much more ordinary and flat. At any rate, this change of perspective is one of many substantial textual alterations that Nin made, and it may stand as an example of the care that she took in revising her works through the years. Nin's decision to place "Winter of Artifice" after "Stella" was logical; it demonstrates as well her care in organizing materials. Although "Stella" was published six years after the original version of "Winter of Artifice," it is well to have it precede the second novelette. Stella's story is only partly concerned with her father, but his importance is so great to her that the reader may wish to know more about this man who deserted his family, thereby leaving indelible emotional scars on his only daughter. His full portrait is revealed in "Winter of Artifice" after having been introduced to the reader in "Stella."

In "Winter of Artifice" neither the father nor the daughter is named, but this fact does not detract from the sense of continuity that extends from the first novelette to the second, because the basic nature of the two is the same: the daughter is devoted to the superficial father, and in both stories the father is married to a woman named Laura. Instead of an actor the father is now a pianist.

For the twenty years since he had abandoned her when she was eleven, this daughter, whom we shall call Stella, has yearned to be reunited with her father, a man who has been her ideal for those two decades. The present events in the story depict their reunion and their new life together, though the reader is frequently taken into the daughter's youth and the intervening years so that one might see the effect of the father's absence upon her. A key cluster of symbols informs the daughter's existence during these years of waiting: "This glass bowl with the glass fish and the glass ship—it has been the sea for her and the ship which carried her away from him after he had abandoned her. Why has she loved ships so deeply, why has she always wanted to sail away from this world? Why has she always dreamed of flight, of departure?" (*Artifice*, p. 55). An abandoned child would understandably love or hate (or love and hate) a delinquent parent, and perhaps especially one of the opposite sex, but the effect on Stella is to isolate her from humanity, just as the characters from *House of Incest* are isolated, and just as Stella cannot find authentic relationships with Bruno and Philip. Ever since her father left her, Stella has tried to flee from the past and from real life by means of the glass ship in the glass bowl. This necessarily fragile mode of transportation may be linked to one of her chief memories of her father, his standing isolated behind a window, showing obvious disgust at being bothered by his family. She has taken this glass window, transformed it into a boat, and, embracing her father psychologically, has sought refuge from this world. But when she is actually reunited with him and he promises to take her with him to the south of France, "she leaned backwards, pushing the crystal bowl against the wall. It cracked and the water gushed forth as from a fountain, splashing all over the floor. The glass ship could no longer sail away—it was lying on its side, on the rock-crystal stones" (ibid., p. 69). Her father has returned, the lost love has supposedly been recaptured, and their future together appears promising; so her fragile evasions of life no longer seem necessary. At the end of the story, however, the "rock-crystal stones" that demolished her insular life have turned into a destructive force that not only destroys fragile ships but also substantial loves. When the bowl breaks, the daughter observes, "Perhaps I've arrived at my port at last. . . . Perhaps I've come to the end of my wanderings" (ibid.). But this is not to be the case, because only the illusion of a better future lies before her upon her father's return.

Only infrequently in Nin's work is a male character developed in such detail as Stella's father is in "Winter of Artifice." Usually men—

husbands and lovers—are present to help point up certain characteristics of the women with whom they are associated. This is an artistically sound device, for it is the women who function as the chief characters. In this story the man is neither a husband nor a lover to Stella, although there are suggestions and impulses of these relationships; here, rather, the father is a highly symbolic character who is presented fully because he is at the core of Stella's problems. In a sense he may stand for the father image that is so important to Nin herself in the *Diary*. Stella's father is a musician of some reputation who, ironically, is unable to transfer to life any of the sensitivity he displays in his art. He walks out of step with the rest of humanity. He has been loved by women and he has fathered children, but he is unsuccessful as a husband, lover, and father because he is unable to give of himself in a human relationship. He views women as sexual conveniences and has little regard for them as human beings; he views his own children as casually and impersonally as he does women and other human beings. He tends to be cold, superficial, and insensitive to the feelings of others; a man who is elegant in his gloves and filter-tipped cigarettes, but one whose elegance betrays a goodness basic to people (love, compassion, feeling) and so leads ultimately to his isolation from others. He is a man of the mind and not of the heart; he is reminiscent of many other characters in literature, including Hawthorne's Chillingworth, Aylmer, and Ethan Brand; Joyce's James Duffy; as well as a number of Henry James's characters.

Stella, in contrast, is a woman of feelings and of the heart, but she has not been able to love as she ought because of the destructive impact upon her of the father's desertion. The natural love of the daughter for the father was violently crushed, and the vividness with which Nin portrays the entire desertion scene is powerful, thereby providing heightened expectations from the daughter (and consequently from the reader) when the father is about to return. "Since that day she had not seen her father. Twenty years have passed. He is coming today" (*Artifice*, p. 60). But during these past twenty years she has been an unfulfilled woman, incapable of loving others fully (as she herself was unloved). Even though he treated her coldly and critically—sometimes cruelly so— when he was part of the family, at least then he was accessible to her; it is his absence rather than his typical inhumaneness that has oppressed her for so long.

As a youth Stella wanted to be an artist because her father was one;

but rather than pursue her desires and talents, she established a barrier between herself and life. When her father left, she tied herself to him emotionally in a lengthy letter that became her diary and that "was a monologue, or dialogue, dedicated to him, inspired by the superabundance of thoughts and feelings caused by the pain of leaving him" (*Artifice*, p. 60). The letter becomes more than she had intended; although it had been meant to be an avenue for the revelation of her love for her father, by accident it became a place for seclusion, a wall behind which she could escape pains and frustrations, and so she was shut off from the explorations that are a part of a normal childhood. At that time her mother had great difficulty keeping her family together in the United States, which was a new country to them, and therefore the mother was not as sensitive to the needs of her daughter as she might otherwise have been. And so, with both parents absent, as it were, Stella found it necessary to pursue at least one of them rather than to face alone the alien world of New York City. This pursuit took the form of writing and living in the diary, the letter to her father, where increasingly she found happiness and security in her solitude. Her love for him flourished because he remained an ideal in her mind, and for twenty years he was to be one of the most important persons in her life and perhaps the most important one of all. She began to realize the dangers of her insular existence in the diary as she grew into womanhood, and indeed it had become to some extent her shadow, or her double, functioning in the same way that the concepts of incest and narcissism operate in *House of Incest*. She awaits her father in Paris at the age of thirty-one, hoping he will become once again her real father and thus permit her to cease writing and living in her diary.

As one might expect, she is totally disappointed. Just as her father could not accept the responsibility of parenthood years before, so is he no more capable of responsible fatherhood now. When he and his daughter are reunited, he is the possessive, jealous lover (like the dancer in *House of Incest*) who wants his daughter's love exclusively for himself. At long last, in a scene of heightened intensity, she is able to present to him the diary that had been intended to be "a revelation of her love for him" (*Artifice*, p. 66). His reaction is precisely the opposite of what she had intended and hoped for.

> Her father's jealousy began with the reading of her diary. He observed that after two years of obsessional yearning for him she had finally exhausted her suffering and obtained serenity. After serenity she had fallen

in love with an Irish boy and then with a violinist. He was offended that she had not died completely, that she had not spent the rest of her life yearning for him. He did not understand that she had continued to love him better by living than by dying for him. She had loved him in life, lived for him and created for him. She had written the diary for him. . . . She had loved him in life creatively by writing about him. [Ibid., p. 79]

There is no response of affection or love from him. And Stella responds predictably to this criticism, disavowing her love of others and subordinating her real self to him. This possessiveness further suggests the father's cruelty and insensitivity: he wants her entirely for himself, but he seems to want to give her nothing. If he could have his wish, she would be something like an Amazon who could care for herself and not need to depend upon him for anything. But Stella is now a woman and responds much differently to her father and his attitudes than the way she had reacted as a child; she now sees that the father she has loved and yearned for is neither a father nor a man; he is a child who tries to evade all human contact and adult responsibilities. She finally understands his shortcomings: "He was now as incapable of an impulse as his body was incapable of moving, incapable of abandoning himself to the great uneven flow of life with its *necessary* disorder and ugliness" (ibid., p. 82, italics added). After looking for the father and loving his every symbol, she had awaited him and had found a child.

The climax of the story is a four-page section describing the union of the father and the daughter, which takes place while a mistral is blowing. Normally cold, this mistral is hot, suggesting perhaps the confusion or tumult of their relationship. A sexual union may be suggested, but it is a mystical rather than a physical relationship that is consummated in the form of symbolic orchestration. Trembling violins, pounding drums, and mocking flutes fuse in rhythm for an instant and elevate father and daughter from the pain of the earth to a place *"where pain is a long, smooth song that does not cut through the flesh"* (*Artifice*, p. 86). They are seeking serenity through music as Stella sought to find it in order to avoid the pain of Bruno; but the answer to the final set of questions (*"Can we live in rhythm, my father? Can we feel in rhythm, my father? Can we think in rhythm, my father? Rhythm—rhythm—rhythm"* [ibid., p. 88]) is no. They may unite temporarily in the mystical dream state or through emotional elevation, but not in reality. She now sees him too clearly to love him humanly. She can tell herself intellectually that she loves him, but her heart will not permit her to live that lie. She finally comes to understand fully her former yearning for him at a point in the narrative when she slips into a mood between sleep and dream, discovering that what she loved all along was not her father but herself mirrored in him. Her attraction to him was the same as that of the narrator's to Sabina in *House of Incest*; it was narcissistic, inhuman, and therefore sterile. Falsity has characterized her father and her love for him, and together they constitute a winter of artifice. Just as the glass bell functions as an image of sealing off human beings from each other, an artificiality keeps the father safely sealed from the distasteful or undesirable, and while the unpleasant aspects of life are conveniently lost, "with the bad was lost the human warmth, the nearness" (ibid., p. 95). She rejects the pattern of his artificial life. She rejects his fear of emotion, of closeness, and sees him as a very sick man. And although she regrets having loved him and trusted him again, she feels ambivalent about the reunion and recognizes that she had to obey the need to join him once more. But Stella comes to realize still more that together they were "slaves of a pattern," for as the story moves quickly to its ending after the climax, she completes "the fatal circle of desertion" (ibid., p. 118) by reversing their roles. When she leaves on a trip, he accuses her of desertion, and Stella now understands her earlier difficulties to the degree that she is able to gain some distance from them and to reflect upon their significance for her. She sees clearly that her former love of her father was manifested to satisfy a myth, not life, and she absolves herself of any guilt by believing that "the feelings they had begun with twenty years back, he of guilt and she of love, had been like railroad tracks on which they had been launched at full speed by their obsessions" (ibid.). Her emotional development had been preordained, determined by the same force, the iron rails, that sent Ahab on his monomaniacal quest for the white whale. Now she has emerged out of the unreflecting "ether of the past," has gained maturity, and is able to stand alone as a woman. Truth finally is possible. Her father was able to see their relationship when he recognized in himself a truth: "Now I see that all these women I pursued are all in you, and you are my daughter, and I can't marry you! You are the synthesis of all the women I loved" (ibid., p. 84).

The ether of the past envelopes them both; they are seeking the self in the other, and they enter a dream state where they fuse. But the ether— and the dream—must wear off, and the daughter in her maturity and understanding is able to cope with it. The father is not. Their separation is to him what it had been to the daughter in her childhood. She had needed him and he left; now he (emotionally a child) needs her, who is very much as a mother to him. She had given herself to him, he had hurt her, and she no longer has any faith in him. She soon recognizes that she would be happy only when separated from him. He reacts predictably: " 'Go on,' he said. 'Now tell me, tell me I have no talent, tell me I don't know how to love, tell me *all that your mother used to tell me*' " (*Artifice*, p. 115). When the daughter replies, "I have never thought any of these things," she suddenly realizes that he has, in fact, failed to achieve the fatherhood she had idealized; he is still the judge. If she has risen in status to the level of her mother, she is also explicitly now his antagonist as well.

In the final lines of the story, Stella is depicted as coming out of that ether of the past that had fogged her mind.

> The last time she had come out of the ether it was to look at her dead child, a little girl with long eyelashes and slender hands. She was dead.
> The little girl in her was dead too. The woman was saved. And with the little girl died the need of a father. [*Artifice*, p. 119]

Although Nin uses the death of a child more powerfully elsewhere, here the implication is clearly that the symbolic child in Stella has gone, that the emotional child at the core of the woman Stella has now ceased to be as she has outgrown her need of the father and has transcended, finally, the arrested emotional development visited upon her by her father in her childhood. The natural process in which Stella can now participate—and which the artificialities of her father precluded—is "the process of growth, fruition, decay, disintegration, which is organic and inevitable" (ibid., p. 101). It is the process of the living, of life itself.

"THE VOICE"

"The Voice," the third section of the volume, has always been a part of *Winter of Artifice*, just as the second section has been, and it, too, was rewritten subsequent to its appearance in that 1939 volume. It has always been placed last in the collection with good reason: it is an attempt to show several troubled characters solving their problems with the aid of a modern priest (the Voice, a psychiatrist) and finding wholeness and relative peace of mind. The focus is no longer directed on one or two chief characters; the narration presents the difficulties of all four of the Voice's patients, as well as the difficulties of the Voice himself, for the possibility of a modern tragedy lies in the tragic aspects of the healer himself who needs help more desperately than do his patients. The title and the thrust of the narrative both point toward this tragedy, but, as we shall see, Nin pursues it to only a limited degree, letting his story lie under the surface, to be inferred by the reader rather than developing it as a primary element. This is not to say that the story is a failure; the four patients are fairly well drawn and fully presented, and two of them (Djuna and Lillian) will become central to Nin's lengthy continuous novel. Also, Lillian emerges at the end of *Seduction of the Minotaur* as the one woman examined in depth in Nin's fiction who achieves a permanent wholeness and true contentment in life.

Djuna is the first character to be introduced. Unable to exist comfortably in a middle position between extremes, she is compared to the elevator that explodes through the ceiling and plummets through the bottom floor into the hysteria of tombs. She lives in a hotel, in a cell-shaped room; her existence there is insular. The hotel itself (appropriately designated as Hotel Chaotica) is like the Tower of Babel in which communication between people is not possible and confusion consequently results. As the hotel contains all this inner confusion, so too does Djuna with her inner conflicts and her inability to fuse into a whole woman. She stands outside of life. She observes others caught in life's current and ferment, but what obsesses her is the residue and debris of real life: dead flowers, punctured broken dolls, wilted vegetables, dead cats. She concludes that human effort and movement lead only to waste. Fortunately, Djuna is aware that she is ill at ease with herself, and she seeks the Voice through whom she understands that the waste and death that interest her are really symbolic of the immobility and detachment from life that she sees in herself. The Voice counsels, "If you were in the current, in love, in ecstasy, the motion would not show just its death aspect. You see what life throws out because you stand outside, shut out from the ferment itself" (*Artifice,* p. 124). In every instance in which stasis occurs in Nin's work, it is tantamount to death. With the Voice's aid, however, Djuna learns that she is dependent on other people, and she begins to move, to flow: "She was moving faster than the slowly flowing rivers carrying detritus. Moving, moving. Flowing, flowing, flowing. When she was watching, everything that moved seemed to be moving away, but when moving, this was only a tide, and the self turning, rotating, was feeding the rotation of desire" (ibid.). She is now filled with music (Nin's symbol of unification) and is able to ride the elevator, attaining fullness and satisfaction at the top floor rather than bursting through it in a quest of some unattainable absolute as she had done before.

Djuna is not left in this state of completion for long. Before her story resumes, however, the short tale of Lillian and her relationship to the Voice is told. Lillian thinks that she is perverse because she is at least superficially masculine and has had such women as Hazel and Georgia as lovers. Since youth she has acted like a male and has had an aversion to feminine accoutrements, and yet she feels guilty for these feelings and for believing that she killed a woman to keep her from marrying a man, for all men are harsh in her eyes. She feels guilty for being caught passing a violin bow between her legs and for thinking that she caused the death of a boy by giving him an enema with a straw. But her seeming masculinity becomes more than just a psychological quirk when she is deprived of her reproductive organs; as she says about her operation, "I was told it was for appendicitis, and when I got well I found out I had no more woman's parts" (*Artifice*, p. 128). She then feels that no man would want her because she is incapable of bearing children. In order to simulate the sexual act she uses a toothbrush. Lillian is uncertain about herself, but like Djuna she becomes a patient of the Voice and appears to be cured by him: "I have something now which you can't take from me [;] ever since I came here I have [*sic*] a feeling so warm and sweet and life-giving which belongs to me, I know you gave it to me, but it is inside of me now, and you can't take it away" (ibid., p. 130). Although the reader does not see Lillian interacting with people or performing sexually with men, the warmth she feels after her experience with the Voice suggests that even if she is not completely healed she is at least well on her way to becoming a psychologically whole woman who is content with herself.

Lillian interacts with none of the Voice's other patients, and her tale is a set piece that could as easily be deleted as included; but although the next patient, Mischa, is presented in only a few pages, he functions as the introducer of the fourth patient, Lilith, and thus introduces the remainder of the tale to the reader. Mischa is necessary to "The Voice"; Lillian is not, and yet they share several characteristics. Both are musicians (Lillian is a violinist, Mischa is a cellist) whose discipline teaches harmony and rhythm but who, like Stella's father, cannot function harmoniously with life. Both have confused notions of their own sexual identities. (Lillian likes to act as men do, Mischa likes to hide in women.) Mischa is much like the paralytic who introduces the modern Christ and the lame Jeanne in *House of Incest*: all three are kept from movement and human interaction by physical disabilities that are probably psychosomatic in nature. Mischa was a child prodigy who was unable to continue his musical artistry past youth (and therefore was unable to develop into manhood), because his hand became stiff, preventing him from manipulating the instrument. Like most physical ailments in Nin's works, Mischa's was a result of a psychological injury, in this case one he had incurred from what he perceived to be a hostile relationship, with sexual overtones, between his parents. Shortly after he had viewed his father bloodied by the animals he had killed, he awakened in the night to see his mother in a white robe stained with blood. Believing that the stain was caused violently by his father, Mischa struck him with a riding whip to keep him from her. As a result of this impetuous act, the arm used to strike the father became stiff and useless.

One can understand why Mischa's hand should become paralyzed, but the true cause of the ailment is more difficult to discern. His stiffness developed to take attention away from his lame leg that contains a fragment of death because it is incapable of functioning naturally. It is the crippled leg that leads women to treat him dispassionately. And so he grows to hate them. It is this deadness of emotion (suggested by the deadness of the leg) that is the cause of his inability to love, and it is this that he wishes to conceal. The lameness, Mischa feels, is the cause of the rejection he perceives, and so he shows his hand "so no one would notice the lameness" (*Artifice*, p. 133). Once the Voice helps him to understand the cause of his physical difficulties, Mischa is liberated, walks with confidence, and sings as he walks into the street and into the flow of life. Psychological awareness has brought understanding that in turn has freed Mischa from his internal turmoil.

One woman who feels tenderness toward Mischa and exhibits a need to protect him is Lilith Pellan, the last of the Voice's patients to be presented. Tenderness and protection are, of course, precisely what Mischa does not want, and, for that matter, they are also not what Lilith herself wants to provide. Her actions toward Mischa and all people are dictated by the experiences of her youth, the most vivid of which was her wandering with her father who came to destroy her childhood by deserting his family. This is exactly what happens to Stella in "Winter of Artifice," but Lilith grows, from the time of the desertion, to detest change, and she comes to live life very conservatively; she becomes an island, a fixed center, a person mistrusting pain and loss. And so she becomes unable to depend on others and to interact with them. The tenor of her relationship with Mischa and her brother Eric is thus established. Djuna, Lillian, and Mischa all are aware of their incomplete selves and go to the Voice for assistance; so does Lilith. It does not take him long to bring her to see the cause of her problems, and she is soon "breathing with the day, moving with the wind, in accord with it, with the sky, undulating like water, flowing and stirring to the life about her, opening like the night" (*Artifice*, p. 145). She is now able to cope with life maturely, but she continues to fear the Voice and Djuna, because they do not permit her to lean on them for assistance as much as she would like; she is therefore no longer able to love herself in them as she has done and can do with others. A result of this is that she begins to love the Voice for himself; she becomes interested in his needs and deficiencies; his detective work in making all the discoveries in her lead her to become sensitive to his feelings as well. He

> took her back, with his questions and his probings, back to the beginning. She told him all she could remember about her father, ending with: "the need of a father is over."
>
> The Voice said: "I am not entirely sure that the little girl in you ever died, or her need of a father. What am I to you?"
>
> "The other night I dreamed you were immense, towering over everyone. You carried me in your arms and I felt no harm could come to me. I have no more fears since I talk to you like this every day. But lately I have become aware that it is you who are not happy. [Ibid., p. 149]

Consequently he begins to confess to her, for no one prior to Lilith had been concerned with him as a person, and the stage is set for his tragic tale.

The Voice not only confides in and confesses to Lilith, but also to Djuna as he tells her of his problems (jealousy and fear) and of his love for Lilith. Instead of pursuing his inner turmoil, the narrative shifts again to Djuna and Lilith, both of whom have slipped back from their new wholeness (acquired through the help of the Voice) into a regression that may be associated with their increasing closeness to the Voice. Djuna becomes associated with the moon, loses her identity, and is alone within herself as she drinks in "the jungle of desire" (*Artifice*, p. 156). Lilith has experienced similar difficulties. She is unable to sleep because "she lived in the myth," in the dream, and "found the absolute only in fragments, in multiplicity" (ibid., p. 157). She yearns for the absolute as Djuna had earlier and so is unable to spend the passion that has accumulated within her. Djuna is in greater control of herself, however, and is able to counsel the anguished Lilith; she loves only a mirage in the Voice. The qualities that she, Lilith, loves in Djuna are only the qualities that she possesses in herself, and so they ought not to be sought: "But none of this is love, Lilith. We are the same woman. There is always the moment when all the outlines, the differences between women disappear, and we enter a world where all feelings, yours and mine, seem to issue from the same source. We lose our separate identities. What happens to you is the same as what happens to me. Listening to you is not entering a world different from my own, it's a kind of communion" (ibid., p. 161). Lilith does not heed Djuna's advice about the Voice, and she therefore helps to cause what passes for his tragedy in the antepenultimate section of the story. There he and Lilith try to love each other, but their attempt is unsuccessful because each wants what the other person no longer is willing or able to offer. Lilith continues to transcend reality in human relationships as she searches for a god, some ideal to fill the void created by her father's desertion many years before. Although the Voice can offer her fatherly impulses (for he can be paternalistic, oracular, and supportive), by this time he is weary of being loved for those qualities; he wants to be loved as a man, as an individual, as a human being. Lilith finally eludes the Voice, and when he loses the power that he has been able to maintain as a doctor, he is unable to function and becomes a virtual nonentity, a child, merely a voice.

One sympathizes with the Voice. He is able to cure, or help to cure, the emotional ills of his patients, but he never is able to achieve wholeness or fullness himself. When he attempts to live his own life, he fails and desperately needs another Voice to aid him. One wants to know what his weakness is, what flaw in the construction of his personality enables him to be a helper but never to be the rich, fulfilled person toward whom he can at least help others incline. The novelette does not supply information on this point. Though ironic as well as tragic possibilities abound in the very nature and fabric of the tale, Nin avoids examining him fully, shifts away from his relationship with Lilith, and fixes upon Djuna instead. She, like most of Nin's characters, has been hurt by life and discovers that dreams are not painful. Her dream is revealed in the final six pages of the story, where she finds that the dream, though painless, is nonetheless dangerous. She learns the lesson promulgated in *House of Incest*: the dream state is a necessary part of one's life, but exclusive residence in it forces one out of life's current and into isolation and sterility. Fortunately for Djuna she is not lost in the dream; she finds that life begins there *"behind the curtain of closed eyelashes"* (*Artifice*, p. 172), and that *"to catch up, to live for a moment in unison with it, that was the miracle. The life on the stage, the life of the legend dovetailed with the daylight, and out of this marriage sparked the great birds of divinity, the eternal moments"* (ibid., p. 175). This is an orthodox statement about the nature of the relationship between the dream and reality, but "The Voice" is not much concerned with that problem. One is gratified that Djuna reaches this awareness, and perhaps it symbolizes the fusion of all of her parts; but it leaves one with the feeling that the author did not wish to pursue the Voice's story. Perhaps she wanted to emphasize the other characters and wished to heighten their own dramas for the reader.

The three parts of *Winter of Artifice* concern women attempting to understand themselves and to make themselves complete human beings after having had their emotional and psychological growth stunted early in life. This is the subject of *House of Incest*, and it was to remain Nin's primary concern throughout all of her other works.

3

Under a Glass Bell

As quickly as *Winter of Artifice* disappeared from public
view after its publication in 1939, so too did Nin
emigrate from Paris to New York at the outset of
World War II. It will be seen that New York functions symbolically in
her work as a town of metal and concrete; a pragmatic, cold, and
inhuman place; so it is therefore not surprising that she was unable to
find commercial publishers for her works there. This was to remain a
problem (although Dutton published three of her books in successive
years beginning in 1946) until Alan Swallow, in Denver, became her
publisher in 1961 and eventually got all of her books in print. But
Swallow was still two decades into the future when Nin returned to
America in 1939. By that time she had published her book on Lawrence,
a prose poem, and a collection of novelettes. From 1937 to 1942,
however, she was writing and publishing fiction in yet another genre—
short stories—and the second and handsomest of her Gemor Press
publications was a collection of them in 1944 called *Under a Glass Bell*.

This book caught the attention of Edmund Wilson, who reviewed it
in the *New Yorker*. He was the first important American critic to
comment knowledgeably and favorably on her work.[1] Perhaps because
of his review, a second edition appeared within four months of the first.[2]
In editions after 1944 the contents of *Under a Glass Bell* were changed
from time to time until the issuance of a 1958 paperback that remains in
print today under the imprint of the Swallow Press. The eight stories
included in the first two editions were written during the late 1930s and

early 1940s; they rank just behind *House of Incest* as Nin's best fiction, and five or six of the stories are quite superb. Those stories later added to the original eight are on the whole inferior to the earlier ones; they will be treated separately near the end of this chapter.

Like her friend Henry Miller, Nin has had the ability to give accurate and provocative titles to her creations, and nowhere is this better exemplified than in this collection. Although the title of nearly any one of the stories could serve as a title for the whole, the one she chose is the most appropriate. A glass bell seems to encase all the characters of the stories; the characters are struggling to emerge from incompleteness into wholeness. Their impediments are usually unseen, being largely psychological, but they can possibly be removed once their causes are identified and once a character decides not to be restrained any further from experiencing life. Like a glass bell, the context in which the characters move is often one of fragility, transparency, and delicacy; and yet in only one of the stories do the characters come close to breaking out (a feature that is characteristic of most of Nin's characters in all her fiction). At their best, the short stories, sketches, and vignettes combine fine stylistics and narrative skill with imaginative originality. If the stories sometimes rise a bit too much into the airy reaches of surrealism, still they can seldom be arbitrarily classified as being surrealistic; rather, such a fictional mode is usually employed when it is an appropriate technique to describe human relationships that can best be described evocatively and symbolically rather than realistically.

One critical problem that might well be introduced at this time (but which will be dealt with in more detail in our discussion of the *Diary*) is the distinction between fact and fiction in Nin's work. The reader will find that the full title of the book (in the later editions) is *Under a Glass Bell and Other Stories*. One is bound to receive the material as short fictional pieces, but one finds that some of the short stories appear later in the *Diary*, and that the material is altered only minimally: the same stories appear under the implicit guise of fiction, and later, again implicitly, as fact. Obviously a strict and hard distinction between so-called fact and fiction will not obtain in this situation. Nin used similar techniques in the *Diary* and the fiction, so that an incident taken from her experience may well turn out to be—to the author's way of thinking—suitable material for inclusion in a book of short stories, so long as it meets the test of quality writing and not simply the consideration of content, which is whether it is "true" or not. One may then conclude that the inclusion of true-to-life stories in *Under a Glass Bell* is a sign of the author's faith in their quality as literature.

When the volume first appeared it carried with it a preface of some interest that was Nin's explanation for her publishing the stories when, in a sense, they represented a period of her development that had passed. It will be useful, as will be indicated later, to read the stories in the light of the preface (which was not reprinted in editions published after the 1940s).

> Because these stories were written before the Spanish war I had thought first of all to destroy them, and then I understood a truth which it might be good to state for others. The stories must be placed in their proper light for those who fail to see the relation between fantasy and reality, the past and the present. Everything is related and inter-active but at times we fail to see how, and consequently, fail to make a higher synthesis.
>
> These stories represent the moment when many like myself had found only one answer to the suffering of the world: to dream, to tell fairytales, to elaborate and to follow the labyrinth of fantasy. All this I see now was the passive poet's only answer to the torments he witnessed. Being ignorant of the causes and therefore of a possibility of change, he sought merely a balm—art, the drug.
>
> . . . .
>
> I did not stay in the world of the isolated dream or become permanently identified with it. The Spanish war awakened me. I passed out of romanticism, mysticism and neurosis into reality.
>
> I see now there was no need to destroy the art that was produced under an evil social structure. But it is necessary to understand, to be aware of what caused the suffering which made such an opium essential and what this fantasy world concealed. And to this task I will devote the rest of my writing.[3]

One will note immediately that the themes presented by Nin in the earlier works (*House of Incest, Winter of Artifice*) are to be presented in the stories of *Under a Glass Bell*. The search for the dream and the cultivation of the painkilling drug recur throughout Nin's works as goals often sought by her characters. However, omnipresent—even if sometimes unreachable—is the existence of the other world, not the impossible dream, but just the antithesis of it, which is inescapable reality, although there are some characters in her fiction who never have to confront the pain of reality so long as they can maintain their unhealthy dream state.

To make the Spanish civil war a pivotal point in Nin's movement from romance to reality is perhaps analogous to the political truth of

World War II: the spiritual erosion begun by the first World War was in a sense completed by the second. The horrors of inhumaneness reached a peak in modern times through the narrowness of nationalism, with the added bonus of a nuclear holocaust permanently threatening persons everywhere. The fairy tales and fantasies of nationalism were no longer accessible to thinking people; the painful political facts of life and of nations learning to live together peacefully became more urgent than ever if life was to endure. One might, then, see Nin's own awakening as being similar to a general awakening in the Western world; the fears concealed in the fantasy world were indeed real, but they had to be confronted, not buried and ignored. The facts of human suffering, of the one life shared by human beings, and of the general nature of the human condition could no longer be ignored by sensitive artists.

One might expect the title story to appear at the beginning of the book, but it does not. Instead, "Houseboat," a story whose theme is reminiscent of that of *House of Incest*, is placed first, and in it the unnamed narrator confronts reality only with difficulty. The general setting is Paris, though its ambience is more implied than felt; the specific setting is the Seine and the people who live on it or near it. There is a current of life in Paris that sweeps most people along with it, but the narrator breaks from it to seek a painless dream life in her houseboat on the river. It will be recalled that Djuna was alienated from a similar current in "The Voice," but she was aware of the dangers accompanying her isolation and sought aid from a psychiatrist. The narrator of this story is not so advanced as Djuna, however, and continues to believe that the painlessness of the dream state is not only a satisfactory alternative to real life, but that it is also a distinct improvement over it. She is not alone in her escape; the others who have broken from the current—the tramps, hoboes, and prostitutes—line the quays where "they sat alone, but not unique, for they all seemed to have been born brothers" (*Glass Bell*, p. 11). These people wish for the somnolence that the river can produce, but the closest they can come to it is to throw newspapers into it and swim vicariously with the papers as they float down the Seine. More successful are the fishermen who have direct contact with the river through their fishing poles; the hypnotic nature of the river is transferred to them through these umbilicals. The person who achieves total union with the river is the narrator. She, who has satisfied her wish to live on a houseboat, finds it responding to every movement of the river; the shutters facing the shore are closed, and poles keep the boat from touching the shore.

The story is especially interesting in that the organizational pattern mirrors the theme, which is the entry into the dream and the eventual freedom from it, or loss of it. A familiar archetypal pattern lies behind the story, symbolizing the universal experience of wish fulfillment and the subsequent disillusionment that follows, at least in the broad pattern. It is, perhaps, a hint of the theme suggested by Vronsky in Tolstoy's *Anna Karenina* who, in spite of the fulfillment of his long-term wishes, realizes "the eternal error men make by imagining that happiness consists in the gratification of their wishes."[4] Nin chooses to represent this universal experience through the primary metaphor of the houseboat itself, the vehicle that puts the narrator directly in touch with the rhythms, currents, and pulsating movements of the water. Her escape from the solid ground of reality is obvious. The quality of the river that the narrator admires most is its continuity; there may be surface disruptions and even momentary feelings of anger, but they remain on the surface and are assuaged by the water's depths. Here as in *House of Incest* the water functions as the subconscious dream soothing those who need solace, drugging those who suffer the pains of life.

It is in quest of a journey out of consciousness that the narrator leaves the shore for her houseboat.

> As soon as I was inside of the houseboat, I no longer knew the name of the river or the city. Once inside the walls of old wood, under the heavy beams, I might be inside a Norwegian sailing ship traversing fjords, in a Dutch boyer sailing to Bali, a jute boat on the Brahmaputra. At night the lights on the shore were those of Constantinople or the Neva. The giant bells ringing the hours were those of the sunken Cathedral. Every time I inserted the key in the lock, I felt this snapping of cords, this lifting of anchor, this fever of departure. Once inside the houseboat, all the voyages began. Even at night with its shutters closed, no smoke coming out of its chimney, asleep and secret, it had an air of mysteriously sailing somewhere. [*Glass Bell*, p. 13]

The narrator assures the reader that she seeks in the dream "not merely a dust flower born like a rose out of the desert sands and destroyed by a gust of wind. When I lie down to dream it is to plant the seed for the miracle and the fulfillment" (ibid., p. 15). But doubts persist. She closes the first section awaiting her phantom lover, an unattainable ideal who makes each mortal man seem unsatisfactory in comparison. Consequently, real love can never be consummated.

Dreams are beneficial in Nin's work—they are, in fact, sine qua non—but they may also be harmful, as this story illustrates. The second section begins with the boat in "a dissonant climate," and the narrator infers from this hostile environment that the boat must have traveled during the night. Daylight has come; illusion—the sense of peace and absence of violence—has fled. A shrieking woman is about to drown in the river. Those tramps that are still not drunk are washing at a fountain. Three men quarrel. Other equally sordid characters appear, including a street cleaner and a young boy abandoned by his mother; and the narrator's voyage has therefore obviously turned from one of exoticism, fantasy, and desire into one of despair, a nightmare.

In the next section "the houseboat traveled out of the landscape of despair" (*Glass Bell*, p. 19) to what appears to be the island of joy. But when the narrator runs up the stairs of the quay, feeling so elated that she believes it must be a holiday, she finds that no one else is participating in the happiness and no one can understand her joy. She returns, devastated, to her houseboat to find men cutting algae with scythes. Another illusion and voyage is completed: "So passed the barge out of the island of joy" (ibid., p. 21). This is the end of the dream portion of the story as well as the end of the beneficence of the dream. No matter how attractive it is, the narrator has found the dream transitory and realizes that it will necessarily be replaced by its opposite, a painful return to reality.

This notion that the positive powers of living completely in the dream are short-lived is borne out in the last section, the only traditionally realistic part of the story,[5] which is introduced with a single explicit sentence that dictates all the action that follows: "One morning what I found in the letter box was an order from the river police to move on" (*Glass Bell*, p. 21). The ostensible cause of this banishment is an expected visit from the king of England, who, the authorities believe, would be offended by the unsightliness of houseboats, laundry, and scenes of poverty. The contentment the narrator has found while living on the barge in Paris is ended; new moorings have to be found outside the city. The narrator's trip up the Seine is like a dream to her: "Only in a dream could I move so gently along with the small human heartbeat in rhythm with the tug tug heartbeat of the tugboat, and Paris unfolding, uncurling, in beautiful undulations" (ibid., p. 23). The final destination is a boat cemetery, and although the narrator hopes that her houseboat will remain there only temporarily, no law was made to permit the return of the boats, even after the king returned home. "So passed the barge into exile" (ibid., p. 25), and so passes the narrator's belief in the beneficence of a total existence in the dream. The dream (escape from pain) passes; reality (return to pain) comes once more. The cycle is completed.

A houseboat on the Seine is the setting for the next story, "The Mouse," but it is not as crucial to the theme as it is in the first story. Here the focus is rather upon the characters and their relationships with each other. Chiefly a character sketch of a small, frightened maid, the story is enhanced also by a rich subtheme that revolves around the narrator's feelings. The maid, unnamed but referred to as "the Mouse," exists in the glass bell of her self-doubt, sense of worthlessness, and quiet fear. In her attitudes and actions she is mousy: she wears mouse-colored clothes, scurries around, and is so frightened and apprehensive that "no gentleness could cross the border of [her] fear" (Glass Bell, p. 27). She is a domestic whose identity is shaped by others, and when she finally asserts herself and performs sexually with her fiancé, not only does she find it unenjoyable, but she becomes pregnant, loses the baby, and nearly dies. There is no indication that she will ever break the glass bell of her fearful personality.

The Mouse is the focal point of the story, but she functions also as a sounding board against which the inhumanity and misunderstandings of the other characters reverberate. She has been treated badly by her former employers (she was made to eat eggs while the others had meat, she had to pay for the dishes she accidentally broke, and so forth) and her own mother was insensitive to her plight and wanted to borrow the money her daughter saved for her marriage. Although the hoboes on the quay are pleasant with her during the day, at night they threaten her with sexual abuse. But as a group, it is the medical profession that is characterized as being the most cruel, and it is the peg-legged doctor, a "grand blesse de guerre," who is especially insensitive to her.

The narrator wishes to find some way of making the Mouse feel secure and lose her sense of fear; although she talks with the Mouse on subjects such as home, family, or places where she once worked that are intended to make the maid feel comfortable, the maid's suspiciousness is never conquered; her defense is never lowered. In this setting of strained domesticity the story progresses through a routine of daily affairs until the Mouse reveals that she is pregnant; but even the pregnancy came about through her fear of being left alone one night, not through the love of a man. After the Mouse has taken measures to perform a dangerous abortion, the narrator finally coaxes the maimed doctor to minister to her, but, unfortunately, "everything about him said clearly: you are only a servant, just a little servant, and like all of them you get into trouble, and it's your own fault. Now he said aloud: 'All you servants make trouble for us doctors' " (*Glass Bell*, p. 31). The Mouse must go to a hospital, and as she and the narrator leave, the latter discovers that the Mouse had been stealing small items from her, the very person who has been her chief supporter and benefactor. In a stroke of irony that is not, unfortunately, fantasy, the hospital refuses to take in the hemorrhaging maid. As she continues to bleed and as her fever mounts, the hospital bureaucrats want to know where she had worked, and where before that.

> The woman bleeding there on the bench meant nothing to them. The little round moist eyes, the tiny worn piece of fur around her neck, the panic in her. The brand-new Sunday hat and the torn valise with a string for a handle. The oily pocketbook, and the soldier's letters pressed between the leaves of a Child's Reader. Even this pregnancy, accomplished in the dark, out of fear. A gesture of panic, that of a mouse falling into a trap. [Ibid., p. 34]

In the denouement the two chief complementary threads of the story, the Mouse's fear and the outrageous inhumanity of the social institutions mired in bureaucracy, come together. This small creature is at the mercy of the universe, and even those people in the medical profession, who ought to be most dedicated to helping another human being, reject her need for help. For the purpose of fiction, Nin has condensed this aspect of dehumanization (quite ironically) largely into the single part of society that ministers to the sick. So formidable is the bureaucracy that one could hardly help another if one wished to. In the tale, however, the problem is compounded by the Mouse's own personality. The maid's mousy appearance, which might seem superficial at the beginning of the story, becomes central to the action later. Her mousiness of behavior and her acting out of fear are reflected when the physicians treat her according to their perception of her as a common servant, a nobody, a suspicious-looking little creature who is probably trying to dupe them. The Mouse herself is so frightened of life that even love and sympathy cannot penetrate her barriers. She finds all efforts at sincerity and expressions of kindness totally foreign, things to be wondered at. The Mouse's nameless designation is the very key to the story: her stereotypical role has made her subhuman in her own eyes as well as in the eyes of others, and she acts out her fear.

One important subtheme to be considered is the role and attitude of the narrator of the story. A significant irony is her inability to rise to a level where she assigns more than a label to the Mouse; and although the narrator makes several attempts to be helpful, her usefulness remains in doubt. As Nin wrote in the preface to the volume, "It is in The Mouse [the story] that first appears the thread of humanity which was to lead me out of the dream: my feeling for the maid was human but I did not know what to do for her."[6] Certainly the narrator in the story tells us a good deal about herself when she consistently subordinates the Mouse to her low rank among human beings. Why is it, in fact, that the narrator fails to help the Mouse? If society is partly to blame, surely the narrator participates in the guilt that society must bear. She does not yet have a proper perspective on her own actions, although she is able to see how the Mouse suffers at the hands of an unfeeling system. The narrator's humaneness, though sincere, tends to be superficial, for she views the maid only as a mouse, a woman who warrants little respect and esteem. The narrator tries as best she can to aid the Mouse and tries to break down her shell of fear and suspicion, but when it is time to express true compassion for her, she can utter her feeling only in the form of litotes: "You ought to know by now that I don't want you to be unhappy here" (*Glass Bell*, p. 28). She does not state unequivocally and positively that she wants her to be happy. And the tone of the narrator's observation (when the Mouse leaves the houseboat for the hospital) is not an encouraging one: "She was carried out of the houseboat. She looked very small. She insisted on wearing a hat, her Sunday hat taken out of its tomb of tissue paper, and the very small fur neckpiece the color of her mouse eyes" (ibid., p. 33). Certainly no one is more genuinely concerned about the Mouse than the narrator, and yet we recognize that she is unable to participate as fully as she might like in the sympathy and understanding that will bring about the cessation of convenient stereotyping.

One of Nin's most successful stories is doubtlessly "Under a Glass Bell," which first appeared in different form in *House of Incest.* In the earlier work, Jeanne and her problems are put in the context of the larger prose poem where they add greatly to the whole and also benefit from it. In the story, however, Jeanne and her problems are isolated and are held up for examination by the narrator for the reader.

Jeanne and her brothers Jean and Paul live together in a house so precious that it is about to vanish. It is quite exquisite. The curtains are stiff, a glass chandelier hovers over all, and the porcelain figurines on the mantelpiece symbolize the inhabitants of the house as they "all seemed to have been caught while in motion by a secret enchantment and put to sleep with a dust of white sleep" (*Glass Bell,* p. 35). It all seems to be delicacy created in a void.

> No violence here, no tears, no great suffering, no shouting, no destruction, no anarchy. The secret silences, the muted pains brought about by great riches, a conspiracy of tranquillity to preserve this flowerlike fragility in crystal, wood, and damask. The violins were muted, the hands were gloved, carpets were unrolled forever under the feet, and the gardens cottoned the sound from the world.
>
> The light from the icicle bushes [chandeliers] threw a patina over all objects, and turned them into bouquets of still flowers kept under a glass bell. The glass bell covered the flowers, the chairs, the whole room, the panoplied beds, the statues, the butlers, all the people living in the house. The glass bell covered the entire house. [Ibid., p. 36]

The house and the people are fragile and isolated; their existences are joined, and they will either die or endure a living death together as the Ushers do with their abode in Poe's classic story. Their house is a miniature house of incest in which the nature of love is incestuous, but even that perversity is perverted; because Jeanne and her brothers do not like to see each other, they communicate only from one room to another and thus are unable to consummate their love. All three of them have been married in the past (and still may be), and Jeanne has borne children; but their concerns are not for their unfortunate spouses or children, but for themselves and the mirror images of themselves in their siblings. Jeanne's goal—and what leads to her difficulty—is to seek an unattainable purity in human existence; consequently she is ill at ease when interacting with human beings (who are tainted, naturally). Therefore she seeks the purity within herself and her family.

All is not hopeless for Jeanne, however. After she recounts the story of her mother's passions and subsequent wasted life, Jeanne admits that her own life began badly because of her mother (she never mentions her father), and it is this admission that permits one to think Jeanne capable of being saved from her insular existence. Immediately a new character enters to offer assistance to Jeanne: it is the narrator. Until this point the narrator has been quietly and unobtrusively relating the story, but when the Georgian prince Mahreb falls in love with Jeanne, the narrator wants to see the relationship developed, and so she enters the tale in the first person, manipulating events so that Mahreb seems to be Jeanne's ideal. The narrator is unable to sustain Jeanne's interest in the prince, and as Jeanne reverts to her former inconspicuousness, she returns to her house of mirrors where she is a woman of fragments. She is dissatisfied being a woman of parts; she earnestly desires to be whole, but because she sees her false self in a mirror, she is unable to achieve that wholeness. In the climax of the story, Jeanne seeks to escape the mirrors and her fragmented self as she realizes her need for human warmth. She flees the mirrors, and dashes toward the garden where "the glass bell which separated them from the world was visible in the light" (*Glass Bell*, p. 42). The narrator urges her on, from a distance, but Jeanne does not see the glass bell, does not break it, and does not find the human warmth she is seeking; instead, she finds the shadow of her sleeping brother and remains a fragmented woman. To show her final isolation from humanity, Nin ends the story with the snapping of the string of Jeanne's untouched guitar, a symbol that Nin used frequently to represent an individual's isolation.

The story could be read easily as the most succinct statement of Nin's basic concerns, techniques, and symbols. Incest, isolation, narcissism, and dreams are all treated explicitly or implicitly; the writing is surrealistic, and the narrator is fairly typical in that she never quite succeeds in her quest to bring relief to those in need. The broken guitar string, the juxtaposition of mirrors (coldness, death) and gardens (life, fecundity), and of course the bell (isolation, detachment) are used to comment symbolically on the actions of the characters. As mentioned earlier in this chapter, a glass bell covers not only this story and its characters, but all the stories in the volume and virtually all of Nin's fiction.

The first two stories are tied together by a houseboat; the third stands alone as a comment, an example of a recurring theme in Nin's work; and the fourth and fifth are joined by their focus on demented men. The Mohican, following the Voice and the Mouse as characters identified only by descriptive nouns, is another character who is unable to function in reality. He is a scholar, historian, and cartographer whose existence lies in books and in the past. "He looked like a white Indian. He believed himself the last of the Mohicans, a faded, high-cheeked Indian transplanted from lost continents, whitened by long research in the Bibliotheque Nationale where he studied esoteric writings" (*Glass Bell*, p. 43). He turns out to be an astrologer who works hard at the trade that obsesses him, until the outbreak of war forces him to stop. The Mohican is a clairvoyant; but ironically he is unable to see into human beings who are near him, and he is incapable of interpreting his own horoscope. His talk is "spherical, making enormous ellipses" (ibid., p. 45), and, much like the characters in "Under a Glass Bell," he is a fatalist and somnambulist who already seems to be dead. He was forced into the past by the auctioning of all his possessions, which was the same thing that helped to cause Lilith's problems in "The Voice." The Mohican's end is sad: the Nazis arrest him because he had predicted Hitler's death. How laughable, this; if they knew the Mohican at all they would have known that his predictions are invariably incorrect and that he is a harmless man. His basic problem (a common one in Nin's works) is that he "could not distinguish between potentiality and fulfillment, between the dream and the actuality" (ibid., p. 47). This is far from being Nin's best story. For one thing, the narrator is not much in evidence and plays an ambiguous role in the story. And, although it is another statement dealing with the dangers of absenting oneself too long from reality, the story lacks some of the dramatic tension and interest—and character relationships—that are present in most of the other stories, though it must be admitted that this one is chiefly a character sketch rather than a narrative piece.

More successful than "The Mohican" is "Je Suis le Plus Malade des Surrealistes" (subtitled "Antonin Artaud" in early editions). It is a better story partly because Pierre, the protagonist, attempts to develop something for the future, but also because it is a better narrative. "The Mohican" is totally lacking in dialogue, even though the Mohican's conversational skill is praised highly; in this other story Nin employs dialogue in generous quantities that results in a very fine—and terrifying—description, a self-portrait, of the man through his dialogue with a woman, the narrator. A living portrait emerges in a way that "The Mohican" could not hope to provide.

Pierre is an eccentric who finally goes insane, a character modeled upon Antonin Artaud, the initiator of the powerful Theater of Cruelty. It is Pierre's belief that the traditional mode of presenting drama, with the actors on the stage, safely away from any real interaction with the audience, is self-defeating because there is a barrier between the performer and the observer. What he proposes to call the Theater of Cruelty is one in which the audience will participate in the performance and will thereby be shattered "with ecstasy and terror" (*Glass Bell*, p. 49). Such a desire has caused considerable frustration for Pierre, because his intense quest has resulted in others simply laughing at him; but he does have one follower, and it is the narrator. She is a woman who has great faith in the dream, who seems to champion the underdog, the ridiculed, the downtrodden (as preceding narrators have done), and so it is only natural that she should embrace this dream of Pierre. Once they both understand his dream, however, the narrator cannot subscribe wholly to all he believes in. He is calcined, like a mineral; she is warm, supple, languorous. She can follow him into the dream, but he is not to touch her. Withdrawn from real life under the guise of the dream, Pierre reveals that it is no existence at all. When he misunderstands her endorsement to be an avowal of physical love, she shrinks from him; but in the final portion of the story she relates movingly—and clinically— his maltreatment at the hands of those who have been under attack earlier, the doctors. If her attitude toward Pierre is genuine, it is still true that apparently her efforts to help lead him closer than ever toward suicide. This last section of the story takes an entirely different tone from the first, mainly because the narrator is not present (and need not be) as a character. Here Pierre is brought in a straitjacket to a team of doctors who examine him and find him insane. He thinks he is a white phoenix that is being chased by a black eagle, announces incorrectly that the president died that day, states that he sees in the mirror not himself but "a monk who is castrated and who sometimes takes the form of a woman" (ibid., p. 55), and avers that he tried to commit suicide by drowning because the narrator did not return his love. The story concludes with no analysis of the causes of his difficulties, or of the narrator's reaction to his present plight, but with a bald description of the inhumane treatment he receives at the hands of a doctor. After the doctor tells him he may leave, the madman gets up, watched by two aides who know his feet are bound. "They let him take two steps on his way out of the room. The doctor let him take two steps with his bound feet and smiled at the way he was tangled and bound. The madman took two steps and fell. He was permitted to fall" (ibid., p. 57). Once again those who have been entrusted to help become the villains of the story.

Pierre is in desperate need of help. His theories of the theater may indeed be valid, as history has in part shown, but it is ironic that he is able to espouse with such vehemence a philosophy whose end is to bring people together (in many ways) while he is himself so isolated from humanity. Perhaps if he could have controlled his fervor he might have become more human. Pierre's ideas are nicely presented in his dialogue with the narrator; his insanity is related objectively, without the presence of the narrator, which is a wise decision on the author's part, for there is no need to have those incidents filtered through the mind of another unless she were to have the narrator respond or comment on the doctor's inhumaneness. The actions are damning enough without comment. The shift from the first section to the second does create a problem in emphasis or balance, though; it is difficult to discern whether the story is, finally, more concerned with Pierre's psychological condition or with the evils of the medical profession, but in the end it holds together as a sad commentary on a man of genius who cannot function in life and whose plight can only worsen as he is taken away from the tasks he has set for himself.

More often than not in Nin's fiction the character who resides too long in the dream will find it turned into nightmare, and this is the case in "Ragtime." The setting seems to be Paris, but it could be any modern city that draws toward itself a race of ragpickers who sift through the discarded objects of others. In this agitated and surrealistic city, an unnamed ragpicker goes about, finding pleasure in the fragmented objects he comes across: "His eyes sought the broken, the worn, the faded, the fragmented. A complete object made him sad. What could one do with a complete object? Put it in a museum. Not touch it" (*Glass Bell*, p. 58). But partial objects could be transformed into something new and wonderful; thus he is creating life out of death. This notion of transmutation and of the continual evolution of things is an optimistic and attractive one, but in this nightmare it becomes distorted and undesirable. The ragpicker appears to be a spokesman for basic and unsophisticated pleasures, but what he does with his fragments does not suggest the fecundity or transmutation one is led to expect. In the first place, his band of drifters resides in shacks on the edge of Paris where there are "no trees. No bridge. No pavement. Earth. Plain earth trodden dead. Shacks of smoke-stained wood from demolished buildings. Between the shacks gypsy carts. . . . Inside the shack rags. Rags for beds. Rags for chairs. Rags for tables. On the rags men, women, brats. Inside the women more brats. Fleas" (ibid., p. 59). Although such language surely reinforces the aura of fragmentation in the story, it is difficult at this point to assign positive value to the ragpicker that was implied earlier. There is not much virtue in converting rags and fragments into squalor.

As is the case with the Voice and the Mouse, the character of the ragpicker remains static and actually becomes an essential figure in the story only as his relationship with the narrator develops; the ragpicker functions chiefly as a teacher to the narrator in her dream. Clearly she has been contemplating regeneration, rebirth, the use of the past in the present; and the ragpicker is her cicerone into certain negative aspects of those ideas. She describes him first from a distance, but a page into this very short story we find her sitting on the hump of his ragpicker's bag, accompanying him to his home where she sees many grotesqueries but where, more significantly, she finds an item out of her own past. It is a blue dancing dress that had fallen apart when she was seventeen. Its demise had caused her much grief. Here is an opportunity for her to recapture the fond memories of the past, to transform the tattered dress into a new one that will set her feet dancing once more; but when she puts it on, she immediately dances through it. She cannot live in the past and the dress cannot be transformed into a new whole one. As if to prove to her that she can never totally escape her past, however, the ragpicker returns to her other personal possessions that she thought she had parted from permanently, including a wisdom tooth and her sheared long hair. These lead her to ask where all the other things are that she has lost, all the things she had thought dead. Instead of an answer, she sees the ragpicker sink into a pile of rags, and when she tries to pick him up, she finds a scarecrow in her hands with sleeves full of straw and a top hat with a bullet hole through it. The other grotesque ragpickers are sitting around a fire made from their rummaging. "Can't one throw anything away forever? I asked" (*Glass Bell*, p. 61). The ragpicker then sings his famous serpentine song of affirmation:

> Nothing is lost but it changes
> into the new string old string
> in the new bag old bag
> in the new pan old tin
> in the new shoe old leather
> in the new silk old hair
> in the new hat old straw
> in the new man the child
> and the new not new
> the new not new
> the new not new

> [Ibid., pp. 61-62]

"All night the ragpicker sang the new not new the new not new until I fell asleep and they picked me up and put me in a bag" (ibid., p. 62). The narrator, weary, has become one more fragmented object to them. So the story revolves around reversals: the ragpicker speaks of transforming death into life, but what he produces is squalor and incompleteness. The narrator seems to be having a nightmare as she tries unsuccessfully to recapture her past, and in this she learns a truth central to Nin's work: that the past cannot be recaptured and that one must make the most of the present. And yet the idea that nothing is lost—perhaps even that nothing can be lost, but only altered—is in one sense very hopeful. The cycle of life is unending; regeneration is a principle of life, as is recurrence. It may require that one look at the process somewhat differently from the way one normally does, but it remains true that we are what we were.

The mature narrator looks back on herself at age eleven in "The Labyrinth," a story much like *House of Incest* in its meaning and design; it is actually a sustained metaphor describing a young girl who walked into the labyrinth of her diary, and as she walked, she followed a design in the maze that she was sure to remember. That is, she kept her diary because "I wanted to remember in order to be able to return. As I walked, I walked with the desire to see all things twice so as to find my way back into them again" (*Glass Bell*, p. 63). At one level, the story is about the narrator as a girl losing a great love in her life and writing down in her diary what she recalls about that love so that she will be able to return to it frequently. She is attempting to recreate, to preserve, to live in the past, which may be a deadly thing to do. One quickly sees the dangers of such an endeavor, for soon after she enters her diary (which is treated surrealistically as a kind of dream), the narrator's obsessions become infinite and she becomes lost. She finds that a life in the diary apart from real life is one that is buffered and therefore protects her—as it should not—against the necessary pains of life. "I was lost," says the narrator, "in the labyrinth of my confessions, among the veiled faces of my acts unveiled only in the diary" (ibid., p. 67). Finally she opens each of the volumes of her diary with her "rusty keys" and finds that "the figures passed armless, headless, mutilated. The white orifice of the endless cave opened. On the rim of it stood a girl eleven years old carrying the diary in a little basket" (ibid.). It may be that at the distance of many years the narrator is tempted once again to relive her first love in the diary, but she finally becomes aware that love or life in general cannot be captured and contained, and that she has grown psychologically mature enough not to need the diary any longer. The dream has brought a renewed sense of her own present worth to the narrator, just as it did in "Ragtime."

In the first two editions of *Under a Glass Bell*, the story "Birth" follows "The Labyrinth" and concludes those volumes. But as it is now constituted, there are five stories that have been added to the original eight; they are positioned after "The Labyrinth" and before "Birth." The five additions generally suffer in comparison to the original eight, although there are clearly exceptions. One of the additions, "The Child Born Out of the Fog," for example, is at least superior to "The Mohican." "Through the Streets of My Own Labyrinth" is logically placed after "The Labyrinth," but it is little more than a fragmentary restatement of the more ambitious story that precedes it, at least thematically. It is a story of revelation and self-understanding.

"The All-Seeing" is the first of two stories dealing with eyes and vision; it is a pastiche of elements from earlier stories. Jean may be the same character who is one of Jeanne's brothers in "Under a Glass Bell." He is a musician, a violinist. Like Mischa in "The Voice," his musical talent is destroyed when his mother gloats over his failure to win a prize.

> "Now you will stop playing the violin and wasting your life. You will be a man like your father, not a fiddler. I'm very glad you did not win the prize. You would have gone to Paris to study and become a good-for-nothing. We never had musicians in our family."
> With one phrase she had destroyed his first passion. He hung his violin on a wall. The strings snapped gradually and hung dead. [*Glass Bell*, p. 72]

His wound drives him into a dream where all is distilled into essences and mirages, where bloodless and passionless legends exist. "After he pursued so ardently only the atmosphere of the dream . . . he lamented the absence of warmth and humanity" (ibid., p. 74). The more he cut himself off from all that was sick, poor, and animal, as well as ugly and sordid and undesirable, the more anguish he felt, for he found no contentment in the dream. In his loneliness he falls in love with the same Unknown Woman of the Seine who was first introduced in "Houseboat," but still his loneliness is not dispelled. The altruistic narrator enters his dream with him, as she did with Pierre in his story, but when Jean begins to speak to her of love—by which he means love of the twin—she is able to recite the dangers of such love as are enumerated in *House of Incest*. " 'People who are twins,' [the narrator] said, 'there is a curse upon their love. Love is made of differences and suffering and apartness, and of the struggle to overcome this apartness. Two people who love the dream above all else would soon both vanish altogether' " (ibid., pp. 75-76). Jean praises the narrator for being the one who will always prepare the flight for others, but does not venture forth alone herself; she sees the one that is not free and retraces her steps to stand by him. " 'But of course, Jean,' [says the narrator], 'we have the dream, this drug given to prisoners of distinction' " (ibid., p. 77). Once again a character is used for the apotheosis of a narrator.

The narrator does not interact with Hans in "The Eye's Journey," which is another very short story dealing with a painter who has difficulty living in reality. Through his paintings he lives in a mirage at the bottom of the sea, but, as one might expect, because he lives there permanently (rather than visiting in order to restore balance to his life), what he finds are weeds, mildew, stagnation, and objects from shipwrecks. After finding the harshness of day (ordinary life) unbearable, he turns to drink where he hopes to find the warmth he finds in the dream. His bottle becomes empty; he becomes paranoid and is committed to an asylum, as Jean is in "The All-Seeing." He loses one eye because of his excessive drinking, and as though to compensate for this loss, he becomes the Watcher instead of the Watched; he is no longer the mouse but the snake, and because his eye is fixed so absolutely on the world, he only stares at the flames in the asylum as they consume him. Hans's eye has journeyed from a focus on the dream (the escape from life) to a focus on reality. As is the case in all other such instances in Nin's fiction, extremism, such as living totally either in the dream or in reality, can lead only to a physical or psychological demise. Hans suffers both kinds of death in this story, but the power it has as an individual work is dissipated if one compares it to others dealing with the same theme.

The asylum fire introduces "The Child Born Out of the Fog." Charred doorways from the fire do not seem out of place among the loiterers, the trash of newspapers and tin cans, broken windows, and the meager shops. Accompanying the litter and squalor and people with concave stomachs of hunger, one approaches what seems to be the equally squalid home of Sarah, but one finds also that she is a woman of some pride who will not let herself be drawn down by the shabbiness of her surroundings. Don, her lover, is a guitarist who performs at a night club. The rhythmic music from his instrument is noteworthy, for until this point in the collection of stories no stringed instrument has produced music; instead, strings snap to show the inability of an individual to flow rhythmically with life. The result of the harmonious union between Sarah and Don is their daughter Pony, whose "two hands stretched towards the white mother and the dark father for equal consolation" (*Glass Bell*, p. 83).

Although there is a unity, a wholeness, and a love in this family that is unique in Nin's works, it is not a family whose emotional success came easily or survives without difficulty. And although there is some confusion concerning Don's race, the love he and Sarah have shared has not been tolerated by society because of its hostility toward miscegenation. Pony was conceived in a fog that served as a buffer between their love and society, and even as the story ends, Don has to travel to a common destination separately from Sarah and Pony, and as the bus in which they are riding passes him, they "were not allowed to wave to each other" (ibid., p. 85).

This is not the only one of Nin's stories that deals with social problems, although it is probably the one that attacks a problem most directly. In an oblique or indirect fashion, "The Mouse" reveals some of Nin's social conscience, as the story, like the present one, deals earnestly with human problems in a tangible and concrete manner, placing the burden of guilt upon a culture that is willing to tolerate inequities, stereotypes, and bias.

"The unveiling of women is a delicate matter. It will not happen overnight. We are all afraid of what we shall find" (*Glass Bell*, p. 86). So begins the tale of Hejda, a child of the Orient who as a primitivistic child found herself inhibited by her society. The story of her unveiling is not a pleasant one. When she marries Molnar, she is repressed by his insensitivity to her real self and to certain aspects of her body. By the end of the story, the two people are separated and Hejda is free, finally, of all restraints. But what she has not learned is that one needs restraints, although they should come from within, not from without. She abuses her new freedom and instead of achieving rhythm and harmony with life, she reverts to the impulsive behavior of her youth. She becomes bold, even brazen; she has discovered that she is very gifted in lovemaking.

> Her friendships with women are simply one long underground rivalry: to excel in startling dress or behavior. She enters a strained, intense competition. When everything fails she resorts to lifting her dress and arranging her garters.
> Where are the veils and labyrinthian evasions?
> She is back in the garden of her childhood, back to the native original Hejda, child of nature and succulence and sweets, of pillows and erotic literature.

The frogs leap away in fear of her again. [Ibid., p. 95]

There is little doubt that Hejda's story is that of many women, and she herself is made into something like the universal woman, not necessarily through the boldness she acquires when free, but through her very impulse "to speak . . . after centuries of confinement and repression" (*Glass Bell*, p. 88). Nin shows clearly how inhibition causes the layers of her veil to form, and therefore Hejda's plight is one with which the reader can sympathize. But it may be that the enumerating of the details is so direct as to be overpowering. It may be, of course, that Nin intended for the rejuvenation of Hejda to be radical to impress upon the reader the sense that the reaction will be as violent as the original action upon the character's personality. Usually Nin shows obliquely, symbolically, or unrealistically a character's problems, which is a technique well suited to the subject of much of what she has written: the entry into the dream, the fantasy, the unconscious, especially as depicted in a fragmented character who is seeking wholeness. Such a straightforward presentation of her philosophy borders on the didactic and violates the fusion of manner and matter that is so successful in, for example, *House of Incest*.

"Birth" is the most moving of Nin's stories. This first-person narrative relates, on the surface, a woman's effort to give birth to a dead child. She becomes exhausted during her four difficult hours in the delivery room where impatient doctors and nurses predictably treat her cruelly; at last, and with no assistance, she is able to emit the child, a perfectly formed girl. After the pain of the stillbirth she has enough strength to fight successfully to see the dead child that her attendants are keeping from her. Such are the events in the story, but to read it only as a powerfully written tale of this woman's physical anguish is to miss its ultimate meaning.

The story's title refers most obviously to the stillbirth, but it also suggests the narrator's birth into selfhood. From the start she is aware of her ambivalent feelings toward the child that is herself.

A part of me did not want to push out the child. . . . A part of me lay passive, did not want to push out anyone, not even *this dead fragment of myself*, out in the cold, outside of me. All in me which chose to keep, to lull, to embrace, to love, all in me which carried, preserved, and protected, all in me which imprisoned the whole world in its passionate tenderness, this part of me would not thrust out the child, even though *it had died in me*. Even though *it threatened my life*, I could not break, tear out, separate, surrender, open and dilate and yield up a fragment of a life *like a fragment of the past*, this part of me rebelled against pushing out the child, or anyone, out in the cold, to be picked up by strange hands, to be buried in strange places, to be lost, lost, lost. [*Glass Bell*, p. 96; italics added]

The narrator is obviously bearing a child, but that female deadness symbolizes a dead part of the mother that hinders her from knowing her true, full, present self. She is comfortable with this part of her being that belongs to former times, and she is understandably frightened to leave the familiar old for the unknown new. This dead fragment threatens the woman's life. She desires "to remember all the time why I should want to live," and she knows that "the child is not a child, it is a demon strangling me. The demon lies inert at the door of the womb, blocking life, and I cannot rid myself of it" (ibid., p. 100). Of course she cannot pass the dead fetus with the assistance of the barbaric doctors and nurses (with outside intervention), but when left to her own devices she is able to become one with nature and drum rhythmically on her stomach; the girl that is her dead self comes out of the tunnel of the womb just as the dancer leaves the house of incest through a similar aperture. In ridding herself of the old, the past, her nonliving self, this woman will be able to confront life as a fully living being; she has been born into adult life by shedding her dead self. This is one of the most recurrent themes in Nin's work, and in placing such an affirmative story last in *Under a Glass Bell* Nin suggests that while one will certainly encounter psychological difficulties, one might well overcome them ultimately. Such is the theme of Nin's continuous novel that would occupy her for the next fifteen years.

One final word may be said about an element of this story's structure, and to do so reference must be made to Nin's *Diary*. All the stories in *Under a Glass Bell* might be said to appear in one form or another in her *Diary*, and special problems that accrue because of these dual appearances will be discussed later. In the *Diary* treatment of "Birth," however, the reader does not learn until the end of the episode that the child is born dead. Although the *Diary* version might contain, in a sense, more suspense and possibly more residual intensity, it is simply narrated chronologically; in the fictionalized version, the end is explicitly connected to the beginning. The powerful ending, the birth of the stillborn child, begins, dominates, and controls the whole story and is a fact that stands behind it, making each painful detail all the more intense because the reader knows ahead of time that the issue will be lifeless.

Under A Glass Bell is surely one of Nin's best fictional achievements.[7]

Most of the stories are short, well crafted pieces that relate effectively her basic concerns, in particular the problem of dream versus reality, but underlying them all is a sense that no matter how distant one might be from life, one must never quit seeking one's place in it. Living is difficult, and at times painful, but only from living life and not escaping from it can one hope to improve it and live fruitfully.

4

Ladders to Fire

After experimenting with different literary genres in each of her first four books, Nin wrote only novels (and two pamphlets) during the next two decades. In these, as in the novelettes and stories, she reworked the themes that were first stated and exploited fully in *House of Incest*, but here her scope is much broader and her result is less successful than in the earliest effort. The first five of the six novels constitute what Nin called her continuous novel. Although they were written separately and published at irregular intervals between 1946 and 1961, she intended them to be a series of interrelated tales about recurring characters. She later was explicit on this point in the introduction to the English edition of *Ladders to Fire* (1963).

> My original concept was a *Roman Fleuve*, a series of novels on various aspects of relationships, portraying four women in a continuous symphony of experience. All the characters are presented fully in the first volume, *Ladders to Fire*. They are developed later in the succeeding volumes, *Children of the Albatross, The Four Chambered Heart, Spy in the House of Love*, and *Seduction of the Minotaur*.
>
> The complete series has been published in America under the title of *Cities of the Interior*.
>
> As each book came out, however, it was reviewed as if it were an independent novel. Naturally the interrelation and interdependence of the total design were lost and obscured. Cross references and allusions lost their cumulative effect and some characters seemed to appear out of nowhere.[1]

The author's intended sense of continuity presents a critical problem that must be kept in mind by any serious reader who approaches the novels. Another problem of which the reader is less likely to be aware is the matter of text in the first and the last of the five novels, namely, *Ladders to Fire* and *Seduction of the Minotaur*. We shall discuss the textual changes in the latter novel in chapter 8. With regard to *Ladders to Fire*, however, one who has observed the changing and shifting contents of *Under a Glass Bell* and *Winter of Artifice* may not be surprised to find a similar textual situation here. When it first appeared in 1946, *Ladders to Fire* was made up of two main sections; the first, "This Hunger," contained two subsections, "Stella" and "Lillian and Djuna."[2] "Stella," as we have seen, now is the first of the three novelettes in *Winter of Artifice*, and "Lillian and Djuna" has since been retitled "This Hunger." "Bread and the Wafer," the second section of the first edition of *Ladders to Fire*, remains in its original position. The original edition carried a dedication to Gore Vidal that has not appeared in subsequent editions. The question may then be raised that if the contents of the continuous novel have been rearranged and altered after publication, then how organic and cohesive can the whole be considered to be? One tentative answer that a careful reading of the novels may reveal is that there is indeed an organic quality and cohesion to the novels, for the artistry of this lengthy work does not lie in its adherence to realism or outer reality; instead, its concern is with the psyches or inner realities of its characters, especially the women. To excise a section (or a characater), to add a conclusion (and Nin accomplished all of these in either *Ladders to Fire* or *Seduction of the Minotaur*) may help give a more satisfactory final shape to the whole. It shows us an artist continuing to be concerned with the nature, fabric, and quality of her work. And although Stella (the character) still appears briefly in the continuous novel, her story fits as well in *Winter of Artifice* as it did in *Ladders to Fire*.

A comparison of the first and subsequent editions of *Ladders to Fire* reveals several textual differences, but the most noteworthy is that Nin's prologue printed in the first edition was deleted from all later editions.[3] In that prologue of five brief paragraphs the author sets forth her topic for the continuous novel, explains the nature of the women she will investigate, indicates why men are treated peripherally in the book, and offers her interpretation of the episode that concludes "This Hunger." In addition, this extraordinary prologue hearkens back to *House of Incest, Winter of Artifice*, and *Under a Glass Bell* and ties together all of her fiction, with the possible exception of *Collages*, into a unified whole. The complete prologue follows.

I have to begin where everything begins, in the blindness and in the shadows. I have to begin the story of women's development where all things begin: in nature, at the roots. It is necessary to return to the origin of confusion, which is woman's struggle to understand her own nature. Man struggled with nature, fought the elements with his objectivity, his inventions, and mastered them. Woman has not been able to organize her own nature, her simoons, her tornadoes, her obscurantisms, because she lacked the eye of consciousness. She was nature. Man did not help her in this because his interpretations, whether psychological, or intellectual, or artistic, did not seize her. And she could not speak for herself.

Today marvellous women speak for themselves in terms of heroic action, integrating the woman, mother, wife, in harmonious relation to history, to larger worlds of art and science. But many more, when entering action or creation, followed man's patterns and could not carry along or integrate within them the feminine part of themselves. Action and creation, for woman, was man—or an imitation of man. In this imitation of man she lost contact with her nature and her relation to man.

Man appears only partially in this volume, because for the woman at war with herself, he can only appear thus, not as an entity. Woman at war with herself, has not yet been related to man, only to the child in man, being capable only of maternity.

This novel deals with the negative pole, the pole of confused and twisted nature.

The mirrors in the garden are the mirrors women must look into before they can go further. This is only the story of the mirrors and nature in opposition, and in the mirrors is only what woman dares to see . . . so far an incomplete woman.[4]

All of the first five novels deal with the psychic problems of the female characters and to a lesser degree with similar problems of the men. "This Hunger," the first section of *Ladders to Fire* (the first novel), introduces representative characters with representative problems. Lillian and Djuna are the two major female characters who have difficulties that are different and yet similar, and the ebullient Jay is the most important male character. Less significant characters are Lillian's husband Larry; her housekeeper, the dutiful Nanny; and her lover Gerard. Lillian is the major character throughout most of the novel, but as the tale progresses, Djuna gains in importance and the conclusion belongs to her. (One may recognize that this technique is similar to the shifting of the story's focal point away from the title character to Djuna at the end of "The Voice," the novelette in which Lillian and Djuna are first introduced.)

In "The Voice" Lillian is a woman whose feminine core is entrapped in a masculine exterior. In that state she has women as lovers, has had her "woman's parts" removed, but finally is able to achieve a certain warmth and contentment with the aid of the Voice. She continues "with her straightforward manly soul" in "This Hunger," but she is also much more aggressive than she was in the earlier tale. "Lillian was always in a state of fermentation" and "seemed to trapeze from one climax to another, from one paroxysm of anxiety to another, skipping always the peaceful region in between, the deserts and the pauses" (*Ladders*, p. 7). She is married to the unchanging Larry whose two children, Paul and Adele, she has borne; so one must infer that her operation took place well after her marriage and even after the time of "This Hunger" in which she is impregnated by Jay. But she is unhappy being a conventional wife, mother, and housekeeper. She seeks lovers in Gerard and Jay and seeks a friend and lover in Djuna.

One of the hallmarks of Nin's fiction, and one of the qualities that makes her work "modern," is its effective lack of adherence to strict chronology, an example of which occurs at the outset of "This Hunger." The novel begins with Lillian's affair with Gerard, and not until later is the reader told that Lillian has a husband; two children; and a seemingly stable, satisfactory home life. This technique of withholding information needed as a context in which to place the affair with Gerard serves the story very effectively, chiefly because it stands in such striking contrast to what appears later as the normalcy of her home life and her own mental condition. This undercutting of the normalcy is therefore shown to us rather than told to us, by the author, which is always an effective fictional device. We learn that it is, in fact, partly because of her relationship with her family that Lillian needs a lover, one who is similar to the phantom lover of the Seine in "Houseboat"; one who is an ideal and therefore unattainable. Even if the reader had not been given this much information, it is obvious that Lillian will not find happiness with Gerard, a nebulous and nonassertive man. Gerard succeeds only in arousing Lillian's doubts within herself. When he fades out of sight, as a dream must, she is left—as she must be—with her dream of an ideal lover unfulfilled.

Gerard, and what he represents, is one alternative to Lillian's unhappy existence with her family, but it is not a satisfactory one. After he vanishes she becomes an Amazon, a warrior whose victories are numerous but insignificant, because she is unable to discriminate between large and small issues and so attacks them all with equal fervor.

She lives on a "plane of war" and is out of the "flow of life," but although her greatest fear is that she will have to submit to a lover, the hunger she really craves is "to be made to yield" to a man (*Ladders*, p. 15). The more battles she wins, then, the more she loses, because she stands isolated from the stream of life. She can interact positively with no one.

An alternative to her family and Gerard is Djuna, a woman who has had to face many hardships, especially in her youth, but who has been able to emerge as something approaching a whole woman because of her ability to draw upon her dreams for sustenance. She is a vibrant woman who is as enthusiastic as Lillian is aggressive; when they meet it is "like a meeting of two chemicals exactly balanced, fusing and foaming with the pleasure of achieved proportions" (*Ladders*, p. 17). Because of this balance they are able to fuse into one being and elevate themselves above the rest of humanity into the painlessness of the dream. This fusion of similarities and the exclusion of life suggests the theme of *House of Incest*, and, indeed, is a recurring theme in Nin's work. Here, as elsewhere, a relationship based on the dream but actually out of touch with reality falsely appears to be fulfilling and desirable. Lillian's feminine core is shrouded in masculine trappings, whereas Djuna is feminine in her appearance and actions; Lillian is unable to control her chaotic inner nature, whereas Djuna dominates hers. But these differences are superficial and do not negate the fact that both of them are women whose natures are similar. A wedding of similarities produces nothing; it is the joining of opposites that may produce fecundity.

Despite her relationship with Lillian, Djuna is fairly well able to cope with life and to live in relative contentment. With a consumptive mother, an alcoholic father, and four hungry siblings, Djuna's youth was unpleasant. After her mother's death, Djuna and a sister were placed in an orphanage. Life there was hardly more tolerable than it had been with their family, but it was after Djuna had been taken in by pseudoadoptive parents, people who took children into their families and were paid the sum of thirty-five dollars per month toward the feeding of each child, that her hardships really began. Until that time she was able to escape reality by going into her dreams and then returning to life refreshed and renewed, but when the adoptive parents offered the promise of love while lavishing love and goods on their natural children, Djuna lost the ability to endure reality, for "the space between actuality, absolute deprivation, and the sumptuosity of her imagination could never be entirely covered." She found that what "she had created in the void, in the emptiness, in the bareness continued to shame all that was offered to her"; her long-felt hunger "alchemized into love," and "whatever was missing she became: she became mother, father, cousin, brother, friend, confidant, guide, companion to all" (*Ladders*, p. 36). But as a woman Djuna was able to renew her fruitful trips into her dreams, and in doing so she avoided the tendency of staying in them, as some of Nin's characters do. Instead, while they certainly offer a trap as well as a "wealth of Byzantine imagery," her dreams "willed her their wisdom of life and death, of past and future; [death] was postponed by living, by suffering, by risking, by losing, by error" (ibid., p. 19). When she regained her ability to exist in reality with the aid of her dreams, her hunger for love turned into love, and she was able to love both men and women in their softness, their hungers, and their needs.

Lillian possesses none of these qualities. She seems not to have experienced anything comparable to the difficulties of Djuna's youth; she is married to a man who is basically good, she has two children who do not appear to burden her, and she has enough money to avoid making material sacrifices. With such a traditionally good life, however, Lillian is miserable. It sounds like a common modern complaint. Part of the cause of her difficulties is her husband Larry who, although he is kind and considerate, cannot view her as a woman who has evolved since their wedding day ten years earlier. Nanny, the maid, aids further in the repression of the real Lillian, reiterating in actions and words that the family is more important as a whole than any one of its members. As if to prove her point, Nanny functions somewhat as a surrogate wife and mother in the family while Lillian is gone, and even refuses offers of marriage because of what she perceives to be her duty to hold the family together. Whatever her other qualities might be, Nanny is the most sensitive of the family members in noting a change in Lillian. When Lillian decides to leave the bed that she and Larry have shared and to move into a separate room, Nanny senses Lillian's unhappiness and sees that the end of the family may be at hand. Her estimate is correct, of course, and Lillian soon after takes a lover who is this time an aggressive manifestation of Gerard; nature provides the accompaniment of a chirping cricket as though to applaud her action. In an interesting mirror image, the author suggests one of Larry's difficulties in perceiving changes in Lillian. There is next door to Larry and Lillian a doctor living with his wife; but the wife has been dead for six months, though the doctor refuses to acknowledge the fact. So does Larry avoid facing necessary facts about changes that are essential in Lillian's psychological growth.

Of all the members of the family, the author is most concerned with Lillian, and one naturally sympathizes with this woman whose psychological development had been stunted a decade earlier. She warrants compassion. She ought to be encouraged to express her true self after years of silence; and it is tempting to view Larry as the chief culprit in the matter, as a stereotypically insensitive husband who had been content with the Lillian he married and therefore did not aid in her need to achieve more fullness. And though, given the text of the novel, he cannot be held blameless, there is no evidence that Lillian confronted him with her problems so that he could be of assistance. Perhaps this is begging the question, for one cannot always realize one's own problems. Larry appears to be a fairly good husband who offers his wife considerable freedom and does not question her numerous journeys; but he does fail Lillian as a lover because he comes to her to be renewed, not to satisfy her. It is Djuna who gives the best insight into Larry's behavior toward Lillian, believing that

> life tended to crystallize into patterns which became traps and webs. That people tended to see each other in their first "state" or "form" and to adopt a rhythm in consequence. That they had greatest difficulty in seeing the transformations of the loved one, in seeing the becoming. If they did finally perceive the new self, they had the greatest difficulty nevertheless in changing the rhythm. The strong one was condemned to perpetual strength, the weak to perpetual weakness. The one who loved you best condemned you to a static role because he had adapted his being to the past self. [*Ladders*, p. 28]

Her comments continue, and her insights offer understanding into what appears to be Larry's insensitive behavior.[5]

As we have seen, one way in which Lillian has tried to find happiness and fulfillment away from her husband and family is with Djuna in a relationship that is doomed to failure. Lillian begins to court Djuna and to bring her gifts representing anything but love; for to those gifts are tied the strings forming a web to trap Djuna, which would enable Lillian to possess her entirely. When she was young, Lillian was frightened by a demon jack-in-the-box; it is a similar demon that is in her and in the gifts she brings. But instead of being repulsed by this poison (although she is certainly aware of it), Djuna chooses not to see a demon but a woman who needs the help and love that she, Djuna, has to offer. Lillian tests Djuna's love severely. When Djuna looks with telling eyes on a can-can dancer, Lillian becomes jealous; when Djuna is busy elsewhere, Lillian becomes ill and needs Djuna to help her.[6] Djuna understandably begins to feel the strain of caring for Lillian and treats her in a condescending manner similar to the narrator's treatment of the Mouse in the story of that title. Lillian cannot help herself, however, because the one thing she needs is love, and in order to try to achieve it she resorts to seduction, which is a tactic that is antithetical to love. Although she is a woman of considerable passion, she is unable to expend it as she reaches the point where she thrives on a "hysterical undercurrent without culmination," and her state is compared to a sirocco that lasted for two days at the end of which there was "no respite, no climax, no great loosening as in other storms. A tension that gathered force but had no release, . . . it was not attached to anything, it was not creating anything, it was a trap of negation" (*Ladders*, pp. 45–46). Djuna realizes that a man and not a woman can save Lillian, but in order to be saved from herself Lillian needs to restore her rhythm with humanity by subduing her aggressiveness.

Midway through this story of Lillian's hunger for life and of Djuna's hunger for love without pain comes Jay, the most recurrent and important man in Nin's fiction. He enters in the tenth of the twenty sections; his name (or a pronoun for it) appears in the first sentence of every subsequent section except the fifteenth (in which he first appears in the second paragraph) and the last. There is no better way than to introduce him with his name, "Jay!" That single word, that single sentence, is all inclusive; Jay is Jay, and he is unique unto himself. He sits at a wine-stained table, ends his phrases with a hum, and creates "a climate, a tropical day" that melts Lillian's aggressiveness (*Ladders*, p. 50). Many of Nin's characters are artists and so is Jay, but his versatility and his numerous talents (painting, writing, acting, music) do not enable him to create great works because he is lazy and hedonistic; if he is confronted with working or idly conversing with someone, he will always choose the latter. But despite the likelihood that he will never produce great art, he is able to produce some results in his relationship with Lillian, soothing her and causing in her a rebirth of sorts. She may have reservations about his indifference, but she notices in him what appears to be a "spark of faith"; it is to this that she clings in her relationship with him.

Jay and Larry have been the two most important men in Lillian's life, but to understand why she prefers Jay is to understand the woman Lillian. The two men are compared in the short fifteenth section of the story. Larry had provided her with security, stability, and protection; he "stood erect, and self-sufficient, and manly" [*Ladders*, p. 59]. But he has not been able to enter her as a true love because, in part, she could not open herself to him; his "upstanding protectiveness" [ibid.] kept her from achieving the human rhythm that Djuna suggested she needed so badly. In fact Lillian had liked every aspect of Larry except "the aspect of lover" (ibid., p. 58). Strangely it is Jay who is in almost every detail Larry's opposite, and it is Jay who will be able to help her regain the necessary rhythm.

> But Jay . . . came towards her almost as a man who limps and whom one instinctively wishes to sustain. He came as the man who did not see very well, slightly awkward, slightly stumbling. In this helplessness, in spite of his actual stature (he was the same height as her husband) he gave the air of being smaller, more fragile, more vulnerable. It was this fear in the man, who seemed inadequate in regard to life, trapped in it, the victim of it, which somehow affected her. In a smaller, weaker dimension he seemed to reach the right proportion for his being able to enter into hers. He entered by the route of her compassion. She opened as the refuge opens; not conscious that it was a man who entered (man of whom she had a certain suspicion) but a child in need. Because he knocked as a beggar begging for a retreat, as a victim seeking solace, as a weakling seeking sustenance, she opened the door without suspicion.
>
> It was in her frenzy to shelter, cover, defend him that she laid her strength over his head like an enormous starry roof, and the stretching immensity of the boundless mother was substituted for the normal image of the man covering the woman. [Ibid., p. 59]

She is able to open herself for Jay. But just as she had been too aggressive with the bicyclist-lover of her youth (ibid., pp. 48-49), so is she too aggressive with Jay; this quality is portrayed symbolically during their lovemaking as she assumes the dominant position. Jay makes it difficult for her to see and to understand her own problems, because he is content to reside within her on her terms.

> His taking her was not to take her or master her. He was the lover inside of the woman, as the child is inside of the woman. His caresses were as if he yearned and craved to be taken in not only as a lover; not merely to satisfy his desire but to remain within her. And her yearning answered this, by her

desire to be filled. She never felt him outside of herself. Her husband had stood outside of her, and had come to visit her as a man, sensually. But he had not lodged himself as Jay had done, by reposing in her, by losing himself in her, by melting within her, with such feeling of physical intermingling as she had had with her child. Her husband had come to be renewed, to emerge again, to leave her and go to his male activities, to his struggles with the world.

The maternal and the feminine cravings were all confused in her, and all she felt was that it was through this softening and through this maternal yieldingness that Jay had penetrated where she had not allowed her husband's manliness to enter, only to visit her. [Ibid., pp. 60–61]

So even though Lillian and Jay believe they function well together, their relationship suggests symbolic incestuousness, the son being his mother's lover.

Until this point Lillian has been of chief concern in her relationship with Jay; but in the antepenultimate section of "This Hunger" Jay encounters Djuna, and through her his true feelings are revealed. There is little doubt that he is truly attracted to Lillian's passions, but the seemingly simple Jay needs more than that: he needs a balance that Djuna is able to provide for him. She is understanding with him, just as she had been earlier with Lillian. She is a woman who is his friend and not his lover, a woman in whom he can confide, a woman who functions in a sense as the hub of his life. With Lillian and Djuna Jay has the balance he needs for psychic survival. But his oversimplified view of the two women, his not allowing reason to enter the passionate Lillian, his not allowing passion to enter into Djuna's relation to him, disserves them as women and as human beings. He is fulfilling only his own needs in these situations and only half the needs of the women who are emotionally dependent on him. Certainly he possesses considerable charm, but it conceals a man who is much more dangerous, probably, than someone like Lillian's husband.

After Jay's character is well established, he introduces a new character, Helen, to Lillian; the women's interaction further elucidates Lillian's difficulties. More extreme than Lillian, Helen is masculine, aggressive, and "immobilized by a fear" (*Ladders*, p. 71). She is one who borders on the inhuman and the mythic.[7] Their situations are similar: Helen felt repressed in her family, and to free herself, to attain life, she fled her husband and children. But she has found (as Henry James's Isabel Archer learned) that fleeing from one's unhappiness is not necessarily to escape it. Guilt and regrets remain, and her body and soul are not free. The one thing Helen needs immediately is consolation, but because Jay is unable to give it to her, Lillian must.

Lillian has feared Helen because she felt that Helen would take Jay from her; but to her amazement Lillian finds herself acting like a lover toward Helen, just as she was afraid Jay might. But Lillian is more like Djuna than Jay in her relationship with Helen, and she now assumes a role toward Helen similar to the one that Djuna had assumed toward Lillian earlier. After Lillian helps her loosen her rigidity and feel a renewed hunger for life, Helen begins to make demands on the person who had helped her; she plays upon Lillian's emotions, dramatizes small incidents, and in general becomes dependent on her. Lillian reacts in a manner similar to the way Djuna had reacted. She feels that she is being swamped by Helen, and, feeling that she can no longer help her, Lillian encourages her to travel in order to leave the scene of her anguish. Although Lillian had helped her as best she could, and even though she feels free after she leaves, Lillian's positive actions toward Helen are undercut because she "had worn the warrior armor to protect a core of love. Once again she had worn the man's costume." She has served Jay, but "Jay had not made her woman, but the husband and mother of his weakness" (*Ladders*, p. 77).

During their last meeting Lillian reveals her pregnancy to Jay. The confession suggests that she may feel herself responsible for the pregnancy and that there is guilt to be expiated. Instead of receiving solace from Jay, the father of her child, he becomes irritated at this possible intrusion into his carefree life and urges Lillian to have an abortion. As a result of his lack of feeling for either her or their child, Lillian, sitting alone in a dark room, addresses the unborn child in the most moving part of the story. She is disillusioned, and in that darkened room she seeks the life without pain that is such a dominant quest in Nin's work. The child is in a pleasurable state, the state of prebirth, but it is kicking at Lillian's womb, eager to live and to face the difficulties of life. In language reminiscent of Djuna's in "Winter of Artifice," Lillian implies that her own father had not been large enough to protect her from life and that her own child will surely suffer because of Jay's inadequacies. Instead of resolving to aid the child through the early years of life, Lillian believes it would be better for the child to die while still protected by the warmth and darkness of the womb. As in "Birth" and "Winter of Artifice," the child is born dead, having been spared a life of difficulties. The miscarriage of the child is physical, and yet in this case it seems to have been induced by Lillian's troubled psyche.

After the hungers of the various characters have been identified and discussed, "This Hunger" concludes with an episode symbolizing the individual hungers of Lillian and Djuna and the collective hungers of all women, as Nin saw them. Lillian has been asked to play the piano at a party in a private home that is as icy and fragile as Jeanne's residence in "Under a Glass Bell." The people are perfumed in their stiff dress; the golden salon is adorned with crystal lamps. Lillian performs passionately in this stifling environment in an attempt to reach some climax that both men and women can share in a "moment of pleasure, a moment of fusion." She is attempting to regain her rhythm with life, but she is unable to do so, for what emits from her and the piano is her plea "to be stormed with equal strength and fervor" (*Ladders*, p. 79), and so she remains frustrated and unable to give satisfactory vent to her passions. The guests politely congratulate her on her performance.

Djuna is also at the party, but instead of sitting among the guests she is situated on their fringe next to a garden recently bathed in rain, amidst a "sensual humidity as if leaves, trees, grass and wind were all in a state of caress" (*Ladders*, p. 80). The fertile garden contrasts sharply with the falsity and artificiality of the people and the gilded room; it functions symbolically to suggest the possibility of wholeness and fertility for the people in general and for Lillian and Djuna especially. But while the garden may be a symbol of hope and fecundity, it is perverted, Djuna discovers, by the presence of three mirrors that have been placed in it by the people who cannot bear the garden's dangerous truth and who delight only in the "fragility of reflections" (ibid., p. 81). Unfelt by the people at the party is a rumbling in the subterranean passages beneath the house and garden, reminiscent of similar rumblings amid another paradisal scene in Coleridge's "Kubla Khan," even to the point of Kubla's hearing ancestral voices from afar prophesying war. The rumblings here seem to be a warning to the guests: beware of the dangers accompanying the perverting of nature. More specifically, they represent "the humiliated, the defeated, the oppressed, the enslaved. Woman's misused and twisted strength" (ibid.), the women whose natures have for so long been twisted out of shape and who will abide those distortions no longer. Not only will Lillian and Djuna assert their true natures, but so too will the finely toileted women who insensitively fawn over Lillian as she plays the piano. This hunger, this desire of women for freedom, is about to occur, and when it does, the precious house and other such artifices will slip into oblivion, as does Poe's house of Usher.

The second and final part of *Ladders to Fire*, as it now stands, is entitled "Bread and the Wafer" to symbolize the "physical and metaphysical fulfillment" of the hungers described in the first section.[8] But instead of progressing toward real fulfillment the characters, with the possible exception of Djuna, once again are struggling to attain a wholeness that is just beyond their grasp. Lillian and Sabina are the two female characters examined most thoroughly, but Jay is equally as important because both of them are in love with him and also because he brings them, through his absences, to love each other. Nowhere here is there mention of Lillian's family, but to insist on constant or even occasional references to the life she is attempting to escape is to demand realism, not reality, an artifice instead of actuality. It is her growth as a woman that is kept in focus rather than the welfare of her family. Throughout Nin's works one can perceive a consistent investigation into her characters' psychological states (reality) and not of their inconsequential physical trappings (realism). As we shall see, the same emphasis obtains, though in a lesser degree, in Nin's *Diary*.

Lillian and Jay remain lovers, although tempestuous ones, and in this section their relationship, along with Jay's character, is examined in considerable detail. He continues to be the voracious man/animal accepting everything and attempting to understand nothing, whose carefree nature demands a flow and freedom suggesting the dancer's at the end of *House of Incest*. But the natural charm and appeal of this hedonistic, indiscriminate individual is undercut by his need for a mooring in his chaos. Not just any mooring will do, and when Jay is instructed that chaos "turns out to be the greatest trap of all," he turns "automatically towards Lillian and read[s] in her eyes that fixed, immutable love which was his compass" (*Ladders*, p. 87), without which he would surely drown in his own existence. Because of her he can live as he desires, but the reverse is true as well: she is able to experience a world larger than herself through her relationship with Jay, and when he is gone she can view life only at a distance. Each helps the other, and each is able to live because of the other. But although Jay is indeed dependent on Lillian, she is in even greater need of him; he therefore functions as her iron lung, as one responsible for every breath she takes. The one thing that Lillian has desired is to be devoured, to be made to submit to a man; when Jay is able to serve her needs, he does so with an intensity unknown to her previously. She feels "caught in the immense jaws of his desire" (ibid., p. 91) into which she throws everything she has. In a splendidly written scene of sexuality, Lillian gives herself entirely, until "she slept, she fell into trances, she was lost, she was renewed, she was blessed, pierced by joy, lulled, burned, consumed, purified, born and reborn within the whale belly of the night" (ibid., p. 92).

Their relationship is an unusual one, however. Superficially it satisfies both but actually leaves Lillian very hungry. It would be easy to find fault with Jay even while granting his irrepressibility, but Nin is careful to offer an explanation for how he became the man he is. His scars are deep from the betrayal by his parents in his youth. Only two examples of their destructive behavior are cited, and while they are bad enough, they also suggest that such cruel actions were not isolated. Jay's father inflicted one early scar. It was the young boy's dream to visit a new battleship at the Brooklyn Navy yard that all his friends had seen. He was jubilant when his father offered to take him to it, and he gladly consented to his father's demand to wash carefully and to wear a good suit. But instead of going to the battleship, they went to a doctor's office where the boy's tonsils were removed. One can imagine the jolt that the six-year-old felt: "The pain was a million times multiplied by the shock of disillusion, of betrayal, by the violent contrast between my dream, my expectations, and the brutal reality of the operation" (*Ladders*, p. 93). Even before that experience, however, Jay had been betrayed by his mother. On a very cold night, when the boy was five, he was walking quickly with her toward the river, feeling terribly cold. She would occasionally take his hand when they crossed streets, and the warmth of her hand warmed him all through, but then she put her hand back in the warm muff she was carrying. The warmth he experienced was not just physical, and to gain more of it he attempted to place his own hands in the sexually symbolic muff, only to have his mother slap them away. These and other damaging experiences left Jay a person yearning for warmth; as a man he devours everything indiscriminately in search of the warmth he desires. Jay tells Lillian of his youth, and she quite naturally feels that she must perform as Jay's mother should have, providing him with the warmth and understanding that he received from neither of his parents. Their relationship, however, is that of lovers, not of mother and son, and so while Lillian is able to perform as a surrogate mother and fulfill the needs of her "son," her own needs go unmet because he cannot offer the psychological comfort that she needs. Above all else, Jay needs to fill the void that his parents created in him, but that void can never be filled; his life with Lillian is therefore destined to be unsatisfactory for both of them, for Lillian will constantly be forced to play the role of the mother and will necessarily feel guilty if she tries to satisfy her own needs instead of Jay's.

Jay's greatest quality flows when Lillian is asleep, but this creative energy does not always have the most positive result if one is to judge it according to its product. When he approaches his work he explodes in creativity, but what he creates is "a spectacle of carnage" in which the whole world is shattered into fragments and in which "bodies, objects, cities, trees, animals were all splintered, pierced, impaled" (*Ladders*, p. 101). This explosion of creativity resembles the act of giving birth, but what he fathers are abortions, freaks, incomplete children that are like animals because "the substance that could weld them together again was absent" (ibid., p. 102). Jay's art does not function only as a comment on his temperament or perception, for when Lillian sees it she is aghast because she realizes, subconsciously, that what he creates are her nightmares, and she is frightened to see herself exposed in such a manner. Jay might create such hostility and ugliness in his art, but once he expresses it there it seems to act as a kind of catharsis for him; he is able to move away from it and become something like a normal man once again. Unfortunately, the effect upon Lillian is the opposite, for she appears to be placid on the surface while in fact she cannot escape from the unsightliness of Jay's art, a mirroring of her inner self. Even Jay in his insensitivity to the feelings of others can "see how Lillian was a prolongation of this warfare on canvas, how at the point where he left violence and became a simple, anonymous, mild-mannered man, it was she who took up the thread and enacted the violence directly upon people" (ibid., p. 103). He can vent his anger and then go on to function in life, and she cannot; therefore, when he leaves her each day, she thinks he is deserting her (as Stella similarly misinterprets Bruno's absences). The ever-salutary Djuna is left to suggest that perhaps Jay is not locking Lillian out but, rather, is locking her in to save her for their nights of ectasy together. Once again Djuna comes to Lillian's aid, and again Djuna is given the role of being the one to help the others with problems and provide insights that they cannot achieve for themselves.

The reasons for Jay's behavior have been discussed; his strange actions have been put in a negative light because of his fragmented vision. The fifth section of "Bread and the Wafer" is largely an interior monologue in which he examines life and reveals his attitude toward it. Even

Djuna's bland reassurances to Lillian cannot discount the fact that when Jay is absent from her, he is not only apart from her but from himself as well. When he enters the street, a microcosm of the larger world, he loses himself in it and becomes akin to Emerson's transparent eyeball. But instead of finding that nature's appearance is never mean, he finds ugliness and squalor all around him. There, all people and things are interchangeable, and if one has lost a child, as appears to be the case with Jay, it is of little consequence because there are other children to be had. He thus faults Lillian for her reliance on the one (that he, for example, is irreplaceable) when no one and nothing is unique.

On his mental trip through the streets, Jay makes two stops. The first, his encounter with a retired legionnaire, is more highly suggestive than the surface narrative implies. The legionnaire has accomplished what Jay has missed: while in the service he received letters from his unknown godmother, letters so warm with feeling that he could almost use them to heat his hands. On his first furlough he searched for and found this poor woman; she sold bananas from a cart and slept under bridges at night. He was so jubilant to be with her, who cared for him so much (as much as his unmentioned real mother should have), that he deserted the Legion to live with her. Jay does not make the connection consciously, but he must know that the legionnaire was able to find warmth in a woman just as Jay himself has been seeking the same thing since the age of five when he was denied his mother's muff. His encounter with the legionnaire therefore suggests that he does not desire an ugly or loveless world at all, but that because of painful experiences in childhood, when his needs went unfulfilled, he is unable to see the beauty and sanguinity that others more fortunate than he can perceive naturally.

After this Jay crosses the Rue Dolent, the street of sadness, the sign of which is nailed to a prison wall, suggesting the unhappiness that the prisoners experience. What Jay finds, however, is that the prisoners are more free than most people who lead lives of quiet desperation.

> *On one side are men whose crimes were accomplished in a moment of rage, rebellion, violence. On the other, grey figures too afraid to hate, to rebel, to kill openly. On the free side of the wall they walk with iron bars in their hearts and stones on their feet carrying the balls and chains of their obsessions. Prisoners of their weakness, of their self-inflicted illnesses and slaveries. No need of guards and keys! They will never escape from themselves, and they only kill others with the invisible death rays of their impotence.* [*Ladders,* p. 106.]

This is essentially the theme of most of Nin's fiction: one may be imprisoned and still be free, and one may walk the streets a legally free person but really be imprisoned behind the bars of one's own mind. All of Nin's major fictional women are attempting to escape from their inner prisons, though not necessarily their outer ones. Jay's stroll down the Rue Dolent concludes when he meets a series of ugly and misshapen people resembling the grotesqueries in his paintings, those distortions for which he has been criticized by the artistic establishment. He does not mind such criticism, however, because it keeps him from attaining fame and wealth, and therefore he is forced to continue living in the streets, exposing life's ugliness that others do not wish to acknowledge. In her art, Nin wished to reveal her characters' inner turmoil to complacent readers and to critics who found her work unrealistic; in his art, Jay attempts to show the underside of life to a too-proper society. In both cases *"the artist is there to keep accounts"* (ibid., p. 108).

Jay brought Helen to Lillian in "This Hunger," and as important as Helen is, she is evanescent and never again appears in Nin's work. But in "Bread and the Wafer" Jay introduces another woman to Lillian, and this time the new character does not fade from sight but remains to become, with Lillian and Djuna, one of the most important women in the continuous novel. Sabina first appeared in *House of Incest*, but in this novel (published ten years after the prose poem) she is described in great detail for the first time. She is a female Jay, a Dona Juana to his Don Juan, and Jay hates her because she is as free in love as he is and because she views all people as he does, as possible lovers. But although he considers her "the woman without fidelity, capable of all desecrations" (*Ladders*, p. 112), he is also able to meet her demands, which are obviously sexual, as he cannot meet Lillian's. When Lillian meets Sabina, though, she feels as though Sabina is the woman she wants to be (as is the case with the narrator and Sabina in *House of Incest*). Sabina is the woman with burning eyes and a rusty voice who dresses in red and silver and enters a scene like a fire engine that signals catastrophe. She is impatient and incapable of resting easily in one place. Like Jay, she is not reflective; she lives in and creates chaos wherever she goes. The title of the novel is hers: as she enters she erects a ladder in the middle of the city and orders all to climb it to the top where they will encounter fire, which is the symbol for Sabina herself.

Lillian wishes to imitate Sabina's audaciousness because it is a hidden part of herself. But she finds herself not in a totally honest relationship with this new woman when she realizes that Sabina is feverishly creating the reverse of what she acted out: "a woman of loyalty and faithfulness" (*Ladders*, p. 115). Lillian, as we have seen, is not known for her analytical powers, but she sees through Sabina's costumes and façades and hears a "child within Sabina whining, tired of its inventions grown too cumbersome, weary of its adornments, of its disguises" (ibid., p. 116). Lillian can see this schism in Sabina, but because it resembles her own, she ignores it and takes Sabina to herself, wearing her bracelet, walking with her arm-in-arm down the street, resting her hand on Sabina's breasts, dancing with her in a café; she is even tempted to take drugs with her. Together they think they have caught a glimpse of love "through a slit in the dream" (ibid., p. 122). Sabina herself is a ladder that Lillian climbs to the fire of Sabina's passion.

Lillian and Sabina attempt to consummate their love, being alone without the encumbrances of the past or of friends. They face the night without a sense of sin, and as they attempt to fashion their own reality they become awkward and somewhat timid. Each wishes to become like the other in order to gain the love of Jay, but as they disrobe and attempt to consume one another they find that such an exchange is impossible, for what each embraces is a mirror image of the inner self: Lillian's newness and Sabina's marked body. A woman cannot find wholeness by uniting with another woman; it is a man who is the complement and completion of woman, just as a woman is of man. Both Lillian and Sabina realize their relationship will not lead to fulfillment; Lillian throws Sabina's bracelets out the window. Lillian also sees that Sabina has really loved Jay and has been using Lillian to gain Jay's love. Because she can gain the love of neither Jay nor Lillian, Sabina becomes "like a foaming sea, churning up wreckage, the debris of all her doubts and fears" (*Ladders*, p. 127).

Lillian's victory over Sabina for Jay's love is pyrrhic, however, for she discovers that her plight with him is what she should have expected from the outset. Although he swears his love for her, what he means by love is not concern, adoration, softness, or the wish to confer real happiness on the beloved; instead, it means that he has a need, a desire, an appetite for her; in short, it means self-gratification. He is heartless, and yet because his mere presence glows, it is easy to see how Lillian could mistake that for the heat of love, which it assuredly is not. Lillian is trapped: she is aware of Jay's qualities and the manner in which he is using her; she knows he will eventually die of hardness, as she will from an excess of feeling. Her love for him is immutable, but she has no such love to act as her mooring; she is strangling in her own roots while he lives out every whim. He and Sabina are indeed similar, but Lillian is different in kind from both of them.

It is no surprise that Djuna consoles Lillian and listens to her describe her incomplete state with Jay. Lillian sought Jay as a guide because he is a man, and indeed "this was a fear all women had known . . . seeking the guide in men, not in the past, or in mythology, but a guide with a living breath who might create one"; the "guide for woman was still inextricably woven with man and with man's creation" (*Ladders*, pp. 132–33). Because Jay is a painter, Lillian thought he could "create her," bring her to life, mold and fashion her; especially because this is a world in which women must take on man's values and attitudes. But Jay's chaos had made it impossible for him to mold Lillian. Djuna admonishes her and directs her toward real independence, fulfillment, and awareness.

> "Lillian, no one should be entrusted with one's image to fashion, with one's self-creation. Women are moving from one circle to another, rising towards independence and self-creation. What you're really suffering from is from the pain of parting with your faith, with your old love when you wish to renew this faith and preserve the passion. You're being thrust out of one circle into another and it is this which causes you so much fear. You know you cannot lean on Jay, but you don't know what awaits you, and you don't trust your own awareness." [Ibid., p. 133]

She could not help Lillian emerge from her pain, "and so they continued to walk unsteadily over what Lillian saw merely as the dead leaves of his indifference" (ibid., p. 134). Thus Djuna cannot solve Lillian's problem for her after all, but she attempts to bring her to a point of fresh insight into the structure of her problem and her personality.

"This Hunger" ends with the great symbolic scene of the party at which Lillian is playing the piano and Djuna is observing the mirrors in the garden. "Bread and the Wafer" and the entire novel close in a similar fashion. The conclusion is what Nin has termed the "nonparty or the antiparty"[9] that is held in Lillian and Jay's studio but which flows out into all the apartments and buildings along Montparnasse. The major character at this party is a wooden, polished man known as the Chess Player. His role is to manipulate people, and in that capacity he is concerned only with their displacement and not at all with their development. One of his pawns is Faustin, the Zombie, who died when he faced experience. He is inert and submissive, and he believes that one ought to cultivate inertia. The Chess Player wants to observe the effect of the dead Faustin on the others at the party, but when his voice falls upon Sabina, it has no effect; she simply turns away. Faustin is disappointed; he enjoyed collecting Jay's discarded mistresses.

Djuna is immune to the Chess Player's manipulations because she lives in her own cities of the interior, keeping no permanent abode, arriving and leaving undetected, "as through a series of trap doors" (*Ladders*, p. 139). She sits close to the guitarist, Rango, who will become of great importance in *The Four-Chambered Heart*. Jay and his friends arrive, and when Sabina observes him and Lillian exchanging telling glances, she decides to leave but finds herself lost and alone with her cape (soul) becalmed. For her, stillness is death. Jealousy now clogs her body and pain lodges itself inside of her; she has become lost in her stories and fantasies, but there is hope for her as the "withered leaves of her being detach[ed] themselves" (ibid., p. 145). Stella appears, still unable to give herself fully to a man, still filled with mistrust, but at this party mistrust is advantageous, for the participants present only invented false selves to each other in order to protect their own vulnerabilities. Just as Jay is heartless, so too are the people here hiding their hearts, the "one uninvaded cell" (ibid., p. 147); therefore, they offer only artifice to the others. Lillian is one of the victims; although she has saved others by shaking them out of their lethargy, she lacks faith and confidence and finds herself alone in her chess square feeling inferior to the others, sensitive to her imagined defects and weaknesses, defeated and humiliated, "a little pile of ashes from a bonfire of self-criticism" (ibid., p. 148). The Chess Player simply smiles at her drunkenness and takes no note of her internal suicide.

The party has the greatest importance for Djuna. As she begins to slip away from it, the Chess Player encourages her to become acquainted with some of Jay's unattractive friends. While she realizes that one may derive great pleasure from the collision of opposites, she is unable to experience it: her dream of the ideal party does not permit her to enjoy the present one (just as a phantom lover occasionally keeps Nin's women from finding a good relationship with a mere mortal). Djuna had, in fact, witnessed a fantastically colorful party, people splendid and gay, the ideal (unattainable) party taking place across the way, but her dream prohibited her from observing or participating in a party approximating that one in grandeur. At the present party, a new danger threatening her is a mood provoked by two phrases from a dream: "This is not the place" and "He is not the one." These "fatal" phrases lock her out instantly, "thrust out by no one but herself, by a mood which cut her off from fraternity" (*Ladders*, p. 150). Her dream, her ideal, has gotten in the way of reality, and she realizes it: "Bring me one who will rescue me! Am I dreaming or dying? Bring me one who knows that between the dream and death there is only one frail step, one who senses that between this murder of the present by a dream, and death, there is only one shallow breath. Bring me one who knows that the dream without exit, without explosion, without awakening, is the passageway to the world of the dead! I want my dress torn and stained!" (ibid., p. 151). As she makes her impassioned plea for salvation, a drunken man emerges bringing a gold chair with a red brocade top on which he transports her back "to the dark room of her adolescence, to the long white nightgown and hair brush, and to her dream of a Party that she could never attend" (ibid., p. 152). All other people at the party have lost contact with themselves and with others, but in the end Djuna returns to the source of her difficulty; in confronting it, one hopes she can become a completed woman who will not forget the hardships of her youth, but instead will keep them in perspective so they will not dictate her present actions.

Lillian, Jay, and Sabina all climb ladders to fire in this novel, but the one who does not, the reflective Djuna, has traveled furthest toward a fulfilling identity.

5

Children of the
Albatross

Children of the Albatross, the second contribution to Nin's
continuous novel, was published originally by Dutton
in 1947.[1] The novel is divided into two sections: the
first, "The Sealed Room," is a fairly coherent story focusing on Djuna
and a set of characters, chiefly male, who encircle her; the second, "The
Café ," is in a superficial way the most obviously structured of any of
the longer pieces of fiction, and yet it contains a looseness of
construction that looks ahead toward Nin's last novel, *Collages.*

Djuna has appeared as regularly, to this point, as any other female
character in Nin's fiction, and her role has been a consistent one: she is
often cast as an important yet peripheral character who emerges, like
Hawthorne's gray champion, when her friends, especially Lillian, need
her assistance. In these instances Djuna is the voice of reason and
reflection who bolsters others. But as has been noted elsewhere, her
comments sometime seem to be condescending, and it is not always
clear whether she evinces true compassion for her confidantes or
whether she is simply gifted with the ability to specify and analyze the
problems of others. One might suspect that like all Nin's women Djuna
has difficulties of her own and has no one to help her with them. Such is
indeed the case, and her history is presented in "The Sealed Room."

Djuna's story is, of course, a psychological one. The most important
event in it is her father's desertion of his family when she was sixteen.
There are hints and allusions to the desertion and to her subsequent life

in an orphanage as the story progresses, but once again chronology is not adhered to strictly, so much so that it is difficult to discern at times which actions are taking place in the present and which took place in the past. It is only after reading the whole of "The Sealed Room" that a clear picture of Djuna emerges. Few facts are presented about her, but we do learn that she is or has been married (although her husband is never mentioned), that she lives in a house on the edge of Paris, that she is or has been a dancer of considerable potential, and that she prefers (or thinks she prefers) to be in the company of adolescent boys instead of mature men. Facts, however, are always anathema to Nin, and it is the inner and not the outer Djuna, reality and not realism, that is investigated through this story, just as it has been in the earlier fiction.

"The Sealed Room" begins with Djuna's arriving at a fair in Montmartre. The instant she leaves her bus the carousel and its music begin, changing her into a happy woman. There is no evidence that an outwardly real fair is in progress. It exists rather in Djuna's mind, and when "she felt the whole scene, her mood, her body [were] transformed by its gaiety exactly as in her childhood her life in the orphan asylum had been suddenly transformed from a heavy nightmare to freedom by her winning of a dance scholarship" (*Albatross*, p. 7). But as important as the scholarship and the freedom it led to were, even more important to Djuna is "her interior monologue set to music [that] led her feet into the dance" (ibid.). That is, although her confinement certainly was physical, it was much more intensely mental, and to free herself she had to take refuge in her cities of the interior, her dreams, to gain sustenance to do battle once more with reality and the mental anguish that she suffered from it. She is constantly bolstered by this inner resource, which is musical, harmonic, rhythmic, that now frees her outer self, creating the gay Djuna who appears at the beginning of the story.

It may be that Nin's second of five novels is too soon a time to present a woman who has overcome her obstacles and has achieved wholeness in life; so despite Djuna's possessing qualities that, if developed further, could well lead to the desired state, she is still struggling and will continue to do so throughout the remainder of the continuous novel. Because she is reflective and rational, however, Djuna always seems to be in less difficulty than do the more obviously troubled Lillian and Sabina. Djuna's present problems have their source in the past. Her dancing teacher, "stylized man of forty" (*Albatross*, p. 11), was able to bring her to submission at an earlier time; through his domination she was able to reach a kind of perfection in dancing. In what appears to be a fusion of past and present, Djuna recalls his attentions to her, his attempts to rule her body, his following her into the dressing room, his invitation to take her with him on tour throughout Europe. The music at the novel's beginning permist her to recall the joyous music of the past, the body dancing, and how to deal with the dancing instructor: "How to explain to this simple man, how to explain. *There is something broken inside of me*. I cannot dance, live, love as easily as others. . . . *I am the dancer who falls*, always, into traps of depression, breaking my heart and my body almost at every turn, losing my tempo and my lightness, falling out of groups, out of grace, out of perfection" (ibid., p. 15). Her inner turmoil prevents her from achieving the happiness she craves. Her difficulty actually lies in her solitude, in her inability to achieve intimacy with another; when the carousel stops, so too does the ecstasy and the remembrance of the dancing master.

This solitude dates, predictably, from her youth, from her time at the orphanage when she was sixteen (and even before that, as we shall see). In the orphanage Djuna formed an attachment from afar with a boy about her own age; she was kept from him, however, by a watchman, a man who was the orphanage directress's lover (and so in a position of great power). In order for Djuna to meet with her boy friend she needed to submit to the watchman's advances, but again, although she was subjected to physical indignities, the more pernicious mental damage resulted in her mistrusting and disliking men of authority. Even this attitude had its roots farther back in her experience, but its feeling is one that Djuna carries with her into the present of this novel. Throughout "The Sealed Room" Djuna is surrounded by adolescent males whose youth and homosexuality appeal to her because those two qualities are exactly opposite to the ones she found so distasteful in the watchman; but by living exclusively in their company she is merely exchanging one extreme for another, and consequently she is unable to open herself to a man like her dancing instructor, even though he is as understanding and gentle as the watchman was insensitive and harsh.

Before introducing the young men, however, Nin presents a picture of Djuna's home to serve as a symbolic introduction to her character. She has wanted a garden ever since she saw the one with the mirrors at the end of "This Hunger," but the one she now possesses is not one she can live in; it is much too calm for the turmoil raging within her and therefore stands as what one hopes the fully developed Djuna will approximate: "Happiness was an absence of fever" (*Albatross*, p. 24). One enters the grounds of Djuna's home through gates that seem, to her inner self, prison gates. When she studies them, she notices that the larger one is rusty and formidable, like the watchman of her youth, but the smaller one is never locked and is therefore always available for entry. It is this openness that she wants her house to suggest about herself to others; she even illuminates the entire house to indicate the passion burning within. Once one is enticed by the house, one quickly finds it is, like Gatsby's, a myth. The house is fanciful, but there is one part that frightens Djuna because it suggests what her trouble is. When all the rooms are lighted, one notices a dark window that has behind it a closed room, one so hermetically sealed that it emits not the least bit of light. This sealed room is Djuna's inner core that is protected from the hurts of invasion, though in the process it isolates her from companionship and love.

Given this background one understands why Djuna prefers the friends she does. The first one to be presented is Michael. He is a year or two her senior, and we later learn that he was the previously unidentified boy friend during her stay in the orphanage. What he offered her then was softness and a lack of aggressiveness, which were qualities opposite the watchman's. But it does not take Djuna long to realize that although Michael is painless to her, he is painless to a fault; instead of interacting they simply parallel each other; they are twins dancing without touching in "a deft dance of unpossession" (*Albatross*, p. 39).

About a year later, when Michael returns from college, their relationship is the same as it had been before, but this time there is a change in Djuna. Instead of feeling comfortable with the nonaggressive Michael, she begins to feel sexually aroused and then frustrated because he will not or cannot fulfill her emerging feelings. At a party she dances off with another. Michael then becomes jealously assertive as he reclaims her for himself, but once she returns to him he quickly reestablishes the old distance so that he will not have to fulfill her physical or psychological needs. He then reveals that while they were at the "dance he had discovered an intermediate world from which all the figures of women were absent. A world of boys like himself in flight away from woman, mother, sister, wife or mistress" (*Albatross*, p.45).

Instead of accepting his homosexuality, Michael blames Djuna for it, and she accepts the blame. She tries desperately to accommodate him, fails, and in time she marries; finally, she forgets Michael's image. But to understand Djuna, the reader must understand Michael's lasting influence upon her.

> But she continued to relate to other Michaels in the world. Some part of her being continued to recognize the same gentleness, the same elusiveness, the same mystery.
>
> Michael reappeared under different bodies, guises, and each time she responded to him, discovering each time a little more until she pierced the entire mystery open.
>
> But the same little dance took place each time, a little dance of insolence, a dance which said to the woman: "I dance alone, I will not be possessed by a woman."
>
> The kind of dance tradition had taught woman as a ritual to provoke aggression! But this dance made by young men before the women left them at a loss for it was not intended to be answered. [*Albatross*, p. 46]

Years later (presumably in the present of the novel), Djuna is sitting with Michael and his friend Donald in a Paris café; she is not an active participant in their relationship at first, but they form a kind of trinity for the moment: "love flowing now between the three, shared, transmitted, contagious, as if Michael were at last free to love Djuna in the form of a boy, through the body of Donald to reach Djuna whom he could never touch directly, and Djuna through the body of Donald reached Michael" (ibid., p. 52). But Djuna recognizes that all their movements continue to be as "a ballet of unreality and unpossession" (ibid., p. 53), and the lingering fear of authority and aggressiveness leads her to continue in the company of these young men.

The remainder of "The Sealed Room" concerns the twenty-seven-year-old Djuna and two seventeen-year-old boys, Paul and Lawrence. Both boys have trouble confronting life, but Paul is of most concern because he was injured (as Jay was) by parents who are now typically insensitive and thoughtlessly demanding adults (the mother made Paul kill his pet guinea pig). Because he feared his parents' response, he destroyed a diary he had kept. Recently they have prohibited him from associating with dancers like Djuna, but he has decided to spend the last month of his vacation with his new friends prior to his going to India (at the request of his father). This decision is unacceptable to his parents; rather than showing him any love, compassion, or confidence, they eventually attempt to have him brought home to safety by a private detective.

There are elements of Jay in Paul, but so too are there in Lawrence, a young man characterized by impulsive actions including an ability to dissolve even the most somber moods of those around him. He is active, voracious, and affirmative. He is able to heal and be healed by Djuna as they participate in a fiery dance, and as a result she attains a belief in the possibilities of life. Lawrence's entrance is like a gust of fresh air that enlivens moribund people, and he reinforces his presence by painting her room with a phosphorescent paint that excludes darkness. This phosphorescence, suggesting "the magic world of childhood" (*Albatross*, p. 68), further symbolizes the fair of these three individuals that "shines from their bodies like phosphorescence from the albatross" (ibid. p. 69). It is this quality and this situation to which the book's title most obviously refers.

A mature adult, of the sort Djuna would abhor, would pay little heed to the puerilities of a Paul or a Lawrence. She not only heeds them, she is much more comfortable with them than she is with the so-called adult behavior of those her own age. Djuna finds the world too cruel, partly because it lacks the phosphorescence of her adolescent friends, the sons who are always beginning and flowing, who have a malleability their fathers lack.

> They treat me as one of their own, because I believe what they believe, I feel as they do. I hate the father, authority, men of power, men of wealth, all tyranny, all authority, all crystallizations. . . . I want to stay in this room forever not with man the father but with man the son, carving, painting, dancing, dreaming, and always beginning, born anew every day, never aging, full of faith and impulse, turning and changing to every wind like the mobiles. I do not love those who have ceased to flow, to believe, to feel. Those who can no longer melt, exult, who cannot let themselves be cheated, laugh at loss, those who are bound and frozen.[*Albatross*, pp. 65-66]

This avoidance of permanence, in its strictest sense, appears to have been formulated as early as "Ragtime," and it continues to be a theme through Nin's fiction and into the *Diary*. Djuna goes on, however, to allow that she has been playing a role as woman, but that now she is entering, with Paul, a house of faith.

The house she enters with him turns out to be more than one of faith; she discovers the next day that a private detective keeps him from coming to her. She begins to think of the boy as an adult now, one who is sensitive and extraordinary, a man containing youthful qualities. She begins to melt before this ideal image she is creating, but when he arrives at her house she is careful to keep at a distance, knowing that she must not love him. Nevertheless, Paul kisses her, asserts himself, and they make love. Symbolically mirroring the experience, Djuna opens the petals of a tulip; he is uneasy with the representation because it suggests her forcing him to engage in an act of love for which he is not ready. He is tentative, and after she has dressed, he feels more comfortable, approaches her again, and again they make love. The result of this initiation is a telephone call from his father, at which time Paul declares his manhood. But the father cannot perceive this metamorphosis that Djuna has helped generate in his son.

Paul fortunately has had Djuna to assist with his first steps into manhood, but in doing so she realizes that his interest in her is merely fleeting and that she must give him up to the larger world he must confront. She has functioned as his ocean, caressing, nurturing, shaping this infant who will be overwhelmed and drowned by her if he does not grow away from her. Certainly this giving of self in such a dramatic and intense fashion is a catharsis of sorts for her (she is a mother giving birth), but Paul feels a similar kind of purity when he is withdrawing from people, not when he is giving to them. Djuna seems to have lost her tendency to retreat into her cities of the interior whenever the harshnesses of reality become too great for her, but in doing so her protégé develops the same response to life. In her symbolical giving birth, Djuna has passed on to her creation her own psychic difficulties.

Paul returns home for his eighteenth birthday and plays chess with his father; his mother makes a formal birthday cake (with strict borders) for the occasion. But when she refuses to launder the clothes he soiled while with Djuna, he returns to Djuna's house where she cleans them for him. She notices the smallness of his shirts and concludes that "he was still slender enough, young enough to be subjected to tyranny" (*Albatross*, p. 103). They remain together at Djuna's listening to Franck's Symphony in D Minor in which "there was immediate exaltation, dissolution in feeling and the evasion of violence. Over and over again in this musical ascension of emotion, the stairway of fever was climbed and deserted before one reached explosion" (ibid., p. 104). The irresolution, non-consummation, and absence of pain suggest that Djuna is once again reverting to her tendency to avoid life by visiting her dreams.

The story concludes with Djuna meeting Matilda, a woman who has awaited her lover for twenty years and whose life has therefore essentially stopped. Matilda's plight is an extreme example of what happens to a person who waits for the ideal instead of recognizing that the acceptance of imperfection is one of life's necessities (as Jay suggested in "Bread and the Wafer"). But more importantly, it is upon reflecting on Matilda's situation that Djuna realizes that her own psychological difficulties antedate her experiences with the watchman and actually stem from her desertion by her father (the original cause of her having been sent to the orphanage). When her father left, he destroyed a cell in his daughter; when he told her that he would return, she believed him, and her wound has therefore remained open. All the windows in her house but one, it will be recalled, emit a strong light, and that sealed room stands as a symbol of this atrophied cell "in which was lodged violence as having been shut and condemned within her out of fear of disaster" (*Albatross*, p. 109). As a result, whenever Djuna has encountered men of authority they have activated this cell of childhood that is filled with anger, and so she has felt insignificant and helpless. Consequently, she has avoided such men, cultivating instead their sons, like Paul. Djuna's father had promised to return, and this hope has made her dependent on these rigid men who are his surrogates; "knowing the tragic outcome of this dependence she felt hostility and her route towards the man of power bristled with this hostility — an immediate need to shut out violence" (ibid., p. 110). The story ends with Franck's symphony, Djuna and Paul together seeking gentleness to protect them from the violence and treachery of the world. Djuna still suffers from the wound incurred when her father left, and she will continue to suffer until he returns to her, as the father does to the unnamed woman in "Winter of Artifice." The reader can thus perceive that Nin's fiction (of which "The Sealed Room" is typical) contains a high degree of consistency and psychological reality, as Djuna carries with her problems inherited by the destructive acts of adults in her past.

"The Café ," the second part of *Children of the Albatross,* is more structured (at least in a superficial manner) than any other of Nin's fictional pieces of substantial length written by 1947. Most of her stock company of diverse characters are present here, but it is their meeting place, the café, that serves as the focal point in the story; seven of the ten parts deal with different characters who leave for the café at the end of their respective sections of the story. Of the remaining three sections, the first describes the café, the penultimate presents all the characters together there, and the short last section focuses attention on one woman, Djuna, whose novel this obviously is, setting her apart from the crowd.

There are occasional visits to cafés in Nin's earlier works, but never before has one café been so thoroughly examined as here. The method of description is similar to the one she employs in her presentation of characters, with external details being included only when they cannot conveniently be avoided or when they reveal something about the inner reality. Despite this café's importance, we do not know its name, what it looks like, or where in Paris it is located; but we do know about some of its real (as opposed to realistic) details.

> The cafés were the wells of treasures, the caves of Ali Baba.
> The cafés were richer even than the oriental cities where all living was plied openly under your eyes so that you were offered all the activities of the world to touch and smell. . . .
> And so in the café, with one franc for a glass of wine and even less for coffee, you could hear stories from the Pampas, share in African voodoo secrets, read the pages of a book being written, listen to a poem, to the death rattles of an aristocrat, the life story of a revolutionary. You could hear the hummed theme of a symphony, watch the fingers of a jazz drummer drumming on the table, accept an invitation from a painter who would take you to the Zoo to watch the serpents eat their daily ration of white mice, consult a secretive Hindu on his explorations of occult streets, or meet an explorer who would take you on his sailboat around the world. [*Albatross,* pp. 113-114]

The cafés are exotic microcosms where the essential aspects of life with the philosophers, writers, and other assorted types of persons are available for the patrons. This particular café is also a musical one where jazz is performed. This music has at its core improvisation, and it is this technique that Nin's own story parallels with its introduction of the café (theme), introduction of a character (improvisation), character going to café (theme), introduction of another character (improvisation), that character going to café (theme), and so on, the variations on the theme continuing within the framework of the café until all the characters meet there (final statement of theme), and where Djuna leaves alone (coda).

It is a rainy autumn day, the weather shutting out the sun and sealing off the city much as Djuna's room was closed off earlier, but with different results. Within this isolated city, people are pushed "gently to live under the surface" in the hothouse of the café; here is none of the insularity of the house of incest, but rather an "easy intermingling of man's inner landscapes" (*Albatross,* p. 114). This interaction is a mirror of the gentle colliding of night and day that produces "erotic sparks" (ibid., p. 115) in the city. For once Nin's characters live in a protected place where they are able not only to avoid the pitfalls of insulation, but where they can actually produce their own erotic sparks. Such a state need not be undesirable or unhealthy; the danger comes when one lives exclusively in it, just as it is unhealthy finally to live out of balance in any way on a permanent basis. Here all the characters come from their daily lives to gain sustenance that this intermingling can offer; then they will return to the places from which they came, renewed by their experience.

Sabina is the first character presented, and she is the same incendiary woman whose belief that ladders to fire lead to love gave title to the first novel. She still communicates with others by seduction, lives unmoored in the present, is malleable in the hands of men, and is willing to become whatever they want her to be. But because of these qualities she is unable to find rest in life and cannot find love, which demands the equal sharing and understanding of the two people involved. Each dawning of a new day finds her alone with the ashes of the people and things she burned the day before, and to renew herself she leaves for the café where her diurnal cycle of passion and destruction begins anew.

Lillian, the next character to be presented, continues to live with Jay and to be unfulfilled by him. He takes from her, goes forth into the world at peace with himself, open to all experience, while she remains "unfree" and filled with "retentions, residues, sediments" (*Albatross*, p. 121). She serves as Jay's bread, but after feeding him, she clings to him, not for mere possession but to keep from drowning in herself. As if to compound her difficulty, the woman Jay paints in his portraits is not Lillian but Sabina, and he does his best work of all when Djuna is there, though he does not paint her. Lillian could tolerate his use of the other women and perhaps even his unattractive friends if only he would give assurance that he regards her as an individual, but as far as she knows he would be as content with any other woman as he is with her. Together Lillian, Sabina, and Djuna (devotion, consumption, and reflection) constitute the bread, fire, and light he needs, but the one he acknowledges the least is Lillian, the only one of the three who is not present in his paintings (for even Djuna's eyes serve as a color chart). Ironically, however, Lillian makes it possible for the others to be helpful to him. So far as Jay is concerned, his relationship with Lillian is entirely one of passion, but she begins to suspect that passion devoid of love cannot endure; it is an attempt to fuse unfusable elements, and so she attempts to escape him first through the wholeness that music provides and then by visiting her lover Edgar in a Montparnasse hotel.[2] That tryst is not totally satisfactory; despite Edgar's bringing her flowers, thereby at least acknowledging the attention she craves, she is not herself with him. Rather than offering herself, she dresses falsely, donning a cape, encircling her wrists in bracelets, presenting herself, and acting as though she is Sabina. Lillian fortunately realizes that this evasion will not benefit her, and so she becomes herself again. Discarding her charade she leaves for the café where Sabina has been drinking for some time.

While Lillian is left at the café, the story continues with Djuna and Jay. Here an explanation is offered for Jay's attitude toward and treatment of women in general and Lillian in particular. Because many women use cosmetic makeup and other such artifices, Jay always considered them to be false, and in order to avoid this falsity he regards them all as sexual objects; no matter what else they might be (or might not be), they are certainly sexual beings. Be they queens, maids, doctors, or artists, all women are the same to Jay; and he wants to destroy any illusions that they create. Djuna, however, is not so easy to categorize. Jay knows that she conceals herself by presenting patterns and then escaping from them. When he is tired, he wants to see Djuna: she reminds him of Florentine paintings; she is the depository of his dream; she is capable of being totally honest, understanding art and man's language; in short, she is "more than a woman" (*Albatross*, p. 134). He feels confident of Djuna when he walks away from her, and as he goes to meet Sabina and Lillian at the café, he compares Paris, the city of love and feminine beauty, to New York, the city of masculine and aggressive beauty, a comparison that is one of the dominant themes in the *Diary*.

Djuna is the last of the major characters to be presented. After Jay has gone into the café we see her emerging from a dream, thinking that later this day she will be cut off from humanity, a situation in which she frequently finds herself. While in such an isolated state she believes she has the greatest amount of insight into other people, into the potentialities of what they might have achieved with their flawed lives. These people, however, true to human nature, are more or less comfortable with themselves, and they become irritated when Djuna points out the disparity between their real and potential selves. A problem develops at this point. Djuna is in a sense violating the sanctity of their hearts, but at the same time she is hiding her real self in her cities of the interior; it is Djuna, therefore, who comes closer than they to being a culprit and who feels uneasy with herself. She believes she presents an image of the complete self to these incomplete people; she has the ability to transform dark into light, sickness into health, and, with her faith in the dream, she believes herself somehow to have superior insight into the human psyche. It is no wonder, then, that she senses she will soon be isolated from humanity: her attitudes explicitly dictate that she will be cut off from mankind. As a critic who cannot accept faults, she is one therefore who cannot accept the human condition, and we have seen many times before that Nin believed that in order for one to be healthy, the realities and fallibilities (and the pain) of the human condition must be recognized and dealt with, not conveniently eliminated. Despite Djuna's critical attitude toward others, she feels a need to be rescued; "she would have liked to escape from her own demands upon herself" (*Albatross*, p. 141), and it is Jay, the embodiment of the ordinary that she rejects, to whom she turns for assistance. For her he is "the living proof that it was in this acceptance of the ordinary that pleasure lay. She would learn from him. She would learn to like daily bread. He gave her everything in its untransformed state: food, houses, streets, cafés, people. A way back to the simplicities" (ibid., p. 144). Pleasure does not lie in the ideal, the solitary isolated cell of the dream to which she perpetually returns. After visiting a shoemaker she goes to the café where Sabina, Lillian, and Jay have been joined by Donald, Michael, and Rango.

Faustin the Zombie first appeared in *Ladders to Fire* and is the next character to be presented here. He fits naturally into this sequence of characters because he is the embodiment of an extreme Djuna. Just as she is critical of others and reverts to her dream, so too does he fail to live a full life, choosing rather to remain isolated in his room. Its furnishings reflect his inertia (just as Djuna's house reflects her inner being in "The Sealed Room"), and if Djuna might be labeled more a psychic voyeur than a physical one, Faustin is both. Ironically, the one example we have of his voyeurism takes place when he overhears a husband cruelly and insensitively questioning his wife about her fidelity to him. When the couple conclude their arguing, Faustin, in his wisdom, anonymously (but audibly) passes judgment on their difficulties and sides with the wife against the husband. Of course the husband has acted boorishly, but at least he and his wife have experienced love and once cared enough for each other to consummate their relationship in marriage. He may be cruel, but the couple have confronted life and have not avoided it, as Faustin has. They have lived and met the realities of life face to face; they have not achieved the ideal, but they have participated in life with some fullness. Faustin's verdict in favor of the wife is humorously pathetic; however, there may be hope for him as he dresses to join the ever-growing crowd at the café.

Still another type of voyeur is Uncle Philip, a man who has an international family to which he is not related and to which he pays his respects at every wedding, birth, journey, or other such festive occasion. He is forgotten, nonetheless, by the recipients of his good will the moment he leaves them; he is entirely innocuous and neutral. He is careful, formal, gray, genteel, and an omnipresent witness to (but not a participant in) all the events he attends. His family is colorful and large, but none of its vibrancy contaminates his sterility. He is a kind of Everyman who has relatives of every vocation in every country one can mention; yet one never thinks to inquire about Uncle Philip's own vocation. When he attends his relatives' ceremonies, we recognize him instantly. He is, in short, that unknown relative who appears for the special family ceremonies in one's existence. When one of Uncle Philip's relatives is leaving to take a surreptitious voyage across the Atlantic without her husband but with her lover, who is there to see her off at the dock with a small bouquet? We know. "The only surprising fact was that Uncle Philip failed to greet them at their arrival on the other side" (*Albatross*, p. 156), a pleasant enough touch of cynical humor. Although he clearly is an abstract type, Nin almost makes him human when she designates him (with some irony) as the only one of the café group who has roots of family, "and yet he felt they were bound to each other, and related to each other as if they had founded new ties, a new kind of family, a new country," but he remains the lonely one, he the *"esprit de famille"* (ibid., p. 157). Though always present, he remains outside the symbolic family that he senses exists in the café. He seems not to have experienced real passion and so cannot function as one of the members of the family there, even though he goes there at the end of his section of the story.

Michael and Donald, who performed their phallic dance in "The Sealed Room," were mentioned as being at the café when Djuna arrived there, but following upon the heels of Uncle Philip, they are the last characters to be discussed prior to the narrative's return to the café itself, with all the congregated characters, as the focus of the story.

These two characters, Donald and Michael, continue to live their lives as they had in the first part of the novel, Michael craving Donald's attention and affection but receiving it only at night. Their situation is comparable in some ways to Lillian's and Jay's, for one of them needs love and assurance from another who is insensitive to those needs. Donald is of especial interest here because it is he who sings a song (actually the refrain that ends "Ragtime"), reminding Michael that "in the new man the child" (*Albatross*, p. 161), a message he had been hearing for some time but had not been acknowledging. In addition to his treatment of Michael and his song, Donald is important because he is an isolated being who will admit no partner. In this quality he is related to Faustin and to Uncle Philip, who are not only without partners but without friends. Michael realizes that his love for Donald will always be frustrated; for that reason he finds himself envying a loving blind couple.

> There was no darkness dark enough to prevent Michael from seeing the eyes of the lover turning away, empty of remembrance, never dark enough not to see the death of a love, the defect of a love, the end of the night of desire.
> No love blind enough for him to escape the sorrows of lucidity.
> "And now," said Donald, his arms full of presents, "let's go to the café."
> [Ibid., p. 164]

Throughout this story characters have been leaving their routine existences to congregate at the café, and when they all arrive (though not all of them are considered to be present) Jay is the center of attention because he is the most open to them. All the others have secret selves or inner chambers serving as reservoirs of the present, but Jay is entirely of the present and interacts directly with the others with no distance between them. He achieved this state of freedom by fleeing home at age fourteen, never to return, and also by renouncing all, "to relinquish, to dispossess one's self of all wishes, to renounce, to be attached to no one, to hold no dream, to live in a state of anarchy" (*Albatross*, p. 167). All these served as a kind of ideal for him, though he has not yet reached the last stage. At the café he functions as the great leveler, examining the inner cores of the others, not permitting secrets to exist or shells to hide in. Like Melville, he encourages his friends to dive deeply, and, like Hawthorne at the end of *The Scarlet Letter*, he advises them to display their worst to others, or at least enough of themselves so that the worst might be inferred. He is a natural man wanting to share his own flaws with those of his friends.

While he is expounding his philosophy of life, the long-suffering Lillian becomes aware that Jay is Jay in that he not only does not care about her, he cares about nothing or no one. Such a disregard for others can be strangely charming, mysterious, and superficially attractive in someone like him; but when one begins to care about such a person, one can only become disillusioned and hurt, as Lillian is with him. When she realizes that her love for him is a cul de sac, the cords that have been tying her to him—and also to her husband Larry and others—suddenly snap, and she feels elated. From this point forward, perhaps, Lillian will be able to develop herself into a whole woman without strangling in the alliances that entangled her previously.

The remainder of the scene at the café and the remainder of the story belongs to Djuna. Michael comes to her suffering because Donald is keeping him at a distance (Donald represents the adolescence that the grown Michael wishes to recapture). With Djuna's compassion and understanding, Michael is able to regain his own identity and Donald becomes a mere shell, a façade, what Djuna calls a clay pigeon. Her affinity with male homosexuals is not totally convincing in the novel, nor is it made especially authentic when it is stated that they perceive the essences in each other. They can interact, but their "enchantment would have no ordinary culmination" (*Albatross,* p. 171). When Michael sees that Djuna is anxious over Paul's pending trip to India (mentioned in the first part of the novel), the atmosphere in the café suddenly changes for her from one of love and freedom to one of "sediments and dregs of false beatitudes" (ibid., p. 172). An organ grinder's monkey conjures up in her mind the images of imprisonment and the orphanage, apparently, for the pathetic monkey dancing a "pleading dance," tied to a loudspeaker tree, attempts a gesture of gratitude as mere pennies fall to him. Her perceptions change and she walks "back again into her labyrinthian cities of the interior" (ibid., p. 173).

Earlier this day Djuna felt she would be possessed by a mood that would cut her off from fraternity; with her thoughts of Paul, that is exactly what happens in the story's coda. As is her practice, Djuna protects herself when she is hurt by entering her dream world where all appears to be painless and safe, and although she is aware that some consider such a visit dangerous she convinces herself that it is in that state detached from "real" life that one can be swayed rootlessly, and of course painlessly, back and forth, in ecstasy. But as we have seen in the works written from *House of Incest* to this novel, such a belief has only partial truth, for the dream world can be very dangerous and destructive. It is not only safe to visit those inner cities, it is mandatory to enter the dream world in order to live a complete life in reality; but when one cultivates the dream exclusively, the sustenance one finds there turns to ashes.

Children of the Albatross continues the stories of the women (especially that of Djuna) that were begun in *Ladders to Fire*. At the end of "The Café," however, only Lillian appears to be moving toward wholeness. Sabina continues her incendiary actions; Djuna returns to her cities of the interior; Jay remains Jay; and Michael gains independence from Donald, with Djuna's assistance. The novel's title refers most obviously to those adolescents in "The Sealed Room," but it refers as well to all of the characters, whose emotional development has not yet reached maturity.

6

The Four-Chambered Heart

The first two volumes of the continuous novel are arguably not novels at all, because each is divided into two distinct, titled, and relatively short parts. But the third, *The Four-Chambered Heart*, presents what is for Nin a long work with only a brief interruption near the end.[1] We have seen that in her fiction published before 1950 she wrote short stories and novelettes of necessarily limited scope; so with this work she afforded herself an opportunity to relate on a grander scale the themes of her earlier works. In so doing she chose to concentrate on her most engaging female character, Djuna, in the company of the Guatemalan Rango and his wife Zora, an invalid. Such an unlikely cast of characters suggests that their story will be unique, but it does not take long to realize that something is amiss: that the story of Djuna's inner turmoil is undercut by the plodding Gonzalo on his interminable journey to awareness of the obvious. For the first time Nin is writing a novel and for the first time her focus is not solely on one or more of her usual female characters; the result of these two factors is a work that is on the whole less satisfactory than its predecessors.

Rango is mentioned only briefly in the first two volumes of the continuous novel, and he functions there as a Hans, a Colette, or a Serge, as a character who obviously shares some degree of intimacy with the main characters but who is little more than a prop. It is somewhat of a surprise, then, when he emerges from his anonymity to become the object of Djuna's interest and, with her, the major character in *The Four-*

Chambered Heart. He is obviously Djuna's opposite: she is a woman of the mind, but he is mindless and a man of the senses, of the body. Together they resemble Lawrence's virgin and the gypsy and constitute a sort of allegory of form and nature. He is the idol of many women who hear him play his guitar in a nightclub where he infuses them with the sensual freedom of gypsy life and of the open road. But when they respond physically to his music and approach him at dawn, he casually leaves them unfulfilled and gives them not a moment's thought. Either through her persistence or her appeal to him, one woman is able to gain Rango's attention, whereupon she asks if he might play for her dancing. This is of course Djuna, and she is drawn to him because he represents the "unattainable island of joy" (*Heart*, p. 6) that she has pursued since she observed the party from afar as a youth and that Nin first mentioned in "Houseboat." To Djuna he is freedom, openness, an individual who knows not shackles of self-doubt nor feels the necessity to find refuge from life in anything like her cities of the interior. But the moment they meet, the ideal that he represents begins to decay and the "island of joy" that she has sought remains unattained. Instead of being a gypsy, Rango is a Guatemalan who has lived with the gypsies for several years; and instead of being the free and unburdened individual that others take him to be, he is almost totally imprisoned by his wife Zora who, in her hypochondria, makes great demands on him.

Djuna recoils from Rango's reality, but soon she is at ease with him again as their previous relationship of infatuation develops into one of love that is blessed by the Seine and is attested to by an organ-grinder's performance of *Carmen*. As they consummate their relationship physically, the narrator expatiates on the nature of love (which is one of the novel's major themes) and describes it as "the great narcotic" (*Heart*, p. 10) that frees those whom it touches from going outside its grasp for stimulants to heighten their enjoyment of life. One never blooms more fully than when in love, the narrator relates, because it causes one to reveal one's total self to another as it decimates all shells and artifices. Hawthorne's Reverend Hooper donned his black veil in order to encourage such openness, but in doing so he isolated himself from his community, congregation, and fiancée and became the most secretive of men. It is in similar terms that one might regard Djuna's love for Rango. She obviously desires to break out of her inner turmoil, but in choosing Rango as a lover to help her achieve that goal she has picked a man who, because of his numerous insensitivities and shortcomings, will not be the partner she needs for her blossoming into a whole, mature woman.

Djuna considers their love so special that it cannot flourish in ordinary surroundings but needs an isolated place where they can fuse into "a solitary cell, where we can dream in peace together" (*Heart*, p. 12). Solitude is consistently dangerous in Nin's work, but Djuna perceives her retreat with Rango not as a sterile absence from life but "the mysterious, the padded, the fecund cell in which everything is born" (ibid., p. 14). She does not realize that dreaming peacefully with another leads to nothing, but she is deluded into thinking that it does because of her experiences with the rest of the world, as it is epitomized by her father. He is alone in life, even though she lives with him, but his isolation resulted from his taking love too casually and therefore killing it. Djuna's difficulty is just the opposite: in order to avoid the desecration of love by considering it lightly she gives it her complete dedication and wants to protect it at all costs against the dangers of the rest of the world. In so doing, however, she is ignoring certain basic realities, and her love for Rango can therefore not endure.

To provide the proper setting for their love Djuna finds a barge that once had been used by a group of touring actors as a houseboat, and Rango's first response to it is, "It's like the Tales of Hoffmann. It's a dream. It's a fairy tale" (*Heart*, p. 17). It thus complements Djuna's conception of their love, and when they are on the barge they are "out of the world. All the dangers are outside, out in the world" (ibid., p. 18). They do not yet know that the greatest danger comes from being apart from the world that they are so gaily fleeing, and this is stated symbolically just after they make love for the first time in their new abode. Rango's caresses are, as expected, so vigorous that he accidentally knocks a lantern to the floor and a fire ensues. Djuna is intrigued by the flames, but they avoid danger when the floor absorbs the oil and so extinguishes the fire. The blazing oil is their passionate love that will soon be absorbed by the floor that is the parasitic Zora. Oblivious to the significance of this event, Djuna and Rango blissfully fall asleep believing that their love will endure.

Djuna and Rango are not alone on the barge. There also resides in one of the cabins a former yacht captain who now serves as watchman for the barge. He resembles the doctor in "The Mouse" in that he lost one of his legs, and he has come to be known as the "drunken grandfather of the river" (*Heart*, p. 20). Grouchy and lecherous, he intrudes on Djuna and Rango's solitary cell with his eccentric behavior. Rango threatens the old man and asks him to leave the barge, but when he promises to remain quiet Rango permits him to remain on board. This man is certainly a nuisance, but he is a contact with humanity and therefore a saviour of sorts for the lovers. Hawthorne's Ethan Brand could find nothing worthwhile in his old friends the doctor, the stage agent, and Lawyer Giles; and as a result he committed the unpardonable sin of breaking the magnetic chain of humanity. But while Djuna and Rango find the old man disgusting, they permit him to remain and to function, unbeknownst to them, as their contact with that magnetic chain.

One other character also makes it difficult for them to achieve their isolated state, and that is the Seine that, swollen with rain water, causes other inhabitants of boats to seek refuge on the firm ground where most people exist. If the river is unsuccessful in forcing people to shore by its swelling, it then becomes tumultuous in order to shake the laggards from either their complacency or defiance. These tactics only make Djuna and Rango more determined than ever to achieve their life together on the barge, and Rango becomes a Valkyrian hero in her eyes as he takes her from the shore to the boat of love. Djuna is as impressed with this display of masculine force as she was when he subdued the watchman earlier, and because their love has apparently overcome the numerous difficulties it has had to face, they are rewarded that evening with what will be their only time of wholeness. In this brief moment of ecstasy they are "content, having attained all lovers' dream of a desert island, a cell, a cocoon, in which to create a world together from the beginning" (Heart, p. 32), but what they present to each other is their past selves, their innocence that once gone is lost forever and can only be recaptured in a state of innocent awareness. Djuna and Rango are not dealing with this latter, mature form of innocence but the former, adolescent one. The paradise they build upon it is therefore evanescent.

The young Djuna has been presented throughout Nin's earlier work. Rango's youth is presented here as one of poverty in the Guatemalan mountains where he was born on an extinct volcano (suggesting his success as a lover). He was reared in nature, the enormity of which caused a certain melancholy in him, and the twentieth century was unknown to his people who lived as though they were sixteenth-century Spaniards. His two sustaining dreams were of cities and of a slender, pale woman (his opposite), both of which he has achieved in this book with Paris and Djuna. He could survive in his native environment, but what caused him to leave it for his present Bohemian life was his love of music in general and of the piano in particular. But this primitive is not comfortable in Paris because he finds it a city of the mind, not of the body, and its tempos subdue individuals' rhythms. Rango of course fights the dominance of this city that encourages abstraction at the expense of sinew, and by his counterrhythm he destroys the pattern that Paris has woven for him. Because he has had to sacrifice his natural movements in order to defeat the city, he loses the quality that originally made him so attractive to Djuna: his earthy sexuality. He is now inert at night, so he destroys during the day the one dream and at night the other that he has had since youth. His difficulty was prefigured in his youth by a black child who was born in the jungle the same day as he and who Rango's father presented to him as a birthday gift. The black youth, away from his natural hot climate, died almost immediately from the cold of the high mountains. In like manner Rango is not suited to life in the city and would likely succumb to it if he were not so diligent in asserting himself and if he did not have Djuna attempting to revive his body at night.

Djuna and Rango's love is destined to fail, and so it does. She observes that it is not a cataclysm or some other great and definite event that destroys love, but small, seemingly inconsequential acts such as her taking great pleasure in cutting Rango's hair only to have that pleasure taken from her when Zora is once again capable of caring for him. The loss of this pleasure that, trivial though it might seem, symbolizes the intimacy of the lovers, is by itself not too painful, but when it is joined by other actions of similar quality, such as Rango's habitual tardiness, they form a bedrock of doubt against which Djuna shall judge Rango's future actions. On another level this inability to fulfill her desire to share total intimacy with him suggests, through the organ-grinder's *Carmen,* her childhood desires that went similarly unsatisfied because of her father's insensitivity toward her. One will recall that he could not understand her childish yet important dreams and desires just as Rango cannot fathom why she is upset at not being permitted to continue cutting his hair. Rango's obtuseness, then, is just the most recent obstacle in Djuna's difficult journey toward love and understanding, and even though she can do nothing about her plight at this time she understands perfectly what is happening to her love with him.

She wanted to say: "Oh, Rango, beware. Love never dies of a natural death. It dies because we don't know how to replenish its source, it dies of blindness and errors and betrayals. It dies of illnesses and wounds, it dies of weariness, of witherings, of tarnishings, but never of natural death. Every lover could be brought to trial as the murderer of his own love. When something hurts you, saddens you, I rush to avoid it, to alter it, to feel as you do, but you turn away with a gesture of impatience and say: 'I don't understand.' "

It was never one scene which took place between human beings, but many scenes converging like great intersections of rivers. Rango believed this scene contained nothing but a whim of Djuna's to be denied.

He failed to see that it contained at once all of Djuna's wishes which had been denied, and these wishes had flown from all directions to meet at this intersection and to plead once more for understanding. [*Heart*, p. 48]

Djuna's plea for understanding will again go unheeded and she will therefore continue to quest for it.

Rango further compounds the difficulty of their love's survival by becoming jealous of Djuna's former lovers and of Jay and Paul in particular, and in so doing he destroys their best moments together, which are when they are making love. He is using the past to destroy the present because Djuna admits that her relationship with Paul is finished. They were, finally, not good for each other. He is in India and inaccessible even if she were interested in him. Rango's malevolence, his urge to destroy, saps the fecundity from their relationship and directs it not toward the fertile cell on the barge but toward a desert island where they might embrace each other's ruined bodies. His notion of love as something to be achieved in isolation (a state created by destroying the past and all differences between the lovers) is, then, self-defeating because it causes Djuna to continue feeling affection for such men as Jay and Paul with whom she has had comfortable and, for her, quite normal relationships. To preserve her feelings for them she stores them in a chamber of her heart where eternal love flows and to which Rango therefore has no access. The book's title suggests that one, and here Djuna, is capable of myriad relationships, and once an insensitive person such as Rango tries to suppress them, one may preserve them in one's heart that can accommodate the love of many. Once again Djuna turns to the cities of her interior, but this time to preserve life and not to hide from it.

Rango's renewed interest in pursuing the ideal soon overshadows his jealousy. He has already fulfilled the two dominant dreams of his youth, to reside in a city and to possess a woman like Djuna, and it is the successful realization of the second one that leads directly to his dissatisfaction with the younger Rango who was content to settle for Zora, the opposite of the ideal woman, and who, with his wife, disintegrated badly. Djuna has renewed his thirst for the ideal, but in so doing she has assured for herself a role as an oasis or as only a purveyor of sustenance to this man who will soon be planting his seed with political revolutionaries instead of with her. She is aware of what is happening to her relationship with Rango, as she is with whatever concerns her, and she is being far from selfish when she reveals that political revolutions, no matter how legitimate, are practically worthless because it is seldom politics that cause one's real life—one's inner life—to change. True change, she avers, must begin with a man and a woman whose love is symbolized by and consummated in the sexual act, and in slighting his intimacy with her he is subverting the larger concern with which he is becoming preoccupied.

> She smiled at man's great need to build cities when it was so much harder to build relationships, his need to conquer countries when it was so much harder to conquer one heart, to satisfy a child, to create a perfect human life. Man's need to invent, to circumnavigate space when it is so much harder to overcome space between human beings, man's need to organize systems of philosophy when it was so much harder to understand one human being, and when the greatest depths of human character lay but half explored." [*Heart*, p. 73]

What Djuna hopes, of course, is that Rango's energy will soon break the chains that confine him to destruction (including his emerging fatalism) and will permit him to build, to create, to give life as she knows him to be capable of doing.

One might wonder why Djuna continues to love Rango and suffer at his hand. He was first attracted to her because she was his ideal, his opposite; and she is attracted to him because he is her opposite as well. From her youth to the present, Djuna has lived in the cities of her interior that are adorned with art of her own making (dreams), the entirety of which is finally inaccessible, and unlike the characters in *House of Incest* or "Under a Glass Bell" she wishes to escape from her insularity and find fecundity and wholeness by means of a man who is her opposite and not by means of a woman who is the mirror-image of herself. She is at all times aware of the dangers of her internal cities, so it is only natural that she grants Rango the benefit of every doubt because he, her long-buried self, is at present the promise of salvation from herself: "This bond with Rango, this patience with his violent temper, this tacit fraternity of her gentleness and his roughness, this collaboration of light and shadow, this responsibility for Rango which she felt, her compulsion to rescue him from the consequences of his blind rages, were because Rango lived out for her this self she had buried in her childhood. All that she had denied and repressed: chaos, disorder, caprice, destruction" (*Heart,* p. 86). Her need for Rango is the same as Hejda's after she escapes from the strangling relationship with Molnar in an earlier story.

Rango's most crucial error with Djuna is one of judgment, and after he makes it the fate of their relationship is sealed. Until this point Zora has been in the background as a pathetic figure who makes inordinate demands on her husband; but when he decides that the two women to whom he is tied should become friends, he is asking for a fusion of life and death, a fusion of opposites that is impossible. Zora, though bedridden, will dominate the remainder of the novel and will destroy not only Djuna and Rango's love but perhaps their lives as well: "Her black hair was uncombed and straggled around her parchment-colored skin. She had no Indian blood, and her face was almost a direct contrast to Rango's. She had heavy, pronounced features, a wide full mouth, all cast in length, in sadness, a defeated pull downward which only changed when she raised her eyelids; then the eyes had in them an unexpected shrewdness which Rango did not have" (*Heart,* p. 89). From this point all will descend toward Zora, the lowest common denominator, and that one great moment of love between Djuna and Rango will recede further and further into the past and practically out of memory. The three become what the narrator calls a "trinity" (ibid., p. 92). The religious connotation of this is ironically implied, but like other groupings of three in Nin's fiction (Djuna, Michael, and Donald, for example), this one will be unsuccessful. Two and not three is the sacred number to Nin, but one must be careful not to assume that just because a man and woman are alone together their relationship is necessarily a good one, as Rango and Zora amply illustrate.

When Djuna and Zora first meet, the latter is friendly and talkative and relates that she is pleased a woman such as Djuna is able to form a sexual relationship with Rango because she and Rango have lived together fraternally for years. Now that Rango's physical needs are accommodated he treats Zora more kindly than he has in the past, and Djuna is no threat to her because she does not intend to take him from her. In fact, Djuna not only is incapable of taking Rango for herself entirely, she joins him in bearing the heavy burden of Zora. This strange ménage à trois is far from Djuna's ideal, but she realizes that "all great flights away from life land one in such places of atonement as this room, with Zora sewing rags and talking about dandruff, about ovarian insufficiency, about gastritis, about thyroid and neuritis" (*Heart*, p. 94). From this moment forward every ecstatic moment Djuna spends with Rango will have to be paid for by duty to the demanding Zora.

Zora cultivates her avowed illnesses carefully by reading in medical books for symptoms of diseases that she might have, by refusing to combat her illnesses, and by doubting the doctors who attend her and the medicines they recommend. She acts in this manner to gain the sympathy of others and especially to gain control over Djuna and Rango. Rango is much more susceptible to her wiles than is Djuna; he refuses to consider the reality of Zora's situation as he walks miles to a drug store at her behest to determine the freshness of a recently prescribed medicine. Djuna's relationship with Rango has been in progress for three years, and it is not until that third year—the present—that she fully understands the position in which she finds herself with him and Zora (and Rango does not yet understand the situation). Only now does Zora begin to encroach upon Djuna's life with him on the barge, and those once frequent nights together are reduced to one each week because of the demands that Zora makes on her husband. Even during that one night Zora often appears at the barge ill and in need of Rango's immediate assistance. His accessibility to Djuna, which was not altogether satisfactory before Zora entered the story, ceases to exist.

Djuna is in the uncomfortable position of feeling the need to continue her relationship with Rango while realizing that in so doing she is becoming caught in the web that Zora is spinning. Being in this position saps her emotional vigor and practically strips her of her worldly possessions. Her insensitive father, who noticed few things about his daughter in the past, perceives that she is dressing poorly and is compelled to ask about the nature of her friends. Little does he realize that she is giving her clothes to the seemingly needy Zora, but the ignorance turns out not to be his but hers as she soon discovers that these sacrifices she has made for Zora have not only been unnecessary but foolish, because Zora accepts the gifts of clothing and stores them in a trunk instead of substituting them for the tattered clothing in which she dresses herself. The irony of Djuna's position becomes even greater when one learns that it is not her natural inclination to be charitable: "Djuna wanted to forget her intuition, in favor of the tradition which dictated that a beggar's needs cannot be judged, because there is a noblesse oblige which dictates: his cup is empty and yours is full, therefore there is only one action possible; and even if an investigation revealed the beggar not to be blind and to have amassed a fortune under his pallet, even then, such hesitations before an empty cup are so distressing that the role of the believer is easier, easier to be deceived than to doubt" (*Heart*, p. 101). Her instinct is to question the receiver of charity, and in acting against her basic belief she is assuming a burden that is not hers to bear and that, if she continues with it, will lead her to an ignominious end similar to Melville's Pierre who also assumes responsibilities that are clearly not his.

Djuna attempts to be a benefactress to Rango as well as Zora, and here, as with his wife, she is unfaithful to herself. Rango is frustrated by his wife's actions, and to counteract them he revolts not against Zora but against situations (mostly societal) that do not pertain at all to his sufferings. But Rango needs comfort from and understanding of his difficulties, and the individual who offers both is Djuna, although she thinks Rango blind to Zora's hypochondria and cruelty and does not believe political actions can assuage a person's discontent. When the tired Rango wishes to lean on her for support she is there, but in always being available she has to conceal her own needs; as a result Rango conceives of her as a woman of infinite energy and strength who can overcome any obstacle. Her predicament is difficult: she loves Rango, her opposite, and believes their interaction will bring her completeness; Rango's dedication to fulfilling Zora's needs causes frustrations in him that lead to his relying on Djuna as a support rather than as a partner; and in fulfilling Rango's needs Djuna's own are left wanting. Djuna decides that the best way to preserve herself is to flee this situation, but after leaving Rango on occasion only to return to him, she leaves for London by boat. While resting on deck, however, she is approached by a *grand blessé de guerre* (reminiscent of the doctor in "The Mouse") who sees in her face a woman open to the problems of others, and he burdens her with his throughout the trip. She therefore arrives in London exhausted, and, after sleeping for twelve hours, returns to Paris convinced that she cannot escape her destiny.

> No more questioning, no more interpretations, no more examinations of her life. She was resigned to her destiny. It was her destiny. The *grand blessé de guerre* on the ship had made her feel it, had convinced her.
> So she made a pirouette charged with sadness, on the revolving stages of

awareness, and returned to this role she had been fashioned for, even down to the face, even when asleep.

But when people play a role motivated by false impulses, moved by compulsions formed by fear, by distortions, rather than by a deep need, the only symptom which reveals that it is a role and that acts do not correspond to the true nature, is the sense of unbearable tension.

The ways to measure one's insincerities are few, but Djuna knew that the most infallible one was joylessness. Any task accomplished without joy was a falsity to one's true nature. [*Heart*, p. 122]

Djuna remains trapped in a situation where she feels uncomfortable and unhappy, and the remainder of the novel is the story of her attempts to escape her plight.

Djuna takes Rango and Zora to the Mediterranean to help restore Zora's health (or mind) and therefore free them all from the trap she has set. But just as politics are no panacea, neither is geography as Zora remains Zora and Rango feels obligated to assist her while Djuna is left yearning for the color and activity of the port as she desired the party she observed from a distance as a youth. Instead of remaining passive to and tolerant of Rango's misplaced presence, she bicycles alone to the festivities only to be met by Rango's jealous rage when she returns to her room. They spend that evening together "*as if* to resolder all that his violence broke" (*Heart*, p. 127; italics added), but by this time their physical union does not compensate for their psychological distance from each other. Rango is now angered by a new Djuna: he sees in her a woman who is unavailable to him, one who is playful and in harmony with people and nature and who "believed understanding could be reached by effort, by an examination of one's behavior, and that destiny could be reshaped, one's twisted course redirected with lucidity." This woman Rango perceives is one who is renewing her quest for paradise and therefore attracts such people as Paul of old who know "how to escape the realm of sorrow by fantasy" (ibid., p. 128), and in so doing her desire to free Rango from his entangling alliances diminishes, as does her reliance on him for her wholeness. Her four-chambered heart, then, serves her well, because it can house and protect affection for both Rango and Paul. The latter offers her the hope of a flawless father, which she needs as much as she needs the nature that Rango offers her. What she finds in Rango's nature, however, is vultures: "To love he brought only his fierce anxieties; she had embraced, kissed, possessed a mirage. She had walked and walked, not into the fiestas and the music, not into laughter, but into the heart of an Indian volcano" (ibid., p. 136).

There is a break in the text at this point in the Swallow edition; the first two editions of this novel designate the following forty-nine pages as "Part Two."[2] This break serves as a rest, a pause before the final, quick working out of Djuna's life with Rango, and the novel's conclusion does not constitute a shift in focus as do the concluding sections of Nin's first two novels. Djuna is now totally aware that she is entrapped by Rango and especially by Zora, and she is so frustrated in her untenable position that she wishes Zora would die so that she, Djuna, could live a full life and her now infrequent nights of passion with Rango could be extended into days as well. One therefore expects Djuna eventually to defect from Rango and Zora, so it is something of a shock when not she but Rango escapes as he goes from her to the revolution. The narrator comments that men leave the difficulties of love for seemingly more important political and social causes much more easily than women, but while Djuna would never make such a choice she nonetheless halfheartedly attempts to mold herself into the proper mate for a revolutionary so she might keep alive the diminishing flame of their love. Rango had little enough time for her when he had also to care for Zora, but now that he directs his energies toward the revolution he has no time for her at all.

There is little possibility that Djuna will succeed in transforming herself into a proper mate for a revolutionary because she believes that all life and all improvement of life begin with a man and a woman together. When Rango leaves her for his larger and ill-defined cause he therefore subverts the very changes he wishes to achieve, and in order to preserve herself from the death he is courting she reverts, as she has always done in a time of stress, to the cities of her interior, to her dreams housed in another chamber of her heart. She is reverting to the dream not to reside there permanently, as do the characters in House of Incest, but to gain the sustenance needed to exist in life.

When she returns to the barge she is a woman who is generally aware of her complete self. The narrator points out that most people recognize their physical mishaps but few perceive that psychic injuries are at least as serious as the more obvious physical ones. In recognizing both, Djuna resembles the multilayered woman in Duchamp's "Nude Descending a Staircase": "the multiple selves grown in various proportions, not singly, not evenly developed, not moving in one direction, but composed of multiple juxtapositions revealing endless spirals of character as the earth revealed its strata, an infinite constellation of feelings expanding as mysteriously as space and light in the realm of the planets" (*Heart*, p. 164). Because of this awareness Djuna becomes even more disenchanted with Rango and defends Sabina, whom he has verbally attacked, by stating that her love of many instead of one is not only acceptable but necessary, because, like Djuna, Sabina is a woman of many parts, all of which need to be fulfilled.

This open disagreement with Rango leads directly to Djuna's escape from the trap in which she has been caught throughout her relationship with him and Zora. Djuna reveals that at one time she related a dream in which she killed Zora with a hatpin to Zora, but that revelation only caused Zora to attempt to kill Djuna in a similar manner on board the barge. Zora thinks Djuna the person responsible for Rango joining the revolution and therefore ignoring her, and in order to reclaim her husband's attention she desires to eradicate the force that moves him. Luckily the wounds she inflicts are superficial, and she becomes subdued by the passion and the honesty of Djuna's words to her, words identifying Rango as a man divided between destruction and construction and who therefore needs one woman to satisfy the former urge (Zora) and another to fulfill the latter (Djuna). This is obviously the correct analysis of Rango, and even if Zora were to kill Djuna, Rango would require another woman to replace her.

When Rango arrives he does not know what to say, but after escorting Zora home he returns to the barge and relates that he is, at long last, aware of his shortcomings and that all of Djuna's love has been given largely in vain. The impetus for this awareness is lent by his fellow revolutionaries who, in evaluating their associates, told him loudly and forcefully what Djuna has been telling him gently and softly for some time: that he is temperamentally unsuited for the life of a revolutionary. His energy is sapped, and he falls asleep like a large child. Djuna is alone, then, on this barge, and as she looks through the barred windows—from her cell, as it were—she tears a board from the barge's floor and awaits her death and escape from unhappiness. She lies on her back beside Rango and begins to see from a new and deeper perspective through a curtain of water that it was not her love for him that entrapped her, but

the static pause in growth, the arrested self caught in its own web of obstinacy and obsession. . . . you grow, as in the water the algae grow taller and heavier and are carried by their own weight into different currents. . . .

. . . I was afraid to grow or move away, Rango, I was ashamed to desert you in your torment, but now I know your choice is your own, as mine was my own. . . .

. . . fixation is death . . . death is fixation. [*Heart*, p. 179]

In preparing for death Djuna discovers basic truths about life, and she realizes that "time and the river" (ibid., p. 182) will eventually heal most wounds and that the barge she is destroying is a "refuge for faith" (ibid., p. 183) (similar to her own four-chambered heart) in which many loves may be housed. With these new awarenesses she realizes that death, like life lived totally in a dream, is a selfish escape from the demands of a difficult yet fecund life, and she thereupon calls to Rango to stop the leak. He awakens in stages, as Djuna had become aware of her different layers earlier, and repairs the damage. As he and Djuna walk to the quays with the dawn of a new day, they spy a fisherman dangling from his pole the doll of Djuna's youth that had committed suicide by drowning. With that event the novel ends, as does the adolescent Djuna (the doll). The barge, Noah's Ark, has survived Djuna's attempt to destroy it, and the faith it represents and the wisdom Djuna attains constitute the good that has come from this sordid tale of Djuna, Rango, and Zora.

7

A Spy in the
House of Love

A Spy in the House of Love (1954) is the best known of
Nin's novels because of its suggestive title and because
it has gone through more editions than any other of her
works, but it is only in its New York setting that it is substantially
different from the other titles in the continuous novel of which it is an
integral part.[1] Here, as elsewhere, the author is concerned with the
psychological anguish of a female character, Sabina, and with her
attempts to grasp the nature of her difficulties, deal with them, and
reach a state of wholeness or contentment that leads to happiness in life.
Sabina's appearance in this novel constitutes Nin's most detailed
analysis of her.

  In her earlier appearances in Nin's fiction (she has been in every novel
and *House of Incest*) Sabina has been a woman in search of passion, a
woman whose ladders lead to fire, and in this novel she continues her
misdirected quest for fulfillment even though she seems to be more
controlled and less impetuous than heretofore as the book progresses. At
the outset, however, she is a tormented woman in a bar who is so
disturbed that she randomly dials a telephone and reaches a psychiatrist,
the lie detector, who frames the novel and who, in his own pathetic need
to be wanted , is a lineal descendant of the titular character in "The
Voice." He is quickly able to diagnose her problem as one of guilt, "the
one burden human beings can't bear alone" (*Spy,* p. 6), but when she
finds his words too painful and abruptly terminates the conversation

113

that was becoming the lie detector's monologue, he then is frustrated both at being unable to help her further and at being no longer needed by her. He has the call traced and goes to the bar where he views her voyeuristically. There he observes her dressed in her usual red and silver, evoking the imagery of fire engines, but above all else she is evasive and uncertain in her words and actions, as though she were enacting a dream. This type of behavior both intrigues and befuddles the lie detector, but the narrator must make the best analysis of the troubled Sabina.

> She was compelled by a confessional fever which forced her into lifting a corner of the veil, and then frightened when anyone listened too attentively. She repeatedly took a giant sponge and erased all she had said by absolute denial, as if this confusion were in itself a mantle of protection.
> At first she beckoned and lured one into her world; then, she blurred the passageways, confused all the images, as if to elude detection. [Ibid., p. 10]

As the dawn appears Sabina must defend herself against the clarity that it brings, and to do so she wraps herself within her cape and angrily leaves the bar with the unseen lie detector following her.[2] Unfortunately for Sabina, her escape from the harshnesses of daylight and reality cannot be achieved by sleep because of her haunting nightmares; she can find balance and symmetry, a calm, only when she awakens and rearranges her outer self with makeup to conceal her inner chaos. Her final accoutrement is of course the cape that permits her to face the vagaries of the night with confidence, but its effect, as well as that of the makeup, subsides as the night wanes.[3]

The cape prepares her for contact with reality, but her preparation is one of hostility and defiance that reinforces her arhythmic relationship with life and does not protect her from the large, harsh trucks that she encounters along Eighteenth Street. Her smallness in relation to the enormity of the trucks is more than just a disturbing episode, because immediately after feeling dwarfed by them she notices walking beside her a woman who is her twin but who, in her magnitude, walks with assurance. Both the trucks and this other woman suggest the woman Sabina truly is and offer evidence that she is not so meager and insignificant as she feels herself to be. Her problem, like that of Stella earlier, is one of self-perception, a sense of unwarranted selfworthlessness that leads her to confront life with excessive gusto to compensate for her supposed inadequacies.

Offering some solace from her problem and yet compounding it is her husband of ten years, Alan, a man of stability who in his reliability and lack of imagination resembles Lillian's husband Larry. Sabina lives with Alan at 55 Fifth Avenue, she goes from him to meet lovers in hotels, and she returns to him after those trysts in order to assauge her guilt. At thirty-five, five years her senior, Alan is dutifully and naïvely trusting of his wayward wife who deceives him (there is no evidence that he is aware of her unfaithfulness) as she explains her absence of eight days by stating that she, an actress, was performing the role of Madame Bovary in Provincetown, Rhode Island.[4] He receives her warmly, listens to her recounting of the past week, and sleeps contentedly, a basically good man at peace with himself and therefore Sabina's emotional opposite. He is not cruel to her in any outward way, and she could have been much less fortunate in her choice of a husband; but in his paternalistic attitude and in his desire for her to be an eternal ingenue, he demands a false Sabina in a manner similar to the insensitive Molnar's refusal to acknowledge the real Hejda in an earlier story. Sabina genuinely loves Alan (primarily because she believes he is kind to her), and because she does she is willing to shape herself into the woman he desires. She is, then, only half present with her husband, and the guilt that she suffers from betraying him keeps her from being her whole self with her lovers as well. The real Sabina is not discernible in either of these two important parts of her life.

In bed in the darkness with Alan she relives the days of freedom (except for freedom from guilt) spent in Provincetown, and her first memory is of lying naked on the sand in a state of complete repose, a state that brings to her not the image of death but happiness. Her calm is interrupted by the voice of Philip who, in his singing of opera to the sea, resembles a modern day Demosthenes, and whose voice transports the supine Sabina to the Black Forest of Tristan and Isolde. Part of Philip's appeal is his sense of the past, the echos of experience and memories that his singing evokes, and because she feels uncomfortable with her tendency to live wholly in the present she spends the day with him on the beach. Sabina has heretofore been a seductress in Nin's work, a woman confident and aggressive in sexual situations, but with Philip she becomes nervous and insecure because his eyes "were impersonal and seemed to gaze beyond her at all women who had dissolved into one, but who might, at any moment again become dissolved into all. This was the gaze Sabina had always encountered in Don Juan, everywhere, it was the gaze she mistrusted. It was the alchemy of desire fixing itself upon the incarnation of all women into Sabina for a moment but as easily by a second process able to alchemize Sabina into many others" (*Spy*, p. 30). Her wish is to escape this lover and reestablish her false but by now fairly comfortable role as Alan's wife, but even as Philip speaks to her ironically, she promises to meet him later that evening. Sabina's confidence is somewhat restored as they walk to town and she realizes when she sees him walking that she has charmed a man of some power, but as her self-esteem improves her "core" anticipates a certain catastrophe. Philip seems an ideal, a man too good to be true, but he becomes more human in her eyes when he appears to be uncertain that she will meet him that evening. This hesitancy permits her to think him attainable, so when they meet she is at ease and his caresses cause her "volcanic lava [to flow], desire incandescent, and where it burned the voices of the blues being sung became a harsh wilderness cry, bird and animal's untamed cry of pleasure and cry of danger and cry of fear and cry of childbirth and cry of wound pain from the same hoarse delta of nature's pits." They thereupon flee the club to "the undergrounds of the night" where all is absent except "one ritual, a joyous, joyous, joyous, joyous impaling of woman on man's sensual mast" (ibid., p. 38). But Sabina's joyousness remains one of anticipation; while Philip lies beside her in the bottom of a boat contented after his sexual release, she is unfulfilled, having failed to reach a climax, and becomes angry because sexually she is unable either to give or receive fully. This continual frustration has led and continues to lead her to desire to act in a traditionally masculine manner; by compensating for this lack with her idea of male behavior, she supposes she will be able to love without attachment as men can.

Sabina and Philip finally part, although she knows he will return when he is in need of sexual activity, because the anonymous woman he truly loves is relatively passionless.

Much of the reason for Sabina's inability to perceive of herself accurately and to melt with a man in sexual union is her long-held affinity for the moon and things remote. As a child she took what were thought to be dangerous moon baths and often lay naked in bed as the moon's rays caressed her body. She thus became discontent with her ordinary surroundings as she became convinced of her own multiplicity, timelessness, and immortality. These new perceptions caused a flame, a fever, that made her restless and made her look consumptive to her mother but which attracted people to her nonetheless. Sabina relives her meeting with Philip as she lies abed with Alan, and the narrative returns to that situation, to the present, to amplify the nature of her relationship with the moon. She is by her own suggestion a woman of considerable depth, energy, and complexity; so when Alan closes the windows, provides artificial light from lamps, and locks the door,[5] she feels confined and flees her reality by following her dream and Debussy's "Ile Joyeuse" toward an ideal sexuality. In pursuing this escape Sabina opens herself to the dangers of the dream that Nin examined fully in *House of Incest*; that is, excessive existence in the dream leads to an unsatisfactory life in reality. And so it appears to be with Sabina as her dream destroys her present reality with Alan. She wants exotic lovers and not Alan, Paris and not New York; but Debussy's music fades, she returns to reality from her dream before she is trapped within it, and from it she has gained the sustenance to live another week with her husband who does not know her and who forces her to be what she is not.

That sustenance is short-lived as Sabina leaves Alan for a rendezvous with Philip. As soon as she leaves her home she removes her wedding ring and replaces it with a musical one that Philip has given her, walks with gusto (as opposed to the manner in which she trudges practically inertly back to Alan), and feels as alive as the newly lighted and vibrant city about her as she leaves her world of security and falsity for one of insecurity and what she believes is truth. The forcefulness exhibited in her walk does not diminish in Philip's presence; instead, if anything, it develops into a juggernaut that completely overwhelms her cool lover, to his obvious dismay. He desires a passionate woman, but one whose passion is internal so it will not threaten him, and he fantasizes about making love to a woman whose arms are tied behind her.[6] In an earlier novel Jay had no use for Sabina because she was his equal in lovemaking, and in this novel Philip also wants to be the aggressor. But Sabina, who has been struggling to regain her lost sexual self, discovers that with Philip she is at last liberated because she is able to consummate their relationship sexually without feeling love for him. To Sabina this ability to love without commitment is the essence of freedom, but the narrator is quick to point out what is immediately obvious: Sabina's conception of love is puerile and self-deluding; her love is one of war for which she assembles treacheries so she will not be surprised by the actions of others; real, mature love is a house in which she is a spy, as much a voyeur as the lie detector who watches her. With her companion, she is an onlooker wishing to participate, but she cannot because of her incapacity of giving herself openly and without defenses. After she and Philip have loved, as she dresses and he lies asleep in a breeze that is growing progressively cooler, she feels "no desire to cover or shelter him, or to give him warmth" (Spy, p. 52); that is, she cares for him only as an object and not as a human being. She wishes to receive heat from her partner, but she is unwilling to give warmth in return, and in her attitude toward the opposite sex, as exemplified here, she is indeed the twin of Jay, whose creative energy and vitality seem to exist at the expense of sensitivity to the feelings of others.

Sabina senses that her new, free self may not be her true self at all, and with that in mind she returns to Alan after five days with Philip. Alan is, not surprisingly, exactly the same as he had been when she was last with him, but in her absence he purchased for her phonograph records of singing and drumming from "Ile Joyeuse."[7] They listen to them together and Sabina is transported aurally to the jungle village of the dark-skinned people who made the rhythmic music, but when she expresses a wish to visit those people with Alan he demurs because of the work his job demands he perform. Undeterred, Sabina senses that, while she is already there in her mind, she will soon be made an offer to visit those sensual people, and when the invitation arrives she will certainly accept it. Such an invitation comes, predictably and somewhat melodramatically, when she soon hears the sound of drums emanating from a cellar club as she is walking along MacDougall Street. This club, with its black performers and patrons, constitutes the realization of her dream, and as she listens to the music her eyes meet and become affixed to those of a drummer who caresses his drums as he would a woman's body. She is attracted by this symbolic sexuality, but when she and the drummer (unfortunately named Mambo) dance, their bodies fuse into one until, for what appears to be an inexplicable reason, he becomes angry and leaves her. Subdued, he approaches her again to relate that other white women respond to him sexually solely because he is black. But Mambo is a proud and serious man, a mathematician, composer, and writer in addition to being a drummer in the club; this treatment of him as a mere sex object by white women has embittered him. Sabina assures him that she has had black lovers before, but that it was not their blackness that kept her with them. Convinced of her honesty Mambo resumes the dance with this woman who seems to have matured since her encounter with Philip.

His pride is one deterrent to her love for him, but so too is Mambo's studio whose entrance is half blocked by an iron railing and is located on Patchen Place where all houses are identical and where any display of idiosyncrasy or individuality is treated as an aberration from a narrow norm. Once Sabina gains entrance to the studio and access to Mambo, however, her problem then becomes one of escape because of the guilt she feels at betraying her husband. Instead of enjoying her time with Mambo she worries that the lie detector has seen her enter the studio and that a man she notices lurking in the stairway is Alan. Neither man is there, but they will continue to follow her as embodiments of her guilt until she becomes one with herself. Alan is of particular importance because he is the core of her life, and if he were to remove himself from her, her life, she believes, would crumble. But Sabina's view of her relationship with Alan is inaccurate because he is the core of only one aspect of the multifaceted Sabina: he is the father whom she is trying to please and not the lover she is seeking in such men as Mambo. Her nascent awareness of her true attitude toward Alan is suggested as she avows his place of central importance to her life. When the narrator mentions that "Alan was the core of her life" (*Spy,* p. 63), she is stating what the conscious Sabina believes to be true. But when Sabina reflects on her inability to sustain a passionate relationship with others, she concludes that her shortcomings have been caused by her fear of losing "Alan *as if* this love were the core of her existence" (ibid., p. 64, italics added). This shift to a qualified statement on the centrality of Alan to Sabina's life is not accidental; rather, it evinces the beginning of doubt, an awareness by Sabina as she begins to grow from considering herself a one- to a multi-dimensional woman who no longer needs to be defined by the acceptance of her paternalistic husband.

With this first spark of awareness Sabina returns to Mambo able to achieve a moment of true and free passion with him, but it is only a moment and vanishes as both of them retreat within their own protective shells, violating the openness that had made that moment of ecstasy possible. This openness with Mambo cannot be sustained, but one must keep in mind that it augurs well for Sabina and that Mambo, with his own psychological problems, is not an ideal partner for her.

Concurrent with this early step toward wholeness is a flashback to Sabina's visit to an ancient South American city that had been destroyed by an earthquake, leaving only façades of buildings and limitless space. Her reflection on this sight leads her to understand yet another aspect of her difficulty, which is her expectation that every lover will provide her the freedom and openness that she saw in that ravaged city. Such an idealistic expectation is of course beyond human capability and therefore causes her to find all men inadequate. She has felt herself to be a captive of her lovers, but now she is beginning to understand that what she has taken for captivity is in fact the human condition of imperfection.

> No place, no human being could bear to be gazed at with the critical eye of the absolute, as if they were obstacles to the reaching of a place or person of greater value created by the imagination. This was the blight she inflicted upon each room when she asked herself: "Am I to live here forever?["] This was the blight, the application of the irrevocable, the endless fixation upon a place or relationship. It aged it prematurely, it accelerated the process of decay by staleness. A chemical death ray, this concentrate of time, inflicting the fear of stasis like a consuming ray, deteriorating at the high speed of a hundred years per minute.
>
> At this moment she was aware of her evil, of an invisible crime equal to murder in life. It was her secret sickness, one she believed incurable, unnamable. [*Spy*, pp. 68-69]

After realizing this shortcoming in herself she is able to begin to recapture her lost emotional self in Stravinsky's *Firebird*, which serves as "her unerring musical autobiography" (ibid., p. 69).

These awarenesses are indeed crucial for Sabina, but they constitute at best a first step toward a reconciliation with her real self, as is illustrated by her last meeting with Mambo. When they go to a movie, an outing that should be relatively carefree, Sabina becomes frightened because of the possibility of their encountering Alan, whereupon she would feel her affections divided between her husband and her lover. She desires to accompany Mambo, but to avoid the possible confrontation she plans carefully the part of the city to which they should go and the precise movie they should see, basing the choices on the unlikelihood of Alan's presence there. Once in the theater she is not safe either, and to avoid detection she takes her seat only after others are settled so she can examine them carefully to determine Alan's presence. This tension comes to a climax when she views spy movies and observes on the screen tensions in the actors that are analogous to her own; they fear to commit themselves too unreservedly to something as ordinary as sleep lest they be discovered, and when she realizes this she identifies herself as "*an international spy in the house of love*" (*Spy*, p. 72) (hence the novel's title). She may view love only from a distance. She attempts to overcome this anxiety by becoming witty and ironical (a quality that she detested in Philip), but when she does she isolates herself even further from her human connections and becomes susceptible to the death that is the fate of every spy. Sabina has learned much during her affair with Mambo, but this knowledge is difficult to assimilate; she evinces little improvement during her relationship with her next lover, John, the aviator.

After Mambo and Patchen Place, Sabina goes to a beach town on Long Island where, standing on a corner, she meets a youthful twenty-two year-old named John whose large eyes reveal a panic different from hers only in that it is more immediately noticeable. In his adolescent appearance he resembles the children of the albatross of an earlier novel, but unlike them he has had the experiences of a man and bears the resultant emotional scars. After becoming disgusted with the sterility of this new town (a quality it shares with Patchen Place) as she awaits Alan's tardy arrival, and as a humane Irish policeman cares for her while she cannot sleep, she learns that the cyclist is a young man who enlisted in the English Air Corps at seventeen and is now grounded. He is not permitted, therefore, to do what he loves best, his vision is reduced from the open spaces to a small scale, and in that sense he and Sabina share a common problem. Later that same evening she again meets the aviator-cum-cyclist and listens to him recount his military experiences. John, like Hemingway's Harold Krebs, has difficulty adapting to civilian life, and he is attracted to Sabina because she does not giggle and because she hates the town they share. They go together to her room and make love with "a long, prolonged, deep thrusting ecstasy" (*Spy*, p. 83), after which he states that "Life is flying, flying" (ibid., p. 84). But Sabina, now having consummated a physical love with great satisfaction, avers that love and nothing else is at the core of life. The mood, the experience, is thus denigrated by John's insensitivity. Sabina assumes the role of his analyst as Djuna has been hers, and John, believing their sexual union to be bad, tucks her in bed before taking leave of her. What he cares for, however, is not the body that has joined with his in sensual delight, but rather one "in which he had injected the poison which was killing him, the madness of hunger, guilt and death by proxy which tormented him. He had injected into her body his own venomous guilt for living and desiring. He had mingled poison with every drop of pleasure, a drop of poison in every kiss, every thrust of sensual pleasure the thrust of a knife killing what he desired, killing with guilt" (ibid., pp. 85–86). Once again Sabina has been unsuccessful in love, but this time John's shortcomings, not hers, are responsible for the failure.

There is some hope that Sabina will be able to recapture that magic the next day when Alan arrives, but his love continues to be paternalistic and her sexual appetite goes unfulfilled, as does her desire to rid her body of the poison that John put there. But if she cannot be cleansed by Alan, at least she thinks herself able to cleanse John, the purveyor of poison. In so doing she will save herself as well, because his obsession with flying is similar to her desire to experience foreign lands and the unfamiliar through her love and because his being grounded is analogous to her repeatedly returning to the mundane Alan. As might be expected, though, this messianic urge is frustrated. When John meets her walking with Alan, Sabina realizes that her young lover now thinks her an evil woman and therefore wants to avoid her, but instead of accepting his decision she stays in town after Alan has returned to New York City and frantically attempts to recapture John's faith so she may cleanse them both. Her aggressiveness not only does not conquer him, but it also causes her to be ridiculed by the moon, the celestial body with which she has some affinity. She is left alone in this unpleasant town without either John or Alan, but even though she was not able to discover the antidote to the poison that infested her and her lover, she has nonetheless not lost sight of one of her basic problems: *"I want the impossible, I want to fly all the time, I destroy ordinary life, I run towards all the dangers of love as he ran towards all the dangers of war. He runs away, war is less terrifying to him than life"* (*Spy*, p. 91). She still seeks the ideal, the unreachable, the inhuman, and as long as she continues to do so she will be unsuccessful in the love that she considers to be the panacea for her own difficulties.

Because her love for John is aborted there remains within Sabina a desire for someone like him so that earlier love may be consummated. This feeling is not new; rather, it has been her method of progressing from lover to lover throughout her life. Little is known of her first lover in the hotel, but Philip is a Viennese singer; Mambo is an African musician; John is a youthful English aviator (suggesting the freedom and improvisation of jazz music in particular which, it is implied, is the type of music preferred and performed by Mambo); and her new lover, Donald, is an adolescent much like John. But in his innocence he is the most dangerous of all. There is another development in these men as well: they decrease in emotional and sexual stature. Philip is most experienced in love and is most comfortable with it; he is threatened only when his lover is too aggressive. Mambo also has experienced many women, but he has increasing difficulty consummating those relationships because he feels that he is being used for his mythical racial sexuality instead of being loved for the human being he truly is or believes he is. Even less secure with his masculinity is John. He functions well with Sabina until after they make love when he thinks that any woman who would perform the sexual act must be bad.

The least satisfactory of these men is the last one, Donald, who is the personification of innocence. He hardly qualifies as a candidate for the designation "man." Sabina is attracted to him because of his similarity to John, but "she did not observe the differences, that Donald's skin was even more transparent, his hair silkier, that he did not spring, but glided, dragging his feet a little, that his voice was passive, indolent, slightly whining" (*Spy*, p. 93). The real Donald is difficult to locate and define because he conceals himself in the masquerade of others so that he can safely ridicule the people he is pretending to be, especially the women. But even though she perceives the puerility and danger of this posturing, Sabina sees his threat: he reverts to innocence in order to gain material for his future mockeries.

Donald's problem resulted, as Jay's did in large part, from a mother who abused him with her insensitivity, and Sabina, understanding how it happened, attempts to help him by offering love and sympathy. This selfless behavior is in one sense commendable, but it so obviously perverts Sabina's true nature that it is destined to fail, as it does. In her relationship with him the absent mother acts, for him, as a filter, as one who discards the love that Sabina offers and changes it into his mother's original insensitivities toward him. As a result Donald is repulsed when he encounters Sabina physically because he thinks he is touching his mother, and in the few instances in which he is aroused, his passion is quickly subdued and he returns to his neutral (neuter) territory. Sabina, however, refuses to let those sparks die, but her pursuit causes him to feel all the more defenseless and adolescent and to think that he must stop her encroachment or he, or his manhood, will become entangled within her, as was the case years before with his mother whom he also loved. He is able to avoid her pursuit deftly, but in so doing he causes her considerable frustration.

As if to offer a symbolic explanation for himself Donald shows Sabina the empty bird cages that he collects to house a bird about which he once dreamed. The cages would offer the *appearance* of freedom to a bird contained within them, but the real freedom, Sabina sees, is neither in his ideal bird nor the confining cages; rather, it is in the passion evoked by

The Firebird. She plays that music on a phonograph, but when she stops it unfinished and approaches him with open arms, he embraces not Sabina the woman of sexual desire but Sabina the mother who can provide the nourishment he needs. She feels strangely serene, but in so doing her passionate breasts cool; she has become the ideal bird that Donald keeps in his cage of innocence. In doing this she has sacrificed herself to her own mother: "What Donald had achieved by capturing her into his net of fantasy as the firebird . . . was not only to reach his own need's fulfillment but to enable her to rejoin her mother's image which was her image of goodness: her mother, dispenser of food, of solace, soft warm and fecund" (*Spy,* p. 101). Sabina, as her mother, is able to shed her feelings of guilt for a moment. Because of Donald she has returned to her lost innocent state that will hopefully permit her to discover peace; but such a result seems unlikely, especially if one attempts to project the innocent Donald into a peaceful manhood. One senses that Sabina desires innocence and peace in her relationship with him because those are qualities that have for so long been alien to her. Her basic nature is not docile; she must learn to accept her complexities, and becoming a surrogate mother to Donald only delays the hopeful inevitability of that acceptance. For this reason the passive Donald is the most dangerous of her male friends, but even with him there is a lesson for her to learn, and it has to do with Alan. She has found her husband inadequate throughout their marriage because of his paternalistic attitude toward her, yet when Donald asks her to perform as a mother instead of as a lover, she readily consents (although she has not much choice) and feels comfortable in that maternal role. As she is fulfilled, in a sense, as mother to Donald, so too is Alan in his role as her father. This of course does not absolve Alan of the charge of being an unsatisfactory husband, but it does suggest that Sabina is possibly as insensitive to him as he is to her.

One aspect of Sabina is certainly the motherhood that Donald causes her to recognize (although she evidently has no children of her own), but so too is her desire for passionate relationships, for the unique love of Alan, and for all of life. Basic to Sabina, however, and the cause of all of her difficulties, is an inability to assimilate her various selves into a congealed whole. She resembles Duchamp's "Nude Descending a Staircase," but once she defines herself as one particular woman (for example, as mother) she has difficulty stepping outside that identity to take advantage of her other Sabinas. As she becomes gradually aware of this problem she is able to envy actors because of their ability to perform passionately as single characters and then emerge from that performance as whole, unique individuals. This analogy is an apt one, of course, because Sabina is herself an actress, and her difficulty at this point suggests Stella's problem that occurred earlier.

As there is great danger in living too unreservedly in a dream in much of Nin's work, there is also as great a danger in living too exclusively in only one of one's many facets or personalities. Sabina believes that when she is the mother she must only be protective and understanding, but when she again hears *The Firebird* she is fearful that she as mother will be destroyed and that she will become too much like her promiscuous father, and "she was afraid because there was no Sabina, not ONE, but a multitude of Sabinas lying down yielding and being dismembered, constellating in all directions and breaking" (*Spy*, p. 109). As she sits alone looking pensively from her window, "she looked at the ending nights and the passersby with the keen alertness of the voyager who can never reach termination as ordinary people reach peaceful terminals at the end of each day, accepting pauses, deserts, havens, as she could not accept them" (ibid., p. 110). Sabina remains as frustrated as ever.

While Sabina grows slowly aware of her difficulties, her anxieties have increased to the point that she finally feels lost: she has found solace with neither Alan nor her five lovers, and the cumulative unhappiness causes her to lose her immunity to pain and to become becalmed in it. Her cape is no longer a shield, and she is left defenseless to wallow in her chaos. But while she is floundering, her external body is being killed so the real Sabina, her essence, will become accessible. It is her core, the whole Sabina, that she has been unable to identify, and its baring coincides with a reunion with the artist Jay in Mambo's club where Jay's paintings are on display. Sabina had been familiar with Jay's work in Paris seven years before, but only now, with her inner self exposed, is she able to see herself in his figures. His people are fragmented, but the pieces are not strewn over such a distance that they are irretrievable into the whole once again. As she views these paintings with new insight she realizes that her small insincerities of the past have accumulated with such force as to fragment her; her search for fire, heat, and passion to weld her parts into the whole Sabina has failed. Jay drew these people to show the "atomic pile in which men and women are bombarded to find the mysterious source of power in them, a new source of strength" (*Spy*, p. 114), and if Sabina is able to understand that with a recognition and acceptance of one's many faces comes power, strength, wholeness, and happiness, she will then be the true self she has been trying with so little success to become.

At this point Jay recounts his early impression of Sabina in language almost identical to that in passages early in the novel (*Spy,* pp. 7–10, in particular). This repeated portrayal of the reckless Sabina takes on new significance, however, because it reinforces both how deep-seated her problems are and what difficulties she has had to endure. Above all else this recapitulation emphasizes her habit of concealing, because of her guilt, her real self. This evasiveness was and is attractive to Jay (his desire is like "the desire of a man to violate a woman who resists him, to violate a virginity which creates a barrier to his possession" [ibid., p. 123]), and as he reflects on their passionate and frenzied ascent and descent in an elevator years ago, he correctly concludes that at her core is not Donald's maternal Sabina but a woman whose ardent frenzy is for desire, for passion. Despite this identification of her true self, she is unable to accept it, and she braces herself against the impending daylight with her cape as she leaves the club alone.

Sabina wants to go home to Alan who will assuredly comfort her, but she cannot because she is too full of experiences that are alien to him and because she is especially concerned about the lie detector whom she has noticed recording her actions in the club. A certain awareness is also hers: her understanding of Jay's work leads her to comprehend Duchamp's famous painting of the parts of a multilayered woman walking down a staircase, and because of this awareness she thinks that her going to Alan would be tantamount to detaching one of her layers from the unison of the whole and presenting him with a limited and therefore false Sabina (as she has been doing). But she is a tired woman, enervated from attempting to hold her frightened self together and wearied from bearing her guilt, and she goes to a hotel across from Mambo's club for rest. One night's (or day's) sleep will not soothe her, however, because it is more her mind than her body that is fatigued. Realizing this, she goes to Jay and the other artists in Mambo's club knowing that they will be sympathetic listeners to her. Sabina and Djuna arrive at the same time. Djuna above all others grasps reality and helps Sabina most effectively. As soon as she is with Djuna, Sabina's anxiety subsides, her rhythm is restored to her blood, and she is able to sit quietly without agitation. But this hopeful situation is quickly dashed when, noticing the lie detector taking notes, she confronts him antagonistically. In her harangue to him she finally pushes back her consciousness to her first crime and therefore sets the stage for the new Sabina who, disappointingly, does not emerge. Her first crime was against herself when, in search of the marvelous, she corrupted truth. This corruption created delusions that led to wishing for and believing in the ideal; that in turn led to her dissatisfaction, in her present life, with permanency. One result of this has been her desire to have several loves instead of one; and that has led to her lies, deception, and finally loneliness. Despite such awareness, Sabina persists in fearing detection of her true self.

First Djuna and then the lie detector analyze Sabina's situation. Djuna points out that Alan, to whom Sabina has always been able to go for consolation, has been more father than husband because that is precisely what Sabina expected of him; but although Alan may not have fulfilled his role as husband as well as he might, what has caused that marriage to be unsuccessful is Sabina herself: "The enemy of love is never outside, it's not a man or woman, it's what we lack in ourselves" (*Spy,* p. 135). Sabina is predictably not pleased to hear such talk, as she is not when Djuna tells her, in another psychological verity, that the lie detector is not attempting to arrest her, but that she projects her guilt onto every person of authority and therefore only imagines their hostility toward her. Djuna further asserts that the blame for Sabina's failures in love rests solely with her; instead of permitting her lovers to be their true selves she made them "either crusaders who would fight your battles for you, or judges continuing your parent's [sic] duties, or princes who had not yet come of age, and therefore could not be husbands" (ibid., pp. 135-36).

This information is difficult for Sabina to accept, and when she tells the lie detector that she has loved not once but many times, he accurately points out that she has never loved at all.

> You've only been trying to love, beginning to love. Trust alone is not love, desire alone is not love, illusion is not love, dreaming is not love. All these were paths leading you out of yourself, it is true, and so you thought they led to another, but you never reached the other. You were only on the way. Could you go out now and find the other faces of Alan, which you never struggled to see, or accept? Would you find the other face of Mambo which he so delicately hid from you? Would you struggle to find the other face of Philip? [*Spy,* p. 136]

The lie detector sees her as a dangerous person because she considers all others such as Philip and Mambo as myths, and the irony of her situation is that in managing her affairs so as always to win, she has in fact always lost because she never truly loved. He further reveals that she has never desired to free herself from the guilt that resulted both from loving many and from not loving at all. She distrusted a single, mature love, and to be safe from it she gave a minimal amount of herself to many.

Music has been an important part of Sabina's life, and at the novel's conclusion Djuna plays a recording of one of Beethoven's quartets that encourages an interpretation much different from that of *The Firebird*. The music suggests

> the continuity of existence and of the chain of summits, of elevations by which such continuity is reached. By elevation the consciousness reached a perpetual movement, transcending death, and in the same manner attained the continuity of love by seizing upon its impersonal essence, which was a summation of all the alchemies producing life and birth, a child, a work of art, a work of science, a heroic act, an act of love. The identity of the human couple was not eternal but interchangeable, to protect this exchange of spirits, transmissions of character, all the fecundations of new selves being born, and faithfulness only to the continuity[;] the extensions and expansions of love achieving their crystallizations into high moments and summits equal to the high moments and summits of art or religion. [*Spy*, p. 139]

The comprehension of the idea that one achieves something like immortality by attaining an elevated existence through love causes the remorseful Sabina to crumple to the floor in despair and to dissolve in her own tears as though returning to a prenatal existence. The lie detector can only reach out feebly to assist her and offer her hope—through music—for the future.

In this novel devoted entirely to her, Sabina emerges as a typical Nin woman who has difficulty finding wholeness and peace in life. She, like the others before her, does not attain what the real Sabina desires, but because of the harsh but necessary words of Djuna and the lie detector she finally possesses the facts of her situation, and one may hope that after having gone through this lengthy nightmare she will awaken a mature and loving woman.

Sabina appears later in the conclusion to *Seduction of the Minotaur*, the final volume in the continuous novel, but she is also present in a curious story entitled "Sabina" that was published in a magazine as "a portion of the unpublished conclusion of *Cities of the Interior*."[8] There is no evidence that other portions of an unpublished conclusion exist, were written, or were ever planned; but regardless of authorial intention this story may be read most beneficially either as an equally unsatisfactory introduction or conclusion to *A Spy in the House of Love,* even though it takes place in Paris before the novel begins.

Her novel ends with Sabina crushed by the awareness of her shortcomings. In "Sabina," however, Djuna attempts to convince Jay that if he only would understand Sabina their relationship would flourish. In the novel Djuna and the lie detector help Sabina understand the guilt that has caused her such unhappiness so she can, in effect, cure herself, but in the later story Djuna's attitude is to accept Sabina with only minimal concern for her obvious psychological difficulties. It matters not, vis-à-vis the novel, when the story is read; in her glib treatment of Sabina, Djuna accepts as fairly normal the behavior that has caused Sabina so much travail, and in so doing perverts the real Sabina who is finally revealed at the end of the novel. Sabina is too deep a woman to be dealt with superficially, and Djuna has shown herself to be too sensitive to treat her friend in such a manner. "Sabina" is perhaps best forgotten, at least as an appendage to *A Spy in the House of Love.*

8

Seduction of the Minotaur

In 1958 Nin published at her own expense a novel about Lillian entitled *Solar Barque*. Shortly thereafter she decided to conclude her continuous novel, but instead of writing a new volume she presented the text of *Solar Barque* and a lengthy, previously unpublished coda to Alan Swallow who published them together as *Seduction of the Minotaur* in 1961.[1] This book serves now as both a self-contained novel and as the conclusion to the much larger whole that began in 1946 with *Ladders to Fire*.

Ladders to Fire, Children of the Albatross, and *The Four-Chambered Heart* are all set primarily in Paris; *A Spy in the House of Love* takes place largely in New York City; but the events in *Seduction of the Minotaur* occur in Mexico, a country that offers a perfect backdrop for the final development of Lillian from a troubled, unsettled woman into one who, at the end, is content in life with herself and her husband, Larry. Paris is certainly superior to New York in Nin's work, but unsophisticated Mexico is the best of all possible places with its casual, rhythmic living and a tropical climate that drugs its inhabitants into a wonderful state of forgetfulness while at the same time encouraging a recognition of the body. Here one may, as Hemingway's Nick Adams does in the more barren area around the Big Two-Hearted River, step aside from the hectic activity and complexity of society and confront nature's primal elements as well as one's basic self. If one is able to discover essence there, one may build oneself anew on a firm foundation and reenter society as a complete human being as Lillian does here (and as Nick Adams is not quite ready to do as he contemplates the dense swamp across the river).

Lillian, a jazz pianist, arrives in Golconda (her name for a town in southern Mexico resembling Acapulco) to perform at Mr. Hansen's Black Pearl Hotel. Jazz, with its multirhythms and improvisational nature, has been present in the background of most of Nin's work, and it surfaced with Mambo as an important element in *A Spy in the House of Love*. Its function, of course, has been primarily symbolic of freedom, openness, slight irreverence, eventual harmony, but so too has its presence been felt more subtly as an almost hidden structure for many of Nin's works in that most of them are impressionistically or improvisationally developed after the sense of a character or place is established (which is analogous to improvising on the chords in jazz). So when Lillian (now surnamed Beye) is presented as a jazz musician, the force of the jazz that has gone before culminates in her and she thus appears to be, even at the outset of this novel, a woman who not only possibly but probably will overcome her difficulties if she so desires, as she assuredly does.

The chord on which Nin improvises in this novel is the one that has resonated within Lillian for many years: her recurrent dream of a boat lost in the streets of a city, struggling desperately, with her assistance, to reach its natural home, the water. The misplaced boat symbolizes the lost Lillian, and that there is movement from unnaturalness toward naturalness foreshadows her development into a woman at peace with herself. The dream of the boat disturbs Lillian, but in the end it is a dream of hope and promise because it portrays her actively assisting herself. An important step in achieving this end is her decision to accept a musical engagement in Mexico. This novel is concerned, then, with the dream, Lillian's realization of its importance, her experiences in Mexico, and her final steps into the Lillian who finds happiness in life.

Lillian's development demands more than her going to Mexico, absorbing its nuances, and more or less passively becoming her true self. Upon her arrival in Golconda she meets three men who represent in different ways certain unfavorable types of characters inhabiting that country. One, the American Hatcher, is, as her own father was, an engineer who came to Mexico originally to build roads and bridges, but who married a Mexican woman and has remained there ever since. He speaks Spanish fluently, wears the casual dress that the climate dictates, but feels uncomfortable in those clothes and laments what he sees as the ruin of Golconda by tourism. He has therefore never submitted entirely to the tropics as one must, and to escape commercialization he and his family live on the beach in a house he is building. Another of these men, Hansen, is less well defined than Hatcher, but he assists the growing commercialization of Golconda by promoting his Black Pearl and bringing foreign artists to perform there. He is a blonde Austrian with a smileless face who shows his disdain for Mexico and its people by speaking Spanish harshly but authoritatively; he is the stereotypical businessman in a foreign country whose sole concern is making money. Hatcher has given himself largely but not completely to Mexico, and Hansen shall always remain an outsider, but both are insidious in their desire to shape Lillian's perceptions of Mexico before she is able to experience it and judge its qualities for herself.

The third of these men also wishes to shape her impressions of Golconda, but unlike Hatcher and Hansen his reason for so doing is not selfish. Dr. Hernandez, of Indian-Spanish heritage, attended a Mexican medical school and, at eighteen after some medical training, settled permanently in Golconda where his constant concern has been for the welfare of the people of that area. He attempts to convey knowledge of their generally ill health to Lillian, but while he is doing her a disservice in helping deny her the opportunity to experience the native life and draw her own conclusions about it, his own selflessness is so appealing that one (and especially Lillian) easily forgives that transgression and sympathizes with his seemingly futile one-man effort to cleanse his people. Unlike Hansen who employs musicians but has no sense of rhythm himself, Hernandez's words are accompanied, symbolically, by a guitar suggesting his natural attachment to this tropical area and its inhabitants. Only slowly does Lillian grow to admire him, and her development as a woman in this novel parallels the growth of her understanding of this man whose death and her acceptance of it leads directly to her successful reunion with Larry. Lillian is first attracted to Hernandez because he reminds her of the lie detector of the earlier novel. He is able to assist Lillian at the outset by seeing through her pleasing exterior to the troubled woman within. He helps her realize that her difficulties, no matter what they are, emanate from within herself, and that to purge herself of them she must understand "that we live by a series of repetitions until the experience is solved, understood, liquidated" (*Seduction*, p. 19), which is exactly what she does.

Lillian is also attracted to Hernandez because he, like no other in Golconda, has serious problems threatening him emotionally and physically; the languorous qualities of the region do not permit him to ignore or flee them. He is comfortable living in and treating the people of Golconda, but this doctor who attended schools in Paris and New York and who is also a published poet is unable to persuade his wife and three children to leave the relative comfort of Mexico City to live with him in Golconda. This absence from the family he loves causes him great anguish, but of immediate danger to him is a group of unseen people who, in their desire for the drugs that he alone may dispense, make attempts on his life until they are finally successful. Hernandez is an intelligent, sophisticated man who is able to balance satisfactorily his own advanced development with the fairly primitive nature of the people to whom he tends. He, unlike one like Hatcher, is therefore able to avoid the traditionally untenable existence of experienced man in an Edenic setting: he does not wilt and he does not surrender his true self to simpler verities; but it comes as no surprise when he dies, because this paradise of simplicity cannot permit something as complex as Hernandez to threaten its existence. It is permissible, alternatively, for Lillian to visit Golconda to recapture her true self by shedding all pretense and artifice, but if she is to develop herself anew, she must do so in a society that encourages such growth. Hernandez, then, must fail in Golconda, but as he does Lillian is able to benefit from observing his heroic struggle.

Shortly after leaving Hansen and Hatcher, Lillian accompanies Hernandez on a visit to a patient in a secluded area. As they navigate the river they are surrounded and almost strangled by nature, but because they are in a handcrafted canoe (native, simple, and therefore not threatening) they flow easily with the river. This success with the canoe goes exactly counter to Lillian's dream of the futility of her actions in assisting a boat reach water from its unnatural presence in the streets of a city, and because in Golconda she has learned to flow with the rhythm of the people and their land and to live solely in the present, her dream of futility ends. She sees her new awareness as analogous to the solar barques of ancient Egyptian rulers who had entombed with them two barques, one for traveling to the moon at night, and the other for a celestial journey to the sun at day. Lillian also has two barques, one, like the former, is static and is for a "voyage of memories," and the other, like the latter and like the canoe, is one that flows effortlessly toward discoveries of things remote. This journey to the sun is broken when Lillian, in the canoe, sacrifices her true thoughts and submits to Hernandez's anguish; and when she removes her hand from the water (breaks from nature), his enemies begin shooting at him. Man's relationship with nature is delicate, and when it is broken havoc reigns.

The dominance of nature over man in Golconda with the necessity of man being in tune with nature is one of the novel's major themes. Hatcher and Hansen will never be at home in Mexico because they are foreigners unwilling or unable to give of themselves wholly to their new environment; Hernandez is a native, but one who has been formed in part by foreign, sophisticated influences and is therefore impure and cannot survive; and Lillian is a visitor who will submit to Golconda for a moment, not to intrude, but to take from it the openness that she needs to complete her own humanity. Golconda is jealous and will embrace only those who are its own without reservation. But behind this notion is another suggesting that nature alone is not sufficient; there is a greater good that comes from the interaction of man and his creations with nature. One of Lillian's favorite spots, for example, and the place to which she likes to go before retiring for the evening, is the hotel's swimming pool that is just ten feet above sea level. Much of the charm of this man-made pool is that it is dominated by the sea, by nature, so that it achieves a life of its own. Thus, when man's creation is conjoined with undiluted nature, two disparate elements are fused into a whole that is greater than the sum of its parts and affords an ideal setting for one who is in turn seeking wholeness.

The pool provides Lillian with a backdrop against which she might develop wholeness, but it does not provide her with her completed self. Her immediate gratification there is a sense of gentleness and reassurance that she has lacked since childhood when she needed the comforting words of a night watchman in order to fall asleep, but she also submerges herself in the pool to avoid confronting the nature of her difficulty. Yet Hernandez, who on one occasion is there with her, will not let her escape the reality of her situation and finally tells her that she acts like a fugitive. She is hurt by this revelation, and she attempts to ignore it by again going under the water, but when she leaves the water, as she must, she returns to Hernandez "gleaming, smooth, but not free" (*Seduction*, p. 28). Nature will assist her, but it will not permit her to achieve her goal passively.

Lillian knows subconsciously that Hernandez is correct, that she is a fugitive from feeling and from truth and as such has sought protection in a chaos that has become her life (although she does not appear to be chaotic in this novel). Hernandez uses an Eastern example to show Lillian the necessity of understanding her past actions before moving on to new experiences such as Golconda offers. She thinks she can start anew there, but if she attempts to she will be unsuccessful because the foundation on which it will be based (that is, her past life) will be of an unknown quality. Hernandez's argument is that one does not change by placing oneself in a new environment or with new friends, because one's past life repeats itself until it is understood and transcended.

His analysis of Lillian is correct: she is a fugitive fleeing her past life, but because she is now in the salubrious town of Golconda she is more confident of her life there than is her new acquaintance. She looks, for example, at the people she has met there and sees no parallel between them and her former friends. Fred, an American student, is a typical Nin adolescent who is unable to enjoy life because his timidity prohibits him from interacting with others. He can express great joy when he is pleased with events or people at a distance, but he is reluctant to return home to his fiancée, Shelley, because he needs to prove himself a man before he marries her. He soon meets Diana, a sensual artist, and when he views her and Lillian from the distance of a docked ship that might take him to the United States, he realizes that Diana offers him Golconda and that Lillian offers him life itself. Rather than return home to Shelley he stays in Golconda hoping to grow into manhood with his new friends. Lillian reflects upon Fred as a person who is unlike any she has known before. She does not, however, attempt a real comparison with her other acquaintances, and had she done so she would have recalled that her first lover (or so he appears to be in the continuous novel) was Gerard who was always preparing to leave, just as Fred plans his escape from his commitment to Shelley. Lillian's past does repeat itself; she is blind to the fugitive nature of her existence in Golconda.

More light is shed on Lillian's predicament, and she begins to understand it a little better shortly after paying for a bird to pick a forecast from among many pieces of paper that hold numerous predictions for the future. She learns that "you will find what you are seeking" (*Seduction*, p. 37). Immediately after that assurance she is approached by a guide whom she had noticed before and disliked. This anonymous purveyor of legitimate and illegitimate delights is a confidence man whose ploy is to locate unsuspecting American tourists and have them come to the financial aid of his confederate, an American who appears to be a prisoner long forgotten in the Golconda jail. Lillian's opinion of the guide is accurate, but when she sees her fellow countryman behind bars she subconsciously realizes that they are fellow prisoners inasmuch as she, a seemingly free woman, is imprisoned within herself. (The jail was once a church; this perversion is analogous to Lillian, with her pure motives, being duped by the confidence men.) Because of this incident in which she is bilked out of fifty dollars she grows increasingly convinced of the accuracy of Hernandez's analysis of her, and she begins to perceive that she feels like a new, whole woman in Golconda, a town that keeps her from returning to her past life. Her Mexican freedom, then, is merely the *appearance* of freedom. This is illustrated in the hour just before dinner each day when many free women prepare for the pursuit of love but when she is filled with doubt because of her timidity and her anxieties. Even when she is courted in the evening she is unable to reciprocate because she is so fearful of solitude that she is unable to take advantage of the antidote when it appears. Upon discovering that she was duped by the confidence men, she meets an Irishman named O'Connor who, like Uncle Philip in an earlier novel, lives the lives of others. He is close to a mirror-image of Lillian in that he came to Golconda to forget himself, and he spends much of his time freeing foreigners who are in real trouble in Mexico. Lillian analyzes him as she has been unable successfully to analyze herself: he frees prisoners because he yearns to be free from his own imprisonment that was imposed upon him as a youth, and he cannot avoid his real self. But O'Connor cannot tolerate the truth coming from outside himself, so he leaves the present with Lillian in order to shield his lost self from detection. She is not that evasive, but her handling of Hernandez's analysis of her parallels O'Connor's reaction to her.

Lillian's awareness of herself increases as she becomes less self-centered and more cognizant of her relationship to her surroundings. She has heretofore thought that Golconda's festivities began with her jazz music in the evening, but she now sees, as she contemplates nature from her hammock, that the festivities never stop because they consist of the sun's effulgence and the moon's softness: Golconda is a perpetual festival of natural opulence, hers to have for a while if she will, and her momentary possession of it will lead directly to her possession of herself. That nature dominates all (that her music, as beautiful and free as it is, is subservient to a larger beauty) is illustrated by the presence of musicians on the beach. This spontaneous performance inspires both the musicians and the bathers, but it also attracts the waves that ebb and flow in a rhythm that makes insignificant the unheard notes from the violin with one string missing. Throughout Nin's work a broken string on a guitar or some similar instrument functions as a symbol of incompleteness and hopelessness, but here the same image suggests past meaning while showing its new significance in the presence of a beneficent nature. This notion of traditionally unpleasant occurrences becoming not only bearable but pleasurable may be seen in Lillian's encounter with a photographer on the beach. She has never enjoyed being photographed, and to avoid this man she swims in the ocean. He is one of such patience and dignity that when she finally returns to the shore, as she must, she apologizes for her action and listens to his cryptic response, "We all have much more time than we have life" (*Seduction*, p. 51), by which he means that while one's life is short, time (nature) is endless. Lillian learns that he, as is Hernandez, is correct.

Lillian meets Edward on the beach. He is a former violinist who has been married many times and who now is a distributor of Coca Cola calendars across Mexico. (He views his life as a calendar, with a different wife representing different parts of his life.) He functions to repudiate art and formality; he has lived in Golconda so long that his children have become indistinguishable from the natives, and he sees Golconda's *natural* artistic creations of higher quality than man can be taught to create. Lillian concurs with his aesthetic pronouncements and avers that in the past when she would feel cold she would go to the tropical birds and plants section at Sears Roebuck or to Botanical Gardens to find the warmth of a miniature Golconda. In those places, however, the trees would be inhibited by glass domes (exactly as Jeanne is kept outside real life in "Under a Glass Bell"), while at the real Golconda the trees grow as they should, unfettered by artifice.

Edward's children, and astute ones they are, help fill a void in Lillian as she fills one in them. These youngsters want a permanent and loving mother and are concerned that their father might choose as his next wife someone with whom they are incompatible. They are attracted to Lillian because of her openness and sensitivity, and they therefore confide in her. She likes them, conversely, because she once lost children of their age and they therefore fulfill her frustrated maternal feelings. Details are not given about her own children, but in *Ladders to Fire* she and Larry were the parents of Paul and Adele. That they are missing does not mean they are dead; when Lillian chose to leave Larry she left her children as well.

One possibility as Edward's next wife is a beauty queen whose plasticity seemingly cannot survive in Golconda and who is unattractive to his children. Fortunately for them this woman joins the company of her physical opposite, an ex-Marine who volunteered to expose himself to an atomic blast and was damaged inside, but they are psychological twins who are typical Nin voyeurs unable to reveal their true selves to each other. Edward ignores this couple, but Lillian analyzes them correctly when she observes that they are cold because they do not know their own selves. When she contemplates introducing them to each other, however, she recalls Hernandez's words that the basic philosophy of Mexicans is "passivity and fatalism" (*Seduction*, p. 55), and even though more sophisticated people believe that man's nature or condition can be altered, to attempt to change them is dangerous, and he who attempts change will suffer, as Hernandez assuredly does. Lillian therefore does not interefere in the sterile lives of the beauty queen and the ex-Marine.

A masquerade party aboard a Mexican general's yacht soon thereafter provides a means for transforming the participants into their hidden selves. Hernandez the healer, for example, is dressed as an Aztec warrior and ruthless lover who wounds people; Diana appears as a grotesquerie with her head within a picture frame; and Fred (now called Christmas exclusively) is a man from another planet whose distance is counteracted by Diana and her frame. Lillian's attire is not described. The atmosphere is dizzying, and when Hernandez takes the dancing partner from a young man who is later identified as Michael Lomax, Lillian, sharing the deserted one's mood of sobriety, consoles him and decides to accompany him to his home. En route she dreams of a native guide standing before an Aztec tomb, and her dream is fulfilled when she finds Lomax's city an ancient one destroyed some years before by the lava from a neighboring volcano. The town is tomblike in its fragmentation and stillness; it is the embodiment of what she thought was another dream, this time of a Chirico painting of ruins. Lomax's sumptuous home among the ruins parallels the peaceful coexistence of the Mayans and the Spaniards who inhabit the town, and they in turn suggest Nin's encouragement of the fusing of opposites that is present in her fiction as early as *House of Incest*: the Indians will never forgive the Spaniards' transgressions, but in their passivity and resistance to change they maintain their identity while living with their traditional enemies.

This fusion of opposites is also present in the aesthetic nature of the town itself. It is a city of ruins, but its incompleteness causes it to be more poetic than it might otherwise be, because each individual is permitted to fill in the voids with his own imagination and thus be the architect of his own myths. (This is largely the theme of "Ragtime.")

There is obviously charm in such ruins, but Lillian finds the lifelessness of the town offensive. For the third time since she has been with Lomax, Lillian thinks she is dreaming but finds she is not when she is pecked by a vulture that symbolizes the living death of the town. Some life does appear there with a display of fireworks, but when Lillian attempts to join in the attendant festivities Lomax stops her because the fiesta is traditionally for men only. She defies his wish and joins the men, to their initial satisfaction, but when they begin to threaten her she escapes back to Lomax. Before she leaves his city Lillian learns it is a perfect symbol for Lomax's inner self; that he had "selected a magnificent tomb, to live among the ruins of his past loves" (*Seduction*, p. 66). Many years ago he decided to live anonymously and never again to fall in love. He therefore buried his emotions and became, like the town, ruined. Lomax offers Lillian passivity and an existence away from life. She leaves as he is courting one of the male students of the town and as she recalls his earlier words to her: "All I ask, since I can't keep you here, is that in your next incarnation you be born a boy, and then I will love you" (ibid., p. 67). Lomax is unable to fuse the opposites (in this case male and female) in order to make himself whole. Lillian, who has developed quickly past him, can only flee from his stultifying personality.

Shortly after leaving the oppressive Lomax, Lillian boards a bus in Golconda that is going to Hatcher's town, San Luis. The scene in the bus is a humorous one with a curious admixture of people—a bullfighter, an old woman carrying eggs, someone transporting candelabras, a man with turkeys and one with chickens, an English schoolmarm, Edward's daughter Lietta, and numerous Mexicans—who witness a leaking bag of corn, a frocked priest falling from his bicycle, and other such events that they do not consider extraordinary. What her fellow passengers offer Lillian is a view of real, honest people behaving naturally and with no sense of embarrassment. She is interested in the bullfighter, Miguelito, whom she had seen perform recently, because his natural and somewhat ruffled appearance in the bus is so different from his stylized dress in the arena. But of all the passengers, she is most engrossed with the young Lietta. Lietta is a child who is completely honest and open and who does not care that the driver to whom she is speaking ignores her. As the bus passes through a tunnel (as it symbolically takes Lillian back to her own youth), she sees Adele, her own daughter, in Lietta and finally Lillian herself at a comparable age. She is doing what she must do psychologically: in order to understand why she is as she is she must understand the early events that gave her shape. Lillian spent much of her youth in Mexico because her father, like Hatcher now (and it is no accident that she is traveling to see him when this return to her youth takes place), was there to build roads and bridges. In Mexico the young Lillian often played in an underground labyrinth that was to house a subway system. She and her friends had been forbidden to play there because of certain obvious dangers, so their life there was more intense than it was when they played above ground. The greatest danger was getting lost, and, as might be expected, Lillian was the one to lose her way when she ignored her mother's whistle to return home. She tried desperately to escape from her underground city, but she was unsuccessful and was ready to accept death (even though she could hear the voices of her family above her) when her mother rescued her. This episode is melodramatic, to be sure, but it symbolizes one of Nin's most consistent themes: that escape into the dream or into one's inner self is not only acceptable but necessary, but to reside there exclusively is fatal. This scene also helps define the collective title, *Cities of the Interior*, that Nin gave to her first five novels, and, most importantly for Lillian, it permits her to understand the event in her life that led to her opaqueness, to her loss of transparency, and caused her to become an actress in life. Her parents were humorless, insensitive, overly practical people who detested Mexico; and their most lasting lesson to Lillian was the one that followed her rescue from under the ground: when you seek pleasure and ignore your sense of duty you are courting death. Until that time Lillian had been a free child pursuing her desire even in the face of danger, but after that she became inhibited and cloaked her real self from the pain that it led her to experience at the hands of her parents. Even nature condemned the parents as it destroyed one of Lillian's father's bridges and a road, and as a result the entire family left Mexico for the United States, away from possible freedom to Lillian's exile in her native land. She can now only wonder what she would be had the family remained in Mexico, but while she will never know the answer to that, at least she understands what made her the woman she is, and she can hopefully move on to an even more complete understanding of herself.

More comprehension is hers when she meets Hatcher and notices that he shares not only her father's profession but also his same hairy fingers, his dominant personality, and his inability to radiate warmth. Because of her experience on the bus and the awareness it encourages, Lillian immediately realizes that her trip to Hatcher is one of memory in her lunar barque and that she must eradicate the past by understanding, as she has just done, and move on to a whole life in the present and future in her solar barque. She arrives with an inhumane Dr. Palas and Hatcher at his shell of a house on a beach where his heavy Mexican wife Maria holds forth passively. Hatcher, it turns out, is a dead man who lives in the past with the memory of his svelte first wife and with a storage room filled with American junk. Lillian had envisioned him as free, but she soon realizes that he is tightly and permanently tied to the past and to the protection that his native land offers him. Hatcher's effect on Lillian is to make her question her own freedom, and she realizes that no matter what it is, a new experience is always accompanied by a parallel experience from her past. With the aid of the ocean and all of its natural force she is able finally to leave the past for the everlasting present.

> She was speeding at the same rhythm along several dusty roads, as a child with parents, as a wife driving her husband, as a mother taking her children to school, as a pianist touring the world, and all these roads intersected noiselessly and without damage.
>
> Swinging between the drug of forgetfulness and the drug of awareness, she closed her eyes, she closed the eyes of memory. [*Seduction*, p. 81]

Lillian has eradicated the past that has held her captive since her youth. She must yet fully analyze the past and come to a complete understanding of what caused her years of turmoil and frustration, and before she leaves Hatcher for Golconda she sees him as one who is totally dependent upon his past (the United States, "Woolworth dishes," "paper napkins" [ibid.]) and preoccupied with his first wife whom Lillian resembles. He cannot face the present and he abhors the efforts being made to commercialize Mexico, yet his fondest dream is that one day his now incomplete home will become a haven for the American movie colony. While his dream will obviously never be fulfilled, its contrast to his reality points up just how far Lillian has progressed, psychologically, past someone like him.

She is not so far advanced in worldliness and sophistication, however, to close her understanding and appreciation of the natives and their passive, thoughtless state resembling the chaos of prelife. Perhaps she cannot return from experience to innocence, but in being in its proximity, she is approached by (and she correctly interprets) the mother of her youth whose eyes have followed her into this Mexican jungle that parallels Lillian's past chaos. She is now able to see her mother as the icy, formal, unfeeling person who caused Lillian, in her search for love, to act impetuously in order to gain, if nothing else, some emotional response—wrath or no—from her mother. Lillian, as do all children, saw herself in the mirror of her mother's eyes as small, awkward, impudent, insignificant; and it has been only during her stay in Mexico, which is a geographical and psychological return to her youth, that she has come to understand that her own self-image has always been warped because she has never seen herself through her own eyes, but always through the glassy eyes of her mother. Lillian has gained this vision, this new sense of self as a mature woman. She is now what she sees herself to be and not the saucy girl she perceived in her mother's eyes.

This awareness coincides with the passing of the old year into the new. She leaves Hatcher on 31 December; she arrives in Golconda on 1 January, the new year, the month of Janus that looks backward and forward (as Lillian looks back to analyze and understand and forward to love). But before she returns to Golconda, to her new self, she experiences the frustrating company of the arrogant Dr. Palas with whom she is traveling. Palas is a young version of Hernandez in that he is just beginning in the medical profession. He is terribly irked when inconvenienced by a peasant in need of his services. He is the most recent in the fairly long list of doctors in Nin's work who are, with the exception of Hernandez, unfeeling and inhumane people. The car in which Palas, Lillian, and the others are riding needs repair even before they reach San Luis, and to get it to that town they need to put it on a ferry to cross a river (recalling Charon and the River Styx). Automobile repair is expectedly slow there, so they are forced to spend New Year's Eve in their rooms while the townsmen revel with their pistols and destroy, among other things, mirrors, an action that further emphasizes Lillian's freedom from her sterile mother. Because it is still the evening before the new year is to begin, Lillian has time to attempt a greater understanding of her past self in her cell-like room in San Luis. She has been able to think herself free when involved with other people, but incarceration in a room such as this one, which symbolizes the psychological cloistering of her past, always forced her into the underground city to which she fled during her years with her parents.

That city was a trap that almost succeeded in claiming her as a victim, but even when she traveled to it she knew what its antidote was: "Life is dreamed, life is a nightmare, you can awaken, and when you awaken you know the monsters were self-created" (*Seduction,* p. 88). She was kept from correct perceptions of life and herself because the eyes through which she looked were not her own, and the nightmare that she saw through those eyes could have been, as they are now, destroyed by proper vision through her own eyes that afford vision into her own being.

Lillian awakens on 1 January to find a mirror broken and with the necessity of using a shared towel to dry herself. The new year and the new Lillian have thus finally begun with the smashed image of her mother and with a willingness, even an eagerness, to share in the tainted human condition that her mother denied. This journey to find her real self has been a long one in psychological time, but it has, in calendar time, taken only the three months during which she has been in Mexico, and that is an extraordinarily brief time to make a trek of that length and complexity. The automobile is finally fixed, Lillian and her companions arrive in Golconda on 1 January, and the new Lillian with her new insight into his need to confess must locate Hernandez and assist in his struggle with his acceptance of himself. But as she awaits his arrival in his office his lights (literally and figuratively) go out because the car he is driving, and in which he has just been shot, crashes into the pole that carries the electric wires to his office. He dies because he fought against "*dangerous* forgetfulness" (*Seduction,* p. 94, italics added) in the form of drugs. Lillian can scarcely believe his death, although she knows it is true, and she can only lament that she was not able to accompany her friend through his own inner cities where his true self lay hidden. With the first day of the new year comes a new Lillian who has to confront immediately the death of her best friend, the person she most wanted to assist. Such newness is not often severely tested so soon, and while Hernandez's death is a test for her, she is able to accept it and keep the new woman she has become because, like the word *tropic* that means "a turning and changing" (ibid., p. 95), she turned completely from the young girl she was through her mother's eyes, smashed the mirror that was their embodiment, freed herself forever from the past, and changed into the woman she always was but never saw herself as being.

Nin ends *Solar Barque* with this final assurance of Lillian's growth, but she evidently felt the need to offer a more fitting conclusion to the whole of *Cities of the Interior,* because *Seduction of the Minotaur* includes roughly forty pages of added material that was not in the earlier novel. The conclusion, a coda, examines Lillian's thoughts as she is flying from Golconda to Larry in their home in White Plains, New York. She is now a complete woman who is about to gain further insight into herself and an understanding of Larry's true nature; she is reaching full maturity as one who realizes that the arena in which human beings develop to their fullest is marriage, or, if not that, then the intimate, caring relationship between a man and a woman.

Her new stature is immediately noticeable when her fellow passengers appear laden with trinkets by which they hope to preserve their impressions of Mexico. Lillian's baggage consists of the emotional and psychological awarenesses she gained there that cannot be preserved in any tangible manner. She learned in Golconda that she was not traveling alone, that even though she had left her family behind they were with her emotionally, and that they actually helped to dictate her actions there. From her new perspective (its exaltation symbolized by her high-flying airplane) she sees, for example, that her affinity for the American in jail was an extension of her first feeling for Larry when she innocently failed to invite him to her eighteenth birthday party and saw him excluded, watching her enjoy the festivities from his position behind the bars of a garden grille. As she then took measures to free Larry, so too did she reenact that event with the prisoner because her marriage had been battered but not broken. Because of its remnants she either became Larry or sought him out during her estrangement from him. By the end of her stay in Golconda she was aware that her earlier perceptions of Larry as a passive, insensitive husband were inaccurate. Her demands on him, stemming from her need for constant reassurance that she was not so inadequate as she thought herself, were extreme. But in appeasing her, Larry sacrificed his own emotional life, and while he enacted her own inner and unacknowledged quiet self, she enacted the turmoil inside him that was caused by insensitive parents, betrayal, and an aborted musical career. When Hernandez died Lillian learned "the preciousness of human love and human life" (*Seduction,* p. 103) and saw for the first time that she and Larry are individuals with their own unique problems and that their marriage had been the fusion only of fragments of each other, not of their complete beings. She finally understands Hernandez's fatalistic message: that the design by which one lives comes from within oneself and is changed only by understanding it. With that knowledge she is able to save herself, Larry, and their lives together. She sees at last that they have both been imprisoned by fear, and that her own fear led to assurance of her own mythic proportions and therefore caused her to compare the more mortal Larry unfavorably with herself. She thought that she was capable of reaching the ideal in life, but she learned, in Golconda, that one may only approach it.

The fear that kept Lillian from wholeness was fear itself, and the avoidance of it caused her to attribute her own weaknesses to others. Her first lover, Gerard, for example, was more passive than she, and to assuage her own fear of sexual consummation she railed against his coldness, safe in the knowledge that he would neither contradict her nor fulfill her sexually. She feared commitment, love, passion, and humanity; the possibility of confronting those qualities or feelings led her to assume the warrior's role. Fear, then, determined her actions in life, and following Hernandez's words, when she understood that fear, as she did in Golconda, she was then able to change the direction of her life for the better. She was lost in the labyrinth and was threatened by a minotaur invisible to all but her; yet it was as real and vivid to her as the beast in John Marcher's jungle. Marcher realized too late the identity of his beast in James' *nouvelle*, but Lillian is more fortunate in seducing her minotaur before it devours her. When she is able to remember back into her childhood, when the only contact she had with her father was the spankings he would administer, the adult Lillian understands that what she has wanted from a man is a continuation of her father, one who offers pain as well as pleasure. The kind Larry offered her no pain; and while Jay, in Paris, provided her with more of a mixture, he was unacceptable because of his childish dependence on others. She finally realized the difference between what she thought was her need of a balance of pain and pleasure and what she truly wanted. Jay fulfilled her need, and made her a woman; but Sabina, the woman of earlier novels whose most obvious characteristic is freedom, threatened Lillian's newly discovered womanhood and turned out to be "a drought of freedom" (*Seduction*, p. 126). Only Djuna, the other major woman in the continuous novel, is able to set Lillian straight and send her toward wholeness. These experiences cumulatively led to her awareness in Golconda, and helped form a base on which she can stand to approach Larry. Lillian at last understands that events in Larry's youth (he was an unwanted child who found warmth only with blacks, his favorite of which ultimately betrayed him) caused him to conceal his true feelings because he had been hurt every time he displayed them. When she realizes this she is in a position as a whole, mature person herself to provide the warmth and understanding that he needs in order to grow as she has just done.

> Together they moved as one living body and Larry was passionately willed into being born, this time permanently. Larry, Larry, what can I bring you? Intimacy with the world? She was on intimate terms with the world. While he maintained a world in which Lillian was the only inhabitant, or at least the reigning one.
>
> Such obsession with reaching the moon, because they had failed to reach each other, each a solitary planet! In silence, in mystery, a human being was formed, was exploded, was struck by other passing bodies, was burned, was deserted. And then it was born in the molten love of the one who cared. [Ibid., p. 136]

The coda brings *Seduction of the Minotaur* to a close, and it also effectively concludes the five works that constitute the continuous novel. The boat in Lillian's dreams that has been stuck in the streets of a town is finally returned to its natural water. She has learned that one of life's most difficult tasks is to know oneself, and that after one does that, one may assist another in a similar quest, the result of which is the true marriage of two complete but different people into a whole. The point of such a quest is happiness, a word that when used casually does not seem to be much of a goal in life, but when it is used in a serious sense (and in the context of the inhabitants of Nin's fiction), it is perhaps the ultimate of life's gifts. Nin presented her characters, who were mostly women and all potentially happy, struggling with their own inner selves, trying to find their places in life, and seeking happiness. Knowledge and acceptance of oneself is the key to Nin's perception of mature life, and that something so seemingly simple is in fact so difficult is the message of Nin's first five novels.

9

Collages

Nin's last novel and last piece of fiction is different from the works that compose the continuous novel in several ways, but what is immediately noticeable is that for the first time none of the familiar characters is present. Nowhere is there mention of Lillian, Djuna, Sabina, Stella, Jay, and the others whom Nin investigated so thoroughly in her earlier works. Also unlike the other novels, this one includes about two dozen important characters (the usual Nin novel has just a few significant ones), takes place across two continents and in six or so towns in California (there is little geographical movement in Nin's other novels), and concentrates on a woman, the artist Renate, who is not consciously seeking psychological wholeness in the manner of Nin's other and more familiar women characters. Nin's dedication of the book to R.P. suggests that she intended the novel to be a humorous one, but although there are characters whose actions evoke smiles, their situations are pathetic and the humor that emerges is therefore of the black variety. This is a book that is so uncharacteristic of Nin that were it not for the cicerone Renate and the book's title, the reader might well not comprehend either the author's intention or the book's meaning. *Collages* is a portfolio of collages, a collection of characters who have some trait (usually a flaw) that makes them interesting.[1] A few of the nineteen brief chapters, or collages, follow logically from their predecessors, but most often there is no transition from chapter to chapter with the expected result that the reader recalls only highlights and has at the end no sense of the novel's

147

wholeness. This impression is reinforced by the tricky ending that attempts to make the disparate parts whole but only frustrates the reader, causing him to conclude that if this book is, as announced, a humorous one, then the humor is that which the author had at the reader's expense as a kind of private joke or confidence game. If one disregards the suggestion to read the novel humorously, one sees a work much more in the Nin mainstream than it at first appears.

The first collage is of Renate's youth in Vienna, a city of statues that gives "an illusion of eternity" (*Collages,* p. 7). Like most of Nin's women, Renate was strongly influenced by her father who, in his involvement with microscopes and telescopes, caused her to view life either too closely or distantly, and in his own blindness to his wife's humanity, treated his daughter as a confidante to whom he could explain his relationship with his wife. Like other Nin women, Renate aspired to be an actress, but when she told her father of her desire (after her first acting performance was awkward and less than totally successful) that cruel and insensitive man pointed out her ineptitude in a mild rage and suffered a heart attack. Feeling guilty at having thus injured her father, Renate disclaimed her interest in acting, submerged that passion, thought that she felt guilty because she had assumed her mother's role, and eventually realized that it was not she who had injured her father, but that he was hurt rather because his secret was revealed: "He had not looked upon Renate as a daughter but as a woman, and his insistence on maintaining her a child was to disguise the companionship he enjoyed" (ibid., p. 9). As a youth in Vienna, then, Renate was surrounded by the statues in the city and also by the statuelike parents with whom she lived. Human companionship seemed not to be hers, and she assuredly did not achieve it when, after refusing to attend school, she became the private student of her father's brother whose madness excluded him as well from life's magnetic chain. Part of Renate's uncle's madness was his belief that his bones contained no marrow, and while that belief was obviously medically illfounded, it was psychologically true: he felt undernourished and deprived because when his mother became pregnant while still nursing him, she took sustenance from him to give to the unborn child, who is his brother and Renate's father. In taking life from his brother, his wife, and his daughter, Renate's father became inhuman, as cold and unfeeling as the statues in Vienna. To escape such nonpeople Renate moves from person to person and from place to place in her life in this novel, and that story concludes where it began, suggesting a fatalism that Lillian, for example, was able to overcome in the continuous novel. When viewed in this manner the otherwise unique *Collages* fits thematically into the Nin canon and in a sense begins, with Renate, woman's quest for wholeness anew. Nin makes several exquisite collages in this novel, but the artist Renate is unable to give shape to her own life.

Renate looks to statues for company in Vienna, and in order for an individual to attract her attention and become her friend he must bear a greater resemblance to the statues than to people. Such a person is Bruce, Renate's most constant companion throughout the story. When she first notices him in Vienna she compares him to the friendly statue of Mercury that she views through her bedroom window. But this silent youth disavows any resemblance to that mystical god and proclaims his affinity with Pan, who is barely a deity at all. Bruce's youthfulness and innocence make him attractive to Renate, but there is also something terribly wrong with him that will inhibit their relationship from maturing past an adolescent level. He is almost mute, but occasionally words will flow from him in rhythmic patterns suggesting an eloquence deep within him. His Norwegian parents inhibited him as a youth and caused him to live a life of silence as they spoke to each other in their native tongue and addressed him only in broken English. They sealed his fate when they left him, at age eleven, to be reared in America by a distant relative while they lived in Norway. The effect of these insensitivities was to cause Bruce to become totally alienated from his true self in a manner that is similar to the women in the continuous novel, but unlike them (as represented by Lillian) there is little hope for his own rediscovery.

Bruce is attracted to Renate because she is compassionate (an unexpected quality when one considers her life with the statues and with perverse people), and when he looks into her friendly eyes he is able to see the smallest core of his real self reflected therein. This beginning of self-understanding is augmented by the portrait that Renate paints of him, although it is not unveiled until long after their stay in Vienna. And because he finds understanding in Renate, he desires her company on his peregrinations that will begin in Mexico, the country in which Lillian found wholeness in *Seduction of the Minotaur*. Renate consents, and as they experience Mexico's charms she becomes giddy and laughs almost constantly at trivialities and at Bruce's pseudosurrealistic stunts, such as placing his wound alarm clock in the middle of a deserted road and letting it ring furiously. Such juvenile behavior might well be expected of someone like Bruce, but this act, as are most actions in Nin's fiction, is symbolic. Bruce's performance with the clock symbolizes his pent-up self. The clock, filled with tension, is, with his help, able to gain a release as it "became unleashed like an angry child . . . , rang like a tantrum, and it shook with fury and protest at neglect" (*Collages*, p. 12). Bruce is unable to give vent to his own hostilities and tensions, but his episode with the clock symbolizes his subconscious desire to do so.

Bruce is unable to unwind, and Renate's laughter soon dies as he proves to be unpredictable. Because of the manner in which his parents treated him, Bruce refuses to be tied to any person, and he therefore begins leaving Renate without warning and without explanation of his actions. Rather than waiting passively for his return, however, Renate at once decides to search for her friend in order to discover his whereabouts and to protect herself from possible danger during the lonely nights alone in a Mexican desert hotel. What she discovers in her search is not pleasant. As she is returning to her hotel from a futile search, she notices two masculine figures beside a road. One is standing erect against a tree, and the other is kneeled before him, performing a homosexual act. The one standing is an anonymous Mexican; the one kneeling is Bruce. Bruce is only the first of Renate's acquaintances who have difficulty consummating a heterosexual relationship. To escape the immediate memory of what she witnessed she drives to Puerta Maria where an opulent coral tree diminishes Bruce's tree of night and where the persistence of the color orange enlivens her anew into a festive mood.[2]

Mexico's tropical splendor is helpful in Renate's desire to overcome the memory of Bruce, but while she submits to nature and even wears a dress resembling the coral tree, she discovers that neither nature nor artifice can cause her truly to forget Bruce and his lover. Her appearance to the natives as a woman at ease with herself is therefore inaccurate, and because she is aware of the discrepancy between what she feels and what she reveals to others, she feels fraudulent, much as Stella does in *Winter of Artifice*. Nin chose not to develop Renate's inner conflict; and before Renate is able to express more than a casual concern for her own mental health and behavior, the focus shifts from her to a new acquaintance, an anonymous man from Los Angeles whose sole concern in life is the comfort of his automobile that he ships, with amusing results, back to America rather than have it exposed to the hazards of the Mexican highways. As silly as this man is, he resembles Renate's family in his perversity and follows Bruce in being other than a heterosexual man. As heinously as Nin presents Bruce's action, his aberration is less appalling than the more symbolic relationship the other man has with his car, using it as a surrogate sexual partner as he fondles, caresses, and sleeps inside it. Bruce's sexual appetite may be sated, but the other man's cannot be because it cannot be reciprocated.

Bruce's sexual interest is limited to Mexican boys, and soon after Renate moves to Malibu, California, he joins her, free from the memory of any earlier unpleasantness. Renate and Bruce never discuss the earlier episode, but in the beginning of his novel that Renate reads Bruce gives his reason for having left her: she was then having an affair with a singer who was enamored of her because she resembled his mother. To counteract such behavior Bruce often left her for Mexican boys in order to balance the hurt she gave him. Renate's explanation of her involvement with the singer is that she locked him in her room because she wished to restrain Bruce from wandering, and by keeping the other man she was expressing her feelings to Bruce symbolically. After temporarily consummating their mutual understanding with the purchase of a peace dove in Malibu (the basic difficulty between them is his jealousy of her and her dissatisfaction with the secrets he keeps from her), Bruce tells her about a dream in which a musical performance transformed him into a column like the statues in Vienna. When she hears of his perverse reaction to sounds that should rather melt than solidify, tears come to her eyes so quickly that she is unable to hide them, whereupon Bruce insensitively smiles at her. Renate's tears and Bruce's realization that they cannot live in Malibu as they had in Mexico lead him to suggest that they sail around the world in a sailboat. This idea is of course ludicrous, but Bruce goes to Holland where boats may be had inexpensively, buys one, and meets Renate when she arrives a month later. Once again an episode is humorous as Renate and Bruce struggle unsuccessfully to master the boat as they need to work its ropes, escape from a becalmed state, and control the rudder. But as with other such episodes, this one is symbolic of something more serious. The difficulties that they experience with the boat parallel those they have with each other. They have been joyous in each other's company, each has been hurt and made immobile by the other's behavior, and they have reacted hastily and unthinkingly to those hurts. Their journey on the boat is therefore bound to be unsuccessful, as it is when they injure an historical bridge, lose the boat's caulking as it is transported by rail to the Mediterranean, and finally put it in dry dock. Renate bemusedly concludes that Bruce's journeys should henceforth be inner ones because he is so inept at physical ones. Such advice has always been sound in Nin's work, but when Renate offers it to someone who is obviously as frivolous as Bruce, it rings hollow, especially when one recalls the seriousness with which Lillian, for example, pursues her inner journey and finds wholeness.

Renate's feelings for Bruce and her patience with him are difficult to understand. His innocence appears to be the only quality to which she is attracted, but instead of leaving him after the boating fiasco, they return together to her Malibu home where Bruce further reveals himself to be of little substance. When a fire threatens her house, for example, his sole concern is with rescuing the nude portrait that Renate had earlier painted of him. He believes that if it were destroyed he would be too. Their relationship at first seems to be consumed in the flames, but after Bruce experiences other women he finds that they were not adequate replacements for Renate, so he returns to her with a set of Chinese puzzle boxes. He had written short pieces about episodes in his life and placed them in the boxes, and he instructs her to open one each time she is perplexed by his behavior. She does this and discovers how his homosexuality began with a friend named Ken and how they pursued their love in Mexico. This removes all doubts she had about Bruce, and she finally severs their relationship as she destroys the Chinese boxes.

To help her forget the bittersweet memories she has of Bruce, Renate takes to a laundromat the sheets on which they had spent much time. She is able to forget Bruce there, not because his stains are removed from the linens, but, rather, because she meets there and is impressed by a mature individual. The laundromat's proprietor is of a quality that his position does not lead Renate to expect. Here is a man (Renate calls him Count Laundromat) who does not idly chat about the weather but rather takes a sincere interest in his patrons and their goods, who takes pride in his work and is not condescending in his treatment of himself or of others, and who is oblivious to the ugliness about him, in part because the rhythm of his machines obliterates it. Renate soon notices a similarity between his ring and a design she recalls having been on a statue in Vienna, and when he reveals that his parents were Austrian nobility, she becomes all the more intrigued and listens carefully as he tells the story of his trek to America, his marriage to a Rhinegold beauty queen, and his eventual employment in his father-in-law's laundromat. Because of her affinity with him the odors of his laundromat become confused with those of her youth in Vienna, and she therefore enjoys her repeated visits to him. Of all of Nin's characters Count Laundromat and Dr. Hernandez are perhaps the only ones who are greater than they appear to be. Most of the female characters are artists who outwardly at least appear to be complete human beings while they suffer considerably internally. Jay and the various husbands and lovers of the women present either a gargantuan or formally secure appearance while possessing idiosyncrasies that make them less than totally attractive human beings. Only the Mexican doctor and Count Laundromat are at least equal to if not greater than the sum of their parts. Renate is fortunate to meet Count Laundromat when she is attempting to forget the adolescent Bruce.

The episode with Count Laundromat is also significant because it is the first time in the novel that Renate is not at least an equal partner in the events that occur; with him she is more of an observer than a participant. This shifting of focus away from her continues when, after she reveals her childhood desire to free all animals from bondage, she paints a portrait of a young woman named Raven who from her youth had wanted a raven of her own. This scene about Raven is similar to much of Nin's earlier fiction, and its roots may be traced as far back as the narrator and Sabina in *House of Incest*. Raven is a gentle and pliable woman who laments that she is not her opposite, which is a raven with the dark strength that it presents. She therefore purchases such a bird, and it arrives in an airplane (a perverse manner of transportation that suggests Renate's and Bruce's boat on a train and the car of the man from Los Angeles on a boat). The creature keeps her from becoming too self-effacing by threatening and intimidating her suitors. Before long Raven and the bird exchange souls, with Raven becoming majestic and the bird becoming timid. This is in a sense a humorous episode, but, like the earlier events in this novel, it bears a striking resemblance to situations in other and more serious of Nin's works; and to present it here frivolously is to undercut the merit of what went before.

Renate is even less obviously present when she relates the story of another anonymous character who, as a young man, was a lifeguard in Malibu and who grew tired of the encumbrances of life with his wife and six children. This man eventually finds life with people on land so unbearable that he begins to spend an inordinate amount of time on the beach with the seals until, as an old man, he lives there exclusively because it affords him the freedom he so desires and because the seals seem to him to be compassionate. He acts as guardian for his animal friends and generally feels comfortable in his new life until his interlude is broken by his children who fear for his well-being and return him to the civilization to which he is unsuited: the first night he sleeps in a bed he falls out and breaks his arm. He therefore returns to his adopted home to die with the seals that he physically resembles, but they are wiser than he and nudge him away as he draws near. Both Raven and this man could have learned from Lillian: she struggles with her problems until she overcomes them within society, but they attempt to find happiness and wholeness in life by communing with animals. They, like Bruce and the man with the car, behave unnaturally and therefore cannot find success, and as Renate recedes further into the background the characters she discusses become more perverse.

Just as Renate is about to disappear entirely from the novel that is hers, Nin reintroduces her and comments specifically on her admirable qualities. As was suggested by her experience in Downey, Renate's art work was not always in demand, and often during slack times she would be a hostess at the Paradise Inn. Here in a club frequented by the Hollywood crowd Renate emerges, like Count Laundromat, a phoenix out of the ashes, a gracious and generous woman observed and admired by all, one who seduces the patrons with her charm. She becomes as the woman she does in part because of the patrons: they are all actors who have lost their real selves and who therefore lead fraudulent lives. Renate, on the other hand, knows exactly who she is, and because she does others look to her as a compass to use in their searches for self-discovery. With Renate all things are natural—her painting, her hostessing, her son—and that naturalness looms especially large next to the pretentions of those about her. But as impressive as she is, there is another who is roughly her equal at the Paradise Inn. The singer Leontine had been a friend of Renate's years earlier, and they are reunited at the club. Renate had always been grateful to Leontine for being among the first to welcome her when she came to the United States, and that kind of openness and generosity has typified Leontine's subsequent life. Of all the characters in the book, she has the best sense of humor, as is displayed in her story of her Parisian lover.

Leontine's maturity is further exemplified by her total acceptance of her blackness. She could be an imposing character, but she is not developed. Renate appears to be a woman of considerable substance in this episode, but the background for that greatness had not been laid. As a result, the picture of these two women is more titillating than substantial, and they stand as magnificent statues against a background of nonpersons.

There is one other person at the Paradise Inn who has a potential for wholeness in life, but inasmuch as he is now past eighty his life is largely spent. Henri is a master chef with a love as intense for the celebrities whom he has fed as for the food he prepares. During his great years he was probably unequalled in his profession, but even then his love of the famous, while innocuous and even charming, caused him to be not quite the man Count Laundromat is. The latter is content with himself among women in curlers; Henri needs love from not just any diners but from famous ones. He is of the old European school of quality, and what is now demanded of him in the United States is quantity, which he dutifully provides to his insensitive diners. He is understandably frustrated (even though his flambées now often resemble cremations), but Renate consoles him by pointing out that Americans have not only lost their taste for fine cuisine, they have also lost their tongue for speaking: they are illiterate both in language and in their appreciation of food. For the aged Henri this information is too late, and he will continue in his life of retrospection.

Renate, Leontine, and Henri all work at the Paradise Inn and are all attractive people, but so too is a man who comes to the club to display his collages. Once he shows them they immediately subdue the effulgent nature in which they are placed: "They eclipsed the sun, the sea and the plants. The laminated blues dimmed the refractions of the ocean and made it seem ponderous and opaque. His treble greens vibrated and made the plants seem dead and the flowers artificial. His shafts of gold made the sunrays pale" (*Collages*, p. 59). The subject of his art is women whom he transforms into myths only dreamed of by mortal men, and they teach "how to remain in a state of grace of love, extract only elixirs, transmute all life into lunisolar fiestas, and all women, by a process of cut-outs, to aphrodisiacs" (ibid., p. 60). Varda believes that only myths endure; but that belief and the validity of his art are severely undercut by the presence of a girl, his daughter, who is impertinent, far from mythic, and a severe test of her father's patience. He views her as "a colorless doll lying inside a magician's trunk" (ibid., p. 61) who needs much work before she is ready for womanhood. This daughter, in her mid teens, is immune to her father's art and charm; she does not comprehend the significance of the touching stories he tells her, and she prefers the mixtures of colors she sees while under the influence of the chemical LSD to those in his collages. After one experience with LSD, however, she awakens in Varda's studio and suddenly understands what her father and his art are about.

> "I looked around at your collages and recognized them. It was as if I had been there for the first time. I saw the colors, the luminosity and the floating, mobile, changeable quality. I understood all your stories, and all you had said to me. I could see why you had made your women transparent, and the houses open like lace so that space and freedom could blow through them."
> When she came home on vacation, she had emerged from her grey cocoon. She was now sixteen and sending forth her first radiations and vibrations dressed in Varda's own rutilant colors. [Ibid., P. 69]

But as good as Varda is, when he and Renate become friendly at the club (she was absent during the story of Varda and his daughter) they cannot quite grasp each other's essence because what Varda needs is an incomplete woman so that he can mold her into the woman and the myth he wants her to be. Nin dealt with this problem of the transmutation of fragments in "Ragtime" and suggested there exactly what Varda is saying here: when something or someone is too complete, too mature, that person cannot be transformed. While that observation is true enough in both the story and in the Varda episode, there is something more important than transformation, and it is one's individual wholeness. In the novel, for example, Renate is superior to Varda because he is unable to communicate with her.[3]

Varda's daughter had to rely on chemicals for vivid dreams until she finally understood her father's art, but one who needs no artificial assistance is Nina Gitana de la Primavera, the first character to be given a full name in this novel and a woman who lives her dreams in real life. Nina is uninhibited, unreflective, impulsive, and completely without pretense. She is a woman who is bound to cause one of two reactions: one either understands that she pursues her vivid dreams in her awakened state, or he attempts to understand her by asking what turn out to be inane and pedestrian questions in order to keep her from figuratively running away from him. (A third response to her would be to dismiss her out of hand as a mental case and not be bothered by her, but no one in this novel is that insensitive.) Nin therefore has both

Renate and Bruce with Nina, the former to accept her and the latter to question her. Nina admits that she has more than a dozen selves (this is reminiscent of Duchamp's "Nude Descending a Staircase" in the continuous novel), has a firm belief that an audience should participate with the actors in stage plays (as espoused by Pierre in "Je Suis le Plus Malade des Surrealistes"), dislikes short American names, and seldom sleeps. She is an amazing woman, and while Nin urges one to accept her as Renate does, one cannot help but sympathize with the often contemptible Bruce who asks the obvious questions of Nina and is then made to be an insensitive boor for so doing. Acceptance of the dream is a basic theme of Nin's that is convincingly developed throughout her early works as well as in the continuous novel. To accept Nina and to question her are both proper responses. (Nina also functions to introduce the Japanese Nobuko to Renate. Nobuko is an actress who in her attempt to become free from her cultural restrictions resembles Nin's Hejda.)

Among the most interesting characters, although they are not the most attractive, are the French consul and his wife who live in Hollywood Hills. The wife is the more appealing of the two, even though she appears to be subordinate to her spouse, and she is the opposite of Nobuko because she uses the present to recapture the past. The present is unpleasant for her: a woman of obvious literary talent who is relatively unknown when compared to her husband's literary and political celebrity, it is her responsibility to entertain at official functions while he stays in his room to write, and she must endure his philandering with young women. The wife's greatest literary success was with a book about four English women wanting to flee their country for the Orient, and the pictures she drew of those women were so vivid, rich, and defiant that Renate wonders how this demure person possessed knowledge of women so obviously different from herself. The wife's demeanor is deceiving, however, because as a consul's spouse she has lived in many different countries and knows a multitude of people well. She habitually reweaves the threads of knowledge that she possesses of these foreign people and places in part to help shield herself from the pain of the present but also to keep fresh in her mind the people of her past that she might use in her books. To help her to avoid the present further she has begun work on a biography of a Turk, the late Shumla. Her interest in him smacks of necrophilia, but to indicate how far she will go to avoid the pain her husband inflicts, she even considers taking Bruce as a lover. Shumla provides a kind of surrogate romance with none of the dangers or entanglements of the real thing, but just after she visits what was his home, gains the confidence of his descendants, and learns the details needed to complete her book, her notes are lost in a fire aboard her airplane, and her affair with the legendary Shumla is therefore not even consummated in the publication of a book. Neither the present nor the past, then, provides solace for this abused woman.

The glamorous culprit is obviously her husband. Fame is his (he has just won a literary award and he was decorated for his military performance), but fame alone cannot make him content, because he acts as he does not to please himself but to fulfill the wishes of his late mother. She wanted him to be a hero in war, so he was; she wanted him to be more successful than Don Juan with women, and he has been and continues to be; she wanted him to be a successful writer, and he is. His successes, then, are empty, because they did not emanate from within himself but were imposed upon him. His mother is dead, so he will be frustrated because he will not be able to show her his successes and then move on to his own genuine interests. He has attempted to bring his mother back to life by having his wife play her role, but that has only led to her greater unhappiness. Because of his mother's lack of acceptance the consul has been unable to grow into adulthood, and he consequently pursues nubile women and is seen with ingenue actresses in pictures in newspapers. This man is an eternal adolescent who is destroying his innocent wife by his inability to mature, and, like so many others, he is a statue, a nonperson.

Like the consul's wife, Colonel Tishnar is an Englishman, and one so stylized that he is almost inhuman. He is glib, his skin and hair are of odd textures, he is sometimes an absentminded raconteur, he refuses to acknowledge unhappiness or pain in his life, and he is a big game hunter. He is also snobbish in his treatment of women, who must meet his specific demands before he will show interest in them. His kind of humor dealing with plain women is not funny, but it follows the consul's treatment of his wife as a comment on some men who, because of either a psychological quirk or a sexist attitude, mistreat women with little thought of maliciousness. In an intrusive manner reminiscent of the narrator of "Under a Glass Bell," Renate introduces Tishnar to her friend Tessa and hopes that these two people will become interested in each other. Tessa is an effervescent woman whose attitude is to accept every challenge that life presents, and because of her varied experiences she is at least the equal of Tishnar. Renate is unsuccessful in her role as matchmaker, because the shallow Tishnar finds Tessa too chaotic and shallow (she favors surrealists). Rather than risk injuring her friend, who has a weak heart, Renate tells her that Tishnar thought she would be too threatening to him and would probably be unfaithful as well. Renate has no right intervening the way she does, but she is trying to protect her friend against Tishnar's venom. She does so successfully, as is evidenced by Tessa's avowal that she would indeed have been unfaithful to him.

Renate is obviously a woman of many interests and talents, and when she tires of her art, her hostessing, and her dress designing (an aspect that is not developed in the novel), she turns her energies toward developing a literary magazine. Its guiding principle is to be freedom; its symbol is a mobile. She quickly discovers talented people who share her enthusiasm for this project; they are all people who are forced to function in a commercial world that not only does not encourage but actually discourages their unique skills and life-giving perspectives. Such people as Max the photographer, John the film critic, Judith Sands the author, Betty the window displayer, Henri the chef, and Harry the jazz authority all join with Renate in contributing to and helping develop a dummy of the first issue. Because they are individually and collectively convinced of the quality and the necessity of their endeavor, they have no qualms about soliciting financial support and giddily accepting it when John Wilkes, a millionaire, offers to underwrite the entire effort. Wilkes, not unexpectedly to the reader, is really a fraud who likes to pretend to be a millionaire and who likes to lead others along to satisfy his own perversity. He is a gardener, but one who cultivates sterility in the false hopes of others, unlike R. P., the "real gardener" of the novel's dedication who created a real world in which Nin's book could be written. Wilkes has broken no civil law, but like John Wilkes Booth (his symbolic ancestor) he is an assassin, and this attack on the dreams of Renate and her friends is as insidious as a physical murder (at least in the context of this episode and of Nin's work in general). Much of one's life is or should be spent in the realm of dreams, and to destroy one's access to dreams is to destroy the person. Wilkes is another statue, another nonhuman whose pleasures in life come from deceiving and hurting others.

After the magazine fiasco Renate recalls her friendship in Acapulco with Lisa, an American woman of great vivacity who became one with Mexico. Lisa had been married several times; had two children; laughed frequently; and, despite her exotic dress, led her acquaintances to believe her natural state was one of nudity. She also possessed "a delicate Toulouse-Lautrec head" that, when combined with her "jungle-luxuriant body" (*Collages*, p. 107) created a paradox. She was still one with nature in Mexico (reminiscent of the theme of *Seduction of the Minotaur*), because it encouraged the pursuit of pleasure that she was able to accept, even though her origins were unknown (or perhaps *because* they were unknown). But sometime after they were together in Acapulco, Renate, in New York City for an exhibition of her own paintings, meets Lisa unexpectedly on Third Avenue where her friend appears to be imprisoned in the shadows of the elevated. She is dressed in a winter coat that conceals her natural radiance, and Renate therefore fears that earlier it was Acapulco that had defined Lisa rather than her having become one with it. The old Lisa is not entirely lost, however, because she has created in her apartment an atmosphere reminiscent of Acapulco, although it is decidedly illusory. The greatest hindrance to Lisa's expression of her true, voluptuous self is her fourth husband, Bill, a man she knew as a youth in New York and met twenty years later in Mexico while he was on assignment for *Field and Stream* magazine. Their life together has not been beneficial for her because he is a miniature man whose temperament makes him at home on Third Avenue and causes him to ridicule his wife's attempts to transform their apartment (and their life) into something effulgent. He is embarrassed because his poker-playing friends are not comfortable in the apartment, and when he and Lisa's unnamed sister speak in their harsh New York accents and show no tolerance for her individuality, and when he stops her Mexican music and kisses her with his cigar-tainted breath, then it is obvious that she must succumb to the insensitivities around her and will therefore become the victim of a more innocent but even more deadly assassin than Wilkes was earlier. Lisa is similar to the women in Nin's other fiction whose sense of self is destroyed and who must struggle diligently to regain it. Lisa did that once in twenty years between her youth in New York and her adult life in Acapulco, but she has returned to the scene of her earlier, unnatural self and will probably have to repeat her cycle of several husbands and geographical changes before she is once again the woman Renate knew and admired in Mexico. When Lisa is last seen she is being made into a statue by hands other than her own.

Nin's book of collages concludes with an intricate one of Judith Sands (who wrote for Renate's magazine) and an Israeli doctor named Mann. Sands had written a novel that gained her some celebrity and that received a small, intensely loyal number of readers who memorized the text and have lived by its precepts. After its publication, however, the author had fled adulation and lives as a recluse in Greenwich Village until she agrees, after considerable persuasion, to meet Mann, an individual of some sensitivity (he brought symbolically correct cigars to Bill and flowers to Lisa), a man whose hobby is visiting women writers, who translated her book into Hebrew while he was a captive in Siberia, and who is the physical embodiment of one of her characters. In order for him to see Sands he must convince her that they need each other. He states that if she refuses to receive him she would "commit spiritual murder" (*Collages*, p. 115), because she created him, and to deny him now would be to starve him and to refuse him his replenishment of self at the source. She also needs him, he explains.

> "We need each other! We are indispensable to each other. I to your work and you to my life. Without me spending your words you may not be incited to mint new ones. I am the spend-thrift and you the coiner. We cannot live completely apart. And if I speak your character on perhaps a lower key than you had intended, even perhaps with a few false notes, it is because I have never met a writer with perfect pitch. If you refuse to talk to a plain man like me, your ambiguities will become intolerably tenuous, like the end of your book, which I do not understand." [*Collages*, p. 116]

When she agrees to accompany him into the world he takes her to the Museum of Modern Art where the artist Tingueley is displaying the Machine that Destroys Itself. The machine is grotesque in its self-destruction and perservse in its negativism and nihilism; yet it is obliquely symbolic of the insularity of Sands's recent life and offers a comment, that is typical of Nin, on the necessity of human interaction and on the absurdity of destruction. The machine consumes itself, the names of authors, a piano that is still capable of producing music, and sends forth a baby carriage from its own holocaust into the crowd to encourage human sacrifice. But before the flames can devour this machine a fireman extinguishes it. The suicide appears to be aborted until Tingueley himself kicks into ruin the remains of his creation, whereupon the onlookers move forward for souvenirs from the fragments. When Mann and Sands leave they meet Renate and Bruce and the four of them go to Sands's room where she shows her friends the fabled manuscript of her next book.

When Mann first spoke to Sands he expressed perplexity over the ending to her famous novel, and the author herself admitted her uncertainty of its meaning. That ambiguity leads directly to the ending of Nin's novel, the last paragraph of which is the opening paragraph of the Sands manuscript that repeats verbatim the opening of *Collages* in which Renate reflects on her youth in Vienna.[4] One is as puzzled attempting to decipher the ending of Nin's novel as Mann and Sands are with Sands's work. Nin offered clues throughout her work, however, that it would be cyclical. For example, at the end Sands and Mann meet Renate and Bruce as they step from a revolving door. The most important clues appear in the episode with the French consul's wife in Morocco. While awaiting her husband she worked on an embroidery that a Moroccan admired and wished to have as his own to commemorate what he saw as the loveliness of her hands. Understandably nonplussed at this request she could say only that her work was not finished and implied that it would not be a satisfactory piece by which to remember her. The Moroccan, undeterred, told her that the Koran says that "nothing is ever finished" (*Collages*, pp. 91, 92), words that reverberate in her mind, that are repeated by Colonel Tishnar (ibid., p. 97), and that announce a certain logic to the book's conclusion because it ends where it began; it begins anew and in fact does not end.

The ending also works on another level that has to do with Nin's fiction vis-à-vis her diary. Most of the people, places, and events in her fiction appeared first (by date of composition, not publication) in the diary. That *Collages* is cyclical and that it begins as does Sands's own unpublished novel suggests at least a parallel between Nin and Sands and implies that, as in Nin's fiction and diary, an episode may be presented in exactly the same way in the two different contexts of fiction and nonfiction, be equally valid in each, and yet have subtle differences of meaning. An example is the situation that Nin presents as fiction in "Birth" and as nonfiction in the diary.

These are only two possible readings of the novel's strange conclusion (another more cynical one is that finding it difficult to make a final statement in her last piece of fiction, Nin chose rather to provide herself a certain immortality by having her last work never end), but neither is totally satisfactory. Nin took such care in creating the wonderful female characters in the continuous novel that her flippancy and inconclusiveness in her last novel are perplexing. Nin announced *Collages* as a comic novel, but the humor is black, unsustained, and generally ineffective. It works best as a flawed extension of the continuous novel; it is a work in which most of the characters are frustrated and pathetic and in which Renate is merely a weak sister to Lillian, Sabina, Djuna, and even Stella.

PART 2

The *Diary*

10

The *Diary*

The diary of Anaïs Nin has a place all its own in the literary history of the twentieth century. The private diary (as distinguished from the published *Diary*, a distinction that we shall carefully observe) was begun in 1914 when Nin was eleven years old. That an eleven-year-old who was under an emotional strain should keep a diary is hardly significant; but that the diary should have survived, grown, and become legendary within two decades of its commencement provokes some curiosity among those who are interested in what might be called loosely the autobiographical mode. Clearly by the early 1930s the private diary had begun to gather a readership, and the transition toward the *Diary* was begun.

There is always something audacious about autobiographical writing. Probably it was the British romantics who were the first professional writers to pay a great deal of attention to themselves in their own works, and as often as not there seems to have been a willingness to cultivate a peculiarly individualistic and narrow (one is tempted to say eccentric) view of one's own life. The nineteenth century is full of examples: Wordsworth's *Prelude* has at its basis a very limited and special kind of selection of details, as does even more that strange work it helped to generate, Coleridge's *Biographia Literaria*. One thinks of De Quincey's writings, Lamb's essays, and even Yeats's so-called *Autobiographies*. What each of these shares (and now it is time to include Nin's) is a special view or vision, as Lawrence would have had it, that goes beyond technique or style but that profoundly affects the kind and nature of the details selected and discussed. There is quite enough in the *Diary* to infer a similar foundation of special detail in the private diary though Nin assures us that the private diary is rougher.

We are told that Nin's private journal was prompted by her wish to keep a record, a kind of personal running letter, to present to her father at the time when he should return to his estranged family; that Nin found herself removed to a new foreign country (the United States) makes her impulse for self-revelation all the more natural, especially as her emotional ties to her father were very strong. The experience of keeping a diary for him seems to have transcended its original purpose (although because we have the published *Diary* to consult and not the private diary, assumptions must be tentative) for the diarist apparently became interested not in self-revelation for her father's sake, or for its own sake, but in self-revelation for *her* own sake. Like her British counterparts a century earlier, she must have felt that her own life and ideas were in themselves valuable enough to record and to detail. As Leon Edel has it, however, the diary was "a way of giving herself concrete proof of her own existence. The diary also became, as it were, her father; and we catch in these pages [of the *Diary*, vol. 1] the straight, questioning look of a little girl interrogating life and trying to be well-behaved and dutiful. But there is something more complicated as well: the diary is that of a daughter, living or imagining a life that would be pleasing to the absent parent."[1] And if the romanticism of the nineteenth century influenced our thinking so thoroughly as some maintain (having become conscious of oneself, one cannot return to unawareness), Edel ironically is correct to place Nin among the romantics (a term she uses disparagingly in *The Novel of the Future*) when he notes that literary "history will probably place her with that last back-water of Romanticism before World War II,"[2] in the family of the Lawrentian revolt and the surrealists.

During the 1930s Henry Miller had begun to praise the diary effusively, especially in "Un Etre Etoilique," where he observed, "As I write these lines Anaïs Nin has begun the fiftieth volume of her diary, the record of a twenty-year struggle towards self-realization. Still a young woman, she has produced on the side, in the midst of an intensely active life, a monumental confession which when given to the world will take its place beside the revelations of St. Augustine, Petronius, Abelard, Rousseau, Proust, and others."[3] The article, written with the enthusiasm so typical of Miller in his nonfiction, was bound to win many over to Nin and to whet their appetite for a chance to sample the diary. For a while it looked as if they might have had their way: inside the cover of the October 1937 issue of *The Booster* (an enterprise of Nin, Miller, and others) was an announcement of the diary's publication.[4] But it was to be nearly thirty years before the enthusiasts were able to see a book-length selection from the work that was already famous in manuscript. During the mid 1940s Edmund Wilson wrote in the *New Yorker* that the "unpublished diary of Anaïs Nin has long been a legend of the literary world, [and] a project to have it published by subscription seems never to have come to anything."[5] The publication of the diary, possibly at Nin's own press, seems to have been considered, but it was not until Harcourt cautiously printed a relatively small first edition in 1966 that the diary achieved the exposure that she had wished it to have (although commercial publishers had considered publishing it). The first printing was followed quickly by many reprintings, and subsequently it has been published in a paperback edition. So, more than fifty years after its traumatic beginning, *The Diary of Anaïs Nin*, heralded for decades, came to light with a selection from the years 1931-34.

Certain aspects of the *Diary*, though difficult to discuss because of their innate nebulousness, must be considered before each of its six volumes can be analyzed as separate entities. Many of the points that we shall discuss have been brought up from time to time by reviewers; so far as we know no reviewer (or critic) has answered these questions with definitiveness, and though we cannot claim ourselves to solve the complex puzzles that face the readers of the *Diary*, neither can we ignore them.

The three areas, which are loosely defined and frequently overlapping, might be segmented in the following aspects to be considered: (1) editorial responsibilities in creating the *Diary*, and the implications of these responsibilities; (2) the question of genre, that is, to what extent is the *Diary* "pure notebook or journal" and to what extent has it been consciously structured, rearranged; and (3) the function of time, composition, and organization upon the finished product. To ask whether the *Diary* is fact or fiction is to miss the point; whether these events happened or are delusions does not help to answer the questions raised above. We do not question the veracity of Nin or of the *Diary*. But certainly it would be interesting to understand Nin's autobiographical technique better (as represented in the *Diary*) by comparing the published version with the private manuscript version.

Let us consider first the problem of the editorship. In each of the six volumes published to this point (1976) it is indicated that Gunther Stuhlmann is the editor; volume 1 (1931–34) states that they have been "Edited and with an Introduction by Gunther Stuhlmann," but the subsequent volumes have been "Edited and with a Preface by Gunther Stuhlmann." It is not evident, however, what Gunther Stuhlmann's role was in the editing, or what the differences are from his writing a single introduction and five prefaces. Nin once was asked what his role had been in editing the *Diary*. Her answer was, "He has been a wonderful editor for me because he is ultimately more objective than I can ever be. So when I have done the small editing, you might say, he has an over-all image—he helps me with the balance, with what is missing, with what is lacking. He has a great sense of structure and he has more objectivity. His criticism is very valuable and helps me a great deal, whereas I might get lost in the detailed work."[6] Because her answer came from an interview, it is not so detailed or structured as it might have been; but does it answer the question as to what Gunther Stuhlmann's role—and for that matter, Nin's role also—had been in editing the *Diary*? Certainly only in a general way. She seems to have attended to the "small editing" or stylistic considerations, whereas it would seem, from what she says, that he has dealt with the broader considerations of characterizations, incidents, themes, subjects—"the balance" and the "sense of structure" in the work—although one must assume, perhaps, that Nin herself was responsible for the initial culling of the manuscript diary in order to come up with a first draft of a published *Diary*. The method of composition, so to speak, of the *Diary* remains obscure; we do not really know what the precise editorial function of Nin or Stuhlman was; in order better to gauge the artistry of either or both, we should like to know. In the introduction to the first published volume, Gunther Stuhlmann states the following concerning the source for the volume.

> The present text represents approximately half of the material contained in the ten original manuscript volumes (No. 30 to No. 40) covering this period. In preparing this volume for publication, Miss Nin, and the editor, still faced certain personal and legal considerations inherent in the nature of the diary. Several persons, when faced with the question of whether they wanted to remain in the diary "as is"—since Miss Nin did not want to change the essential nature of her presentation—chose to be deleted altogether from the manuscript (including her husband and some members of her family). The names of some incidental figures have been omitted or changed, since,

as any reader will soon see, the factual identity of a person is basically unimportant within the context of the diary. Miss Nin's truth, as we have seen, is psychological.[7]

Most of this is straightforward enough, even if it raises some interesting questions about the kind of truth contained in the *Diary*. But so far as editorial policy is concerned, most of the questions we have raised remain unanswered. We do not know the technical details of the initial selection of passages, who controlled the style and the larger pattern affecting tempo, who proposed, who countered, who disposed.

The question of genre is infinitely more complex than that of editorship. Perhaps the most essential point we should like to emphasize in this respect is Nin's revealing statement in *The Novel of the Future*: "I have often said that it was the fiction writer who edited the diary."[8]

The chief values Nin ascribes to her fictional technique obtain here as well: psychological authenticity, the function of the dream, the sense of immediacy, and the use of symbolism. The basic construction of the *Diary* shows the fiction writer's hand, suggesting professional editing and selecting. Characters appear and reappear, their essences often being revealed to the reader through their behavior and psychology. As some reviewers have pointed out, the *Diary* contains more substance, concreteness, and context than her fiction normally does. Nin herself believed that the *Diary*, a product of careful editing and selection, represents a new art form, a synthesis of the fictional with the authentic nonfictional quality of the diary.

But it is not so simple. In both genres, Nin's approach is essentially the same: through the presentation of many characters, revolving around a chief female character, all of them are defined in a coherent, structured piece of literature. What is the difference, then, between the fiction and the *Diary*? One finds that some of the short stories in *Under a Glass Bell*, for example, appear later in the published version of the *Diary*, presumably having been included first in the private diary before appearing in the volume of short stories. But the material is hardly altered: the same stories appear under the implicit guise of fiction and then later, again implicitly, as some kind of objective fact.

In her public writing career, she moves away from the nebulousness of the semisurrealistic novel toward the more objective position of the *Diary*. Standard fictional elements such as structuring, recurring motifs, symbolism, stylized characterizations, and psychological authenticity occur quite as much in the *Diary* as in any of her novels. An incident taken from her experience may well be qualified for inclusion into a book of stories largely on the basis of style and organization, not on the basis of whether the content is true or not. The apparent distinction between fact and fiction, between the diary and the novel, may be illusory. Short stories may be true to life and may be actually taken from real incidents in life. Their existence in a published volume of stories, however, is likely to suggest that the author has faith in their literary value. Is not—or may not—the same be true of the *Diary*? On what basis was the selection of characters and incidents made if not largely on a literary basis? She indicates the standard was "purely a human and personal one" and not a literary one at all.[9] And yet her readers may recognize the literary artist's hand at work.

When asked once if there were not characters in the diary who seemed to correspond with those in her fiction, Nin answered, "Yes, it is true. Some of them were even untransformed. For instance, the story 'Birth' is taken literally from out of the diary. I made hardly any changes in it. Some of the characters usually go through some kind of composite transformation. For example, the portrait of my father is recognizable in 'Winter of Artifice' but it is not altogether my father and the incidents are not written according to the diary. Some are and some are not."[10] When asked if she found any contradiction in writing something in the diary as fact and then publishing it as fiction, her answer was negative, for in fiction she takes the basic idea (from the diary) and expands and amplifies it.[11]

Our conclusions on the matter of genre are these: because of the careful selection, arrangement, and structure, the *Diary*, while possibly being faithful to the original manuscript, fits more into the category of a new and created work of art rather than being simply a reproduction of Nin's private journal. As a piece of literature, with all the elements of fiction, it succeeds as well as if not better than most of her fiction perhaps because it is rooted more firmly in an identifiable and substantial context.

The third point to be considered is the matter of time and its relationship to composition and organization, as well as the relationship of the diarist to her own work. Nonfiction of any sort can be a complex concept to deal with, especially when a diarist may be trying to give us a kind of objective truth. The diarist, the autobiographer, and the letter writer may furnish us with interpretations that are different from those perceived by others. It may be recalled that Thucydides, that most wise of historiographers, recognized the natural human limitation of myopia in himself and guarded against it in a way that many moderns would find radical: "With reference to the narrative of events [taking place in the Peloponnesian War], so far from permitting myself to derive it from the first source that came to hand, *I did not even trust my own impressions* [italics added], but it rests partly on what I saw myself, partly on what others saw for me, the accuracy of the report being always tried by the most severe and detailed tests possible."[12] Which is to say, the writer—even if writing about himself or herself—can do no more than reproduce the conception of oneself that one has. There may or may not be truth in Nin's characterization of herself and others, for example, though we may be sure that she is providing us with her own conception of the truth as she perceived it. William Blake and William Wordsworth grappled with the same problem in the early 1800s; Wordsworth's fine phrase in that excellent poem normally referred to as "Tintern Abbey" is to refer the reader to the external reality in that mixture of subjectivity and objectivity,

> of all the mighty world
> Of eye, and ear,—both what they half create,
> And what perceive.

A filtering takes place. Wordsworth above all, in this poem and in *The Prelude*, is sensitive to the effects of time upon the remembrance of an incident and the effects of time upon composition. What little we know of Nin's *Diary* in its relationship to the private diary suggests a similar kind of recognition of the effect.

For example, she indicates two specific instances when material had to be rearranged to fit the needs of the published *Diary*. In one case she wanted to establish the setting and describe her house at Louveciennes; she places the description at the beginning of the first volume in the *Diary*, though apparently it actually was written in a different part of the original.[13] Similarly, a letter written by Henry Miller in 1938 describing his boyhood is included in the 1931 section because it seemed more appropriate to Nin to place it there, and probably most readers would agree. But as a consequence the reader must know and perhaps has a right to know that alteration and rearrangement have taken place. These are not limited to the adding and changing of language or passages, or with necessary cutting but include the manipulation of incidents and characters in order to develop a more coherent and unified work.

A tangential question to be considered is the effect, then, of time on the *Diary*, as well as on incidents in the private diary. No doubt when editing the *Diary*, thirty years or more after the incidents took place, the published version will be different from the private version, because the editor-author, Nin, has herself changed during those thirty years. (For a suggestion of the truth of this, one need only consult Wordsworth's *Prelude*, the dual-text edition prepared by Ernest de Selincourt, and compare the 1805-06 version of the poem with the latest version, 1850, which Wordsworth worked on and revised his whole life: the man of thirty-five included portions that the man at sixty-five will not let stand.) And so with Nin's *Diary* we assume that a transformation has taken place, that there are substantial differences between the private diary and the selection made for the public *Diary*.

Time acts as a filter. The process of composition is a complex one. Take, for example, the episode in volume 1 of the *Diary* that deals with the birth of Nin's stillborn child (pp. 338–47). The same incident, somewhat revised, appears in the story "Birth" at the end of *Under a Glass Bell*. The incident is recorded as having taken place during August 1934, and probably it did. We do not mean to cast doubt upon chronology. And yet one can see, as we have indicated above, that some liberty has been taken with the arrangements of incidents, and Gunther Stuhlmann himself points out to us in the introduction to the first volume of the *Diary* that the "dates in brackets, given by the editor . . . are merely intended to indicate the flow of time (or date a specific event), and do not always correspond to the numerous dates in the original manuscripts, where retrospective entries sometimes confuse the actual chronology" (*Diary*, 1: xi). What does this mean, exactly? How close are the dates? Which have been changed? Are we to regard the dates as approximate? The birth episode is recorded as having taken place in August 1934. When was it written originally? Not during the birth, though it simulates the events. Probably it was written some time shortly after, perhaps a few days after. What has time done to Nin's perceptions? Undoubtedly it has filtered them, unless, like Thucydides, she has gone out of her way to reproduce as closely as possible a document representing what actually took place. But we expect the diarist to filter events through her own psyche anyway; a diary is supposed to be one person's impressions of events, which is what gives it value and interest.

The diarist gives to events a shape, a structure, and a coherence; the diarist, like the writer of fiction, imposes upon them a kind of unity and order that was not necessarily there to begin with. What we have, then, is perhaps something like a heightened reminiscence. After being confronted with the hundreds of volumes of the private diary, Nin and Stuhlmann were then confronted with the enormous task of finding something worthy and interesting enough for the reading public, and, through selectivity and structuring, the published *Diary* evolved, partly to suit the editors, partly to suit the readers. The birth story must stay: it provides a kind of drama and intensity that will suit all. But was it revised for publication? We do not know. Was it touched up to fit the specific context in which it now appears? Is it closer to fiction than to objective truth? Probably, if by fiction one means the ordering of literary elements to produce a coherent whole. And similarly, the cautious reader will not want to take at face value Nin and other characters who appear in the *Diary*; we assume that they have been subject to selectivity and structuring too, that they may be more fictional than not, and that the factual had to give way at times to the demands of a coherent work of literature. We regard the character of Nin in the *Diary* as a persona, which is not inconsistent with the way Nin later regarded the character herself. For the purposes of dramatizing her experiences, she had to become a character in her own drama; for the purpose of art we would expect the persona to have consistency and psychological authenticity. That Nin, many years later, may have imposed upon the persona particular roles or masks is something we shall consider as we look at the nature of Nin's characterization of herself in each of the volumes of the *Diary*. We ask our readers to remember, however, that diaries written during the 1930s were edited during the 1960s, and that the second and the third volumes of the *Diary* were being edited either during or after the huge success of the first volume. This success may have had a substantial effect on the editing of subsequent volumes. Did Nin consciously or unconsciously characterize herself in a certain way in the first volume, and then change the portrayal in later volumes? What was the psychological effect likely to have been when, after years of trying to have her fiction accepted, she could openly portray in the *Diary* her struggle to gain into the publishing world the entry that she was seeking so desperately? There can be little doubt that the nature of the *Diary* must have changed from what it would have been had she not achieved the fame and exposure denied to her for so many decades. And it is fortunate to be able to record that the values, especially of humaneness and enthusiasm, that she tried to inculcate into her fiction exist quite as prominently in her *Diary* as they had in the novels.

So the journal-letter, one might say, became a journal-novel. In each of the volumes, along with character development and something like a plot, one finds a main character, Nin herself, who is surrounded by minor characters who help to define her. She moves and progresses among these subordinate characters in a way not unlike the hero or heroine in a picaresque novel. Through skillful editing, Nin and Stuhlmann produced an organic, well-wrought work of literature.

11

Volume 1, 1931-1934

The first volume of the *Diary* covers an exciting time in
Nin's life, a time when she was living in Paris and
meeting a fascinating array of people; a time when she
became initiated into the mysteries of psychoanalysis, which were to
have a profound and lasting effect upon her. There is no simple way to
outline the structure of the volume; although one might propose that
there are four broad divisions segmenting the work into categories
according to the chief characters with whom the persona is connected.
The presentation of important characters, and Nin's connection with
them, provides the chief interest in the journal, beginning with her
acquaintance with Henry Miller, and, a short time later, his wife June.
In what might be called part 2 Nin encounters Dr. René Allendy, who
psychoanalyzes her and generates in her a keen interest in the
psychological sciences. At about this time she also encounters Antonin
Artaud, the French actor. Closely connected with the second part is the
portion describing the dramatic return into her life of the father who
abandoned his family many years earlier (part 3). The psychology
surrounding their renewed relationship is organically connected with
the psychoanalysis that she had been going through with Allendy.
Finally there is Nin's association with Dr. Otto Rank, the famous
psychoanalyst, whom she is working with in November 1934, as the
volume closes.

When Nin first met Henry Miller she was taken by his vitality and
enthusiasm.

> When I saw Henry Miller walking towards the door where I stood
> waiting, I closed my eyes for an instant to see him by some other inner eye.
> He was warm, joyous, relaxed, natural.
>
> He would have passed anonymously through a crowd. He was slender,
> lean, not tall. He looked like a Buddhist monk, a rosy-skinned monk, with
> his partly bald head aureoled by lively silver hair, his full sensuous mouth.
> His blue eyes are cool and observant, but his mouth is emotional and
> vulnerable. . . .
>
> He was so different from his brutal, violent, vital writing, his caricatures,
> his Rabelaisian farces, his exaggerations. The smile at the corner of his eyes
> is almost clownish; the mellow tones of his voice are almost like a purring
> content. He is a man whom life intoxicates, who has no need of wine, who is
> floating in a self-created euphoria. [*Diary*, 1:8]

And so does Nin plunge into her role as the record keeper of her
experiences with a series of colorful characters, much in the same way
an articulate innocent, well gifted in expression, can detail in nuance
and eloquence a new universe of people and types. It is chiefly into the
role of an initiate that Nin casts herself in this volume of the *Diary*. We
have the opportunity to read her record of the new, interesting, and
often exciting events, on the one hand, and their effect upon her, on the
other. The progression of the initiate is, after all, from innocence to
some kind of knowledge or experience, and the characterization of Nin
in this volume is true to that kind of development, at least as a broad
pattern. From the lacquered Paris suburb to the shabby quarters of Paris
she sinks, as though to experience firsthand the ugliness, the fearfulness,
the violence of a life unknown to her, a Bohemian existence she
approaches with natural ambivalence, with curiosity and trepidation. Is
it safe, one wonders? Is she really participating in it all, even in the risks,
the violence, the drunkenness, the sexuality, in all of it? In fact we are
not told; details are omitted or neglected. We do not know to what
extent she conveniently retires to the suburbs, so as to make excursions
into the nightlife when desired. As in the novels, some of the context is
missing. But the enjoyment is there, of Miller's power, his acceptance of
the richness in life, his finding "joy in everything, in food, in talk, in
drink, in the sound of the bell at the gate" (*Diary*, 1:11). One need only to
recollect Nin's strong interest in D. H. Lawrence's vitality and principle
of life to see an analogy with her fascination with Miller's way of
living Paris in 1931.

As deftly and adroitly as Conrad preparing his readers for Heyst in
Victory does Nin prepare the foundation for Miller's second wife, June.

"Henry came again today. He talked about his second wife, June. June was full of stories. She told him . . . " (*Diary*, 1: 12). Nin records Miller's detailed reminiscences of bizarre stories told to him by June—accompanied by the tantalizing revelation that June's protective labyrinthine web of tale was created for the sake of safety. The stage is set. The veracity of June's tales has already been questioned and more stories of June are related. The reader can sense, without being told, the imminent entrance of June into the Miller-Nin orbit. June is mysterious; she hates daylight. We receive more tangible evidence. Her illusions and her lies are synonymous to Miller but not to Nin, who keeps silent and observes. Miller does not understand; Nin wants to pursue the matter to the point of motive: What makes the lies necessary? June's entrance, in what would be called the second section, does not disappoint: "As June walked towards me from the darkness of the garden into the light of the door, I saw for the first time the most beautiful woman on earth."

> A startlingly white face, burning dark eyes, a face so alive I felt it would consume itself before my eyes. Years ago I tried to imagine a true beauty; I created in my mind an image of just such a woman. I had never seen her until last night. Yet I knew long ago the phosphorescent color of her skin, her huntress profile, the evenness of her teeth. She is bizarre, fantastic, nervous, like someone in a high fever. Her beauty drowned me. As I sat before her, I felt I would do anything she asked of me. Henry suddenly faded. She was color and brilliance and strangeness. [Ibid., 1: 20]

All this, until June talks; then her enormous ego and posturing come into focus, and Nin believes that everything Henry has said about her is true.

At this point the reader may begin to understand better Nin's assertion that she lived only for the high moments, that she was in accord with the surrealists, that to be fully alive was to live instinctively and unconsciously. These values were noted in and confirmed by her fiction, her stories, and her criticism. As carefully as in a novel, she provides her readers with the tension and energy vibrating between her and Miller, opposites in so many ways; and then June, Nin's female opposite, so to speak, is introduced: she is vibrant, earthy, physical, standing in contrast to Nin who is demure, small, delicate. Nin pursues the tale, quite a good one in itself, of their attraction, their ultimate repulsion, the intricacies of their relationship, and the power of their minds over one another. In short, the psychological authenticity of the relationship is maintained with an expertise that surpasses that of any other delineated in the fiction. The nebulous ("What a secret language we talk. Undertones, overtones, nuances, abstractions, symbols" [*Diary*, 1:34]) is balanced, however, by a rich foundation in the reality of flesh-and-blood people who are colorful and complex.

Dovetailed with this grouping of characters is Nin's association with Dr. René Allendy, who psychoanalyzes her, affording her another excursion into self-knowledge and eventually self-revelation. In an unfortunate and awkward attempt to provide a transition to Allendy and psychoanalysis, Nin refers to her friend Marguerite's trying to persuade her to see the analyst ("She reminds me that in New York I had a breakdown" [*Diary*, 1: 75]). Nin resists at first, feeling no paralysis; however, in time she succumbs and her lengthy encounter with Allendy begins. It is all coherent and integrated: Parisian life, sensitivity to psychological levels, Nin en route from the incitement of Henry and June Miller's lives, through her own barriers, on to a richer life of creativity. It is not to be doubted; no fictional plot has a greater sense of unity than this progress of the *Diary*'s heroine, who is out not to seek her fortune, but rather to find fruitfulness, friendship, self-esteem, and worthy productivity. The *Diary*, possibly through selective editing, maintains these interrelated themes and keeps them steadily before the reader. This is the literary artist's function, we are reminded in *The Novel of the Future*: to express the inexpressible, to see sense and unity in the larger fabric when we are blind to it otherwise because of its immediacy. This is to say that thematically and ideologically the introduction of Dr. Allendy into Nin's life and *Diary* is not certainly inevitable, but it has the aura of truth about it, contributing to what Aristotle refers to as unity of character: the persona is staying in character, and, although the cause of her visit to Allendy is not outlined in detail, the reader might infer that the Miller-June experience with all its psychological violence (Miller's rowdy Bohemianism, his obscenity, June's lies, June's stormy quasi love affair with the persona) provides an appropriate entree into the world of psychoanalysis, doubts having been planted, perhaps, by the physical quality of June and the liveliness of Miller in contrast to the more reserved and quiet nature of Nin. Clearly she wants to pursue analysis, even if with some caution. ("Psychoanalysis does force one to be more truthful. Already I realize certain feelings I was not aware of, like the fear of being hurt" [ibid., 1: 77].) Her innate hypersensitivity and quest for understanding are perfectly consistent with her role as seeker for new experience and for new understanding.

Allendy recognizes the suffering that Nin has endured; he is sensitive to her doubts and fears; he forces her to confess her uneasiness about her fragility, her smallness, and her vulnerability. He reassures her. But he seems to awaken in her a "restlessness, which was vague and lyrical" (*Diary*, 1:89), which prior to this meeting had been only latent. She wanted to be more like June. The diarist traces her emotional progress toward the overcoming of obstacles blocking her way toward liberation, especially her fear of exposure, her uncertainty about herself, her wish to emerge from a protective shell. She begins to sense better her own abilities as well as her value to others, and by 1932 she has reached the point where she feels "loved, fecundated, fecund."

> Dr. Allendy says I do not seem to need him any more. But he does point out to me that by entering Henry's world (poverty, Bohemianism, living by expediencies), I have moved in the opposite direction from my father's world (luxury, society life, aesthetics, security, aristocratic friendships, etc.).
>
> Henry's world seems more sincere to me. I never liked my father's worldliness, his need of luxury, his salon life, his love of titles, his pride in his own aristocracy, his dandyism, his elaborate social life. [Ibid., 1: 98]

Was she beginning already to punish the father who rejected her? It was not yet time for him to reenter her life, though he was in Paris or its vicinity now and then. But she was beginning to come to terms with herself and was beginning to understand her own feelings toward her father.

Continuing to see Allendy, continuing with her introspection (which is grueling, relentless, and kept steadily in focus), Nin depicts her probings and first tentative attempts to discover her true nature.

> Dr. Allendy: "The more you act like yourself, the nearer you will come to the fulfillment of your real needs."
>
> Anaïs: "But I am not sure what this self is. For the moment I seem to be busy tearing down what I was."
>
> Dr. Allendy: "I do not despair of reconciling you to your own image."
>
> What a beautiful phrase! To reconcile me to my own image. And if he can help me to find this image? [*Diary*, 1: 110]

The graphic portrayal of Nin in movement toward self-realization cannot but affect all feeling people. One senses her satisfaction in saying that this was "a time of pleasure, broken only by superimpositions from the past. I want to linger over it" (ibid., 1: 111). She dressed less flashily as she found her confidence being restored; she relived her painful past and saw that she had been hurt so badly that the fear of loss dominated her. In her childhood diary she had written, "I have decided that it is better not to love anyone, because when you love people, then you have to be separated from them, and that hurts too much" (ibid., 1: 115). The motif has been so carefully controlled that one finds the cumulative effect of this pain reaching a high peak of intensity—and just at the end of a chapter. Tempo is assuredly one element that the fiction writer has injected into the *Diary* with skill.

And at this crucial time, a new threat looms, and one that is to recur from time to time: some loss of confidence in or uneasiness with those to whom she has entrusted herself, in this case Miller and Allendy. Allendy begins to make more demands upon Nin than she wants to accede to; Miller continues to need her to nourish his work and his fiction. She begins to feel exploited, as one who is asked to understand everything, accept everything, giving almost to the point of self-annihilation. Increasingly she feels that Allendy is losing his objectivity, and she finds herself telling him small lies to see if he can detect them. When he demands that she cease seeing Miller and June, she says that she has stopped. She leaves Allendy with a web of lies. More significantly, she begins to realize that his brand of analysis fails sufficiently to accommodate the artist, and so she begins reading Otto Rank's *Art and Artist.* The movement away from Allendy, however faint, has begun. This movement coincides also with her poignant realization of the kind of tragedy that is inherent in the life of the analyst, for the analyst must always be on the outside looking into the lives of the patients or clients. But who is looking into the life and the mind of the analyst and taking care of the doctor? This interesting diversion is pursued at some length, and as a motif the relationship of patient and doctor becomes more complex as it comes more clearly into focus, as it does in Nin's connection with both Allendy and Rank.

The narrator/persona indicates that Allendy enabled her to identify more clearly her true nature and to give herself to it. She rejects Miller's down-to-earth friend, Alfred Perlès, because he is too clownish; Nin's friend Jeanne, on the other hand, is more suitable: she is a mysterious character, part of a family that had exhausted, "in five generations, the ordinary joys of fame, fortune, beauty, intelligence, voyages, honors, genius, debauch, power, leaving four heirs who could only love each other" (*Diary*, 1: 169). She is, in short, elusive. Nin is always attracted by the extraordinary, the unusual, the mysterious and elusive of life as it is manifested in human beings. "I want to live only for ecstasy. Small doses, moderate loves, all half-shades, leave me cold. I like extravangance" (ibid., 1: 174). Miller's raucous kind of primitive approach (probably traceable to his Brooklyn-American heritage) stands in contrast to Nin's life with a father who is a cultured artist, performing in the most elegant music chambers in Europe. The persona is interested in her attraction and repulsion to both these worlds. The life toward which she gravitates contains both of these forces to some extent; it represents a kind of reconciliation of these opposite poles, though in a strangely mad way: it is the world of art and originality and enthusiasm as embodied in that fierce and angry man, Antonin Artaud.

This gaunt man with visionary eyes is, one feels, another diversion for Nin on her quest for experience. He seems to encompass an artistry that is analogous to that of her father but assuredly without the salon ambience about it. Artaud's energy and ingenuity in a way match Miller's, but it would seem that this man who was "all nerves," the surrealist disavowed by the surrealists, a ghostly brooding figure, is part and parcel of the café life, a European Bohemian obsessed with his art as much as Miller was.

Allendy introduces Nin to Artaud and brings the actor to see her; the drug habit is ruining him, and Allendy is trying to free him from this destruction. Artaud and Nin begin to correspond, to respond to each other's writing. At the Sorbonne she is able to see his violent brand of theater firsthand and finds its power captivating and incredible, as Artaud discusses "The Theatre and the Plague."

> He asked me to sit in the front row. It seems to me that all he is asking for is intensity, a more heightened form of feeling and living. Is he trying to remind us that it was during the Plague that so many marvelous works of art and theatre came to be, because, whipped by the fear of death, man seeks immortality, or to escape, or to surpass himself? But then, imperceptibly almost, he let go of the thread we were following and began to act out dying by plague. No one quite knew when it began. To illustrate his conference, he was acting out an agony. "*La Peste*" in French is so much more terrible that "The Plague" in English. But no word could describe what Artaud acted on the platform of the Sorbonne. He forgot about his conference, the theatre, his ideas, Dr. Allendy sitting there, the public, the young students, his wife, professors, and directors. [*Diary*, 1: 191]

His face contorted in anguish, the gifted—and possessed—actor played the part too well, to the horror of the onlookers; as his eyes became dilated, his muscles taut, he began to scream in agony, "enacting his own death" (ibid., 1: 192). As though to carry out this violent portrayal, however, the more he continued the more the audience reacted, first gasping, then laughing, and then hissing; finally, jeering, they left. The Allendys and Nin went with Artaud to a café, hurt and wounded by the abuse. He was bitter: people, he claimed, always want to hear about death, but he wanted to give them the experience. The scene, as Nin describes it, is a masterpiece painstakingly depicting herself, Allendy, and Artaud; and describing further the progress of the persona in her exploration for a psychic home or stationary point. The details fit perfectly with the section on Allendy-Artaud and with the larger pattern of the *Diary* and Nin's characterization of herself in it. This integration of scene with scene, the consistency with which the characters are drawn, and the articulateness with which the tale is related all function together to produce an organic quality that binds and unifies the characters for the reader, while providing something like a plot and accompanying development. That the cumulative effect of these elements should strike the reader all at once attests to the skillful editing alluded to earlier. Nin dramatizes the kind of power and intensity in Artaud that she herself had searched for, and yet, as with June, it will not do finally, and Nin is left with her own quest to pursue.

As a kind of welcome interval, Nin's movement from Allendy toward Rank is interrupted by the reappearance in her life of the one man with whom she wished she could have had a close relationship, her father. It is carefully executed. We have been well prepared for his puff and powdery entrance; both his view of himself and himself as others see him are nicely presented; necessary gaps of exposition are provided by Maruca, the father's young wife who had been his piano pupil. The reconciliation is more satisfactory for father and daughter than one might expect: both are adults now, though both are sensitive to the peculiar quality in their own lives that keeps them instinctively separate. Much of this extended episode is moving, a wise inclusion in the *Diary* that always benefits from the dramatic and the colorful. The father, loving luxury, silken shirts, gold-tipped cigarettes, lavish bouquets, and mistresses, who is full of lies and deceptions, almost a villainous chap, we feel, provides one more foil to the character of the persona and helps us to sort out her values, her obstacles, and her development.

A new motif, and one that becomes fully developed in volume 2 of the *Diary*, begins to emerge when Nin observes that somehow or other she always loses her "guide halfway up the mountain, and he becomes [her] child" (*Diary*, 1: 261). She had had to let go of Allendy, too; his usefulness had ended, and she sensed, it seems, the inversion of her relationship with him: he was suffering from lack of affection, also. But chiefly she wanted him to help her create literature, and his supply of imagery and symbolism was limited; one can almost hear Rank rushing in to fill that void. But before Nin reached that stage she needed help in creating and in caring for the "children," her friends, who surrounded her, and she went to Allendy because she needed someone to help her take care of them (ibid., 1: 163).

Nin once noted in the *Diary* that she would be rudderless without Allendy; but an even better doctor to help her find direction was Rank, a gifted analyst who had written many books by 1933. As soon as she meets him, she knows that they share similar perspectives because they each value creativity so much. His insight into her psyche attracts her and overwhelms her. He recognizes her need for mythmaking, for creating herself, but he feels that she is too dependent upon her diary and makes her leave it with him. She is startled, shocked, lost; her opiate has been taken away from her. She writes about it, she says, in retrospect, after she has returned to the diary, which Rank sees as her last defense against analysis. By taking away the diary, he prevents her from analyzing the analysis.

Rank's approach is considerably different from Allendy's; he notes that Allendy was trying to persuade Nin to give up the quest for the marvelous by adapting to ordinary life, whereas Rank sees happiness as the "positive, creative assertion of the will through the consciousness of creation" (*Diary*, 1: 284) that can have its base in artistic enthusiasm. Rank thinks he understands the function of the diary, that while Nin had been playing so many roles, "dutiful daughter, devoted sister, mistress, protector, my father's newfound illusion, Henry's needed all-purpose friend, [she] had to find one place of truth, one dialogue without falsity" (ibid., 1:286). Rank denotes this as a mother concept; the reader has already encountered it in Nin's portrayal of herself as one who, though guided halfway up the hill, then becomes the guide.

Allendy, Henry Miller, Nin's father, Jeanne, all these, and especially the men, remain in varying degrees near the *Diary*'s surface. Nin helps Miller with the publication of *Tropic of Cancer* by paying the printing costs. The birth episode, alluded to earlier, occurs in August 1934; the father of the child is not identified. Rank decides to go to New York, where he is offered "plenty of money and a job" (*Diary*, 1: 336), although he wants to stay in Paris. Soon desperate letters from him arrive to Nin in Paris, begging her to come and work with him there. She believes in Rank; she talks with Miller, pointing out the nature of his work in Rankian terms. She cannot resist.

> Psychoanalysis did save me because it allowed the birth of the real me, a most dangerous and painful one for a woman, filled with dangers; for no one has ever loved an adventurous woman as they have loved adventurous men. The birth of the real me might have ended like that of my unborn child. I may not become a saint, but I am very full and very rich. I cannot install myself anywhere yet; I must climb dizzier heights. But I still love the relative, not the absolute: the cabbage and the warmth of a fire, Bach on the phonograph, and laughter, and talk in the cafés, and a trunk packed for departure, with copies of *Tropic of Cancer*, and Rank's last SOS and the telephone ringing all day, good-bye, good-bye, good-bye . . . [Ibid., 1: 359–60]

It is a warm and personal, even hopeful, conclusion to a tale of three years' worth of the extremes of living. This was the first volume of Nin's real continuous novel.

12

Volume 2, 1934–1939

Published just a year after the first volume of the *Diary*, the second volume is in many ways a coherent extension of the first. Many motifs and themes, as well as characters, reappear here; so that, taken together with the first, this volume depicts Nin's experience over the entire decade of the 1930s. Because war (the Spanish civil war and the advent of World War II) dominates the scene, this volume necessarily has both a political and social cast that is lacking in the first. And yet there are so many new characters and so much new material, along with some new directions, that the present volume quite as much as the first stands as an interesting and largely successful self-contained unit. In some ways it shares characteristics with the traditional roman-fleuve, which is hardly surprising in a private diary and perhaps even more likely in an edited, published version. Like a continuous novel, the *Diary* focuses attention on familiar characters (familiar here from volume 1) and yet introduces new characters who moved into Nin's life. Not the least important of the old characters is the persona of Nin herself, a character who develops significantly as a writer. Otto Rank and Henry Miller continue to figure prominently in the second volume. Of the new characters, the most remarkable are Gonzalo, a Peruvian Marxist; Helba, his wife; and Lawrence Durrell, whose fame as a writer was still before him during the 1930s. Other subsidiary characters are usually participants in the literary life of Paris at this time.

From all appearances, Nin's and Gunther Stuhlmann's editorial techniques remained the same as those employed in the editing of volume 1. In the preface, Stuhlmann deals briefly with the problem of editing this massive diary and recognizes that Nin's dual function as author and editor is imprinted upon the public version.

> To choose from a cohesive, organically developing text like that of the diary, with its weaving and reweaving of time and incident, its natural gaps and duplications, its gradual maturing, is always a precarious undertaking. The author's own initial selectivity in writing her diary is re-enacted, for the second time, in the editorial process. And the original diary itself, in all its fullness, after all is merely a *reflection,* a refraction, of the totality of the author. It is not the full, rounded, day-to-day Anaïs Nin portrayed in place and time with an eye toward presenting herself to the world. In her unabashed, sometimes unflattering exposure of the inner person, of her spontaneous reaction to people, events and ideas, Miss Nin takes us into a confidence undisguised by the art of the writer. [*Diary*, 2:v]

It may be and no doubt is true that the private and secret person lives even in the pages of a diary edited and smoothed for commercial publication; it is likely that the published diary is, however, in every way more controlled, coherent, literate, and steadily focused, having a unity not to be found in the unedited original. One might expect, on the other hand, an original to possess more variety, diversity, and imperfection than could be allowed before the public. Perhaps the best that one may hope for is that the *Diary*, the result of a wise selection, can be presented to the reader as a work with the natural liveliness and interest of the original but without the defects of lapses, repetitions, and other literary weaknesses that are likely to appear in a first draft of notes written hastily and sporadically.

The text of this second volume, we are told, represents about half of the manuscript volumes numbered 40 through 60, covering the years from 1934 to 1939. "Certain people, including Miss Nin's husband and members of her family, again had to be eliminated. The names of some of her analytical patients had to be changed or omitted, and the dates provided by the editor merely summarize the specific and—due to Miss Nin's later reflection of a previous event—sometimes confusing dates in the originals" (*Diary*, 2: vii). No explanation is offered and perhaps none is needed to account for the elimination of those closest to Nin; yet many will wonder at this significant omission: how it has affected the basic nature and quality of the text, how it affects the reader's view of the persona, and how it alters the thrust of the narrative. Because of these omissions and the selective nature of the editing, it would seem to be incautious for one to assume that the *Diary* represents unaltered fact. This is not to imply that the material is unfactual, or that Nin is unjustified in making such excisions; rather, it reinforces our belief that the *Diary,* as an entity and as an aggregate, belongs properly to the genre of the journal-novel, which is similar in some ways to the eighteenth-century epistolary picaresque novel; and because Nin's journal-novel appears in multiple volumes, it can share some qualities of the roman-fleuve with its epic possibilities, lending potential for plot, characterization, and elaborate development at every level. Lord Byron once replied to his publisher, John Murray, "You ask me for the plan of [*Don Juan*]: I *have* no plan—I *had* no plan; but I had or have materials. . . . If it don't take, I will leave it off where it is, with all due respect to the Public; but if continued, it must be in my own way."[1] The spirit of freedom and spontaneity exhibited here is perhaps closer to Nin's *Diary* than one might at first expect. Her own tastes (and Gunther Stuhlmann's) no doubt dictated in part what would be selected for publication; and the nature of the events (the narrative, one might say) is also a primary consideration. But what of the times, the temperament of the reader and the publisher? And do the diaries (*Diary,* too) of 1966 and later years contain reactions to the reception of the *Diary*? Did the reviews of the first and second volumes influence which material would be selected for the third and subsequent volumes? Could praise and criticism *not* have been influential? These speculative questions are introduced chiefly to hint at the complex nature of the subject matter that the journal-novel allows author and editor to present. A work may have its roots in a genre that is quite distinct and different from the continuous novel and yet share attributes of that literary form, although the writer may not have intended to produce a published literary work that was related to that form.

Perhaps the best way to discuss the content of volume 2 is to identify chief themes or emphases in the work rather than to trace the narrative chronologically. Just as the first volume can be approached in terms of the author's relationships (with Miller, June, Allendy, her father, and Rank), so in this volume are there stresses upon key connections with characters that are often generated by and related to broader themes. For example, in volume 2 the diarist's relationship with Rank grows out of her interest in psychoanalysis, and the volume opens with her arrival in New York to work with him (a useful transition from the first volume, which ended with her departure from Europe). The Rankian section, a short one, establishes Nin in the United States in her role as a lay analyst and goes on to trace her subsequent break with psychoanalysis. This decision, which is one of paramount importance, comes about through her recognition of the enormous sacrifices required by analysis, sacrifices that ultimately would require her to give up writing altogether. And so as she breaks with analysis in favor of art, she returns in June 1935, to her artistic home, France; and her house at Louveciennes; and her literary friends, Henry Miller, Alfred Perlès, and Michael Fraenkel. Determined to publish their own works and other worthwhile manuscripts, they found their own press, Siana (*Anais* spelled backward) Editions. Again the abstract theme of the *Diary* (artistry) resides in the diarist's concrete connection with the craft of writing and with those who share her literary interests. Another part, or theme, might be designated as that portion of volume 2 revolving around Gonzalo, the Peruvian Marxist, and perhaps by implication the larger issues of the Spanish civil war, the upheaval in western Europe during the late 1930s, and the progressive political disintegration accompanying the development of new world powers. And finally there is the recurring theme (that is not an identifiable section) of Nin's own development, the depiction of the woman and artist who wishes to persevere in her art, ignoring politics altogether, but who eventually must recognize the reality of war and destruction and the annihilation of a way of life and a literary coterie in Paris. The advent of World War II becomes more and more clearly defined, serving as a backdrop to the central action of the drama that is played out by the character of Nin. This includes her development and artistic progress, her new roles and the growth that she experiences on the houseboat, and the richness of her life as she cultivates new people who function as subsidiary characters: Albertine, her maid; Jean Carteret; Conrad Moricand; and characters from the past, such as her father and Antonin Artaud. It is during this time that Nin's important literary attempts, *The House of Incest* (1936) and *The Winter of Artifice* (1939), are first published.

A chief theme of volume 1 revolves around Nin's initiation into the mysteries of psychoanalysis, particularly in her growing association with Rank. This development reaches its zenith at the end of the first volume, when she leaves the lively Bohemian life of Paris to sail to the United States, at Rank's express wish, to help him in his work. The voyage itself, though not described, serves as the transition from the old life to the new, from the old world to the new.

My ship quite fittingly broke all speed records sailing towards New York. It was night when I arrived. The band was playing, and the skyscrapers were twinkling with a million eyes. I was looking for Dr. Otto Rank on the wharf, staring at the Babylonian city, the tense people, New York a dream wrapped in fog and sea smells.

Rank was there. Through the influence of a powerful patient of his, the formalities were quickly disposed of and I was whisked away, baggage and all, into a taxi and to a room reserved for me at what I immediately called the "Hotel Chaotica." [*Diary*, 2: 3]

The passage is more suggestive than it may first appear, for the overtones apparent here indicate the direction of the persona. The dreamlike and Babylonian qualities of the city are largely negative; and how long can one be expected to live in a Hotel Chaotica? The six- or seven-month stay in the United States seems doomed from the beginning.

Rank helped Nin become established in New York and catered to her needs and wishes, but Nin was unable to respond favorably: it seemed an empty life in New York, where life was "all external, all action, no thought, no meditation, no dreaming, no reflection, only the exuberance of action" (*Diary*, 2: 4). The theatrical plays would not do, but in assisting Rank with his patients she found drama deeper and more terrifying than on the stage. As Rank began to love the dynamic life there, we sense how strongly she reacted against the artificiality and sterility of the life and times, and the contrast between Paris and New York was persistently in her consciousness, "Paris a sensual city which seduced the body, enlivened the senses, New York unnatural, synthetic" (ibid., 2: 7). But there was a richness to New York that Nin recognized and soon cultivated, necessarily recollecting her childhood when she lived on West Seventy-fifth Street. Rank, she indicated, was interested in her history; and he wanted to know more about women, insisting that psychoanalysts as yet knew little about them. Under her influence, he began to rebel against his profession, temporarily wanting to live life for himself instead of for his patients. "I had," she wrote, "awakened in Rank a hunger for life and freedom, as Henry [Miller] and his wife June had awakened it in me! What ironies!" (ibid., 2: 10). She helped Rank through a professional crisis by suggesting that he balance work with recreation, and in time he began to manage his time better, partly by sending her some patients, her first.

During early 1935 Nin continued working with her patients as a lay analyst, but she was not isolated from literary interests. She visited Dreiser and read Lawrence; Henry Miller arrived from Paris, writing

Black Spring in New York (a book dealing in large part with that city). He later dedicated the book to Nin. At the same time, she was dealing with the difficulties and complexities associated with severely disturbed patients whom she needed to treat while Rank was traveling in other parts of the country, falling in love with the West. Rank's work in New York and Philadelphia, Miller's writing, and Nin's work with patients are themes that the diarist discusses in some detail, although often sketchily. Rebecca West, Waldo Frank, Norman Bel Geddes, William Carlos Williams, John Huston, Raymond Massey, and other notables appear in the *Diary* during this residence in New York City. In the meantime, by March or April 1935, Nin was beginning to feel more and more uncomfortable in the analyst's chair. And she began to see Rank more clearly than before, recognizing that his strength of will inevitably created a tragic personal life; but when he asked her to give up her writing in order to rewrite his books, she knew the time had come to leave New York or "be consumed in service and healing" (*Diary,* 2: 38). At a meeting of psychoanalysts in Long Beach, a sordid convention in a sordid resort, Nin resolved the crisis.

> I was not a scientist. I was seeking a form of life which would be continuous like a symphony. The key word was the sea. It was this oceanic life which was being put in bottles and labeled. Underneath my feet, moving restlessly beneath the very floor of the hotel, was the sea, and my nature which would never amalgamate with analysis in any permanent marriage. I could not hear the discussion. I was listening for the sea's roar and pulse.
>
> It was that day I realized once more that I was a writer, and only a writer, a writer and not a psychoanalyst.
>
> I was ready to return home and write a novel.
>
> A few days later I sailed for home. When I left, New York was covered with fog. I could only hear the ship's sirens. [Ibid., 2: 41]

As an introduction to the second volume, the initial section on Rank functions very effectively; it provides a smooth transition between the first and second volumes of the *Diary*, it enables the reader to see how Nin portrays one more stage in her contact with analysis, but more fundamentally useful is that the rejection of Rank (and America) propelled Nin, who was an artist with an artist's mission, once again into the familiar culture of Paris in June 1935. The next four years, sketched out in the remaining 300 pages of this *Diary*, depict Nin the artist meeting a new foe, politics, which was a necessary specter to be faced during the onset of World War II in western Europe.

Nin's return to Paris and her home at Louveciennes after an absence of seven or eight months was an auspicious event for her, for it was not merely a return to the antiquity and charm of Europe, but rather a return to France by the persona who had recognized and felt the strengths of the American experience, the vitality and liveliness of New York, though she found it lacking depth and meaning. Depicting herself as one stirred and quickened to develop a new, uncreated work, she wrote, "I have to grow in a different way, not cover mileage, but in depth. I have to sublimate my love of adventure" (*Diary*, 2: 43). And, most notably, "I dream of a printing press, of publishing" (ibid.). With Henry Miller, Michael Fraenkel, and Alfred Perlès, the idea of the printing press takes hold; it seems that the idea of having a tangible method of reproducing their work served to incite her to concrete achievements. At first Fraenkel "appropriated" the idea of the printing venture and made a list of books they would publish, omitting Nin (although Perlès had named the press Siana). And yet it was potentially a time of great creativity for Nin: she was beginning a new phase. She had left Rank, thinking that she had finally overcome the need for a father. She did not miss him; she did miss the vibrancy of New York. But she felt uneasy about her restlessness. "Adventure is pulling me out. When a man feels this, it is no crime, but let a woman feel this and there is an outcry" (ibid., 2: 46). The literary aspirations of Nin and Miller began to reach fruition through Jack Kahane of the Obelisk Press, who agreed to publish Nin's *Winter of Artifice*.

Miller became a minor celebrity with the growing recognition of *Tropic of Cancer*, and in the meantime he was at work on *Tropic of Capricorn*. Their own press made plans to publish a number of works, including Nin's *House of Incest* and two works by Miller.

The literary pursuits and achievements of the Nin–Miller group, later joined by Lawrence Durrell, occupy a central position in this second volume of the *Diary*, and the working relationship of these writers will be briefly examined. However, it may be pointed out that concurrent with this literary progress is the increasingly frequent characterization of Nin in a role as nurturer and protector. The pattern is apparent in volume 1 of the *Diary*, when Allendy and Nin's father (her erstwhile benefactors) themselves required help from her. The image is naturally reinforced by Nin's strong interest in analysis and her patients in New York City. She recognized that the constant need for "a mother, or a father, or a god (the same thing) is really immaturity" (*Diary*, 2: 21), but she also recognized the need to provide love for those who sought it. And so the portrayal of Nin as benefactor emerges more and more, dominating the larger portion of the book. Of her friends in Paris in July 1935, she wrote, "I am the young mother of the group in the sense that I am giving nourishment and creating life. All of them now in motion. When I look at the changes, the transformations, the expansions I created, I grow afraid, afraid to be left alone, as all mothers are ultimately left alone. To each I gave the strength to fly out of my world, and at times my world looks empty. But they come back" (ibid., 2: 51).

The next year brought further work (Nin was writing *The Winter of Artifice*) and a return trip to New York City. A most remarkable journey to Morocco in the spring of 1936 allowed her to practice in the diary her verbal artistry with skill and delicacy; in terms of sheer flavor and exotic description, it is a passage that is unsurpassed.

Settling in Villa Seurat, Miller continued working on *Tropic of Capricorn*. Nin was a frequent visitor; their talk was ongoing, and ideas were exchanged in what appears to have been a fascinating and instructive literary experience for both of them. On the one hand she was able to discuss the essence and goal of her diary writing, the attempt to capture the "instantaneous vision of the world" that she believed in; on the other hand he was able to introduce her to new ways of using language that were new and experimental verbal techniques employing modes of exuberance, elevation, elation, frenzy. Their ideological give-and-take nourished them both. There is no question that Miller's bald enthusiasm for life was perpetually attractive to her, but she knew him well enough to perceive that his wildness, his childlike receptiveness to life, his warmth and passion, also could lead to a violent and chaotic world that precluded tenderness and softness. In a very oversimplified way he represented for her the masculine quality, while she cultivated the feminine. At this time she saw the diary as "a feminine activity," "a personal and personified creation," whereas other traditional artistic forms (painting, sculpture, pottery, architecture, novels) were "too far from the truth of the moment" (*Diary*, 2: 172). Stories written at this time reveal similar notions, and it was at this time that most of the stories later to appear in *Under a Glass Bell* were conceived and written, some of them growing out of experiences recorded in the diary.

Near the end of 1936 Nin and Miller became involved with a new correspondent, Lawrence Durrell. Durrell sent his *Black Book* to Miller in manuscript, and soon Miller and Nin both corresponded with the English poet, who was living in Greece. A good deal of the literary correspondence that ensued is recorded in the *Diary*. Then in August 1937, Durrell and his wife Nancy arrived in Paris and visited Miller, Nin, and Perlès. The meeting was propitious for them all.

> I walked to Henry's studio to meet Lawrence Durrell and his wife. What first struck me were his eyes of a Mediterranean blue, keen, sparkling, seer, child and old man. In body he is short and stocky, with soft contours like a Hindu, flexible like an Oriental, healthy and humorous. He is a faun, a swimmer, a sail-boat enthusiast. Nancy, his wife, is a long-waisted gamin with beautiful long slanting eyes. With Durrell I had instant communication. We skipped the ordinary stages of friendship, its gradual development. I felt friendship at one bound, with hardly a need of talk. [*Diary*, 2: 223]

Although she sensed very soon that Durrell suffered from the English disease of impersonality, she found him interesting, withdrawn, and warm at the same time, also somewhat cautious, somewhat detached. Soon she, Miller, and the Durrells were spending many hours and evenings together in discussion; a beautiful "flow" existed between them, and they were able "mutually [to] nourish each other, stimulate each other" (*Diary*, 2: 231). Nin reacted against the detachment that she observed in Durrell; he exposed others without feeling for them.

> And Lawrence Durrell, where does he stand? At times I feel he could have been, symbolically speaking, the writer child of Henry and myself. He likes Henry's ruthlessness. He calls it anti-romantic. He calls it the truth. He himself writes without feeling, impersonally. But there is something else there. I think he is a romantic seeking to repudiate or deny this. I think he is a poet and a painter, and that he will never open human beings in the way Henry does. But he will not go into them either, into their feelings as I do. He is too English for that.
> I think he does not know yet where he stands. [Ibid.]

The diarist portrays this small group as unmasking each other and defending their approaches to literature and to life; she reproduces their interesting repartee, preserved from a time and place when a small group of dedicated writers were able to pursue at length the rich ideas that they brought to each other. Woman's role, the detachment of man, the function of the diarist, all are painted for us with verve. One paragraph is nearly classic, for it encompasses Nin's view of woman as one who is in touch with the centrality of life that is forbidden—or taboo, perhaps—to man. Woman's role in the creation of literature should parallel her role in life: "Tragedies, conflicts, mysteries are personal. Man fabricated a detachment which became fatal. Woman must not fabricate. She must descend into the real womb and expose its secrets and its labyrinths. She must describe it as the city of Fez, with its

Arabian Nights gentleness, tranquility and mystery. She must describe the voracious moods, the desires, the worlds contained in each cell of it. For the womb has dreams" (ibid., 2: 235).

In the summer of 1937 the group decided to assume control of a small magazine, *The Booster,* which was something of a literary joke. It reawakened Nin's rebellion against Miller's "atmosphere of begging, stealing, cajoling, school-boy pranks, slapstick humor, burlesque" (*Diary*, 2: 236). Perlès was involved in the enterprise, and she may have been apprehensive, because she disdained his clowning. From her point of view, *The Booster* was never a success. She tried to dissociate herself from it near the time of its inception, determined to leave it to Miller, Durrell, and Perlès. Its brand of humor offended her. She wrote a few months later, "I do not like the *Booster*. It is vulgar and farcical. Strident. Then I feel guilty: 'Perhaps I am too austere' " (ibid., 2: 264). She seems to have entertained some second thoughts about the matter, for later she was a contributor and even went so far as to participate in a plan in November 1937 to edit an issue containing women's writing. Afterward, however, her uneasiness about the magazine seems to have been borne out as she saw the frivolous enterprise draining the energies of her friends.

The intellectual dialogue, especially of Nin and Miller, cannot hope to be reproduced here, nor have we attempted to do more than to hint at its complexity and richness. If it is true that there was mutual admiration and attraction on the part of these writers, it is equally true that there remained a substantially radical difference in their approaches and values in literature, insofar as these approaches are defined by Nin in this volume of the *Diary*. What she perceives to be Miller's callousness, cruelty, and depersonalization she deprecates; sensual dynamism, without humanism, is offensive to her. The variations in their respective approaches are detailed superbly when she comments on portions of *Tropic of Capricorn,* one of the works occupying Miller at this time.

Along with the Miller-Perlès-Durrell coterie, the other people who dominate Nin's *Diary* between 1934 and 1939 are Gonzalo and his wife Helba. At first glance it seems most unusual that these two people should figure so largely in the *Diary*, or, rather, perhaps, that they should have been so closely associated with the diarist, because they were political without being literary. In one sense their presence helps a major theme to emerge that is obscured in the Miller-Nin relationship, namely, the tension or opposition between art and politics. We have seen earlier how psychoanalysis (science) was successfully relegated by Nin to a level in her affairs that was much lower than art, her writing. But the collision between politics and art is not so easily dismissed, chiefly because the intrusion of the political thinking finally could not be resisted in the late 1930s by many people. And so it is Gonzalo, and to a lesser degree Helba, who is assigned the dramatic function of being the vehicle for political solutions to human problems.

When Nin first encountered Gonzalo, the Spanish civil war was imminent. "The Spanish Civil War is in the air. It is as if Gonzalo had come in answer to my question: 'What does it mean, what can I do, as an artist?' " (*Diary*, 2: 86). At parties, Gonzalo, with the withdrawn Helba, a former dancer, conversed with Nin extensively in Spanish. The swarthy Peruvian's low, husky voice awakened what she calls the Spanish in her blood, and her effect upon him was powerful: "Anaïs, what a force you are, spiritual and vital, though you are all wrapped in myths and legends, you are like a whip on me. When I first saw you I felt a shock, you aroused my pride, for the first time I am shedding the fumes of alcohol; I want to *be*, Anaïs" (ibid., 2: 87). He told her of Peru, of his Scottish-Indian background, the Incan culture in which he was reared. He talked "disconnectedly and feverishly, as June did" (ibid.). He and his deaf wife had fallen into poverty; her deafness had cost her her dancing career. He was lost in drinking, but Nin awakened him from his lethargy, he claimed. And he, in turn, imposed his Marxism on her.

The times made it right for Nin to consider politics. She had not been unaware of the political drama going on in Spain but had not taken sides because it all seemed "based on economics, not humanitarianism" (*Diary*, 2: 92), and she did not trust any movement or system. Gonzalo threatened to go to Spain to help with the war effort and talked of sacrifice and dying. Nin could not see it but as a world of death, for art had been her religion, not politics. But it became increasingly difficult for her to see how art could function in a political universe; Gonzalo had, to some extent, been her undoing, as Henry Miller had been several years earlier. "Gonzalo attacks the world I live in. Henry destroyed my bourgeois virtues, Gonzalo my art world" (ibid., 2: 103). But to her, Gonzalo's world of political ideology seemed a deadend both for him personally and for the larger community. And still she could dream, and September 1936 brought one of her dreams to fruition: she moved into a houseboat on the Seine. Through the depiction of Gonzalo and Helba, the reader is persistently drawn into the theme of war, politics, and destruction. The persona of Nin struggles to reconcile the opposing universes. An image of this crumbling universe is represented, in fact, by Gonzalo and Helba themselves, living together in a kind of squalor hitherto foreign to them, living in a "dark, cavelike dwelling" where they sit "like defeated, passive, tragic figures in a Chekhov play" (ibid., 2: 132).

Helba's health was perpetually bad, though her neurosis made it seem worse than it was. Gonzalo was preoccupied with political and economic revolution behind which lay his belief in Marxism as a panacea for injustice and corruption. He felt drawn to the Spanish civil war on principle, but in his own state of weakness of will he resisted going to it. And eventually, if temporarily, the character of Nin could not resist his idealistic portraits and vehement speeches; she became persuaded to his point of view and typed pages of propaganda for Republican Spain. He was allowed to organize political meetings on her houseboat. He was proud to have awakened a kind of political sensitivity in her, and indeed, she recognized his success. It was he who took her to see the desperate poverty of the rag pickers near Paris, but it was she who had made a poem out of them; she wanted to see if she could "make a poem out of an economic revolution" (ibid., 2: 152). But in the deepest sense there was a futility about her becoming seriously engaged in politics, at least in this stage of her life. Although she sympathized and felt very deeply for the hunger and needs of the afflicted, she did not believe that any system would save them. By inclination she was led to reject a Marxist doctrine: "I have fought too much for a spiritually honest and free life to pass from one narrow-mindedness to another, from one dogma into another, from one prejudice into another" (ibid., 2: 274). However, she weakened under the pressure of Gonzalo's urgings and political meetings ensued. Gonzalo's sincerity made her want to believe in his cause; to some extent she shared his view that the life of an artist was a life detached from the realities of living, and that a social and political conscience was necessary to improve the condition of people. She granted some of the argument, but always with reservations. "I have built a rich private world, but I fear I cannot help build the world outside. Deep down, I feel, nothing changes the nature of man. I know too well that man can only change himself psychologically, and that fear and greed make him inhuman, and it is only a change of roles we attain with each revolution, just a change of men in power, that is all. The evil remains. It is guilt, fear, impotence which makes men cruel, and no system will eliminate that" (ibid., 2: 154-55). For all its ideology, however, Gonzalo's approach was superficially anti-intellectual; neurosis, he claimed was for the rich. No one would be neurotic, he asserted, were it not for economic problems that could be solved. Nin's strong faith in psychoanalysis, "the great enemy of Marxism" (ibid., 2: 131), was too powerful for her to reject, even under the pressure of her close relationship with political revolutionaries.

Miller and Gonzalo dominate the volume. Gonzalo's aspirations along with Helba's neurosis and suffering touch Nin. It was a kind of Bohemian life that they lived on the Seine near all the hoboes, in close contact with the Latin American sympathizers of the Spanish, participating in the café life of the artists. Born under the sign of "the giver, Pisces" (*Diary,* 2: 201), she gave at the same time that she pursued her writing. Reflecting on the austere pasts of her friends, she noted that the fewer possessions she had, the richer she felt. But the real difficulties faced by Gonzalo and Miller in their pasts gave her cause to wonder how beneficial poverty actually was. She recognized the pain that necessarily accompanied materialistic scarcities, but she associated spiritual wealth with poverty. She gave up indulging herself and traveling, because

> I have to pay for Henry's rent, Gonzalo's rent, and to feed them all. No rest. No seashore, no travel, no vacation. Voilà. No Heine's beach costume, no mountain air, no sun on the body. But I get pleasure from seeing how my children live. Gonzalo is so good for the present, he is good for life, but that is why he may be of less value in the eternal, in art, than Henry. He is immediate, and that is why he lives in politics. He lives so much in the present that he has the beautiful gift of direct emotion, as a woman has, a beautiful gift of responding with all of himself, as Henry does not. [Ibid.]

Gonzalo was faithful to his cause; Miller was faithful to himself so that he could develop his art and his career as a writer.

It was in many ways a rich life that Nin portrayed during the years 1937 and 1938. Above all, it was an interesting life because she was in touch with interesting people. The episodes revolving around Moricand, Carteret, and Nin's father all give drama and interest to the volume. Special episodes, such as those connected with the maid Albertine or the removal of the houseboat by authorities, later were converted into some of Nin's most effective short stories. As though one were reading a novel, the theme introduced by Gonzalo earlier, the destructive effects of politics, dominates the ending of this volume. As the threat of war builds, disintegration accelerates. "Collective anxiety, panic, rebellion, fear. People packing and running away. People faced with the threat of concentration camps, imprisonment, or bombing. Henry stopped revising *Capricorn*. He became ill at the disruption of his individual life. Black days for the world" (*Diary*, 2: 303). There was no escaping the inevitable confrontation.

> All my actions were concerned with preserving our small world from death.
>
> At the first air raid, I would not hide. I wanted to encounter war and see its burning face. It is at such moments that one becomes fully aware of life, its preciousness.
>
> Before the war, I asserted through art the eternal against the temporal, I set up individual creativity against the decomposition of our historical world.
>
> I had severed my connection with it, but now nothing was left but to recognize my connection with it and to participate humanly in the error. [Ibid., 2: 348]

Nin and her friends fled to various parts of the world: Miller and Durrell to Greece; Nin, Gonzalo and Helba to the United States.

> We all knew we were parting from a pattern of life we would never see again, from friends we might never see again.
>
> I knew it was the end of our romantic life. [Ibid., 2: 349]

Wartime psychology nearly always seems to create significant aberrations when compared with one's way of thinking during the stability of peace. The turmoil of a world reeling with inversions seemed to be one, however, that Nin could accommodate, although she was not invulnerable to its effects. But with the spirit of the Lawrentian flow, she was able to emphasize the living and the continuing, even in September 1939, the month that war was declared. "I see flow and movement. Wherever I see life and growth I follow. All I know is that I am in contact with vital elements. I am not cut off, or lost. I am not sharing with Moricand talk of age, death, the past, the end. Not hiding or escaping. It does not frighten me to have to revise all my values again" (*Diary*, 2: 343–44). This consistent depiction of Nin's persona as one who values creation, expansion, and sympathy of relationships is held steadily before the reader to the end; rigidity and narrowness are consistently rejected. Nin's vision of the artist's transforming the world in some constructive fashion was a view that she clung to and believed in because it seemed a sound basis for beneficent change. The value of the dream is explicit once again.

13

Volume 3, 1939–1944

There is without question a good deal of dovetailing
and interweaving (of both theme and character) in the
first two volumes of the *Diary*. But more re-
markable, perhaps, is the degree of clarity with which each published
volume speaks to the reader, intended, perhaps, to evoke a particular
response through the very selection of materials to be presented to
readers. In volume 1 the new world of art, freedom, and Bohemianism
(Paris style) captivated the young Nin; the convergence of her work on
D. H. Lawrence, the world of Henry Miller, and the initiation into
psychoanalysis provide the foundation for the characterizations. In
volume 2 the woman becomes an artist in her own right, stimulated by
the writings and thoughts of Lawrence, as well as her association with
Miller, Durrell, and Rank. The backdrop of a Europe readying itself for
war introduces a mood of psychological and spiritual desperation, a
disintegrating world in which Nin the writer nonetheless begins to find
her own methods and techniques of fiction writing. Volume 3 seems to
answer the next logical question: How does an avant-garde literary
artist establish contact with an American audience? The war was well
under way, the Paris crowd was dispersed, and Nin found herself back in
a country that was foreign in a number of ways, but particularly
aesthetically. During the years 1939 through 1944, the war itself lies
curiously far in the background, more often than not out of the persona's
consciousness (at least in this published version). Nin presented to an
American readership a fictional technique that seemed singularly

unattractive to commercial American publishers. How she dealt with this problem is one of the chief themes and minor triumphs of these years.

The volume begins with a graphic description of Nin's leaving Paris, Europe, and the Old World behind as she travelled by hydroplane from Portugal to the Western Hemisphere with other refugees. The writer outlined her feelings as she contemplated what she had lost and had left behind, incapable yet of envisioning a future. Exhausted, she arrived in the United States, ill with the flu, according to a physician; but he could not "see the body is empty, the fire is gone, I am a king without a kingdom, an artist without a home, a stranger to luxury, to power, to bigness, to comfort. I lost a world, a small human world of love and friendship. I am no adventurer, I miss my home, familiar streets, those I love and know well" (Diary, 3: 11). This lament is more prophetic than one might at first suspect, for its tone signifies the paradox that Nin sensed (as did Miller) during these years: an America that has a materialistic splendor out of proportion to its psychic emptiness.

One of Nin's first visits was significant: she met with Frances Steloff of the Gotham Book Mart, a champion of the unknown writer for many years, "who played for us the role Sylvia Beach played in Paris" (Diary, 3:11). Nin reestablished herself; she saw her brother Joaquin, who was at that time on the music faculty of Williams College. She met many of the literati who were in New York at the end of 1939: Dorothy Norman; Caresse Crosby; James and Blanche Cooney; Mabel Dodge Luhan; and also other people who attracted her interest such as Robert Duncan, who was then seventeen; and Yves Tanguy, a painter. Miller returned to the United States from Greece, where he had been living after he left France. Rank had died shortly before Nin's return. Gonzalo and Helba had returned by February 1940. The introduction and the setting were established. Like an overture to an opera, the chief themes had been identified and the production began in earnest.

One can perceive a number of recurring motifs that surface in the Diary, and nearly all the themes are interwoven or interconnected; and yet three broad areas receive the most persistent attention and, without damaging the whole, can be separated out and examined. First, there is the consideration of America. The diarist approaches the complex subject from a number of different perspectives and angles, and yet America as a presence is very much a part of the book, just as the advent of World War II had been in volume 2 of the Diary. Nin's perceptions of the American literary scene make up one part of this collage, as does

Henry Miller's contribution (a journey through the nation with his reactions to it) that permeates the *Diary*. Another aspect is represented by the erotica Nin and her friends are writing, a highly symbolic and suggestive writing skill, as though this was the kind of literary energy truly to be valued in this culture. And, finally, lying behind these scenes is the whole splendid and diverse world of New York itself, both unique and in a strange way representative of the country in which it lives. If there is any single unifying symbol in this volume, it is New York City, reflected in its opulence and its decadence, its originality and glitter, from the freedom of the Village to the rhythms of Harlem. These and more are explored and relished by Nin, just as Paris had been during the earlier 1930s in her volumes 1 and 2 of the *Diary*. A second theme or grouping in this *Diary* is Nin's friends, those with whom she shared most of her life and time, or those who were most important in her life: Caresse Crosby, Kenneth Patchen, Luise Rainer, Robert Duncan and Paul (pseudonym), Gonzalo and Helba, and Frances Brown. Finally, as a third theme or motif, is Nin's literary development, her quest to receive recognition in the American literary scene, her methods of pursuing this elusive goal, and the nature of her success in 1944. This quest gives a good deal of order, if not unity, to the entire volume, for the *Diary* itself manifests the very kind of communication and acceptance that Nin was seeking for nearly three decades in the United States; and in describing the quest, she achieves it.

AMERICA, 1939-1944

Plotting out Nin's or rather the persona's response to America of 1940 is no simple matter, for it involves the perceptions of one who was for the second time cast upon these western shores as a refugee, one who was almost by definition an alien because her heart and spirit were elsewhere, and in the most profound sense, whose life was elsewhere. What if the war had not come? Surely the growth and development of the Paris period would have been cultivated and perpetuated. But idle speculation is useless, and it was in the midst of the superficialities, ugliness, and small talk of New York that this diarist found herself. Socially, the only comforts she found were those aspects of the city that recalled Europe to her. Poets, she sensed, were confused; Patchen particularly upset her, but the poets, or poetic personalities she saw around her distressed her because of their prosaic nature. The more the writers (Duncan, Miller, Saroyan, for example) became confused, the less able they were to perform their chief functions, which was not to "preach, seek to convert, philosophize or moralize," but to "reveal magic coincidences and magic possibilities" (*Diary*, 3: 113), to mediate between their vision and their audience rather than to engage in political or practical meddling. "The old communities understood this. Each one had his role allotted to him. The poet to supply his visions, his song, his inspiration (from within) and the others to hunt, fish, build, and the wise men to interpret events, omens, the future. The poet's business is exaltation and how to impart it. I feel the poet is losing this power because he is joining the prosaic, the contingent, the mediocre everyday details, the mechanism" (ibid., 3: 113-114). Anyone who is faintly familiar with Nin's literary principles and the value of D. H. Lawrence to her could have predicted such a response to the contemporary literary scene in the America of 1940. What role had sublimity at that time? Or enthusiasm, even among poets? No wonder, then, that when she seriously began to approach the commercial publishers their reactions were shocking to her. "One of them," she wrote, "called me up after reading *Winter of Artifice* [original text, 1939] and said I was a skillful writer, a fine writer, but could I write for him a novel with a beginning, a middle, and an end? Could I write something like *The Good Earth*?" (ibid., 3: 161). And although she recorded her response as one of laughter, it must have been a bitter laugh. This event, in the fall of 1941, was typical of the new literary reality that had to be faced. The drama was set. An agent says to her, "Put away your European work. It doesn't go here. Read *Collier's, Saturday Evening Post,* see how they do it, and go ahead" (ibid.). The idea was too abhorrent for the diarist to comment on. To Nin's way of thinking, her technique never did partake of the kind of realism or naturalism that seems indigenous to this country. When she was (to anticipate somewhat) able to revise and reprint *Winter of Artifice* (1942) herself, she defined her own vision of her work, as represented in that volume.

> *Winter of Artifice* is the pure essence of the personality, stripped of racial characteristics, time, place, the better to penetrate the innermost being, the deepest self. Description of states: insomnia, obsession, coldness, split. Because I myself was free and beyond nationalism, uprooted, and possessed of an X-ray of the inner life of others, as well as my own. Describe people as composed of climate, elements, race elements, foods they eat, animals they resemble, books they read. As layers, living in past, present or future, in ideas, dreams or daydreaming, absent, or preconscious, conscious, seeing themselves or blind, atrophied or superaware, and then all this must be stripped away in order to reach the subconscious essence which is a

superimposition of all these elements, in a web, a cellular interdependence. [Ibid., p. 247]

Can one seriously imagine the commercial publishers of the 1940s—or even now—warming to such a concept of fiction on behalf of their readers? Even in Joyce one recognizes the literal and the intellectual, although interfused from time to time with the surreal and the psychologically real that language can simulate.

These points may help to establish that the literary scene depicted in the *Diary* was not one receptive to Nin's visionary quality, the psychological and spiritual fusions, the portrayal of the unconscious, that were basic to her art. If an explanation is to be had, one must penetrate far beyond a description of current literary tastes, or even of psychological temperaments (the author's in contrast to that of the larger community's). A sizeable portion of an explanation is found in passages here that recount or react to Henry Miller's journey across America. As deftly presented to the reader as a composer presents a fugue to an audience, this brilliant theme stands out boldly in the pages of this volume as Miller travels on an odyssey in which he intends to collect material for a book for which he had received an advance from Doubleday, only to come up with a manuscript that they find unacceptable. The result, *The Air-Conditioned Nightmare,* is Miller's bizarre and unorthodox product, and many of its moods and sensibilities are reiterated in Nin's pages. This strange country with its varied communities lay before Miller in the fall of 1940 as he began his travels; disappointment is imminent, and at times the book is violent and outraged. "Henry returns from his wanderings. He tells me about America. He reads me sections he has written. He has been looking for something to love. Nature, yes, that was extraordinary. He tells me about the stalactite cave, the wonders of it, and how they placed in it a radio because it was the best place for a receiving station! Henry is not impressed with size, power. He looks for a deeper America. He tells me about the ugly places and the beautiful places" (*Diary*, 3: 55). Nin herself was not impressed with largeness; power was to be felt, but not in mere numbers. Miller, she observed, was angered by what he saw. "I am not angry," she stated, "but I seek desperately for the sensitive and human America. But I feel anger and violence in the air" (ibid.). Traveling to the West, Miller eventually arrived in California. His observations on America, even from Hollywood, are written in delightful Millerese.

> . . . it is only out here that I have begun to get something out of
> America. If I had known I'd have cut a good deal of my itinerary. The good
> and the bad are mixed. You hit all levels here. But the good is good. I am so
> filled up with things to write now. . . . What happens here is that being
> isolated from the rest of the country, being in a favorable climate, the sun,
> water, mountains, life easy and cheap, people broaden out in sympathies,
> become genuinely goodhearted. It can sound cheap and sickly, sentimental,
> or quite noble, according to the person. But just as America is less envious,
> more generous than France, so out here there is a difference between East
> and West—the tendency being to develop the heart and the soul. [Ibid., 3:
> 119]

Nin's reaction was that Americans were busy rejecting Europe; they
borrowed but refused to acknowledge the debt; those in Europe were
grateful for the influences they imbibed, but here she felt "a kind of
shamefaced stealing from the European artists and a quick turnabout to
deny any such influence" (ibid., 3: 120). The realization or perception of
this prejudice (or hostility) was incomprehensible to her: "I cannot
understand when the publisher says that no one will read a novel that
takes place in Europe. There is an atmosphere of separatism. The
foreigner is an outsider. There is no fraternizing. The art patrons invite
all the foreign artists together, as if they should be kept together. I seek
to mingle with American life but I feel a suspicion, a mistrust, an
indifference" (ibid.). But then the persona was not Henry Miller, nor
did she have Miller's immense sense of appreciation, of receptivity, of
delight generally; and so far as the United States is concerned, she was
still too close to her loss of Europe and still too shocked by the altered
literary climate to feel positive about her new circumstances. Miller's
trip, notes, and letters help to exacerbate this condition to some extent,
although she noted and appreciated some of the beautiful parts of his
responses. Miller at his gregarious best received multiple offers of
hospitality from all around the country. Perhaps it is in contrast to his
travels and working that Nin unconsciously sensed she was overwork-
ing and broke down with uncontrollable weeping. To her it seemed
that she was "broken for good, physically and spiritually (ibid., 3: 239).
She had driven herself too far.

Miller found some fascinating acquaintances in his travels through
the United States, but at the same time he was offended by the infernal
quality (worse than Dante, he says) of the stretch from Pittsburgh to
Youngstown; the poverty, filth, ignorance, crime, and a hundred other
evils; the gadgetry and stupidity of materialism at which America, of all

countries, had excelled. And perhaps most unusual of all is that during these years, in an effort to keep ahead financially, Nin, Miller and others, found themselves involved in a literary scheme that lent itself all too readily to a symbolic interpretation: the writing of erotica. It is an activity that is dealt with frequently in this volume, and Nin's participation in the business came about quite by accident. "A private collector offers [Miller] a hundred dollars a month to write erotic stories. It seems like a Dantesque punishment to condemn Henry to write erotica at a dollar a page. Henry rebels, because his mood of the moment is the opposite of Rabelaisian. Because writing to order is a castrating occupation, because to be writing with a voyeur at the keyhole takes all the spontaneity and pleasure out of his fanciful adventures" (*Diary*, 3: 33). A book collector served as the middleman, and because the old and wealthy client insisted on remaining anonymous, the experiment took on added mystery and interest; even after it palled, Miller began to wonder if the wealthy client indeed existed. Planned meetings never took place; a signed copy of one of Miller's books ended up on the book collector's shelf, but with a plausible explanation. Miller later suggested to Nin that she also write something erotic.

> I felt I did not want to give anything genuine, and decided to create a mixture of stories heard, inventions, pretending they were from the diary of a woman.
>   I never met the collector. He was to read my pages and to let me know what he thought.
>   Today I received a telephone call. "It is fine. But leave out the poetry and descriptions of anything but sex. Concentrate on sex."
>   When I gave sensuous or poetic-erotic descriptions, the client would complain, so I began to write tongue-in-cheek, to become outlandish, inventive, and so exaggerated that I thought he would realize I was caricaturing sexuality. But there was no protest. [Ibid., 3: 57-58]

Every morning after breakfast she sat down to write her allotment, and samples of the erotica are provided in the text of the *Diary,* along with the gratified responses of the "old man." In order to meet her own financial needs and those of her friends, she kept the erotica going. Soon many of her friends were submitting copy, and Nin saw herself as "being the madam of this literary, snobbish house of prostitution-writing, from which vulgarity was excluded" (ibid., 3: 151). "I gather poets around me and we all write beautiful erotica," she noted. "As we have to suppress poetry, lyrical flights, and are condemned to focus only on sensuality, we have violent explosions of poetry. Writing erotica becomes a road to sainthood rather than to debauchery" (ibid., 3: 157).

As one suspects, all of this, and especially the good feelings about the erotic composition, was transient. It was demeaning after all, and anyone with even a faint acquaintance with Nin's literary principles as well as her belief in psychological honesty will anticipate her adverse reaction to a kind of composition that was so distant from her fiction of the period, the stories in *Under a Glass Bell* and the revised *Winter of Artifice*. The breaking point occurred when her friend George Barker had to resort to writing erotica to keep himself in drink. She began to think about the old man that they hated and decided to write him, telling him their feelings. "Dear Collector: We hate you. Sex loses all its power and magic when it becomes explicit, mechanical, overdone, when it becomes a mechanistic obsession. It becomes a bore. You have taught us more than anyone I know how wrong it is not to mix it with emotion, hunger, desire, lust, whims, caprices, personal ties, deeper relationships which change its color, flavor, rhythms, intensities" (*Diary*, 3: 177); and she further instructs him that he is shrinking his world of sensations, "withering it, starving it, draining its blood" (ibid.). Given Nin's powerful wish to write and to write well (in her fashion), the energy and time that the erotica took from her fiction writing must have unnerved her. The persona's quest for literary fruition and development must have been subverted by this task, performed, it seems, for money and money alone (and by December 1941 politics and money were all everyone thought about in America, she noted). The picture before us becomes more clear: the converging of these financial needs (the result, erotica), Miller's trip and subsequent depiction (*The Air-Conditioned Nightmare*), the unenthusiastic reception to Nin's writing ("you write skillfully, but could you give us something like *The Good Earth*"?); all these help to portend Nin's literary fate in the United States during the early 1940s. But this, which might be called the context in which she found herself, is only a part of what she had to cope with. Exactly how she did overcome obstacles will be dealt with in the third part of this chapter.

One final aspect of America remains to be examined, and in some ways it was the most important part of Nin's life at this time, insofar as it is related in the *Diary*; it is that great setting, the single unifying symbol of Nin's America, New York City. There was a good deal to like and to detest about the America of the 1940s; "its overwhelming luxury, incredible comforts" (*Diary*, 3: 11) contrasting with the deficits of excessiveness that were at the time probably uniquely American: "No place to sit and talk. You are rushed by the waitress. The radios blare so loudly one is deafened. The lights stun you. Noise and light are amplified until the senses become dulled" (ibid., 3: 34). The harshness of the city contrasted strikingly with the warmth of Paris, and the sterility of the inner life pointed up the superficiality of American life.

But, for all these persisting American weaknesses, Nin found ample rewards in New York life, especially in Harlem and in Greenwich Village. "I danced," she wrote, "until five A.M. at the Savoy Ballroom. I love Harlem. The Savoy is the only genuinely joyous place in New York" (*Diary*, 3: 27). She warmed to the fervor of jazz frequently during these years in the early forties, finding in its world and language a connection with, one may term, the rich and rhythmic possibilities of American life; and on one occasion she told of addressing a friend of hers, " 'If I were American born,' I said, 'I would write the equivalent of jazz' " (ibid., 3: 36). Going to Harlem to drink, talk, and listen to jazz clearly provided Nin the simulated café life of Paris, though perhaps the jazz and its seductiveness made it especially significant for her. One senses a true sensual richness in her descriptions.

> Caresse Crosby came. Canada Lee is starring in *Native Son*. We went to the play together. Then to Harlem, where Canada Lee runs a night club. We talked. Drank. Listened to jazz. Some jazz is flamboyant, some creating tensions not by increased loudness but by the subtlety of its gradations. Some jazz is like velvet, some like silk, some like electric shocks, some like seduction, some like a drug.
>
> How could one not love the people who created such a music, in which the rhythm of the heart and of the body is so human and the voice so warm, emotions so deep. [Ibid., 3: 106]

Nin was consistently attracted by what she saw in blacks. The genuine joys that she experienced in New York at this time were frequently those associated with Harlem, jazz, music, rhythms, and the vitality and humanity of the open, warm blacks.

If there is any single place in New York with which Nin became permanently attached as a place for daily living and not merely occasional excursions, however, it was the Village, representing for her a kind of life closest to her immediate European past. In her words, the Village had character. The old houses, the shops, the parks all had a humanness about them that set them off in a world apart from the garishness of the city. From the first she liked it; later she loved it, and she found it conducive to her work.

> Beautiful autumn days. I love the Village. I love the Italian shops selling homemade spaghetti and fresh cheese, the vegetable carts which sell small fruit, small vegetables, not the tasteless giant ones. Macdougal Street is colorful. The Mews, and Macdougal Alley, with beautiful small houses of another era, cobblestone streets and old street lamps. On Macdougal Street there are night clubs where they play a subtle, low-keyed jazz which occasionally explodes.
>
> I sat on a bench in Washington Square and wrote the story of Artaud, a composite of real fragments from the diary and imaginary conversations. [Diary, 3: 47]

The European sense of leisure brought back a pleasant past but also helped to create a hopeful future, for it was against the backdrop of the Village that Nin perceived "genuine artists and genuine relationships" existing (ibid., 3:134). She allowed that the Village she sensed was not the one that others would necessarily discover, but for her it was the anchor of her life in 1940. It was there that she later set up her own printing press and, with her friend Gonzalo, began to print her own works.

PERSONALITIES

Volume 3 of the Diary lacks the continuity found in the first two volumes chiefly because there is no continuing relationship between Nin and a single set of people in the same way that relationships are described in volumes 1 and 2. Volume 1, focusing on Miller especially but also on June and Allendy, is coherent; volume 2 simulates something of the same with a continuing examination of Miller, but also of Otto Rank, Gonzalo and Helba, Durrell, as well as other friends. Perhaps the most important intrusion into volume 3, and one that makes the work somewhat fragmented, is the prominence of place instead of personality in Nin's consciousness: the shift from Europe to North America is kept in the reader's mind throughout this volume just as Nin found it dominating her own consciousness. The comfort of Paris was gone and she found herself on uneasy terms with America and with Americans. No single continuing group of friends emerged in this volume to help it cohere, yet it is true that there are depicted in these pages a number of valuable relationships. Miller was still important to her, and, indeed, Nin used much of Miller and his responses to this country to frame her own picture of America during these war years. But most of the time these two writers were separated, although they corresponded freely. Some of the people whom Nin found herself engaged with included Caresse Crosby, Kenneth Patchen, Robert Duncan and Paul (pseudonym), Gonzalo and Helba again, Luise Rainer, and Frances Brown, along with many, many others who were New Yorkers as well as visitors to that city. It is, altogether, a graphic depiction of Nin's reentry into the literary culture of New York.

Caresse Crosby commands special attention. She and her husband Harry Crosby had run the Black Sun Press in Paris and knew the important writers of the time. Colorful, "she trail[ed] behind her, like the plume of a peacock, a fabulous legend" (*Diary*, 3: 15). Her connection with D. H. Lawrence especially piqued Nin's interest, it seems, as did Crosby's own magnetism. All life, glitter, and animation, the word *yes* always on her lips, she intrigued Nin. Crosby's home, in Bowling Green, Virginia, had become a kind of center for artists at that time, and Nin's description of a weekend at the home, with the Dalis, Miller, Flo and John Dudley, is a quick glimpse into a surrealistic weekend with surrealists. Crosby was often one of those who went with Nin to Harlem to hear jazz; clearly she was one of Nin's close friends during the early years of the 1940s, possibly because of the Parisian connections both had, and because of her experience with publishing. There was the possibility in 1941 of Crosby's trying to revive the Black Sun Press, but lack of money seems to have prevented her from carrying out her plans until late 1942, though a number of people including Nin, Miller, and Gonzalo helped her with publishing projects. Nin seems to have been in touch during these years a good deal with Crosby, and no doubt the relationship was warm and continuing, but so far as the published *Diary* is concerned, it was not much more than a casual friendship.

Nin's relationship with Kenneth Patchen, the poet, was altogether different. They met through Miller, who admired Patchen's work. Nin was disenchanted from the outset.

> He loomed at my door, large, heavy, pale, and out of his small tight child's mouth a muttering that may have been a greeting. He sat heavy and stony in my small room. His eyes were soft, brilliant, but like those of an animal, with no recognition, no sign of personal focus, merely watchfulness. He saw the papers scattered on the desk, evinced no curiosity or interest. Conversation was arduous. There was an impenetrable wall of sullenness, a desire not to talk. He knew none of the books I knew. He said so little that later I had the greatest difficulty remembering whether he had spoken at all.

> I tried to understand him. I did not share Henry's enthusiasm for his writing. To me it seemed like the mumblings of a prisoner, inarticulate, repeating again and again without hitting the target, a dimly unfocused obsession. [*Diary*, 3:30–31]

When she read some of Patchen's manuscripts, she was reminded of Miller's rebelliousness; she found his work dark and unwholesome. She visited his flat, however, but shortly thereafter she seems to have given up trying to contact him because it was too laborious: "I no longer answered the bell" (ibid., 3: 32). Patchen does not dominate this volume of the *Diary,* but he is a presence whom Nin may have included in the published version because his work and personality seem representative of the spirit of the times. His *Journal of Albion Moonlight* was to her a chaotic piece by a man who was blind to human emotions. The nightmares of war and of the fragmented self that he described she presents as the work of one who can portray violence and destruction, but not birth and creation; his book is full of "groans, cries, but they are all physical, animal. It is a drama of impotence and destruction" (ibid., 3: 63). The three or four pages that she devoted to *Albion Moonlight* contain some of her most sustained descriptive literary criticism of sordid vision in a work of literature.

Patchen, heavy and fleshy, visited her and she gave him some of her notes on his work, but he did not understand them. Visits, lending money, and Robert Duncan's great dedication to him all exacerbated Nin's inability to warm to Patchen; yet, with Duncan, she continued to try to help him, even going so far as to take one of his manuscripts to Maxwell Perkins at Scribners. "In the diary," she wrote, "I may record my coldness towards Patchen, but in life, the absurd code by which I live, I helped him" (*Diary*, 3: 165). Clearly, according to the description of Patchen and Nin's reaction to him, they were never close to appreciating or understanding each other.

Robert Duncan, another poet, was a young man in his early twenties around 1940, and he too is a figure who appears and reappears in the pages of this volume. In some ways his friendship with Nin can stand, unfortunately, as a kind of symbol for the American experience that she encountered during these years: their relationship of warmth and mutual helping deteriorated as Duncan championed Patchen and began to attack Nin's weaknesses. The Duncan–Nin relationship became a "barbaric friendship" that contrasted with the way they all took care of each other in Paris (*Diary*, 3: 187). The past and Paris continually haunt these pages.

Nin first met Duncan, whom she describes as being a beautiful boy of about seventeen, at the house of James and Blanche Cooney in Woodstock, New York. There Duncan read one of his poems, and Nin was introduced to his works and heard how *House of Incest* inspired him. He, too, wrote a diary, and in her published volume Nin includes his portrait of her. She also records her response to his poems. Later, when Duncan found himself with dual allegiances to Nin and Patchen, he pressured her to sacrifice for Patchen and to be responsible for Patchen's welfare. Nin began to form a different picture of Duncan: physically handsome, he spoke as in a trance, but she found his real warmth in his diary.

> By an exchange of diaries we entered each other's private life as we could never have without them, for he goes from me to young men and our love is purely fraternal. He has great charm, seduction. His features are delicate, he has a slender Egyptian body, the shoulders very straight, the waist narrow, the hands stylized.
>   With me he is firm, definite, boyish. He never shows me his feminine side. This I can see only in public, in the presence of men. Then he becomes pliant, undulant, flexible. He deploys coquetries, oblique smiles and oblique phrases. I see the body soften, become woman right under my eyes. [*Diary*, 3: 82-83]

But Nin was hurt when Duncan did not take her side against Patchen, although she perceived that his attachment to him represented a search for violence and fire; a quest for intensity; masculinity, perhaps; and tension. The portrait of Duncan is itself intense and the connection with Patchen gives the passages added drama. Nin's policy of inclusion works admirably with the Duncan-Patchen passages, especially when she presents her view of Patchen and then contrasts the portrait with Duncan's assertion that she has chosen not to understand Patchen. Duncan's feeling of guilt stemmed from his perception that he and she did not have to share Patchen's nightmare. Nin would have none of it: Patchen to her was one who sought to destroy what he did not understand, but Duncan continued to insist that she accept Patchen. "Deep down, I cannot," she wrote, "neither as a writer nor as a human being" (ibid., 3: 90).

Another aspect of Duncan that emerges in the *Diary* is his homosexuality, especially his relationship with Paul (a pseudonym), with whom he masquerades coquettishly. Nin chastised Duncan for his refusal to declare openly his homosexuality in order to avoid military service, thereby striking one blow for honesty of expression (instead of guilt) and another against war. She encouraged him not to withdraw and retreat, but to face real human pain, a necessary ingredient for reaching emotional maturity. Nin was caught in the middle of the love affair of Duncan and Paul, with its series of conflicts and cruelties. Only by reading Duncan's diary could she perceive what his inner life was like, however; outwardly he became more intolerable the more he exploited her. She details her analysis of his psyche, another phase of exploration at which she is adept and which enhances the *Diary*. She traces the decline and cooling of their relationship, all of which is complicated and connected with Paul and Patchen. But the episodes are written interestingly, engagingly even, and as the tension develops in the relationship of Nin and Duncan, the reader becomes a participant in their drama of affection and estrangement. As they withdraw from their friendship, Nin analyzes the movement: Is it the withdrawal that kills the warmth, or was the warmth simply reflected in their friendship? The sense of loss is poignant; the depiction of human beings is very humanly drawn; Nin's principle of simulating one's psychology succeeds well again.

Of other participating characters in the *Diary,* those who deserve notice are Frances Brown, Luise Rainer, and Gonzalo and Helba.

Frances Brown, whom Nin met through the Cooneys, had been a dancer prior to contracting tuberculosis. In the 1940s she was drawing and sculpting, and she seems to have formed an intimate friendship with Nin nearly as soon as they met, talking at length about analysis and dreams. The extended description of Brown's eyes (*Diary*, 3: 207) seems to signify the high degree of sensitivity with which Nin found herself responding to her impact. The opposite of Helba, Brown was gentle and sensitive, one who escaped a childhood of poverty and violence. It seems that Nin shared a sense of the painful childhoods they both experienced and endured, and she pursues the topic at length ("I wanted to know more about her childhood" [ibid., 3: 211]). Tracing the similarities in their lives, they shared the comfort that two human beings can who have been through similar ordeals: "She and I tracked the inception of sorrows where they are truly fashioned, not in events but in our reaction to them, and both of us spent all our energies creating a world according to our own desires and patterns, in disregard of the one the cynical deities had bestowed upon us" (ibid., 3: 213). Constructing, creating, and building, Nin saw herself and Brown engaging in the same general approach to living. It is no surprise that they began to talk about their respective works of literature and a common theme they shared, the development of woman, which, to some extent, appears in all Nin's works. Nin quotes at length scenes from Brown's childhood, which is another device she uses effectively to help characterize an important figure. And Brown continued during these years (and in the pages of the *Diary*) to rise in Nin's estimation, so much so that after being out of town, Nin wrote in Fall 1943, "Return to New York. Activity. Work. Frances the most evolved of women, the most superior, a woman of wisdom, good for the altitudes" (ibid., 3: 293). A fine phrase, that last, and high praise.

Luise Rainer was a different story altogether. Arriving at a dinner given by Dorothy Norman, "Luise Rainer arrived in a long, white, floating dress, her hair floating, her gestures light and graceful, flowing too, a mobile, fluid quality and radiance. Her face expressive, animated, showing as it did in her films a greater sadness than the role called for" (*Diary*, 3: 53). Nin's initial reaction to Rainer was the response of one who sensed that role playing and the need for audience were Rainer's screen personality, but that in real life she was open and vulnerable, that she was authentic, emotional, and authoritarian in a childlike sense; Nin "loved her instantly" (ibid., 3: 54). Several months later, again at Dorothy Norman's, Nin encountered Rainer, who fascinated her with her broad range of gestures, inflections, and behavior. But there was in Rainer's behavior something sinister, a hint of self-destruction, a way of life that was shattering her. As with June, Nin admired Luise Rainer's ability to reveal and express herself instead of being restrained by an innate timidity.

Much of the *Diary* is given to Rainer's unsatisfactory marriage to Clifford Odets, the playwright. Moving quickly from romance to disaster in their marriage, Nin recounts the destructive relationship in some detail, not, we feel, through any sense of sordidness, but out of sympathy for another person, someone whom Nin admired, who was severely wounded in life. More and more, however, Nin perceived a conflict in Rainer's own life, a conflict between the "woman and the actress" (*Diary*, 3: 138). Rainer rebelled against accepting roles when she was with Odets; and when she did act, she often tried to extend herself and her own personality, rather than become the character she was portraying. Some of the passages dealing with Rainer show Nin perhaps at her most wise and sensitive, with impressive psychological insight; that she should concentrate on an actress when discussing role playing is typical of her, and successful. Probably Rainer helped to inspire many of the details that Nin attached to Stella in *Winter of Artifice*. Many aspects of Rainer's life and her conception of herself support this contention, for in real life she was jealous of her screen image, with the screen version being more attractive, seductive, and enchanting than her perception of herself. Her problem was that she wanted to be liked and admired for what she really was, not for appearances. Nin tried to help her, to reassure her, to restore her self-confidence, and to rescue her from neurosis, which was no easy task. And eventually it became an overwhelming enterprise; Nin grew weary of helping the afflicted—Duncan, Patchen, Rainer—and she stayed away from her at times. When Rainer read earlier portions of the journal, she sided with June, then against June, in order to arrive at a sense of her own value vis-à-vis Nin. It was difficult: "I can no longer defend myself against the egotists," notes Nin (ibid., 3: 163); and one gets the sense not that Nin was trying to be the cure-all for those who needed help, but that she sensed in herself, her interests, her intuitions, and her training insight that could be helpful and constructive in the lives of others. Rather than being a meddler, she was a healer, but she could not succeed every time. Conflict with others eventually wore upon her and she could not sustain conflict with them perpetually. "A spiritual punching bag. All this might perhaps be good for Luise but where will I find the strength and the objectivity to play this game? I see my last image of Luise, standing at the top of her stairway, taut, stretching her little figure, made taller by anger, indicating that she is the biggest one of the three, shouting: 'Now write a book in which I, Luise, am both you and June. A different book' " (ibid., 3: 164-165).

The appearance of Gonzalo and Helba in this volume of the *Diary* takes a much different form from what it had in volume 2, and indeed life with them in the United States was undoubtedly strikingly different from what it had been in Europe. For the most part, the role of Helba in this volume (if not in Nin's life in the 1940s) is much diminished; when she appears at all it is usually in her role either as one who was creating obstacles in the lives of those around her (chiefly Nin and Gonzalo), or as someone who was in dire need of help, medicine, money, and food. Hysteria and wild scenes became routine, it seems; her illness, which served as "her strongest weapon against others" (*Diary*, 3: 207), was diagnosed as being pathological and hysterical.

Gonzalo and particularly his childhood memories and his Indian heritage from Peru continued to be an object of great interest to Nin. She carefully noted his political and Marxist inclinations, perhaps because his ideas and arguments were not persuasive for her, though they remained a preoccupation with him. Because Nin's humaneness necessarily made her sympathize with oppressed groups and suffering individuals, it is understandable that he would continue to try to politicize her; but in turn she saw him as overlooking the suffering of those close to him, wanting to be helpful only by solving global problems: "For Gonzalo the solution to all problems lies outside. I go to the other extreme and blame myself for everything and never consider myself a victim of anything but my own weaknesses, my own flaws" (*Diary*, 3: 69). His lack of sympathy toward neurosis and psychology contrasted, of course, with hers. And although he had a great gift of humaneness himself, it was confounded by a high degree of unreliability and irresponsibility. Nin recognized his potential, tried to bring him out of his dark moods, and as an additional benefit, found him to be a rich and interesting source of erotic stories to send to their patron. But because he could not discipline himself, Gonzalo was unable to do any effective political work, his guilt increased, and together he and Nin walked the streets trying to find employment for him. As it turns out, the chief work he was to do, and to do well, was with Nin herself, helping her to print and publish her own writing.

THE LITERARY ACHIEVEMENT, 1939–1944

When Nin returned to the United States in the winter of 1939, she had accumulated some years of successful writing and publishing. Not only had she published the D. H. Lawrence volume with Titus in 1932, but with the Miller-Durrell-Fraenkel enterprise, *The House of Incest* had been published by their own Siana Editions. Additionally there was *The Winter of Artifice,* published in Paris by the Obelisk Press in 1939 and partially destroyed in the war. But also she was publishing shorter pieces of fiction in small journals. Consequently, when she came to the States in 1939, two important incidents took place that were to shape, to a large extent, her mode of publication during the early 1940s. First, as we can tell from the *Diary,* she spent a considerable amount of time assessing the contemporary American landscape. The prospect, to say the least, was not encouraging for her, for at the same time she was assessing her own possible participation in American literature. Probably she was too optimistic and too hopeful; or to put it another way, she underestimated the extent to which her own work would be an aberration from the norm of the American literary scene. This dual assessment, of the work of her contemporaries and of herself, led to the second significant occurrence: with the help of Gonzalo, jobless anyway, she began to print, publish, and distribute her own works. The publication of their second work, *Under a Glass Bell*, finally brought Nin some of the national recognition for which she had been hoping and which she thought she deserved. It is with the publication of that work in 1944, and Edmund Wilson's favorable review in the *New Yorker*, that volume 3 of the *Diary* closes.

The confusion in American writers of the time carried over, she maintained, into their tendency to philosophize and teach rather than to excite by contagion and with vision. We have seen that so long as Nin wrote even vaguely like the "European" surrealists, she was doomed; concrete, realistic details were more in vogue, and one need only to consult the current fiction in *Collier's* and *The Saturday Evening Post* to corroborate the tastes of the times. When Nin tried to present *The Winter of Artifice* to American publishers, the truth is that she had a considerably better chance of having some of it published than she did any of *The House of Incest*, which would have been (and perhaps still is) too obscure to be part of any popular fiction in the United States. Nin began revising *The Winter of Artifice* in the fall of 1941. Her literary agents praised her work, two hopefuls wanted to publish her, but she noted they were "dreamers," and whatever money they had was lost in a book of poems by Patchen that did not sell. Caresse Crosby, it may be remembered, also wanted to reenter publishing but could not get sufficient backing. Nin despaired: "There is no protection for the writer. Anyone can come and say he will publish it, keep it in a drawer for a year, and then return it" (*Diary*, 3: 175). But she continued to have faith in the book, as indeed she had had in her work all along. She began to understand, however, that those whom she was dealing with were not so much interested in the inner drama of her characters as in the realistic trappings of everyday detail. It was a battle she had had to wage time and time again, and even in reviews of the *Diary*, similar criticisms surfaced. "But people," she observed, "still want the old-fashioned stuffing, every door opened and closed, every window opened and closed, every bell rung, every telephone call registered, as in Dreiser, who mentioned the rent paid by each character. I used a roller to squeeze out all superfluous matter. It is compressed, condensed, a meal for modern tempo, even for parachute jumpers!" (ibid., 3: 176). Well, yes and no. As we shall see in *The Novel of the Future*, she was attuned to a mode of presenting psychological realism; but in 1940, James Joyce notwithstanding, the American reading public was still more in the mood for the so-called realistic moderns, such as Dreiser, Hemingway, and Wolfe.

Irony builds upon irony in the *Diary*. How to murder a writer? She advised, after he writes a spontaneous book, and is sent for, he is then asked to write something to order, something similar to the last best seller, such as *The Good Earth*. If that fails, she asserted, he can be led off course with large sums of money. (So far as we know this did not happen to Nin.) She perceived that she was revealing more than her contemporaries wanted revealed in fiction, so that when she cast light upon the human condition with sensitivity, this thrust was counter to the modern tendency that denigrated sensitivity in a culture that had become "calloused by harshness." She pursued her work, first revising *The Winter of Artifice* for publication, tightening and polishing it. To her way of thinking, the revised version represented "the pure essence of the personality, stripped of racial characteristics, time, place, the better to penetrate the innermost being, the deepest self" (*Diary*, 3: 247). She might have expected that the response to it, in the greater world, would be either criticism or silence, as it continues to be with radical innovations.

Dedicated to her vision, she did not slacken in persisting to perfect her fiction techniques, trying to fuse the physical and the spiritual, the conscious and the unconscious. She studied Giraudoux, and her "three gods of the deep: Dostoevsky (instinct-unconscious), Lawrence (instinct-unconscious), Proust (unconscious-analysis)" (ibid., 3: 256).

Determined to enrich her fiction, to base her work on other characters, she began with dreams and their relation to the lives of people she knew, integrating their psyches with their lives. But even when she determined more and more on the proper course for her fiction, there remained the problem of publication.

She states that in September 1941 her works were in demand but were all out of print (which is technically true), and with the war, no doubt few copies of her first three books were available in the United States at that time. She stayed closely in touch with Frances Steloff and with others connected with the Gotham Book Mart, however. Clearly that shop would serve as a useful outlet if she could find some way of having her works printed.

Nin's practical experience with printing seems to have been limited to those years in Paris when Siana Editions were being printed, but the "only work [Gonzalo] responded to was printing, because he had been associated with that on his brother's newspaper in Lima. He loved first editions, fine printing, and everything connected with it" (*Diary*, 3: 179). But apparently his real experience was limited, even if his enthusiasm was not. When they came upon a second-hand treadle-press for sale, they borrowed money from Frances Steloff and Thurema Sokol, rented a top-floor studio at 144 MacDougal Street, bought good paper and type, borrowed a book from the library on printing, and off they went, starting with *Winter of Artifice* in January 1942. The press was a challenge and they learned through experimentation. In addition to setting type, they decided to use line engravings by Ian Hugo. They learned by themselves though James Cooney stopped by and gave them useful advice. Soon the operation was functioning and Nin clearly was gratified at the physical success of being able to produce her own work in a pleasing format. They were able to print two pages a day, increasing their output, until the book was completed on 5 May 1942; then off to the bindery, where they encountered objections because the book was of a nonstandard size. Finally, by 15 May it was delivered, bound and ready to sell. The Gotham Book Mart had a party, and the "book created a sensation by its beauty" (ibid., 3: 196). James Laughlin offered her a review of it in *New Directions*; she chose William Carlos Williams to review it, but it was, she noted later, an "unwise choice" because of his misunderstanding of her work (ibid.). Paul Rosenfeld wrote a review that she considered to be "totally inaccurate" (ibid., 3: 204); Williams evinced antagonism; Harvey Breit would have reviewed it in the *New Republic*, had his editor let him. "Complete silence from the New York *Times*, the *Tribune*. My underground success continues from person to person, fervent, secretly and quietly." And, she noted with some weariness, "I thought the press would solve our economic problems" (ibid., 3: 205), which of course it did not. The failure was a commercial one, she felt, not a literary one.

The rent at the press studio began to be overdue, and in time, about a year after the publication of *Winter of Artifice,* Gonzalo designed "a beautiful book for *Under a Glass Bell*," a collection of short stories. By October they were printing the first page; subscriptions began to come in and they could see their way to print 300 copies. "Reached page sixty-four. Joy at achievement and a certainty that the stories are poetically valuable" (*Diary*, 3: 303), she noted in January 1944. And, with obvious pleasure, she recorded the enthusiastic responses to the stories and to the printed book, highlighted by Edmund Wilson in an important *New Yorker* review, where he alluded to them as "half short stories, half dreams, [mixing] a sometimes exquisite poetry with a homely realistic observation." And he concluded, "But perhaps the main thing to say is that Miss Nin is a very good artist, as perhaps none of the literary Surrealists is. 'The Mouse,' 'Under a Glass Bell,' 'Rag Time,' and 'Birth' are really beautiful little pieces" (ibid., 3: 310-11).

The three pages in volume 3 that follow the quotation of Wilson's review are a kind of epilogue of delight; all sorts of interesting benefits, rewards, and attentions were showered upon Nin; but, looking ahead, she knew that she had a number of supporters who would continue to need her own support. An immense satisfaction accrued after the favorable notice in the *New Yorker*; she had more than a good chance now at pursuing her fiction and being published. "Close the door and window upon the world for a moment," she concluded, "turn to the diary for all its musical notations, and begin another novel" (*Diary*, 3: 314).

14

Volume 4, 1944–1947

The fourth volume of the *Diary* was published in
1971, long enough for the first three volumes to have
achieved considerable popularity and also long enough
to give attentive readers the chance to form a kind of perspective
regarding the relative quality of individual volumes. Probably the first
volume is the strongest: it has unity, coherence, drama, and intensity
that subsequent volumes lack. The extended passages dealing with
Miller and June, and with Nin's initiation into psychoanalysis, provide
the reader with an examination in depth of Nin's persona functioning in
a single ongoing experience. Nowhere in later volumes is her
experience with a person or a pursuit sustained the way it is in volume 1.
Volume 4 is a good case in point. The shortest of all volumes published to
date, it concentrates on a number of interrelated themes, but compared
with volume 1, the fourth is diffuse and fragmented. This is not to say
that it is weak or uninteresting; some of Nin's finest and most poignant
observations about life and literature occur in this volume. But as a
whole it lacks the tight, consistent focus that is provided especially well
in volume 1.

A number of familiar themes reappear in this selection from the
original diary, a grouping (usually month by month) of associated
material from manuscript volumes 68 to 74.[1] Henry Miller and Gonzalo
return, although in this volume they are in the process of vanishing from
Nin's life. Her literary life—printing, writing her fiction—receives
some fascinating attention. Her gravitation toward the young and her

disappointment in the "mature" is dealt with in some detail. A number of minor figures are introduced who are only occasionally interesting. It was, as always, a time for substantial changes in Nin's life as it was in American life; World War II lies in the background, indeed, so far in the background as to be ignored, apart from Nin's noting crucial events in the war's conclusion or in the lives of those who must go off to it; but it does not dominate this volume in the way the Spanish civil war did volume 2. One important and pronounced theme in this volume is the continuing restatement of her values, of how to live. This strong sense of humanism in her *Diary* has made the work consistently attractive to many readers; the clear articulation of her vision of how life may be lived gives, perhaps, more value to volume 4 than any other single theme, although many will find her discussion of fictional techniques to be valuable. It was during these years that Nin was first able to begin publishing her novels commercially with Dutton; the tales of her continuing disagreements with publishers' tastes are integrated well with her steady development of her craft.

"How to Live"

The phrase "how to live" is from Matthew Arnold. In his essay on Wordsworth, published as a preface to Wordsworth's poems in 1879, Arnold wrote this significant critical observation: "It is important, therefore, to hold fast to this: that poetry is at bottom a criticism of life; that the greatness of a poet lies in his powerful and beautiful application of ideas to life—to the question: How to live."[2] Without question Nin's *Diary* may be seen to be analogous with Arnold's view, and time and time again she reiterates the value of humaneness, sympathy, and harmony.[3]

According to Miller, Nin may have had self-doubts frequently (*Diary,* 4: 7), but consistently she seems to have had a firm view of her strengths and her sense of integration: "My only strength is the strength of wholeness, of total feeling" (ibid., 4: 19), she wrote in June 1944, resisting being an unreal idealized figure. She had a mission—many missions, perhaps—that were connected with her past and with her craft of fiction writing. She wanted to help resolve the conflicts of women in the 1940s and states that this "will become in the end the predominant theme of the novel: the effort of woman to find her own psychology, and her own significance, in contradiction to man-made psychology and interpretation" (ibid., 4: 25). She saw herself as one evolving and changing, not hoarding and ceasing to grow. From the beginning of her literary career, growth and change were positive values for Nin, ones that were probably absorbed from D. H. Lawrence. She tended not so much to be didactic as she was willing to establish herself and her values as an example for others. Her life became in 1945 one in which she was integrating her ideas of fiction with psychology; she understood the usefulness of focusing attention on the inner life and no doubt intended to pursue it more, even if certain friends were trying to develop the "realist" in her. And with some pleasure, she noted that the great beauty of her life was that she lived "out what others only dream about, talk about, analyze. I want to go on living the uncensored dream, the free unconscious" (ibid., 4: 62). Specifically it is not possible to understand to what she is alluding; but generally she has in mind her capitalizing upon the intuition as a guide for her life, leading to future possibilities and potentialities. Surely this is one of her chief precepts of how to live.

She was aware that her intuitions carried risks, that they were perhaps illusions, and that, at any rate, they could not be proved to anyone else. But she saw that both were necessary: "To live passionately and blindly, to take risks; and then to interpret later, in order to rescue one's self from disaster if it turns out to be an illusion rather than a creative intuition" (Diary, 4: 70). What she never did was to settle for the safe and secure route in life; always she was involved in a quest to understand the psyche in order to free and liberate people from their neuroses and their limitations. Her connection with symbolism developed in this way, for she felt that there "is a connection between what takes place within us and what takes place outside" (ibid., 4: 71).

In the Diary one can see clearly how much she reacted against the dull, the prosaic, and the unimaginative. This partly explains why there are so many colorful persons described in the published Diary. Many of the others, she claimed, she would not name, though she met them everywhere: dull, down-to-earth, plain, "one-dimensional" men, "always talking of politics, never for one moment in the world of music or pleasure, never free of the weight of daily problems, never joyous, never elated, made of either concrete and steel or like work horses, indifferent to their bodies, obsessed with power" (Diary, 4: 81–82). Little wonder then that she was attracted so strongly to Miller and to other men who had the spirit of life in them. Politics and polemics remained for Nin fruitless parts of life in which she had no wish to participate: she saw them either as destructive or useless; she asserted that argument and struggles were of no interest to her, being antithetical to her makeup. "I seek harmony," she wrote. "If it is not there, I move away" (ibid., 4: 91). She seeks in life what ought to be, not what is: ideas, "experiences, and ideals reflected yet distorted by dreams. Also created by dreams." But in between, she noted, "an all-consuming loneliness" (ibid., 4: 124).

One can understand, then, that increasingly she saw her life and her writing as inseparable, as part of the same experience, integrated through her imagination. The qualities she valued in life were those that she championed or described in the fiction and in the diary. The mode was different, for fiction contained endings, or something like an ending; the diary and life do not.

For Nin the secret of a full life was to live intensely and passionately, as though there might be no tomorrow; the advantage of this inclination, she noted, is that one not only makes the most of every minute, but the vice procrastination is avoided, along with "the sin of postponement, failed communications, failed communions."

> This thought has made me more and more attentive to all encounters, meetings, introductions, which might contain the seed of depth that might be carelessly overlooked. This feeling has become a rarity, and rarer every day now that we have reached a hastier and more superficial rhythm, now that we believe we are in touch with a greater amount of people, more people, more countries. This is the illusion which might cheat us of being in touch deeply with the one breathing next to us. The dangerous time when mechanical voices, radios, telephones, take the place of human intimacies, and the concept of being in touch with millions brings a greater and greater poverty in intimacy and human vision. [*Diary*, 4: 148-49]

The humaneness, authenticity, and deep sincerity of these words ring out. This is Nin at her best and her most engaging, we find. Her words are constructive and are of a kind to encourage constructive relationships, not dehumanized callousness. Lynn Sukenick has written that Nin's gentleness and sympathy are crucial to all of her relationships and that the "most remarkable thing about Nin is how she revives the wisdom of sympathy in an age which tends to be embarrassed by it."[4] The "importance of sympathy and aspiration," as Sukenick terms it, could well stand as a credo for Nin and her answer to the question, How to live?

CHANGES AND DEVELOPMENTS, 1944-1947

There were important changes in Nin's life, many of which were enumerated in the pages of this volume of the *Diary*. But in the context of her life, as it is revealed to us in the first four volumes, a few noteworthy occurrences need to be described, namely, her changing relationships with Henry Miller and with Gonzalo, the initiation of Nin's commercial publishing with Dutton, the beginning of her public lectures, and her journey to the West and to Mexico. Each one of these constituted an important alteration in her life, and the effects of some of them were of dramatic significance.

We have noticed already that Miller's description of Nin bore no resemblance to reality. But she began to sense a different Miller from the one she had known so well in the life of Paris in the 1930s; and Miller was at this time thousands of miles away from Greenwich Village, just making his home in Big Sur, where he was to remain for some years. Rather than writing to her in his characteristic style of liveliness and enthusiasm, he was writing her letters "burdened with guilt, talk of atonement" (*Diary*, 4: 4), she indicated. His endless capacity for receiving and enjoying seemed somewhat diminished. His letters sounded sad to Nin, though Miller was beginning to reap some of the financial support he had been seeking for years. Apparently he dissatisfied his patron, however, and funds were cut off. Nin chastised him for giving away what the patron had meant for him to keep. "Is it guilt," she asked, "that makes you unable to receive? But why do you give always to the wrong person? Futile words. We have discussed this often enough" (ibid., 4: 21). Nin and Miller seemed to feel hesitant about seeing each other, even when he made trips back to the East. Nin suspected some guilt on his part in having overburdened her in the past; she observed that he had not been able to face situations like this openly. "I would have been glad to see him. But perhaps this separation was good for both of us, and we did not want to witness or stress the finality of it," she noted in October 1944 (ibid., 4: 31). Later, when Nin made a car trip to California, she saw Miller with his new wife, Janina Lepska, and noted tension between them. He was embarrassed. The atmosphere was not relaxed and Nin and her companion did not stay. "I should not have visited Miller. As soon as one ceases to know a person intimately, the knowledge of them is from the outside, as if you stood at a window looking in. From this day on I would see Henry from the outside, in that sense which I call not knowing. Through others' eyes, through his writing, or through his wife. Other Henrys. Knowledge is intimacy. Intimacy takes trust and faith. That was over" (ibid., 4: 220). For those whose initial attachment to the *Diary* came at least in part through the introduction of Miller and June, there is some regret to be felt at the estrangement. The truth of human relationships is simulated, however, and in a literary memoir a reader could have expected nothing except changes and developments, including the changing attitudes of friends toward each other.

So it is with Gonzalo, Nin's friend from Paris who played an important part in her life during the late 1930s. Her chief printer and helper, Gonzalo aided her in bringing out her own books during the early 1940s, and the press was given a name made up of a combination of his first initial G and his last name, More—GEMOR Press. Volume 3, it will be recalled, closes with the successful publication of *Under a Glass Bell*, printed by Nin and Gonzalo, the book that received praise in the *New Yorker* from Edmund Wilson. Volume 4 opens in April 1944 with the notation that the first edition of the volume had sold out in three weeks' time. Nin was about to make plans for a reprinting. In fact, a great deal of Nin's day-to-day living during the period from 1944 through 1947 was spent working with the press, printing her own works or works of others, often with specially designed engravings and illustrations by Ian Hugo and others in their coterie. Gonzalo was very proud of the work, as was Nin. Having discovered skills and gifts, he seemed to mature and become responsible. But just as Miller's gaiety seemed to have been diminished, so was Gonzalo's. Together Nin and Gonzalo worked to try to make the press a financial success, an endeavor made all the more difficult when they refused to pay protection money for their shop (an incident that ends happily). But Gonzalo's irresponsibility and poor business judgment continued. Nin began to have doubts more than ever about it being worthwhile to continue with him, and she began seriously to believe that the press might fail. Early in the *Diary* one can see that the groundwork for the break between them has been laid. Eventually Nin tried to persuade him to return to Peru where an inheritance was waiting for him, but because his wife Helba would not go, Gonzalo remained in the United States. He felt he would be regarded as a failure by his highly successful family. Nin assured him that this would not be the case, and that he was not a failure. "I did not want to say: 'You have destroyed everything, the press, my devotion, my faith.' But suddenly I let out a strange, strangled sob at the devastation they had achieved. Gonzalo looked blind and mystified"

(*Diary*, 4: 173). He did not follow up on possible jobs, and eventually Nin had to supply them with money to keep them from starvation. In time he did find part-time work and small jobs to do; he is not heard from again, however, in this volume of the *Diary*.

One of Nin's dreams came true during these years: after struggling with her own press, printing her own works, she was able to have a novel, *Ladders to Fire,* accepted and published by Dutton in 1946. Having published a number of works in this country such as *Winter of Artifice* (1942), *Under a Glass Bell* (1944), *This Hunger* (1945), and others on her own press; and having contributed to various small journals, she began (she indicates) to be approached by commercial publishers in November 1945. Random House, Harper, and Viking all contacted her. And fortuitously she made the acquaintance of the youngest editor at Dutton, Gore Vidal, who was then twenty years old. By December she had a contract and a cash advance from Dutton. It was the beginning of a most curious publishing career for Nin, for her novels were never commercial successes until after the *Diary* was published. But it was a milestone in her life for her to receive recognition from publishers and in a sense to be admitted into the fellowship of American novelists. Nin was able to break into the commercial market on the one hand but refused to imitate what she (and the publishers) perceived to be the kind of so-called realistic writing that the reading public seemed to be willing to purchase. It was a mixed victory that she earned; none of her books went into a second edition in America until Alan Swallow reprinted her novels in the early 1960s. In 1947 Dutton brought out her second novel, *Children of the Albatross.*

Nin must have given hundreds of lectures in her lifetime, but she notes in 1945 that she had a considerable fear of facing an audience. She overcame this fear when she agreed to appear at a poetry reading at the Young Men's Hebrew Association in November 1945, just at the time when commercial publishers were pursuing her. Symbolically, it was a kind of birthday for her. She read a short lecture and a passage from *This Hunger* and also read "Ragtime." The applause was "warm and spontaneous" (*Diary*, 4: 96); she was asked to sign books; she was elated to have mastered her fear, although she wondered whether she was going to be accepted or not. "Last night I took this chance and won" (ibid.). Soon after she lectured at Mills College in New York.

By June 1946, she was making notes for a lecture tour, stressing the theme of relationship and the exploration of all the varieties of relationships for human beings. Concentrating again upon intuition and its benefits, she decided to explore and capitalize upon what she saw as a "feminine concept" (*Diary*, 4: 150), the language of emotion instead of that of the intellect, emphasizing free association, spontaneity, and improvisation. In December she began her lecture tour: Harvard (where two hundred people crowded into a room designed to hold fifty). Nin was impressed with the absolutely quiet attention she received. Then Dartmouth, Goddard, Amherst. Subsequent readings followed, most frequently at colleges and universities.

The other event we should like to explore briefly is Nin's trip to the great West of the United States. The idea seems to have occurred to her in May 1947, when a young man from the West suggested to her that New York City was not representative of the United States. Understandably, Miller's book, *The Air-Conditioned Nightmare,* had not given her any impetus to explore the country. Thinking that she might combine a Western trip with a journey to Mexico, she made plans to leave New York. And so, in the summer of 1947, in a Ford Model A, with the top down (nicely illustrated in the book), she headed toward the West with a friend destined for Las Vegas and a divorce. The itinerary is predictable: through the Smokies, the Shenandoah Valley, the Carolinas, Georgia, Alabama, New Orleans, Arkansas, Oklahoma, Santa Fe; and then for some reason north to Denver and Boulder, over to Utah, Arizona, Las Vegas, and Los Angeles. A number of friends were visited on the way: Weeks Hall in New Orleans, Frieda Lawrence in Taos, Lloyd Wright (son of his more famous father, Frank Lloyd Wright) in Los Angeles. She visited Henry Miller at Big Sur; Jean Varda in Monterey; and George Leite, the publisher of *Circle,* in Berkeley. The result of the trip, Nin points out, was of some importance: "If I had not traveled West I might not have wanted to become a permanent resident [of the United States]" (*Diary*, 4: 222).

She traveled on during this summer to Mexico City and Acapulco, where she met Doctor Hernandez, a person who seems to have captivated her immediately. Remembering that the definition of *tropic* is "turning," she sensed that a new woman would be born on this journey to Mexico. And so the fourth volume concludes.

WRITING FICTION

Nin repeats time and time again that her writing and her life are not separable, that they were both part of the same experience. And during these years her writing was more important to her than ever: she was beginning to make the plunge, in plain view, into the highly visible world of the commercially published novelist. But to do this she had to order her fiction in a new and different way, not to satisfy a publisher, but to satisfy her own ideological and critical ideas of what she wanted her novels to reveal. She knew from good friends (who could be good critics) that her fiction lacked not only conventional realism, but also warmth and humanity, something that got lost in the "metamorphosis into myth, or fiction" (*Diary*, 4: 17). Nin admitted that she got lost in the labyrinth of the diary; she wanted themes found there to emerge in the fiction, however, and particularly wanted to articulate the theme of the woman's "role in the reconstruction of the world" (ibid., 4: 25). In order to manifest this depiction, Nin determined to characterize women in their multiple roles: the masculine and objective woman; the child woman; the maternal woman; the sensation-seeking woman; the cold, egotistical woman; and the healing, intuitive "guide-woman" (ibid.). The evolution, noted Nin, would be from subjectivity and neurosis to objectivity, expansion, and fulfillment. Although the function of the dream is not noted by Nin, one who is familiar with the earlier fiction can see that through subjectivity she may have meant the limitations of the ego, or even of the dream, should it be pursued exclusively. For Nin the dream, if lived out, provided life more abundantly; but the dream could also become a tragic trap. To live within the dream and *not* to bring it into reality, Nin often suggests, would lead to disaster.

Nin began to try fictional techniques that were new to her; she found that she could not make a synthesis of characters she knew but had to associate freely to construct the "underground life" (*Diary*, 4: 28) of the character she was describing. Working on *This Hunger,* she constructed interior portraits of her chief characters and then began to move outward. She sensed the possibility of the mirror as an image that would clarify her meaning. She worked at creating characters, noting the merging of literalness, fictionalization, and her own contributions, feelings, and thoughts; composites were developed. Aware of her inadequacies, she was "guided only by a vision of character infinite in depth and change, in timelessness, and in space" (ibid., 4: 36). Her descriptions of days of writing portray her working at spontaneous creations, freely associating and delving into the unconscious life of emotions, instincts, and dreams. It was, she recalled, as if she "were writing about the night life of woman and it became all one" (ibid., 4:

39); at the subconscious level all were the same. She sensed a new kind of reality and found her creative capabilities to be at their height. She concentrated on what she termed her sixth sense better to find sensations and divinations. Even in writing about her writing one senses her delight and enthusiasm, and perhaps her wonder at her own creativeness. She acknowledged that we play a persona role in the world, and she may have determined to define the persona of each of her characters. It is up to the reader, of course, to define the persona of Nin in each of the *Diaries,* and the attentive reader may find that there are shifts in each *Diary* presented to the public, just as there are shifts in the protagonists of different novels.

To some extent Frances Brown was a speaker for the reading establishment, perpetually urging Nin to be more of a realist. Nin uses the urgings as a podium for her own beliefs (though not in a negative or defensive way): what she leaves out (the so-called realistic details) weighs down her characters like too much upholstery. Nin opted for the inner voyage; indeed, she believed that the America of 1947 suffered from too much realism, too much "Dreiserism, too many Hemingways and Thomas Wolfes" (*Diary*, 4: 66). In order to please Frances Brown, Nin read T. S. Eliot, but she resisted his Puritanism and found him *"déséchant"* (ibid.). True to herself and to her Lawrentian ideals, she felt the "prime morality of literature" to be to teach people "how to live [echoes of Matthew Arnold], expand physically and mentally, how to experience, see, hear, feel, and give birth simultaneously to the soul and the body" (ibid., 4: 66-67).

Ambivalence intruded during the composition of *Ladders to Fire*; Nin rebelled against it even while she was writing it. She sensed that the composite characters were false, which, of course, they were, because they were depictions of exaggerated tendencies in her female characters: Sabina, the passionate woman; Lillian, the inhibited woman of instinct; Djuna, the woman of the psyche; Hejda, "the woman of oriental obliqueness and new freedom; Stella, the actress living by osmosis" (*Diary*, 4: 70). Frances Brown was won over, allowing that Nin created truth in the end, not fantasy; that is, Brown allowed the existence of the very kind of simulated psychological reality that Nin aimed for (and which she champions so enthusiastically in *The Novel of the Future*). "You discard realism," Brown observed, "but not reality" (ibid.).

Nin discusses her fictional techniques at some length in this volume of the *Diary*, and perhaps because it was written during a time of intense literary productivity it contains observations on technique that are as lucid as some of her critical work. She contrasts fiction writing with diary writing, noting the possibilities for other art forms in fiction (such as the ballet in "Bread and the Wafer"). When composing the party scene in *Ladders*, she found a new way to deal with "neurotic vision" and "fused symbols and externals. I was inspired by the dance style of Martha Graham. The placing of the characters, the symbolic enacting, the suggestiveness" (*Diary*, 4: 120). It was at this time that Nin found many aspects of the other arts such as dance, painting, modern music, sculpture, and dress design suggesting literary techniques to her. She resisted telling the simple tales (à la Steinbeck) of a world immersed in physical pain, hunger, and poverty; the inner world of neuroses and symbolic dramas make up the reality that Nin wanted to portray; she may be forgiven for believing that the way of Steinbeck is easier and simpler; they both had their tales to tell, and she was led by her associates and her interest to explore the psychological realms rather than the Gabilan Mountains. Nin's defense is that a sick and maladjusted world cannot feel the poverty and pain in others if the neurosis and self-centeredness are left unattended; hence her devotion to her particular form of revelation.

A short section of six pages headed "June, 1946" (*Diary*, 4: 150–55) contains as concise and yet as full a statement of Nin's literary principles as one could wish, giving added value to volume 4 of the *Diary*. Through the manuscript diary, Nin was able to learn to develop the habit of honesty, of writing intensely with improvisation, spontaneity, enthusiasm, and naturalness. "Dreams pass into the reality of action. From the action stems the dream again; and this interdependence produces the highest form of living. I have been able to make these transitions. I have passed from one to the other" (ibid., 4: 150). With variations on a theme, with expanded expression, she aimed at truth and psychological reality, what she terms "emotional algebra" (ibid., 4: 151), which is the quest to depict emotional reality with the language of emotion and the senses. Her theme is harmony, to restore modern people to basic relationships, and to reduce the separateness and divisions among people. In this quest the diary has been her aid, she tells us, because it means a personal relation to all things and people. Surely this is usually the case and part of the immense attractiveness of the *Diary*, as we are able to encounter it. In volume 4, Nin is writing from the vantage point of the period from 1970 to 1971; she had been able to see what the response was to the first three volumes, and apparently she was not to view the value of the diary in her life in quite the same way that she does in the first three volumes (partly because she may have had different uses for the diary between 1931 and 1934 from the uses during the period from 1944 to 1947). Ironically, Nin introduces the reader so well to the psychological complexities of human beings that one must necessarily respond cautiously to her assertion that "the real Anaïs is in the diary" (ibid., 4: 105). It is impossible for us—or her—to know to what extent the persona in the *Diary* is a reflection of Anaïs Nin's complex human roles in what is sometimes called real life.

THE YOUNG AND THE OLD

Youth and age are amply represented in volume 4; in fact, the dichotomy outlined by Nin is more radical than any she suggests elsewhere. On the one hand we have the younger set, chiefly young men represented by Gore Vidal, Leonard W., Pablo, Kendall, and the recurring allusions to Caspar Hauser. On the other hand we have Edmund Wilson who, though he was once Nin's literary benefactor, increasingly symbolizes for her the dullness and rigidity of an older, more traditional generation than those of her young friends.

Leonard W. and Pablo were young men who gravitated toward the freedom and acceptance that they found with Nin and her friends. Along with other of her "children," they were rebels against ordinary values and cultural taboos. She welcomed their openness and vulnerability; they were, Nin states, a "relief from tight, closed, hard, harsh worlds" (*Diary*, 4: 88). The contrast between them and Wilson was striking, probably because in part he openly expressed his hatred for young writers, and also because he was looking consistently toward the past for his values (read Jane Austen, he told her; you can learn something about how to write novels). All of this points more and more toward one truth: Nin warmed to the adolescents because she found them more accepting of her. She asserted that she was not with them to guide them, but "because I feel as they do, act and think as they do" (ibid., 4: 95). Nin explicitly emphasized the contrast with Wilson, sometimes devoting one paragraph to the adolescents with the next being a contrasting one disparaging Wilson. For her the youths represented fluidity and spontaneity; Wilson, rigidity, heaviness, and tradition. His response to *This Hunger* was lacking, and to let him and his values be made explicit to the reader, Nin reprints virtually all of his review, as she does Diana Trilling's. Anyone who is acquainted with Nin's values will find a high degree of consistency in the antithetical qualities that she perceived in the youths and in Wilson; to some extent she echoes here (and in much of her work) the values she first absorbed from D. H. Lawrence: the positiveness of the physically expansive, the feeling, the subtle, the luminous. Wilson always demanded; his opinions were dogmatically to be subscribed to; and, worst of all, he became for Nin an embodiment of MAN "who misused his power, to dominate woman"(ibid., 4: 142). She saw in him one who would bend her will to his, depriving her of her aspirations, liberty, beliefs, and development. Wilson was not only strong, but hardened.

A recurring motif in the fourth volume of the *Diary* is Nin's continuing allusions to Jakob Wassermann's Caspar Hauser, the story of a dreamer who is destroyed by the world (and far more beautiful than the story of Christ, Nin allows). As a child Hauser was imprisoned, then abandoned to strangers, after which power, "intrigue, evil cynicism join to murder him. Never was the ugliness of the world more clearly depicted. Caspar Hauser died at seventeen" (*Diary*, 4: 64). Hauser's story is that as a child he

> is imprisoned for fifteen years in darkness, through the intrigue of a powerful adult world (royalty here stands for power). Then he is freed, accidentally, in a strange city. His honesty, his direct statements, his acts seem so strange to the adult world. They adopt him, and at the same time seek to convert him to their ways. They feel he is different. He keeps a diary. He destroys the diary because he feels they are trying to violate his secrets. He has a dream (or a recollection) of another world. It is a dream of a castle. Behind the door stands his beautiful mother. He wants to return to this castle and find his mother behind the closed door. The woman who could have loved him and saved his life did not dare transgress the barrier of age. He died because he was unprotected. [Ibid., 4: 101-2]

Though Hauser was no poet, his affinities with the young impressed Nin, as did Wallace Fowlie's dictum that in every poet there is a man, a woman, and a child; in the poet, the child or the adolescent never dies. The rigidities of maturity are never firmly established in the young; change is possible. The innocence of the young is to be encouraged and nurtured; the alternative is the arrogance of Edmund Wilson.

The other important young man in her life at this time was Gore Vidal. Clear, bright, and attractive, he knew of *Under a Glass Bell* before he met Nin at a lecture at the Y.M.H.A. given by Kimon Friar in November 1945. In contrast to the developing adolescents like Leonard W., Vidal was sure of his direction, aspiring to become president of the United States. He identified with Richard II, the king-poet. Nin wrote of Vidal, "He is full of pride, conceals his sensitiveness, and oscillates between hardness and softness. He is dual. He is capable of feeling, but I sense a distortion in his vision" (*Diary*, 4: 105). Rather than being shrouded in the mists of adolescence, Vidal is clear-eyed in his quest for the good life; Nin read the novel he was writing and perceived action in it, but no feeling. She wondered if there were a potential warmth in him, or whether he would be another Hemingway. His detachment and casualness made him distrust close relationships; being involved meant getting hurt. Curiously, Vidal seemed to combine the arrogance and loneliness of age with the vitality of youth; he consciously tried to establish a contrast between himself and the other adolescent young men among Nin's friends. Nin admired his quickness and his intelligence, but the direction of his writing distressed her. His quest for power, conquest, and domination came forth when he was in the outside world; she eventually discovered in his past the beginnings of his defensive shell, which she terms "America's most active contribution to the formation of character. A tough hide. Grow it early" (ibid., 4: 144). His prosaic and literal novel she found very disappointing, cruel, and cynical. Vidal clearly became, for a time, a very close friend of Nin's; but she became disenchanted with him and wondered after some time if she had projected upon him the positive qualities that she thought she had seen in him.

In terms of personalities discussed in volume 4, there is no scarcity of interesting people: Martha Jaeger, a psychoanalyst, figures early in this volume as a confidante, advisor, and friend to Nin; Frances Brown continues her friendship with the diarist, urging Nin always toward more realism in her fiction writing; Wallace Fowlie, a scholar at Yale, impresses her with his knowledge of French literature. Nin and her other friends act from time to time in films for Maya Deren; Kendall, a nineteen-year-old, is another young man with whom she feels a close affinity and with whom she corresponds at length; during her trip to California she meets the great collagist, Jean Varda, in Monterey, and is delighted by him; Lloyd Wright, a superior architect, meets Nin in Los Angeles and shows her some models of buildings he had designed.

A final critical estimate of volume 4 might include some of the following observations. Although the quantity of material printed here is less than in any other volume, the quality is largely the same as in the third. Probably it is inferior to volumes 1 and 2 because of its fragmented nature. The ideas, the humane and psychological perspectives presented to the reader, are quite as enticing and winning as in any of the earlier volumes. The form is less engaging, chiefly because the continuity is not so well sustained as in the earlier volumes. Many characters appear here, but few are presented in any depth; even the persona of the diarist herself is muted and less prominent, perhaps because there are fewer crises presented in this volume than in the earlier ones. The reader is allowed to see the fiction writer at a closer view than ever before, however. Necessarily, some of the ideas seem repetitive because many of them (or variations on them) have appeared previously in other volumes of the *Diary*. Even though high drama is lacking here, the reader may be interested to see Nin moving steadily toward her dream of literary success and acceptance in a culture that she deemed hostile, superficial, and underdeveloped in the qualities that she valued most; her continuing sense of mission is kept before the reader, and one can sense her consistent approach to life, both in her writing and in her personal relationships. This very consistency may suggest that the *Diary* is carefully edited, so that only a sympathetic and controlled persona is allowed to emerge. Such an emergence, however, is not unique to this volume.

15

Volume 5, 1947-1955

The fifth volume of the *Diary* (1974) was taken from the seventy-fifth through the eighty-eighth volumes of the manuscript diaries. Of the first five volumes to appear, this is the most different from the other four; it is far more fragmented and less sustained than earlier contributions to the series. Relative to its predecessors, it lacks coherence and unity, and although some themes such as sympathy, analysis, and fiction writing reappear that are discussed in earlier volumes, no clear focus emerges and no clear theme is developed. It contrasts strikingly with a work like the first volume (1931-34) with its dramatic characterizations of Henry Miller and June and the detailed description of their ambivalent relationship. The highly fragmented nature of volume 5 may echo the disequilibrium in life that is generated by a number of factors. Nin's frequent traveling to Mexico and San Francisco and her trips back and forth between Los Angeles and New York and to Paris must have served to keep her unsettled. The incoherence and lack of sustained development in the *Diary* may well reproduce for the reader the diarist's agitated condition. During these years we see the Nin persona suffer from depression and attendant emotional problems as well as physical illnesses. The death of her parents contributed significantly to problems she already was facing. It is a time when Nin's literary achievement is thought by some to be uneven, signaled by the publication of *The Four-Chambered Heart* (1950) and *A Spy in the House of Love* (1954). The critics continue to serve up a considerable portion of adverse judgment about her work, and though she retains a coterie of admirers who praise her novels, she seems at this time to have begun seriously to turn to the diary as her major work, with an eye toward eventual publication.

In all its fragmentation, it may well be that volume 5, edited carefully, stands as a masterpiece of verisimilitude, imaging in its form with short, undeveloped passages (the Fall 1948 section receives fewer than three full pages)[2] the disconnected nature of her encounters during these years. Other possibilites come to mind: it may be that during the years of editing the fifth volume, presumably between 1971 and 1974, Nin chose to alter or redirect her characterization of herself from earlier volumes. No doubt that self had changed, and the nature of the diary entries must have revealed a different Anaïs Nin to both editors.

TRAVEL, 1947–1955

To designate Nin's traveling during these years as a major aspect of the fifth volume is to indicate that her travels were perhaps an obsession. It is difficult usually to tell what motivation lay behind the extensiveness and especially the frequency with which she visited various areas. Sometimes, as with the journey to Mexico that opens the volume, it was an extension of a trip related earlier, in this case the trip to the west coast of the United States in 1947 and the journey to Mexico serve as well as a transitional device, linking the last episode of volume 4 of the *Diary* to the first in volume 5. At other times her journeys were generated by her need for surgery, or arrangements for lectures, along with a general transplanting from Greenwich Village in New York City to the small community of Sierra Madre near Los Angeles. Frequently no explanation is given for the persona's changing locale or living in a particular city at a specific time. This high rate of movement stands in contrast to the general stability outlined in earlier volumes of the *Diary*; to be sure, there are side excursions in all of them, but for the most part volumes 1 and 2 take place in Paris, and volumes 3 and 4 are set in New York City. In the fifth volume there is no center; rather, the chief motifs of geographical movement and disconnection are graphically represented time and time again, as are Nin's disconnections with the publishers, with her deceased parents, and with aspects of herself, resulting in an ongoing consultation with her revered psychoanalyst, Dr. Inge Bogner. Dr. Bogner's role in the *Diary* is one of a confidante who can reveal to Nin patterns in her behavior and who can account for Nin's recurring depressions. And yet, for all this, Dr. Bogner is kept largely in the background and is used as a device for the diarist to bring the reader revelations passed on to her by the analyst.

The impact of Mexico was particularly strong on Nin; numerous pages are devoted to detailed and colorful descriptions of Acapulco, the people and their way of life, and Nin's own participation in this culture, especially during the winter of 1947–48. She felt at home there with her Spanish-Cuban heritage, could speak Spanish fluently, and sensed an affinity with the people. She found that Mexicans lived much more in the present than New Yorkers did and that Mexicans were more closely in touch with each other than were their urban counterparts in the north. The foliage, beaches, music, fiestas, and colors all conspired to renew in her an appreciation for joyfulness that she had been unable to discover in the United States. The tropics were not a threat to her as they were to so many outsiders; rather, she became strengthened and rejuvenated. A jazz band helped her construct the proper image.

> Jazz is the music of the body. The breath comes through brass. It is the body's breath, and the strings' wails and moans are echoes of the body's music. It is the body's vibrations which ripple from the fingers. And the mystery of the withheld theme, known to jazz musicians alone, is like the mystery of our secret life. We give to others only peripheral improvisations.
>
> I feel like a fugitive from the mysteries of the human labyrinth I was trying to pierce. I escaped my patterns. I escaped familiar and inexorable grooves. The outer world is so overwhelmingly beautiful that I am willing to stay outside, day and night, a wanderer and a pilgrim without abode. [*Diary*, 5:5]

In time Nin made the acquaintance of a physician, Dr. Hernandez, who talked to her at length about his life that he dedicated to serving those in Acapulco who needed him. Eventually Nin purchased a small house high on a rock overlooking the sea. In the relatively short time that she was there, she gave herself over to Acapulco completely, trying to discover as much about it as possible. She notes, with some pleasure, how tourists were routinely defrauded by the residents, and she describes the strong sense of joy, celebration, and festivity of which the residents were capable. It was a different culture from that in the United States, particularly New York. But, perhaps to avoid giving a completely unreal or idealized version of the country, she also notes the squalor and cruelty of the Mexicans. In all, the few months' stay in Mexico had a reviving effect on Nin, because she was reassured "of love's existence, to see people who could dance, sing, swim, laugh in spite of poverty," and perceived anew the existence of life and joy (*Diary*, 5: 22). In Acapulco Nin felt more in touch with people and with nature than before; her life was relieved of the tensions that she suffered in her dealings with the world. So strong was her attachment to Mexico that she scheduled a number of return trips, including ones in spring 1951, fall 1951, spring 1953, and spring 1954.

To some extent, however, Nin's visits to Mexico were aberrations from a newly emerging pattern in her life that led to the establishment of a permanent residence in California at Sierra Madre. It was more obvious in the early 1950s than now that California was the antithesis of New York City, and even life in Los Angeles is described by Nin as being "not as toxic as in New York" (*Diary*, 5:34), a benefit that she attributes to the proximity of the West with Mexico and the Orient. The pleasantness of southern California compensated sufficiently for the vulgarity and banality of Hollywood. Similarities to Cuba became apparent to Nin. And she found San Francisco to be very desirable because she could work well there, not being "dissolved in nature" so much as in the Los Angeles foothills (ibid., 5: 38).

Her removal from New York to the western states was clearly a turning point, although exactly in what way is not made clear in the *Diary*. This dual contact with Los Angeles and New York came at a time when she had begun to realize that her fiction would not be popular and she turned to the diary for artistic expression. Her dual residence, if that is what it was, is almost a symbol of the schizoid nature of Nin's literary life, in which she was drawn to write fiction (having written it for nearly twenty years) but consistently found the unpublished diary to be praised above all. Moreover, she began to travel within the United States more than in any earlier period in her life. Is it an accident that the frequency of her traveling coincides with that of the emotional problems that she was facing? The fragmentary nature of the *Diary* may reflect the disjointedness that surrounded Nin more accurately than we suspect, particularly when we find whole seasons dealt with in a few pages. On a single page she notes events that took place in Los Angeles, New York, and San Francisco during the winter of 1949-50 (*Diary*, 5:53). A reader is bound to find this perplexing and difficult to assimilate. The fragmentary presentation in the *Diary*, however, may be explained in two ways. First, she notes in the section entitled "Winter, 1950-51" that this "year the diary almost expired from too much traveling, too much moving about, too many changes. I felt pulled outward into activity, I did not want to meditate or examine, it was like floating. Several trips to Mexico, several explorations of the West, several trips to New York for the books, a mood of instability and restlessness, and I wrote mostly letters" (ibid., 5: 59). Second, Nin may have felt the need to edit this volume in a different way from the first four, having had the opportunity by the early 1970s to receive and analyze considerable reader response to the early volumes. If it was a sparse diary during these years, her problems no doubt were compounded as she struggled to add one more good volume to the series.

As though to punctuate this impulse to travel, she returned to Paris in the fall of 1954. She had not seen Paris since the war, and a close friend issued her a warning prior to the journey, "The Paris you loved is dead!" (*Diary*, 5: 199). But much of the city remained the same; the nature of Paris had not changed substantially, and Nin was warmed by the "imperfections, discomfort, and patina" (ibid., 5: 201). The contrast with New York impressed itself once more upon her, just as it had when she landed in New York in 1939; and as in 1939, she finds Paris to be far superior. Even the hoboes were better: not dour and frightening as on the Bowery, but comical and ironic. She sought for her old houseboat but was unable to find it. She found many old friends, however, and best of all, she found that the Paris that she had loved was not dead.

> The lovers still love each other. The Seine still glitters with barges and boats. The fountains still play. The shopwindows are still dazzling displays of imagination and style. The galleries are crowded. The bookshops are crowded. The parks are filled with flowers, gardeners, and children. The shops are small and intimate and the shopkeepers attentive. . . . There is a patina of shared lives, through high literary articulateness. It is still the capital of intelligence and creativity, enriched by the passage of all the artists of the world. [Ibid., 5: 207]

EMOTIONAL PROBLEMS, 1947-1955

For Nin to describe her emotional problems so frequently and so openly as she does in volume 5 indicates the high priority and value she places on these aspects of her development or experience during these trying years in her life. It is not that she depicts a series of crises to portray the depth of her problem, but there were crises. One of the first was the death of her father on 20 October 1949. She had not seen him since they met in Paris during the late 1930s. He died in Cuba. She experienced the normal regrets and guilt about aspects of her behavior toward him, feeling that she should have overlooked his selfishness. In retrospect she recognized how radically different she had been from him, for she tried to be in touch with people, whereas he remained disconnected from them. It disturbed her that their relationship had been incomplete and unfulfillable.

Her return to psychoanalysis led her to become a patient of Dr. Bogner in June 1951.

> I felt that my frustration about the publication of my work was doing me harm. It sapped too much of my energy in fruitless anger. I could not resort again to publishing my own books, as I knew this took so much time that it would prevent me from writing. I felt the anger corroding me. I turned once more to psychoanalysis.
>
> I had heard about a woman doctor who had come to America during the war. Several persons talked about her in a way that appealed to me. I had already proved to myself that I was more honest with a woman, because I was not preoccupied with charming the doctor. . . .
>
> I visited Dr. Inge Bogner and liked her instantly. [*Diary*, 5:69]

Feeling suffocated and overwhelmed by the demands put upon her, Nin sought and received help from the analyst. One is reminded of Nin's observation during her early years in analysis that the analyst and the patient sometimes exchange roles; after years of playing the role of helper, the diarist herself needed aid similar to the kind she had striven to give. With Dr. Bogner, Nin reviewed her attitudes (toward America, for example) to try to discover the roots of her uneasiness. It was, she noted, a "long, arduous quest for self-revelation which few would persist in" (ibid., 5: 83). What particularly bothered Nin from the beginning of her American experience in 1939 was directly related to her failure as a writer, at least in terms of gaining an audience: the fraternal literary life was not available in the United States as it had been in Paris, possibly because of the intense spirit of competitiveness among those seeking publication. Nin always felt like an outsider in the artistic community, and the difficulties that she encountered in having her work published during the 1940s exacerbated that problem. There is, after all, a notable contrast in her life between the activity and receptiveness of those around her during the Paris years and the later years in New York. And yet, it seems that it may have been Nin herself who was the chief competitor; for some reason, financial and commercial success seemed not to matter to her so much in Paris as it did after she returned to this country and discovered that publishers found her style to be interesting, her writing talented, but her works counter to the taste of the reading public. The publishers rejected her.

In February 1953, Nin found that she had a tumor the size of an orange. She flew to New York and was admitted to New York University Hospital for surgery. Great pain and weakness followed. A truth imposed itself upon her: "As the physical body healed, I became aware of the psychic illness once more: the fact I cannot face is that I am a failure as a writer. The publishers won't publish me, the bookshops won't carry my books, the critics won't write about me. I am excluded from all anthologies, and completely neglected" (*Diary*, 5: 106). She lamented that she had to pay to have *A Spy in the House of Love* printed in Holland. "What," she asks, "makes my work so difficult to understand? I do not accept ready-made patterns [she answers], I do not practice the accepted integrations, the familiar synthesis. I am evolving a more fluid, flowing life, living out each fragment, each detour without concern for the conclusions. And it all ends, life and writing, in a deeper correlation, interconnection, not synthesis" (ibid., 5: 107-08). The abstractness of the language suggests that the conclusions may have been drawn from an analyst's session; but it may be that her failure to follow familiar patterns kept her detached from a public for years and years. No doubt Nin's anxiety increased as it became more and more explicit that she would never be a popular novelist.

Nin continued in analysis from 1951 through the remaining years covered in this volume, that is, through 1955. She likened the experience to shock treatment, because it threw her back to childhood. Her faith in analysis continued to be as strong as it ever had, so strong that she asserted at one point that neither friendship nor love could penetrate as deeply, alter consciousness, or give awareness in the way that psychoanalysis was able. By the summer of 1953 Nin understood the degree to which she had been projecting her own conflicts upon others, as she had done with Miller and Gonzalo.

> We fight this part of ourselves which is unknown, which we instinctively fear. Because it was feared we stifled it. Because it was stifled we must breathe it through others.(The June in myself? In other women? The Henry in myself, friendly to the whole world? The Gonzalo in myself, rebel and untamed?)
>
> But the revelation of this aspect in those we love becomes the threatening enemy. We cannot come to terms with it. The proof of this truth is the reversals which take place. Henry and I are estranged, and I have to do my own living and writing. Gonzalo returns to France, and I have to achieve my own violence. [*Diary*, 5: 124]

By 1954, however, Nin was feeling as poorly as she ever had about the destruction perpetrated upon her ("America tried to kill me as a writer, with indifference, with insults" [*Diary*, 5: 157]); and what is so strange, she pointed out (to herself, her diary, and the future) was that she had faith in her own work, a fact that made severe criticism and unpopularity still more difficult for her to bear than ever before. She reread *A Spy in the House of Love* and found it to be "a piece of music, and that it [was] full of awareness" (ibid., 5: 158). She was proud of it; again she had to remind herself that she would need to learn to live as an outsider, in "opposition to the trend" (ibid.).

The death of her mother in August 1954 produced an emotional crisis more severe than the death of her father had caused. Because Nin was visiting her mother and her brother Joaquin in Oakland immediately prior to the time of death, the trauma was pronounced; the separation became intense as she had to dispose of her mother's personal belongings. At the same time, she found herself drawn into a new and closer relationship with her brother, and she partly returned to one of her former roles as a substitute mother for him. Frequently she describes Joaquin as a saint in the *Diary*; she seems to have been pleased to nurture and comfort him after their mother's death. In the days that followed, Nin analyzed and reconstructed her relationship with her mother, noting those unique qualities that her mother possessed and particularly the contributions that each of the parents made to Nin's own personality and character.

During these years the persona was able to achieve an understanding of her reactions to criticism, especially in some of her conferences with Dr. Bogner. The truth was that Nin was so dedicated and devoted to her art, that the validity of her vision was simply beyond question ("I am willing to admit errors in my life and relationships, but not in my work" [ibid., 5: 235]). Dr. Bogner's emphasis on the interrelation of the subjective and the objective helped Nin to integrate "the warring factions" inside her (ibid.). Indeed, the depiction of a kind of resolution of Nin's emotional problems helps to give a sense of unity to the latter portion of volume 5; for, according to the diarist, during these years and the conferences with the analyst, neurosis disappeared and health returned. In the fall of 1955 she could write that analysis had brought about an extraordinary change, that she had gone for a month without depressions and anxieties, or at least that there were only occasional or mild visitations. Her response was not to become manic, but it may have been an overreaction to the pain that she had suffered, for it was at this time that she perceived what she took to be a true and permanent change in herself; she noticed that she had fewer fears and hostilities and better feelings about America. It is, in fact, the eventual resolution of these problems that helps give what form there is to the fifth volume, leading her perhaps to choose 1955 as the concluding date for the volume. Near the end she notes, "It took me a lifetime to find happiness in quiet things—not only in the peaks of ecstasy or passion. I feel reintegrated into the human family. I have overcome the neurosis at last" (ibid., 5:253).

This great emotional and psychological climax of the 1947-55 segment came almost simultaneously with her experimentation with LSD and the conclusions that she drew from the experience. In short, she found the chemical unsatisfactory because of her certainty that she had natural access to this unknown world through art. By way of her writing, reveries, waking dreams, and night dreams, she had visited "all those landscapes" (*Diary*, 5: 260). Although LSD produced a fusion of the senses, she felt that one in close contact with one's subconscious life could penetrate to the depths of wonder, life, and joy. That one could achieve this state through drugs was destructive, however, because drugs alienated and separated people from life instead of drawing them into it. The passivity of the drug effect works against the active living out of one's fantasies and dreams that Nin consistently favored; she wanted to bring the dream to life, not to shutter a person off from life through the dream. And so, in what is one of the pinnacles of her expression of faith in the subconscious, her strong reaffirmation of life, dreaming, and the unconscious is expressed at what she perceives to be the end of her journey through psychoanalysis that took so many years.

> I have to go on in my own way, which is a disciplined, arduous, organic way of integrating the dream with creativity in life, a quest for the development of the senses, the vision, the imagination as dynamic elements with which to create a new world, a new kind of human being. Seeking wholeness not by dreaming alone, by a passive dreaming that drugs give, but by an active, dynamic dreaming that is connected with life, interrelated, makes a harmony in which the pleasures of color, texture, vision are a creation in reality, which we can enjoy with the *awakened* senses. What can be more wonderful that the carrying out of our fantasies, the courage to enact them, embody them, live them out instead of depending on the dissolving, dissipating, vanishing quality of the drug dreams.
>
> I will not be just a tourist in the world of images, just watching images passing by which I cannot live in, make love to, possess as permanent sources of joy and ecstasy. [Ibid., 5: 262]

With those words Nin concludes the fifth volume of the *Diary*; implicitly she recognized the strengthening of some ideals that she had maintained with difficulty for years in the face of enemy fire. The psychological and physical disruptions in her life during this time clearly brought her into the depths of depression; apparently through analysis, however, she was able to understand the causes of her anxieties and found herself more fervently than ever believing in a unique artistic orientation that she had trusted for years. That the diary began to emerge during this period as a work of art in which she placed her faith is also a clear indicator that she sensed her direction to be valuable, fruitful, and promising. An artistic reorientation was occurring.

FICTION AND THE *Diary*

During the years from 1947 through 1955 Nin continued to write fiction, even though the response to it was just about as disheartening as it had ever been. *The Four-Chambered Heart*, a fictionalization of Gonzalo into a character called Rango, was published by Duell, Sloan and Pearce in 1950. Originally directed to Dutton, that had published both *Ladders to Fire* and *Children of the Albatross*, the newer novel would have had to wait "for several years" (*Diary*, 5: 49) before Dutton could bring it out, and so eventually it was placed with the alternate house. *A Spy in the House of Love* (1954) was apparently rejected by Duell, Sloan and Pearce and was published by the British Book Centre. Not only did Nin have to pay for some printing (done in Holland), but the so-called publicity for the book was nearly nonexistent, according to the *Diary*.[3] The first of these two novels, *The Four-Chambered Heart*, "quietly sank" (ibid., 5:59) and generated no particular response. As she records in the *Diary*, "There is a very real, very opaque silence around my work" (ibid., 5: 81). From what Nin could see, there was little promoting of the book by the publisher. The second novel, *A Spy in the House of Love*, on the other hand, aroused antagonism and was not well received; it was a financial failure as well. When one considers that Nin had been working toward acceptance in the literary culture since her arrival in New York in 1939, there was painfully little to show by 1954 in the way of success. She had been able to progress from publishing her own works to publication by commercial houses, but, as in the 1940s, her fiction was not received during the 1950s with warmth or enthusiasm by either the reading public or the critics. It may be of some interest to note that during all these years Nin was able to attract and retain a group of supporters who admired her work, and she was apparently popular as a speaker on various college campuses. But as we have seen in the previous section dealing with her psychological problems, the kind of acceptance for which she strove was not in sight at this time.

When *Under a Glass Bell* was printed for the fourth time, it was published by Dutton (1948). Nin's response to the clippings and reviews was that there was not "one line of understanding" (*Diary*, 5: 25). The "ugliest, most prejudiced review was written by Elizabeth Hardwick in *Partisan Review*" (ibid., 5: 36). Nin was unable to understand the vituperation her book generated in the reviewer and perhaps reacted against what might have been the greatest insult of all, that she was a bore and was out of date. At any rate, when one compares her earlier works with *The Four-Chambered Heart*, it may appear that Nin brought to this new novel a concreteness that had been absent from her earlier fiction. The novel represented her attempt to capture the undestroyed image of Gonzalo in a detailed characterization. The portrayal of Sabina in *A Spy in the House of Love* is more typical, however, and she may have felt more comfortable depicting her, just as she had pursued the portraits of other women in elaborate detail in *Ladders to Fire*.

The publishers seem to have responded almost simultaneously in rejecting the manuscript of *A Spy in the House of Love* during the fall of 1951. A number of publishers turned it down at that time, including Pellegrini and Cudahy, Farrar and Straus, Viking, Houghton Mifflin, Doubleday, and Putnam's. After Harper and Macmillan also rejected it, Nin despaired: "I have raged at the wall growing denser between myself and others. I do not want to be exiled, alone, cut off. I wept at being isolated, at the blockade of the publishers" (*Diary*, 5: 83). The novels caused her isolation and estrangement and had led her back into psychoanalysis. She applied for a Guggenheim fellowship during the winter of 1951–52 and was refused. She revealed her feelings toward the reviewers and critics who derided her work by converting them in her dreams into giant snakes, leeches, and tarantulas. Occasionally in the *Diary* discussions of her novels sound painfully like defenses and justifications for the mode of characterization and the standard by which characters were included (or excluded), and for the general esoteric quality that she knew was evident and recognized in her writing.

In a beautiful letter to an unnamed correspondent, she answers the question, Why does one write? Part of her conclusion is that authors write in order to transcend life, to reach beyond, as well as to record the journey into the labyrinth. She believed that the role of the writer is not to say "what we can all say but what we are unable to say" (*Diary*, 5: 171). No doubt the fiction that Nin wrote contained, to her way of thinking, precisely this kind of revelation. But the readers, particularly in America, were unaccustomed to such an elaborate and filigreed style, such subtle and selective characterizations, and the heavily psy-chological nature of the novels. Jazz, the other art form with which Nin liked to compare her fiction, was also not for everybody and also thrived on nuance, elaboration, and improvisation. Ignored by the critics, omitted from the popular magazines and anthologies, she nonetheless felt that there was an audience that she could find, people who were "not intellectual or political snobs, [but who were] those who have feeling and intuition" (ibid., 5: 164). They were the ones, she claimed, who wrote her letters of simplicity and emotion, and it was for them that she hoped to enrich the language, expand vision, and heighten awareness.

It was in the context of these painful years that Nin began to turn more and more to the diary, not as an opiate or secret retreat in which to practice her writing, but as her artistic magnum opus. For years, partly at the urging of Miller and others, she had considered publishing portions of the diary and had once (in the 1930s) prepared a 600-page excerpt to show to Maxwell Perkins, the famous editor at Scribners. His reaction was that the excerpts would not do, that the diary needed to be published in its entirety. In 1948 Nin still was experimenting with the idea of publishing it and tried to find a way of providing a "flow of the diary so that it may not seem like a diary but an inner monologue, a series of free associations accompanying the life of several characters" (*Diary*, 5: 38). She insisted that it could not be published in its entirety, but might it be converted into a "Joycean flow of inner consciousness?" (ibid.). Tense while writing fiction, she would feel at ease while composing the diary. Consequently the diary emerges more and more as a work in which she might flourish spiritually and psychologically, perhaps because it was a private work, could have no systems or values imposed upon it from the outside, and altogether was immune from criticism unless the author wished to share it with select readers. In a letter to Maxwell Geismar, a critic with whom she maintained a most ambivalent friendship, she wrote assertively of her commitment to the diary following her reactions to the adverse criticism from the latest novels.

> I don't need to be published. I only need to continue my personal life, so beautiful and in full bloom, and to do my major work, which is the diary. I merely forgot for a few years what I had set out to do . . . . I have settled down to fill out, round out the diary. I am at work now on what I call the volume of superimpositions, which means that while I copy out volume 60, I write about the developments and conclusions which took place twenty years later. It all falls into place. It is a valuable contribution to the faith in the Freudian system. It can wait for publication. [*Diary*, 5: 217]

The vacillation here between her quiet contentment and faith in the diary on the one hand, and her urge to press it into print on the other, came to be worked out in time. Perhaps her conscious decision can best be summarized by a telling sentence near the end of this volume: "I think what I should do is to devote the rest of my time to preparing diaries for publication, no more novels" (ibid., 5: 237). As it developed, however, it was to be eleven years and two novels later before Swallow and Harcourt jointly published the first volume of the *Diary*.

To say that the writing of the diary—or the preparation of the diary for publication—emerged as Nin's chief literary activity during this period would be quite inaccurate. But one can see that the diarist who edited volume 5 is depicting the beginning of the shift from novel writing and publishing to diary writing, editing, and publishing. The intensity of the pain that Nin felt at the hands of the critics was considerable; the pleasure she felt in recalling her plans to publish the diary, one might speculate, was equally great.

Two characters who were important to Nin's writing and to her personal life figure in volume 5 of the *Diary*. The first, James Leo Herlihy, who became a well-known writer, was a young student when he first met her in 1948. He remained during these years one of her most ardent admirers and enthusiasts. One can sense the immense joy she received from his careful attention to her works and the inspiration in turn that he received from her. As they exchange diaries to read, one is reminded of the literary sharing among the Nin-Miller-Durrell group in Paris during the 1930s. Nin's pleasure at having incited Herlihy to write, having nurtured and nourished him, is one of the few consistently positive aspects of this volume; her novels were success stories that went bad, as were other ventures recorded in these pages. But Herlihy's possibilities excited Nin, and their relationship was mutually beneficial and constructive. As a result of Nin's efforts, Herlihy became first published. He was, she said, her spiritual son, so powerful was her attachment to him.

Nin's relationship to Maxwell Geismar, the critic, approached being the converse of that with Herlihy. Finding Geismar and his wife Anne to be brilliant, witty, and mature, Nin was pleased to spend a pleasant evening with them; but the ominous note of much that was to follow was sounded when she observed that he was a Marxist critic and saw all of literature only as a function of politics. Their relationship was, as we stated earlier, one of great ambivalence, but Nin saw them frequently in New York. Geismar's initial response to portions of the diary was very favorable: "This is literature of the first order," he wrote (*Diary*, 5: 101). But Nin had continuing reservations about him, partly because of her conviction that politics seldom served humanity and so was of low priority, and partly because Geismar's literary interests chiefly lay with writers from the past, not contemporary authors (and Nin fancied herself in touch with the future). When Geismar wrote a review of *A Spy in the House of Love* for *The Nation*, Nin was incredulous at the prejudice she perceived in it and at his gross misunderstanding of the novel. The emotional levels of the novel, she felt, were lost on him; he, too, was part of the unfeeling majority, and Nin's letter responding to the review is defensive and bitter. Her later view of him was that he withdrew into the sterile world of William Dean Howells rather than to try to stay in touch with the living literature of the present. Eventually Nin made her peace with him, and she realized that not only had she overreacted to his critique of her novel, but that she had cast him into the dehumanized role of *critic*. She wished that he had responded in his review in the same way he had to her on the telephone when he told her of the novel, "the book is alive" (ibid., 5: 232). The two portraits of Herlihy and Geismar provide a good context in which Nin was able to present responses to her writing as well as her reaction to them. And for the most part, these two depictions are not characteristic of volume 5 of the *Diary*, which contains an inordinate number of short, often weak, biographical sketches of some persons known to her but who do not always come alive for the reader.

One cannot read the fifth volume of the *Diary* without sympathizing with Nin. By this time she realized that success and popularity as a fiction writer were not going to be hers. The added weight of emotional disturbances and anxieties (the death of her parents, the severity of the reviews) compounded the pain, forcing any sensitive reader to appreciate Nin's feelings. She is, above all, able to communicate time and again her devotion to her writing and her faith in her own version of fiction, which is to say, the consistency of her portrait of the persona of Anaïs Nin is not to be questioned. And yet all the pain that Nin felt during these years is tremendously ameliorated, like the pain of a bad dream, when the reader realizes that it is a nightmare from which she would awaken at a later date, at a time when the *Diary* (the very book the reader is reading) would turn out to be a huge success, the financial and literary success that had eluded Nin for all those years. The complicating imposition of this knowledge backward onto the pains she suffered from the Geismars, Hardwicks, and others, helps to give this fragmentary *Diary* unity of concept and emotion. But the final estimate must remain that as a whole work, volume 5, because of its fragmented nature, is difficult to assimilate, and the chief themes do not emerge so readily as in earlier volumes.

16

Volume 6, 1955–1966

The sixth volume of the *Diary* (1976) covers the period in Nin's career up to the point when volume 1 was favorably received by reviewers during the spring of 1966. The sixth is different from the earlier five volumes in a number of ways: it deals with more years; it has more pages of text; and it has more balance and structure, so far as the entries are concerned (almost to a fault, because the divisions are usually strictly seasonal). It cannot rival the first two volumes, which detail Nin's relationship with her literary associates in Paris; it lacks the unity, coherence, and drama that make those early volumes so powerful and engaging. On the other hand, it is not so fragmentary as volumes 3, 4, and 5. It may move slowly and at times by fits and starts, but move it does from a point in 1955 when the diarist still found her literary career frustrated by hostile publishers (and reviewers) to the time in 1966 when the *Diary* became a published reality, when fame and success finally reached the persevering writer.

Nin claims more than once that during these years the diary had become the Diary of Others: "I have decided to retire as the major character of this diary," she wrote in the winter of 1962/63; from that point on it was to be called the *Journal des Autres* ("Diary of Others") [*Diary*, 6:319]. The suggestion that prior to this time Nin was the central character will be acknowledged by those who have read the first five volumes; that Nin could express this fact so openly in volume 6 may come as a surprise to some. In fact, however, the openness of this disclosure is characteristic of the tone of this volume; the persona

252

retires quietly into the background, the mood is relaxed. Nin does not have to hold center stage, but focuses attention on her friends, neighbors, developments in her career, or obstacles she faced. With what appears to be more candor than in earlier volumes, she discusses the copying and editing of her diary, not just to prepare it for publication, but to round it out and fill it in, as she says. Nin may have felt free to discuss some aspects of editing, because the success and popularity of the *Diary* gave her new confidence. She claims that the tensions and conflicts of early years have become resolved, and certainly the tone of volume 6 confirms her claim. It is surely possible, however, that when she edited the diaries of 1955-66 from the vantage point of the mid seventies, those years that brought the first publication of the *Diary* may have seemed in retrospect more splendid than they actually were at the time; such a view might well affect the tone, along with details selected for publication thought to represent the earlier period.

The centrality of the diary as a topic, its movement from roughness through editing and copying toward publication, is basic to volume 6. The momentum from the doubts about its value in 1955 to the praise of reviewers in 1966 establishes the *Diary* as the one enduring example of Nin's literary achievement; indeed, it may well have been Miller's effusive praise of the diary that led many to seek out Nin's fiction long before the diary was published.[1] Nin's life during these years, however, was hardly dominated by the diary: it was a time when she continued in psychoanalysis with Dr. Inge Bogner and a time when she assiduously pursued the ongoing composition, publication, and distribution of her fiction. During these years she came into contact with writers of the Beat Generation; she wondered at Beckett's *Waiting for Godot*; she renewed her old friendship with Lawrence Durrell; she fulfilled (to some extent) her dream of being a roving editor for a periodical, and traveled to Brussels, Paris, and Venice. A number of new experiences engaged her and frustrated her; working toward the filming of *A Spy in the House of Love* occupied a distressingly large amount of her time and energy, and she found herself dealing with the first critic to attempt a full book-length analysis of her fiction. Her challenge was to find a way of encouraging him to study surrealism and psychoanalysis, which were the sources of her work.[2]

EDITING AND PUBLISHING THE *Diary*

It may be recalled that toward the end of volume 5, in the early 1950s,

Nin began to refer to the diary as her major work and described herself as engaged with what she called "the volume of superimpositions, which means that while I copy out volume 60, I write about the developments and conclusions which took place twenty years later" (*Diary*, 5:217). The precise meaning, or, rather, the implication of these comments is somewhat obscure, but it is clear that Nin was and probably had been for some time recopying the manuscript diaries. For what reason we are not told in detail, although she indicated that she filled in and rounded out portraits of various characters (ibid., 6:36). And as we know from Gunther Stuhlmann's prefaces to the *Diary*, a selection for publication was eventually made, presumably from the copied versions. There is evidence of reorganization of materials and possibly the imposition of neologisms back into a time when the words did not yet exist.[3]

It is in the context of all this—the copying out of the diaries, the movement toward publication, the sense that the diary is her chief work—that the sixth volume begins. By the fall of 1955 psychoanalysis had brought her to the point where she felt gay and free, less critical than before, less fearful and rebellious. She attributed this mellowness to analysis and once again believed that she had overcome neurosis. She was at peace with herself and in a very positive mood: "Every moment you can choose what you wish to see, observe or record. It is your choice. So you create the total aspect according to your vision. We have a right to select our vision of the world" (*Diary*, 6:12). At this time, beauty and love were her choices. Dr. Bogner had told Nin that independence was a feeling, not something literal. Striving for self-sufficiency but wary of aggressiveness, Nin tried to overcome among other things her financial problems. And her emotional difficulties were not solved quite so well as she had thought: "Blow after blow after blow. Strongly tempted to burn the diary. Unless I go to Paris and live the life of a Genêt, openly, criminal and monster, I will die. The atmosphere of America, puritan, middle-class, hypocritical, afraid of reality, is like a total absence of oxygen" (ibid., 6: 22).

Actually, in the pages of the *Diary*, the persona does move steadily toward emotional health, but the more she begins to anticipate the publication of the diary, the more guilt she begins to feel, "guilt and concern about the contents of the diaries and their effect on others" (*Diary*, 6:25). Once again she is tempted to burn the diaries. Her guilt took such extreme forms that she labeled one portion of the diary

"Mea Culpa" month to reflect her sense of fault and responsibility with regard to her role in friendships. These attacks of guilt continued for a few more years and then seem to have stopped when Nin truly could release herself from preoccupations with the past and could redirect herself toward the future and the possible publication of the diary. There can be little surprise that such ambivalence should intrude; she knew that when the diaries were published, pain could conceivably be inflicted on others, and yet she believed in the diary's content and direction, and so looked forward eagerly to the time when they could be made available to a broad readership.

By 1955, we are told, Nin was seriously copying out the diaries; she flew to San Francisco "to collect the diary originals and have them nearby to copy" (*Diary*, 6:27); in January 1956, she noted, "I bought paper, let the house go, and settled into the diary world. I copied volume 68. I was happy. I was in a rich world. The Press. Gonzalo. Frances Field (then Brown). Analysis with Martha Jaeger" (ibid., 6: 35). The diaries were delivered to Bekins Storage, Arcadia, California; Nin then proceeded to copy a volume at a time (apparently in duplicate), would return the original to the file, and would "send one copy to Jim [Herlihy]" (ibid., 6: 36). The concept of organizing the diaries also was introduced at this time and seems to have originated with Herlihy, her confidant then whose thoughtful advice—and appreciation—concerning the diary Nin welcomed. To their mutual pleasure, they frequently exchanged diaries and responded to each other's work. Herlihy's analysis of volume 55 sounds in some ways as though he were analyzing the progress of a novel: "The person and the writing grow steadily in clarity and wisdom and beauty. It is a great saga of an individual, very possibly the greatest that exists. No important step is missing: the floundering, the searching, the backsliding, the bold and magnificent steps forward in consciousness and freedom" (ibid., 6:44). But Herlihy also added the following comment, which registered in an interesting way with Nin: "You have got," he wrote her, "all levels here, Anaïs, I never found this in other books, sensuality, intelligence, mysticism, and through no conscious organization of your own there is a fusion (you do not organize well, I must tell you that, and I must tell you why; it is not your job) that causes one level to comment on another, illuminate mutually" (ibid., 6: 45). Can a diary be organized, and if so, through what mode? The question seems to have tantalized Nin, and her response to Herlihy's observation indicates once again her growing faith in the artistic value of the diary and her view of its potentialities.

> You did say more than you realized, even if you believed you were feverish and drugged with reading. And the sharp awareness, too, when you say: you do not organize well and it is not your job. This is the problem I am trying to solve. I made one failed attempt in the novels. It [the diary] has to be organized, not perhaps as I tried to, but like jazz. As you know from your own diary, the price you pay for improvisation is that it may sound like fragments. What holds jazz together? In the old jazz a trite theme, New Orleans folk tunes known to all. In the progressive, classical music, for they do borrow and embroider upon Bach, etc. A theme. Yes, it is my job, Jim, because no one else can do it for me. And I didn't do it in the novels. [Ibid.]

The thread that she wanted to pursue was the self, but in America, in "the mass age," to be a self was condemned as a great crime. And so, although she understood the chief theme and motifs that she wanted to present, the problem of organization disturbed her. These doubts and reservations were recorded during the winter of 1956–57, not long after she had written Herlihy about organizing the diary.

> I don't know why I can't give the diary the continuity and unity of a Proustian work.
> I would have to leave out incomplete portraits, scenes, too sketchy at times.
> I would have to fill in more details about character outside of the relationships. For example, Albert Mangones, I do not feel he is all there. I also lose sight of people. When Albert returned to Haiti, I no longer knew about his life. I very rarely resort to hearsay. I do not trust others' descriptions.
> Sometimes I feel I concentrate too much on inner feelings and not enough on the outside.
> I typed volume 66 all day, alternating with housework. Gonzalo, Jaeger, Frances Field, Thurema, Josephine Premice, Albert Mangones, etc. This made me grateful for the richness of my life. [Ibid., 6: 66]

Many readers might agree that the problems of unity and continuity were never totally solved, except possibly in the first two volumes. One might not normally expect a diary to possess these qualities; and yet a work that is offered by a writer to a reading public may be expected to offer either unadulterated originals (in the case of a diary either a facsimile, transcript, or the like) or something that has acquired shape, that sustains interest in itself, and that transcends the fragmentary quality likely to be inherent in any daily record of experience. In volume 6, Nin develops to some extent a new focus on others instead of making herself the chief subject of observation; this new focus, however, helps to make the volume fragmented and works against her quest for unity.

As she reread and rewrote portions of the diary during 1957, she sensed accurately that in those pages she was able to "re-create the emotional intensity" of relationships; the "luminous incandescence" preserved in the diaries seldom remained, however, when she reencountered people from out of the past (*Diary*, 6:85). The disappearance and loss of feeling from the past shocked her, perhaps because when she recorded the portraits and experiences with others she was presenting all the characters at heightened moments. It seems that Nin's perception of the very nature of the diary gradually began to shift during these years beyond the change from a self-portrait to a Diary of Others. As though it happened without her quite realizing it, she increasingly saw the diary as a structured work that was similar to a novel. Indeed, she noted that she would write her novels from work in the diary and needed to find a way "to make them flow together" (ibid.). She may have meant this flow to take the form of content, but the stylizations could hardly be separated. To her own surprise the changing nature of the diary—or of her view of the diary—became clearer to her: "I fell asleep the night before, remembering a 'character' in the diary and adding to the portrait, and I realized it was the first time I had looked upon the personages in the diary as 'characters,' and that it revealed I was tending towards the work of art and transcending the personal diary, for I also began to see it as peopled, in fact, crowded as any so-called social novel might be" (ibid., 6: 146).

During the copying of the diaries Nin's imagination was stirred as she relived (and presumably rewrote) descriptions from the past. She continued to construct a unity out of the mass of materials in which she found herself submerged. In her earlier life, prior to the 1930s, she had devoted herself to the diary; and, prodded by Miller, she then attempted fiction (*Diary*, 6:208). The circularity of her literary progress is not lost on anyone who understands that during these years when she was reconstructing the diaries (the 1950s and 1960s), she did so along lines that normally are imposed on, or grow out of, organized prose fiction. One can understand why she admired Proust, especially, as her model: he revered the unconscious in his fiction writing.

During the winter of 1959-60 Nin was copying volume 70, and once again she referred to the diary as her major work (*Diary*, 6:224). She found when she typed a volume that her past life was recreated with "such an intense pleasure" that it was "worth the struggle" (ibid., 6: 243). At times, of course, she was unaware of many aspects of her past, and the reviving of experiences sometimes impressed itself upon her powerfully: "Often I did not know what I had done, or that I had done it. It was when I seemed most careless and casual that I would miraculously give the sensation I had experienced *sur le vif*. Writing is a curse only when there are no readers. Almost every other occupation gives more pleasure: cooking, sewing, gardening, swimming, but *none of them give you back the life which is flowing away from us every moment*" (ibid., 6:243-44). Even more than the fiction, the diary was well designed to preserve and return that life for Nin, and undoubtedly it sets up stirrings and remembrances of things past in her readers as well. She knew, in time, that the intimacy of the diary was double edged. Although it recorded the freshness and strength of high moments, it was limited by the narrowness of its personal quality, and the diarist wanted to try to broaden it and expand it, even though it was locked by time in the past. She wanted to find a way, for example, to correct the past and show that Miller's anger and rebelliousness softened as he gained an admiring readership. In such a way she hoped to bring past impressions more accurately up to date and to note subsequent developments in the lives of certain characters.

Eventually Nin learned how "to handle the diary. After the diary is written roughly like a sketchbook, there has to be a craft like that of the fiction writer in the choice and cutting" (*Diary*, 6:298). Repetitions needed to be eliminated; portraits wanted to be filled out, which meant for the diarist adding material to that which she had recorded initially. Her interest in making it a Diary of Others indicates a willingness to allow it to take on a dimension and purpose different from the diary of her young womanhood. Her statements from the winter of 1931-32, "Ordinary life does not interest me. I seek only the high moments" (ibid., 1:5), contrast strikingly with her phrase, "What I want is a life in depth" (ibid., 6:25), which was written in the winter of 1955-56. The stages of Nin's life depicted in volumes 1 and 6 of the *Diary* seem to be eons apart from each other. The *Diary*, therefore, not only transcends her fiction but in a sense transcends itself: like Keats's Grecian urn, it "dost tease us out of thought/As doth eternity." Like the best in poetry, the diary is symbolic and suggestive of the breadth and richness of life, of the alterations that take place, whether we will or not.

With the skill of an accomplished writer, Nin leads the reader through volume 6 toward the climax and culmination of the whole six-volume series, the publication of the first volume of the *Diary*. Alan Swallow, of Denver, who was printing and distributing Nin's novels in the 1960s, evinced an interest in the diary, but he felt it would be too big a burden for him to carry alone. And so the possibility of a shared publication began to be considered. At this time (fall 1964) Nin had one thousand pages of edited text in hand; she reedited, cut more, and had her agent, Gunther Stuhlmann, show it to publishers who might collaborate with Swallow. Fear of publishing the *Diary* revived when Nin saw the venture as a probability; her fear of criticism, of hurting people through her revelations, of exposing herself to maliciousness, all these needed to be allayed by her analyst, Dr. Bogner, who urged her to look ahead, not back toward fears that arose out of past experiences. "Meanwhile," noted Nin despairingly, "as if to confirm the old fears, several publishers wrote negative letters" (*Diary*, 6:378). Nin faltered and decided not to publish it after all; but at the same time she maintained great faith in the diary that she had tried for years to publish. The ambivalence, she admitted, was painful. Pages describing her torment and reservations, and real fears of hurting her friends, are convincingly depicted here. She determined, through Dr. Bogner's help, to be courageous, to recognize that the diary is "mostly a work of love" (ibid., 6:381). "As I worked to bring all the fears to the surface, the mature writer accepted the challenge. I solved the problems of editing according to my own standards, my own ethics" (ibid.).

Eventually Hiram Haydn, of Harcourt, Brace and World, accepted the diary for publication. "I love it," he said; "I will do it" (*Diary*, 6: 384). Nin had triumphed in the quest to present her treasured and much-admired diary to the world. Immediately she began editing volume 2. Her faith in bringing out the first volume was rewarded when she read strong, positive reviews from notable critics like Karl Shapiro and Harry T. Moore. With pleasure, one knows, she reprinted in the *Diary* one of her favorites, the "deepest and most understanding review" by Robert Kirsch in the Los Angeles *Times* (ibid., 6: 397-99). Nin achieved the literary success and respect that she had sought for so many years.

NIN'S LIFE AND LITERARY CAREER, 1955-1966

Although the editing and publishing of the *Diary* appears to have been Nin's chief concern during these years, and particularly in the 1960s, it was only one of many projects that she was able to fulfill, and the publication of the *Diary* was only one of many causes that she had to fight for. This was a period in which she very actively carried out some of her plans for publishing fiction. *Solar Barque* (1958), a short novel that later was incorporated into *Seduction of the Minotaur*, received some of her most careful attention. The year 1959 brought the publication of *Cities of the Interior*, the one-volume reprinting (through offset) of Nin's first four novels (*Ladders to Fire, Children of the Albatross, The Four-Chambered Heart, A Spy in the House of Love*) as well as *Solar Barque*. Nin published the volume herself. In 1961 Swallow brought out *Seduction of the Minotaur,* and in 1964 he published another novel, *Collages.* In 1965 Putnam's published Henry Miller's *Letters to Anaïs Nin,* a project organized by Nin and her editor-agent, Gunther Stuhlmann.

This was, however, a time of recurring literary difficulties for Nin, quite apart from her frustrated attempts in the 1950s to come to terms with the diary. The French refused to print *Ladders to Fire* unless cuts were made. *A Spy in the House of Love* was sold to Avon paperbacks, but when the ownership of that firm changed, Nin was unable to have them continue to publish her work. She had to resort to publishing and distributing *Solar Barque* herself. She sent no copies to reviewers, because, she said, "they distorted" her work, and without the reviewers, people approached her work "with far more natural intuition"; and so she was able to arrive "at a direct connection with those who read" her (*Diary*, 6: 134). She noted that Gore Vidal was now a critic, "which means he is cremating people" (ibid., 6: 257). She published *House of Incest* and *Under a Glass Bell* by offset and distributed them herself also. Direct sales and distribution were not ideal solutions for Nin, but these methods allowed her to keep some of her books in circulation during the 1950s, and not long after that the Phoenix Bookshop in New York City distributed her books.

It was a rich life that Nin lived during these years. Well established in the Los Angeles area, she found herself part of a neighborhood, even babysitting with neighbors' children. ("The neighbors trust me with their children every time they need to go out. The idea of trusting your children to a surrealist must be encouraged" [*Diary*, 6:34].) Ambivalent about her location, Nin appreciated the tranquility of California while regretting that she was cut off from the publishing activity of New York. Her highest domestic wish came true when she moved into a beautiful house designed by Eric Wright, son of Lloyd Wright and grandson of Frank Lloyd Wright. One large studio, with huge windows, the house nicely combined comfort with aesthetics. But because Nin contracted pneumonia on one occasion and had to undergo surgery on another, her life at this time was far from being perpetually idyllic.

At one level, Nin fulfilled her objectives admirably during the late 1950s and early 1960s: the more the diary grew in importance to her, the less defensive she became about the quality of her fiction. Occasionally she would encounter, with a vague but true curiosity, new experiences and new ideas. She went round and round with Timothy Leary and Aldous Huxley about the value of LSD, Nin's position consistently being that "if we had been properly trained to appreciate music, painting, poetry, meditation, dreams, we would not have needed drugs" (*Diary*, 6: 131), and that such states as drugs produce can be arrived at naturally. Having experimented with LSD (under a doctor's supervision, as she always pointed out), Nin was not unaware of its effects; but she felt that drug users did not go on to the important second step, to try to connect their visions to life.

Nin was also interested in that remarkable drama, Samuel Beckett's *Waiting for Godot*. It had, she admitted, quality, inventiveness, and complexity; but she saw it as a play for intellectuals, a drama that reflected rather than expressed the subconscious. It was "carefully charted" but came "altogether from the mind, and the dissociative process is only a reflection of the true subconscious realm" (*Diary*, 6: 46). She and Herlihy, although apparently attracted by some aspects of the play, decided that they were not finally engaged by it.

Perhaps the most important friendship in terms of Nin's literary career was the one that she formed with Alan Swallow. Born and reared in the Rocky Mountains, Swallow functioned as a small publisher while teaching, but he later devoted full time to his publishing career. Nin respected him as a maverick publisher and as a man of quality, modesty, and integrity. He took over the distribution of her works in 1961 and was of invaluable aid to her during the early 1960s by keeping her books in print.

The variety of other people that Nin became acquainted with during these years is of some note. Her close friendship with Herlihy continued, as one might infer from his close reading of the diary. Her good friend Renate Druks appears frequently; as do Thomas Payne of Avon books; William Goyen, the novelist; and Eve Miller, Henry Miller's latest wife. Nin met Allan Ginsberg (and describes a riotous poetry reading of his) and Jack Kerouac, a writer with whom she could not establish a close relationship for a number of reasons ("A failed meeting because I am not a drinking partner" [*Diary*, 6: 116]). She read Kerouac and judged his work to be "a chaos of meaningless experiences" (ibid., 6: 192).

Like all the *Diary*, volume 6 contains a number of portraits and character sketches. Some of them (for example, Harold Feinstein's or Mildred Johnstone's) are very brief, indeed, and may have had more value for Nin than they do for most readers. At their weakest, these sketches seem only obliquely related to Nin's progress, and they help to contribute to the fragmentary quality that seems to pervade the *Diary* from volume 3 onward. But most of the portraits are devoted to people who were clearly related to her life or literary career. Some, like Lawrence Durrell, emerge from the past; others, like Lawrence Lipton and Jean Fanchette, bring Nin into new professional relationships. There are others, like Marguerite Young and Roger Bloom, who hold a special place in the diarist's life; and still others, like Gunther Stuhlmann and Oliver Evans, who point toward the future of Nin's career in America.

During the summer of 1957 a friend of Nin's brought her a copy of Durrell's *Justine*. There was in progress, as Nin stated, a Durrell epidemic, and she felt that he "was going to write the book of our century, as Proust did for his" (*Diary,* 6: 103). The remembrance of Durrell stirred Nin to write him; and a renewed and very cordial correspondence ensued. Durrell's long letters describing his *Alexandria Quartet* (which he was writing) and relishing his long-sought-for fame, achieved nearly ten years prior to Nin's own eventual success, are quoted. In the spring of 1958 she visited Durrell and his wife Claude in the south of France, and later in the year, Nin recorded, with some uneasiness, "I asked Lawrence Durrell to write a preface for the English edition of *Children of the Albatross*. He wrote one so off the mark that we could only use half of it. He does not understand me or my work" (ibid., 6: 172-73). She delicately explained the problem to him later in a letter (ibid., 6: 182-83).

Through the efforts of Lawrence Lipton and Jane Morrison, Nin found herself participating in a magazine called *Eve* in the fall of 1957. What they wanted from Nin was "a kind of letter [in] editorial form. . . . A kind of diary of your comings and goings, conversations with the people you meet and reports on things you do and places you go—whatever you think will be of interest to our imagined Eve, whom

I am sure you know very well, for after all she is really you. I can think of no better description of the sort of thing we would like to have than your own reportage, to make women feel they have been there" (*Diary*, 6: 106). Nin collected the best material she could for Lipton and his editor Jane Morrison; one sample of Nin's contribution, her "Letter from New York," is quoted at length (ibid., 6: 109-115). After the magazine failed, Nin was still determined to carry out her "romantic fantasy of becoming a roving editor" (ibid., 6: 150), and she made arrangements with magazines to do articles on the Brussels World's Fair in 1958. She made subsequent journeys to Venice and Florence. It was a new experience for Nin to become so mobile, and it agreed with her. She ventured out in other ways too; she spent a good deal of her time dealing with Jean Fanchette, the editor of *Two Cities* in Paris, whom she had met through Durrell. An article by Fanchette on Nin's work brought her great pleasure, and so it was with appreciation that she helped him with material for the magazine. "I was grateful for Fanchette's understanding. I count him my best friend in France. The magic link. It was strange that at the time I felt bad to be returning to the same old constellation, Miller-Durrell. It seemed like regression. But then I realized it was not a return to Miller and Durrell, but to France and Fanchette. The present asserted itself" (ibid., 6: 190). Nin acted as an editor in America for a while, promising to send Fanchette good writing that she came across; however, according to Nin, he neither answered her friends nor returned their material. The friendship was marred and seems to have disintegrated.

In the United States the diarist faced a series of frustrating and fruitless attempts to see *A Spy in the House of Love* made into a motion picture. Robert Wise, "who always wanted to make an art film with his own money" (*Diary*, 6:356), pursued the project in the middle 1960s; but when the script, which was written by Marguerite Duras, arrived, the portrait of Sabina was unrecognizable and Wise did not accept it. "Another deep disappointment," wrote Nin, "when I least expected it" (ibid., 6:361).

However, there were two significant friendships that developed for Nin during these years. One, with Roger Bloom, a convict, came about after Miller had begun a correspondence with him while Bloom was incarcerated in the Missouri State Penitentiary. Of interest is Nin's attempt to lead the convict to her favorite reading material, which she did by sending him books; she also sent a typewriter, but the prison rules allowed inmates to receive only new ones, shipped directly from the shop. When Bloom began to fight for parole, Nin contributed a written estimate of his character, using her authority and experience as a lay analyst for support. The struggle for parole continued for some years; Miller went so far as to visit Bloom in prison. Even though Nin and the convict shared a great deal with each other in their letters (in a correspondence that no doubt was rewarding to them both), their epistolary relationship seems to have ended on a very unfortunate note. During Miller's visit to Bloom at the prison in the summer of 1962, he showed Miller the scrapbook that he kept during his prison years, a collection of letters, photographs and newsclippings. "It was Henry Miller," Nin remarked ruefully, "who made the comment that 'they were worth a lot of money,' which shocked me. Bloom was utterly without thought of using our friendship. In fact, during the publication of *Tropic of Cancer* by Grove Press, when there was talk of a trial, because I knew what the media could make of such a case, I asked Roger Bloom to send me back all my letters temporarily while there was danger of scandal splattering all of us. He did" (*Diary*, 6: 305-6).

Far more important was Nin's long-standing friendship with Marguerite Young, whose novel, *Miss MacIntosh, My Darling*, Nin encountered when a portion of that work appeared in *New World Writing* during 1959. Nin found the fragment from the novel to be so extraordinary, imaginative, and poetic that she looked up Young and found her to be as delightful as her prose. Nin devotes many pages to her in volume 6 of the *Diary*; in fact, no character is dealt with at more length, or with more depth and obvious admiration, than Young is. Her writing is praised, analyzed, and described in detail. If Nin's great love was the diary and the exploration of self, Young's was America, "the comic spirit of America, the poetic imagination of America" (*Diary*, 6: 213). Her work seemed to Nin to resemble Calderon's *La Vida es Sueño*, "all is a dream, in the end, boundaries do not exist" (ibid., 6: 243). On the telephone Young read passages to Nin from the developing novel, and scattered throughout the *Diary* one finds Nin relating bits of the bizarre and delightful conversations. Young's novel was published by Scribners in the winter of 1965-66.

No amateur judge of character, Nin connected the novel and the author, asserting that the portrait of the person held the key to the work.

She is a down-to-earth Middlewesterner whose conversation soars into the infinite. She is, herself, one of her own most fascinating characters. She has a native sense of comedy with a recognition of American imagination. She studied philosophy, is articulate, eloquent, fecund, at ease in the daily world. She has the power of an epic writer, nothing of the minuteness we consider feminine. She has the wide span of America, its vast epic vistas. Her apartment is filled with objects which pay their respect to the past. She loves her roots. [*Diary*, 6: 385–86]

It is a wonderful portrait of a remarkable woman, and it is one of Nin's most engaging character presentations.

The entrance of Oliver Evans into Nin's life probably was something of a worry to her; it was he who was to write the first critical study of her fiction. In the pages of the *Diary* Nin notes her ambivalence toward the project. She patiently tried to answer his questions about the extent to which her novels were autobiographical, chiefly by assuring him that if he were to compare portraits in the diary (not yet published) with those in the novels, he would discover great differences between the two. She admired the balance, solidity, and integrated nature of his work, as she had admired an article Evans published in *Prairie Schooner* on her fiction. The portrait of Evans is written delicately, and at times with humor. It comes as no surprise to the reader, however, to find that as she reads chapters from his book, she had many reservations; she wisely concluded, "I think from now on I should not read chapter by chapter and leave you free to pursue your own interpretations" (*Diary*, 6: 378). Evans's book subsequently was published in Southern Illinois University's Crosscurrents series. Not only was it the first full-length study of Nin's fiction, it remains a valuable one.

So far as Nin's future was concerned, the appearance of Gunther Stuhlmann in her life (noted in the *Diary* as having occurred in fall 1957) was momentous. He seems to have become Nin's literary agent during the ensuing winter. Exactly how he helped her during the next four years, if at all, is not clear, but he helped negotiate an arrangement with Alan Swallow in 1961, helped her circulate the diary to publishers, aided her in the editing of Miller's letters to her, helped with the editing and polishing of a version of the diary suitable for publication, and quite clearly assisted her in bringing to life many of the literary projects that she hoped to see in print.

Volume 6 is the culminating triumph for Nin. In the winter of 1957-58 she had written, "My connection with the world broke twice: the first time when my father left me. The second time when America slammed the door on my writing. What I have been busy reconstructing is my bridge to the world" (*Diary*, 6: 121). Temporarily cheered by the receptiveness of the French in 1964, she was able to see 1966 bring her acceptance in the United States. The description of the struggle and the conquest is moving and deft. The *Diary*, in all its six volumes, details the movement of a writer from her first entrances into serious literary composition, through various successes and failures, until she finds the true voice that a readership in the United States wanted to hear in the *Diary*.

PART 3

Criticism and Non-Fiction

17

D. H. Lawrence: An Unprofessional Study
and The Novel of the Future

D. H. Lawrence: An Unprofessional Study

The writing of literary criticism was never one of
Nin's strengths, and she never was as good a critic as
she was a fiction writer and diarist. She recognized this
in her literary performance. Apart from her first book on D. H.
Lawrence, she published only two critical pamphlets in the 1940s.[1]
Subsequent book-length publication of a critical nature probably can be
attributed to the great popularity that Nin earned through the Diary,
which made her a celebrity as well as something of a speaker for
women. Aside from two typically juvenile pieces in her school
newspaper in 1918, Nin's first published effort was "D.H. Lawrence
Mystic of Sex,"[2] a short, undistinguished essay that is important only
because it anticipated her first genuine sustained attempt at writing, D.
H. Lawrence: An Unprofessional Study.[3] This thin, modest volume was
completed during the winter of 1931-32, having been written,
according to the Diary (1: 5), in sixteen days. The author traveled to
Paris where she presented it to a publisher, Edward Titus. She recorded
the event in her diary: "It will not be published and out by tomorrow,
which is what a writer would like when the book is hot out of the oven,
when it is alive within one's self. He gave it to his assistant to revise."[4]

The study appeared at a crucial time. Lawrence, dead only two years,
had been a controversial writer during his lifetime, and the controversy
continued after his death. Consequently, most of the books about him in

the early 1930s were directed toward Lawrence the person. Nin's was exceptional in that she directed her focus toward his works and ideas, the themes and substance of what she calls "D. H. Lawrence's World."

The book's organization is logical and cogent, although somewhat wooden and mechanical. Nin begins with a broad perspective and moves to selected detailed explications of the works, considering along the way aspects of background, philosophical concepts, themes, elements of style, and problems of technique. She keeps before the reader the organic vision of life that Lawrence promulgated and views the world he created from many levels. But Lawrence's works themselves—with characters, themes, imagery, symbolism, and special language—are her most important consideration. Her technique might be designated as a modified explication de texte of Lawrence's works. The study is divided into these broad units: first she examines and explains the more important philosophical concepts contained in his writings, particularly the themes of love, death, and religion, along with his attention to primitivism and to women; second she provides an analysis of selected works, especially *Women in Love, Kangaroo,* and *Lady Chatterley's Lover.* She discusses *The Rainbow* frequently, but almost entirely ignores *Sons and Lovers*, a curious omission in view of that book's sustained reputation.

Nin does not begin with background information that is necessary to understand the Lawrentian world but begins even further back, discussing the kind of approach that a reader must take to enter Lawrence's world. She argues that "there must be a threefold desire of intellect, of imagination, and of physical feeling, because he erected his world on a fusion of concepts, on a philosophy that was against division, on a plea for whole vision: 'to see with the soul and the body' " (*Lawrence*, p. 13). A "fusion of concepts" upon which Lawrence erected his world has many analogues in Nin's own writing, where she echoes for the next four decades Lawrence's themes of comprehension, understanding, and consciousness, all leading to an organic view of life.

Nin suggests that Lawrence achieved knowledge through a diversity of approaches, imaginative and intuitive, rather than through a single system. Instincts and intuitions led him to his principle of a living dynamic world in which the only rule is not to restrict oneself to one system: systems restrain the life principle. Rather, in Lawrence's view, positive values ought to be assigned to qualities connected with flux, mobility, and creativity. "The secret of all life," he wrote, "is obedience: obedience to the urge that arises in the soul, the urge that is life itself, urging us to new gestures, new embraces, new emotions, new combinations, new creations" (*Lawrence*, p. 14).

Nin defines the axis of Lawrence's world as "livingness," which is directly connected to the plane of the visible universe as well as to the plane of "subconscious life in continuous flow and movement." Through intuition, instinct, and a central "physical vision," he approached his characters, allowing them to act out their lives, though they also function symbolically. Nin sees Lawrence revealing himself most in the character of Somers, a person (much like Nin's own Djuna) who is hypersensitive and self-conscious. Nin observes that Lawrence's characters often reflect his own feelings and contradictions; especially in terms of sexual struggles, the characters are highly symbolical of artistic voraciousness, the *"creator's craving for a climax far bigger than the climaxes life has to offer"* (*Lawrence*, p. 26).

The core of woman, for Lawrence, was her relation to man. One may doubt that Nin subscribed to this view; yet we meet a number of women in her novels, stories, and *Diary* who base their values on a man or who find their anchor in men's lives. Even in 1931 Nin saw the woman-artist, however, as the "artist-builder woman," one who was increasing in proportion to past numbers. One may get the impression that Nin felt Lawrence might have penetrated more deeply into the psyches of women than he did; nonetheless, he was able to recognize that women spent years living up to a masculine pattern that may be unsatisfactory for them (while admitting that the men's patterns *"had not been much good"* [*Lawrence*, p. 50]). Nin quite properly reaches the conclusion that Lawrence had "an extremely sympathetic feeling for the problems of the modern woman" (ibid.). In his "androgynous writing," he was very sensitive to woman's psyche and captured precisely those delicate details that Nin captured so well: "In small descriptions of clothes he does not see the woman's costume flatly, visually, as men do, but he is sensitive to the quality of materials, to the flow and suppleness, and intricacies of coloring. A hat has an angle, a certain mood, a class; so has the handling of an umbrella; so has the manner in which the dress is worn" (ibid., p. 58). In short, he sees with the woman's eyes and perceives as she does; but he also presents the man's point of view, as Nin indicates through examples from *Kangaroo*. She concludes that

Lawrence was not the first artist to come closer to the woman than other men have, but "it is the first time that a man has so wholly and completely expressed woman accurately" (ibid., p. 59).

In other parts of her book, Nin addresses herself briefly to Lawrence's language and style, the rhythms and sense of his language. She insists that his language makes a physical impression as a result of his projecting his own physical response into the object he was describing. The richness of his vision and imagination enabled him to write with admirable descriptive quality. Nin provides a number of extended examples from Lawrence's texts to show the diversity of his stylistic capabilities. Even if he is surprising, or mischievous, or shows bad taste, he is never monotonous or austere, she claims.

Nin defends Lawrence against the attacks of pornography, "mindless sensuality," and morbidity. Certain readers accused him of being enslaved by sex. Nin inquires, "Who was enslaved by sex, the man who could not see anything but sex in Lawrence, or Lawrence—?" (*Lawrence*, p. 69). In some of the best criticism of the book, Nin concentrates on the kinds of adverse criticism traditionally leveled against *Lady Chatterley's Lover*: Why does Lawrence include crude realism? Why the obscenity? Is the novel an attempt to justify sensation for its own sake? Nin pursues the threads of these implied arguments to the point where she can provide cogent psychological replies. Lawrence, she notes, was trying to renew in receptive readers the reality of sexual passion "which the cult of idealism had distorted for us" (ibid., p. 109). In order to break through reticent and evasive language, Lawrence "took the naked words and used them because they conveyed realities which we were to live out not merely in action but in thought" (ibid.). It is not an incitement to sexual action for everyone, but only for those who feel that they must act.

On the whole, Nin's criticism of Lawrence must disappoint a modern reader in some ways because of the narrowness of its approach. On the other hand, she keeps in focus the chief themes of Lawrence and demonstrates the function of many of these in specific works, and she does it candidly, directly, and unpretentiously. The book's self-announced "unprofessional" nature is more refreshing than not.

Nin's debt to Lawrence may be characterized best as a sensitivity to the truths and values of the unconscious, her recognition that the principle of life is severely restricted when one capitulates to systems instead of trusting his intuitions. The values of life, such as newness, dynamism, and movement, that remain primary in Nin's set of values surely are largely attributable to Lawrence's impact upon her. Progression, myth and mystery, and the recognition of the physical all are positive values in Lawrence that Nin echoes in her own works. Nin once wrote, "If I had answered Proust's famous questionnaire: which is your favorite flower, etc.? I would say enthusiasm! It brings things to life."[5]

The Novel of the Future

In 1968, subsequent to the publication of the first two volumes of the *Diary*, Macmillan brought out the volume entitled *The Novel of the Future*.[6] This book contains Nin's thoughts and critical judgments on techniques of writing as well as approaches to literature, and although it deals with particular twentieth-century novelists, Nin pays special attention to her own writing. The result is a book that is very limited. There is a logical reason for this limitation: Nin's critical sense was highly refined in certain areas, but on the whole her critical judgment was selective and parochial, and probably she felt comfortable discussing those writers whose approaches and values had affinities with her own. Of course, her own writing would frequently illustrate best the kind of fictional technique that she believed in.

Nin had published some of her critical opinions earlier, not only in the book on D.H. Lawrence, but in the two pamphlets from the 1940s (*On Writing, Realism and Reality*). Although *The Novel of the Future* contains some expected analogues with these earlier works, especially with regard to themes from Lawrence, this later book-length work amplifies ideas presented in the two pamphlets and attempts to distinguish between the fictional depiction of psychological reality and the so-called objective portrait of a world with specific external details sketched, which is sometimes designated as "realistic."

Although Nin indicated that her intent was "to study the development and techniques of the poetic novel" (*Novel*, pp. 3-4), her accomplishment is considerably different and may be characterized as a loosely organized analysis of her own writing (its genesis, techniques, and goals) along with introductions of other writers when their works illustrate an attempt or an approach that Nin wished to emphasize. Any formal or organized consideration of the history or development of prose (or poetic) fiction is absent. There is, however, as much thematic consistency in this critical volume as one will find in the novels or the *Diary*.

A number of themes recur, woven in and out of the book: (1) the value of psychological realism in fiction; (2) the value of the dream in its relation to fiction; (3) the usefulness of vitality, immediacy, and improvisation when integrated into fiction; and (4) the continuing value of symbolism, with lessons still to be learned from the surrealists and their influence. In her introduction, she explains what led her to write any literary criticism at all. When she came to the United States in 1939 she was astonished at the difference between continental and American literature. In France, "all energies were engaged in innovation" (*Novel*, p. 1), a war against the trite, the conventional, and the traditional. In America, on the other hand, literature seemed to be written "for the masses" and was "in the hands of the social realists, dominated by the social critics, all more concerned with politics than psychology or human beings in particular. In America the aim was not to be original, individualistic, an innovator, but to please the majority, to standardize, to submit to the major trends" (ibid.). The result was the rejection of Nin's work by publishers who felt that "no one would be interested in books dealing with life in Paris, and that the style was too esoteric and subjective" (ibid., p. 2). When her works finally were published, many felt that she had left out too much of the "realistic trappings." Nin determined that these attitudes raised questions that needed answers, and one product was the pamphlet *Realism and Reality* (1946), defending her disregard for traditional fictional realism, commonly regarded as the proper context for so much prose fiction. She began to deliver lectures, and in time she found it necessary to formulate a theory.

> The theory was not an innovation in terms of French literature, but it was to an America which was almost completely Anglo-Saxon in matters of writing in spite of its many expatriates. . . . Surrealism was an unpopular term in the 1940s. Even recently it was confused by academic critics with baroque horror stories.
>
> My main theme was that one could only find reality by discarding realism. I was speaking of psychological reality to an audience conditioned to representational social realism. With time the nature of psychological reality became a subject of controversy. [Ibid., pp. 2–3]

The present book, then, was part of Nin's continued attempt to explain not only the rationale for her own fictional approaches, such as her neglect of ordinary details in the lives of her characters and her preoccupation with relationships among characters; but it was also an attempt to explore the genesis and growth of these techniques in her fiction.

The volume is divided into eight primary sections. In the first she discusses the dream, the unconscious, and their relationship to literature. In the second she explores what she calls *abstraction*, the presentation of only a selection of key details rather than the whole. In the third chapter, "Writing Fiction," she discusses the kind of psychological authenticity invested in her own characters. The fourth, "Genesis," outlines her first attempts at writing and her acquiring of literary values, while the fifth and sixth chapters deal with the relationships, limitations, and freedoms inherent in the writing of the diary and in the composition of fiction. In the seventh she estimates the novel's future and its potentialities, especially as signaled in the fiction of representative contemporary authors. Finally a conclusion (with a highly Lawrentian orientation) not only brings the book to a close, but takes us back to many of the main themes of her first book, *D. H. Lawrence: An Unprofessional Study*.

Hardly any phrase in all of Nin's work carries more significance than the title of chapter 1, "Proceed from the Dream Outward." The essence of this Jungian dictum hinges upon the word "dream," which Nin defines as ideas and images in the mind not under the command of reason: "It is merely an idea or image which escapes the control of reasoning or logical or rational mind. So that dream may include reverie, imagination, daydreaming, the visions and hallucinations under the influence of drugs—any experience which emerges from the realm of the subconscious. These various classifications are merely ways to describe the different states or levels of consciousness. The important thing to learn, from art and from literature in particular, is the easy passageway and relationship between them" (*Novel*, p. 5). The writer who is sensitive and cultivates the subconscious can depict the connection between the conscious and the unconscious, and "the sooner he can achieve a synthesis among intellect, intuition, emotion, and instinct, the sooner his work will be integrated" (ibid., p. 7). One might wish again for more precise definition here, but the point seems to be that the good artist, like the good psychoanalyst, probes deeply enough to bring up the fullness and richness in a character, for example, rather than to be content with superficial half-descriptions of living, the so-called realistic portrayal of existence. The dream is not only instructive but is necessary to creation, and the integration of the physical and the metaphysical, the conscious and the subconscious, is the type of integration that Nin wished to encourage in order to reproduce or simulate a kind of psychological realism in fiction.

Because she placed high value on the dream-unconscious life, Nin reacted strongly to realism, especially representational social realism that ignores the psychological reality of the characters, wherein lies the very basis for the truth of characterization. Rather, Nin chose those external details that revealed the internal, the inner drama, wishing to elucidate some new aspect in the characters and their relationships, better to sharpen our insight. This quest for meaning was to be achieved through the revelation of the "elusive inner structure" (*Novel*, p. 26), and so one can see that some of the positive values in this scheme would be nuance, fluidity, suggestiveness; the artist would be freed from restraints and rigidities, of needing to provide precise details drawn from the physical context of ordinary reality. However, definition fails. The degree to which these concepts are filtered through the author's consciousness is clear when she notes that she has "only discarded the novel's explicit and direct statement in order to match the way we truly see and feel, in images resembling film sequences" (ibid., p. 27). The flow of images without interpretation is what she perceived as confusing those unaccustomed to anything other than a traditional narration.

As *The Novel of the Future* progresses, one senses that even though precise definitions may be scarce, there was a great deal of consistency in Nin's approach to fiction, especially in her quest for reproducing—or simulating—the authenticity and truth of human relationships. The pursuit of the hidden self, as she termed it, is based on the intuition, but it is "checked against reality" (*Novel*, p. 45) in order to be true to the psychological framework she wished to establish. Consequently, she describes in detail her quest for a greater reality than that provided for in the so-called realistic novel. Characters are composites and contain emphases; transitions are lacking ("I do not always put up a road sign: 'here we enter a dream' " [ibid.]). Superficialities of realism are given over to deeper truths of relationships.

Nin time and again voiced her conviction that literature ought to enable people to sympathize with each other, ought to break down barriers instead of creating them. Empathy and sympathy make us human. "The novels born of repulsion, revulsion, hatred are those I consider war novels. They encourage war among human beings and, consequently, universal war" (*Novel*, p. 72). She indicated that the kind of awareness she was seeking in the *Diary* was the sort to remove the mask, to "penetrate through the persona" (ibid., p. 75) and to find the basic emotional self. Ideologically this coincides with her aim in fiction to focus on the truths discovered by the emotions, with a heightened sensitivity to the interconnection of dreams, reveries, and the subconscious. A pattern among these will emerge, she notes, but it is the artist's quest to reveal them to the reader in the form of lifelike characters and relationships. Nowhere in life, she maintains, can one find an O. Henry plot running parallel to the "inner plot" of the psyche. The true novelist records the "true flow of man's thoughts, feelings, reveries" (ibid., p. 83) but has had to develop new forms and techniques to express this elusive new world; the traditionalists then bring the charge of formlessness against the writers of the new fiction. "The old concept of chronological, orderly, symmetrical development of character died when it was discovered that the unconscious motivations are entirely at odds with fabricated conventions" (ibid., p. 84).

Nin seems to have held the idea that the artist is a communicator for the rest of us. This is not a new idea; one of its chief proponents was Thomas Wolfe, who also indicated that the task—and gift—of the writer is to express what all feel but cannot utter, truths that they recognize to be valid but cannot describe.[7] Nin describes exactly the same kind of concept.

> . . . I stress the expansion and elaboration of language. In simplifying it, reducing it, we reduce the power of our expression and our power to communicate. Standardization, the use of worn-out formulas, impedes communication because it does not match the subtlety of our minds or emotions, the multimedia of our unconscious life. The concept that we communicate by simplicity, by denudation is erroneous. The writer's role is *to express what we cannot express*. He is our virtuoso; he can help us out of our prison of inarticulateness. Man's thoughts and feelings are far more subtle than those he can usually formulate himself if the writer fails to endow him with the fullest range of expression. The writer was at one time the magician who broke through the silence barriers until he chose to talk in the way everyone talks (the man in the street), a language that conceals more than it reveals, clutters and finally paralyzes exchange between human beings. [*Novel*, p. 93]

And although every profession and way of life has its own language, the writer's primary role, rather than furnishing us with the ornamental, is to teach us to "speak as we feel and as we see" (ibid., p. 94). As a result Nin asserts that the writers she recommends are those who command the fullest range of "musical notation," exhibiting the richness of the English language.

When Nin began writing fiction she did not realize that her novel would become a continuous one; that it did she attributes to her habit of following characters for years in her diary. As a notebook, the diary provided the real people for her to transform into fictional characters, with modifications of every sort, with improvisations, trusting to her unconscious, she says. She traces the origin of the diary, indicating that its beginnings lay in her wish to keep communication lines open with a father who was lost to the family, especially as they moved to a new country. She barely mentions here the details of the sources of the diary, discussed in ampler detail in other places. But the roots of the diary nourished her wish for the freedom to write that only a diary could provide; she tried fiction, wrote some novels and short stories, but only in the diary could she write about what interested her. She could be open with herself; she could shed her self-consciousness, and she could tell all. "The secrecy of the diary was a great incentive to honesty. In life (and in the novels) I had a painful awareness of the sensitiveness of other human beings, and like the Japanese, I did not like to offend, to hurt others' feelings, shame them, embarrass them. . . . I was not lonely in life. The diary was not my only confidant. But I tended to let others confess, talk, assert themselves. I found it difficult to argue, to differ, to attack, to assert. So I observed and listened and poured it all into the diary" (Novel, p. 143). Written spontaneously and sometimes on the spot (she would carry it with her),[8] the diary provided her with opportunity to be honest, to reveal herself with the authenticity that she tried to imbue in her characterizations, instead of having to play the part of the false persona she had "created for the enjoyment of [her] friends, the gaiety, the buoyant, the receptive, the healing person, always on call, always ready with sympathy" (ibid.).

The benefit of the diary in terms of immediacy, however, was that it normally dealt explicitly with the present, "the warm, the near, being written at white heat" (Novel, p. 147), so that a love of the living moment and of immediate reactions evolved in the diarist who wished to pursue these intellectual or emotional curiosities. Most of us, she notes, adopt a pose, create a persona, as a defense against the world. Whether such a pose or persona is created in a diary, she does not say, but as we have shown in the preceding chapters, the carefully stylized creation of a persona is discernible. Nin believed that her dealing with interesting and "representative" people who were not yet famous made good material for the diary, and when she later came to edit it, she included minor characters who were quite as interesting as the famous ones.

Even in the diary, Nin believed that it was possible to tell the truth and yet avoid being adversely judgmental, to understand rather than to condemn, to respect the lives of the subjects; for such transgressions generate "alienation, self-defensive methods, and a growing dehumanization" (*Novel*, p. 151). Needless to say, attacks on other human beings help to set up barriers rather than break them down. And so, in editing the published version of the *Diary*, Nin attempted to achieve range sufficient to allow the characters to speak for themselves, as it were, even if the person in question must support "a few frailties" (ibid.). In order to give a full portrait, she chose to leave out nothing essential, to seize upon the basic rather than the peripheral, to provide a full psychological portrait rather than to clutter the *Diary* with personal details that are not essential to understanding the relationships existing between people. And for the diarist to be patient, to realize that the final returns are not in, was of paramount importance, because finalities are impossible to achieve. "This portrait [of a character] is only achieved by a cumulative effect because a diary never ends. As the diarist does not know the future, he reaches no conclusion, no synthesis, which is an artificial product of the intellect. The diary is true to *becoming* and *continuum*" (ibid., p. 153). Moreover, the only necessary excisions from the *Diary* were the unimportant, the trivial, and the repetitious. Although an occasional description was worth rewriting, for the most part the *Diary* took form through the expertise of the fiction writer's selectiveness. In one paragraph, Nin provides a powerful testament to the force that the composition of the diary exerted upon her writing.

> I reached a greater reality of feeling and the senses. The preoccupation of the novelist: how to capture the living moments, was answered by the diary. You write while they are *alive*. You do not preserve them in alcohol until the moment you are ready to write about them. I discovered through the diary

several basic elements essential to the vitality of writing. Of these the most important are naturalness and spontaneity. These, in turn, sprang from my freedom of selection. Because I was not forced to write about something, I could write about anything which interested me genuinely, what I felt most strongly about at the moment. The enthusiasm produced a vividness which often withered in the formal work. Improvisation, free association of images and ideas, obedience to mood, impulses, brought forth countless riches. The diary, dealing only with the immediate, the warm, the near, being written at white heat, developed a love of the living moment. [Ibid., p. 160]

During most of the book, Nin answers the questions of why and how one writes. Near the end she returns to those writers she respected and admired, by implication, perhaps, using them as examples for new writers to emulate: Marguerite Young, Maude Hutchins, John Hawkes, Anna Kavan, Marianne Hauser, Jerzy Kosinski, "the early Truman Capote, the early Kerouac," Nathanael West, Djuna Barnes, and William Goyen (*Novel*, p. 166). And of course there remain the masters, Joyce, Proust, and Lawrence, lurking in the background; but they receive no attention in this portion of the book. Rather, the message seems to be that the novel of the future is already here; its creators simply have been ignored. Portions of key novels are discussed in some detail, their writers defended against misinterpreting critics. And the single writer who is praised most highly is Marguerite Young, especially for her *Miss MacIntosh, My Darling*. "Everything I have said about writing, every attitude, theory, technique, suggestions and indications, can be learned from the richest source of all, the work of Marguerite Young. Her work represents the nourishment which every young writer needs. It is endlessly fecund and fecundating, it develops free association, inner monologues, and *psychological reality* to the highest degree. It is a constant feast of images, both profound and comical" (ibid., p. 183). A long appreciative paragraph on Young by William Goyen follows Nin's words of enthusiastic support. Examples from Young's work serve to elucidate Nin's concept of the novel of the future.

The conclusion brings together Nin's summary statements about the subjects presented in the volume. Wishing to be neither "finite" nor "dogmatic," she implies that all she had written earlier constitutes her credo: she saw the need for more freedom and liberation of the imagination, freedom from the binding restrictions of the traditional and conventional novel, and recognized the need to turn against what she sees as a developing pessimism.

The modern novelist must, of course, reject the static imagery of the realist and accept the mobility of the psychological realist. The new novel must deal with the full range and dimensions of human beings: integration, flexibility, the human being as the purest example of relativity—he is fluid, "in a constant state of flux, evolution, reaction and action, negative and positive" (*Novel*, p. 193). Intellect and feeling, disintegration and synthesis; it is all very Lawrentian, and, labels aside, it signals Nin's recognition—in fiction—of the human being as developing, complex, becoming, imperfect, individual, dynamic, always in movement.

Nin concludes:

> The active, fecundating role of the novelist has been forgotten. We have the supine tape-recorder novelist who registers everything and illumines nothing. Passivity and inertia are the opposite of creation. Poetry is the alchemy which teaches us to convert ordinary materials into gold. Poetry, which is our relation to the senses, enables us to retain a living relationship to all things. It is the quickest means of transportation to reach dimensions above or beyond the traps set by the so-called realists. It is a way to learn levitation and travel in liberated continents, to travel by moonlight as well as sunlight. [*Novel*, p. 199]

Nin was above all consistent in her writing. The values that she maintained implicitly in her fiction are described and at times analyzed in the *Diary*. Her literary criticism helps to fill out the statement of these values. If one approaches her criticism expecting to find objective analyses of other authors, that reader will be disappointed. Nin's criticism, like her lectures, does much to express aspects of her own development and techniques, but it does not take priority over her clearer statements in the fiction and in the *Diary*. The looseness and formlessness of *The Novel of the Future* ultimately may seem to be a flaw, and there is a good deal that might have been dispensed with. And yet, for all that, it is one more contribution to the critical and aesthetic canon comprised by all of Nin's works.

18

A Woman Speaks and In Favor of the Sensitive Man

A Woman Speaks

Owing largely to the success of the *Diary* by the mid
1970s, Nin acquired a wide readership, especially
among college students and women; consequently, two
books were published that might never have been brought out were it
not for Nin's newly acquired and growing fame. *A Woman Speaks*,
edited by Evelyn Hinz, is a pastiche of chief ideas and themes drawn
from Nin's lectures, addresses, seminars, discussions, and private
interviews; the material is taken entirely from the years of the *Diary*'s
growing popularity, 1966 through 1973.[1] Lectures and addresses are not
printed in their entirety; instead, the editor has chosen to select from
these diverse sources portions that seem to cohere, or at least deal with
similar themes. These selections, which are sometimes as short as a few
sentences or as long as several pages, have been organized into chapters,
each revolving around a central idea. Questions and answers that
evolved during lectures and discussions have been set at the end of each
chapter, giving each unit the appearance of being a lecture followed by
a question-and-answer session. This organizational concept of Hinz's
book is better in theory than in practice. Inevitably some of the passages
are juxtaposed awkwardly with each other; and because the editor has
had to choose from already existing comments of Nin's, the possibilities
of a clear direction and sense of unity are severely limited. There is

virtually no chance for development of ideas of the kind that Nin as editor paid careful attention to in the *Diary* and in *The Novel of the Future*. All of this is to say that *A Woman Speaks* is uneven and often repetitious, but many of Nin's themes and emphases emerge in interesting new ways, although those who are familiar with the first six volumes of the *Diary* and *The Novel of the Future* will find many old themes rehearsed here.

In the eight chapters that make up the book, the editor concentrates on a number of broad areas that are representative of Nin's messages to the many groups she addressed during these years. Nin's strong belief in faith in oneself as a positive value is presented with clarity in the first two chapters. The relationship of feminism and liberation (that goes beyond feminism) is considered in detail, as is the value of the wish, of pursuing one's desires in life. The editor includes a sizeable portion of material on one of Nin's favorite subjects, the value of the diary and its role in her writing and living.

Nin believed that modern Americans hunger most for faith, and what she wished to present (in the lecture quoted) was "the one faith that has supported and has meant so much to me all through my life" (*A Woman Speaks*, p. 1). The problem, as Nin perceived it, was that faith in oneself as "a creative piece of work" (ibid.) has been tabooed in the United States (as it has been since the time of the Puritans), and instead Americans have been encouraged to live within the group rather than to rely upon their own inner resources. The theme is Lawrentian: "I want to give you a center of gravity in your own soul, an axis in an unstable world, a core so that you will build a one-celled world with a creative will—the world as we would like it" (ibid., p. 3). Nin never had faith in systems, for only through the personal and intimate can one produce compassion for and insight into others. It is a theme that Nin speaks of frequently: when we understand, we do not judge. Sympathy results from sensitivity and humaneness, and it is the kind of faith that the artist has that Nin would like to see developed. It resists negativity and emphasizes the creative will: if I do not like it, I can change it; for the artist "believes that life is changeable, that it can be metamorphosed, and that it can be conquered, that he allies himself much more with the hero" (ibid., p. 4). Nin sees the faith in the power of the individual as having been eroded, so that people feel helpless and consequently have abdicated responsibility for their own actions.

This refusal to despair can be accompanied by creativity and relationships with others. Nin's interest is, after all, developed out of the historic roots of humanism, and one of her announced struggles has been to "involve everyone in this connection, this contact which comes out of feeling for others" (*A Woman Speaks*, p. 11). She recognized explicitly and wanted desperately to communicate to her audience that we all need warmth, encouragement, and nourishment; but that we find ourselves in a culture in which we are ashamed of paying compliments, "of saying beautiful things to other people" (ibid.). A small and intimate universe, highly integrated, provides channels that can keep feelings open from one to another. To be separated from others is a kind of death, but the cure for the distress cannot be accomplished from the outside. Obviously it needs to come from within, deliberately and consciously. The error, as Nin saw it, was that the culture told people to be generous, active, and altruistic, but to deny selfhood and the growth of the individual; and, she asks, what "can you give when there is no self, when you have no sensitivity, no receptivity, no warmth, nothing to contact others *with*? And this error grew and grew" (ibid., p. 16). She suggests that one place to begin is with the recognition, by each person, that all of us can be hurt and troubled. The search for stability leads back to the self, however, for at its worst the external world remains uncertain and threatening. In an era of hopelessness, when people were losing faith in social change, Nin asked them to put their faith rather in themselves, to retain their sensitivity and not to become indifference to life. Each person has skills that can be put to use; even political action is seen as useful to Nin in a way that it was not during the 1930s. But the salvation of the universe must come from within, not from an external social source. So she urges her audience to have faith in what they, as humane and sensitive human beings, can do to make the world less hostile and more constructive.

Much of the text of *A Woman Speaks*, and many of its questions and answers, are related directly to the women's movement that became a powerful force once again during the early 1970s. Two full chapters are devoted to feminism; one of them, the third, deals with what might broadly be described as Nin's views on the contemporary feminist movement; the other, the fourth chapter, deals with the achievements and contributions of some key women, chiefly from the twentieth century. However, as Nin said on a number of occasions, she struggled during much of her life for the women's movement and women's studies, but also for men. She found when the *Diary* was published that it appealed to women and men across the country but apparently mostly to women, from the response she received in the mail. The label "feminist writer" was hardly new to Nin; because her novels had traced the progress of women for the most part, she had acquired some time earlier the reputation of one who was closely in touch with women's feelings and was a writer who expressed a peculiarly feminine point of view in her writing. While admitting to being a feminist, Nin never believed that liberation could be achieved by one segment of the population but contended that it must be simultaneous. She points out that men have learned from the "woman's great quest for her identity" (*A Woman Speaks*, p. 35); she objects to stereotyping in terms of masculine and feminine roles, although she readily admits that everyone, both male and female, is composed of both masculine and feminine qualities. She champions the men who can throw off the taboos of the past, men who can allow their tenderness and intuitiveness to develop. Nin sees the roles imposed by the past as limiting to both men and women: "That," she says, "is why I believe woman has to work at liberation with men, because we can't do it by ourselves. We have to do it really all together. All races. All men. All women. It has to be everybody" (ibid., p. 40). Nin urges women to continue developing their personal lives, which men seem to have neglected in their progress toward professional goals that have kept them separated from the personal in life. Nin believes in marriage, but not in "the dogma that we've made out of it, the rigid dogma" (ibid., p. 48). She avoids rigidities, traps, and imprisonments of any sort. She rejects passivity and instead maintains that everyone is responsible for the failures and defeats that come to him. From Rank she learned that if "you're told that you're responsible that means that you can do something about it. Whereas the people who say society is responsible, or some of the feminist women who say man is responsible, can only complain. You see if you put the blame on another, there is nothing *you* can do. I preferred to take the blame, because that also means that one can *act*, and it's such a relief from passivity, from being the victim" (ibid., p. 49). Anger, for example, can be directed into creative channels instead of being responsible for destructive explosions. In short, Nin suggests that the best way toward liberation is for one to create one's own, preferably to seek the psychological way rather than the political: then one can remove the obstacles and create one's own freedom instead of having to ask for it. Independence in women was what Nin stressed in her female characters, not heroines who demanded or asked for freedom, but who created it for themselves. She was, she emphasized, talking about liberation in inner terms, ridding oneself of guilt, of being aware of one's growth and inclinations, and "the necessity of considering that sometimes the obstacle is not necessarily the man but an obstacle in ourselves created by the childhood, sometimes an obstacle created by the family, sometimes by our own lack of faith in ourselves" (ibid., p. 56). In her characteristic way, however, Nin objects to the rigidities of feminism just as much as she objects to all dogmatic rigidities in other aspects of life; she does not want to see any group, however militant or well intentioned, force others to go against their nature.

In relation to the sensitivity to self and the struggle for liberation, Nin introduces a third theme connected to the first two, which is the value of identifying and developing the wishes and desires in oneself. Along with William Blake and D. H. Lawrence, Nin recognized the importance of allowing one's unconscious to act as one's guide through life. The phrase that Nin frequently liked to emphasize, "to proceed from the dream outward," is a verbal acknowledgment that one's dreams, wishes, and desires can propel a person into action, and that if one has a vision of one's wish, the healthier the pursuit toward fulfillment can become. In this respect she related something of her experience with LSD and psychoanalysis that provided her with insight into human experience and behavior. One of the most efficient models for fulfilling one's desire is, of course, the artist, who, as Rank pointed out, is one compelled to make his dreams public; for the artist is paramountly the person who has creative will and who tries to bring his wishes, desires, and visions to fulfillment. This theme persists in Nin's *Diary* as it does in *The Novel of the Future*; for her the opposite of the artist is the neurotic, who, in Rankian terms, hides his dream from himself. The needs of human beings, of intimacy and being close to experience, are therefore enhanced by the artist, who corroborates our lives, but who takes us beyond them, through the myth, and gives significance to human experience.

Finally, a portion of *A Woman Speaks* is spent directly upon the diary, both the private and public versions. To some extent the diary, from its beginnings, represented for Nin her attempt to overcome her innate shyness and helped in her quest for overcoming the fears, timidities, and obstacles in her emotional nature. She learned, through practice and by writing in the diary, that she could best form human connections by giving "the deepest self, for only then would you receive the deepest self of others" (*A Woman Speaks*, p. 150). The intimate and living quality of the diary enabled her to capture the moment, and by portraying herself and others at first hand, "by accumulation and by accretion a personality emerges in all its ambivalences, contradictions, and paradoxes, and finally in its most living form" (ibid., p. 154). It was a place, Nin claims, where she could always write truthfully and could depict the richness and vacillations of relationships with complete authenticity.

Nin provides a number of interesting details concerning the composition of the original diary, indicating that she never went back to revise and polish the originals, that no alterations were made, that there were, in fact, no erasures: "In the original nothing is erased, nothing is polished really. That's where I learned spontaneity" (*A Woman Speaks*, p. 172). But, as we have seen in the discussion of volume 6 of the *Diary*, there was a time when Nin copied the originals and then presumably edited the copied version for publication. Nin discusses in *A Woman Speaks*, often in ample detail, the considerations that went into the editing of the diary for publication.

As a whole work, *A Woman Speaks* lacks the breadth of a finished or polished publication. It possesses both the strengths and weaknesses of oral communication, from which it was drawn. It contains some brief and detailed passages containing new information that was not to be found in Nin's articles, *Diary*, or critical materials. (There is, for example, a tantalizing and delightful paragraph on page 261 on how to pronounce her first name.) The major themes, however, have been stated before, in the *Diary*, in some of the early pamphlets, or in *The Novel of the Future*; the book develops and amplifies ideas already known to Nin's readers. Those who want to pursue Nin's ideas in depth will want to read it; others will find it interesting perhaps as an informal introduction to her chief themes and ideas presented in colloquial form.

In Favor of the Sensitive Man
and Other Essays

Published in 1976 and compiled, presumably, by Nin herself, *In Favor of the Sensitive Man and Other Essays* consists of articles, lectures, reviews, interviews, and brief portions from her diary that were apparently published for the first time.[2] But except for the diary excerpts, nearly everything else has been published before. It is a curious book. It has a popular tone about it, and it may come as no surprise to find that some of the material has appeared in popular magazines and travel journals, as well as in literary reviews (for example, *Playgirl*, *Vogue*, *Ramparts*, *Westways*, and *Travel & Leisure*). The book has been organized into three broad divisions: the first, "Women and Men," includes articles on eroticism in women, on the new woman, on Nin's views of womanhood, and other articles related to feminism. The second, "Writing, Music, and Films," is made up almost entirely of reviews, articles, or lectures devoted to some of Nin's favorite artists and authors, such as D. H. Lawrence, Marguerite Young, Daniel Stern, Ira Progoff, Edgar Varèse, and Ingmar Bergman. The third and last section, "Enchanted Places," reveals a side of Nin known to most of her readers, but not in such a concentrated manner; she details in these highly descriptive miniature travelogues some exotic areas: Fez, Morocco, Bali, Port Vila (New Hebrides), and Noumea (New Caledonia). A pleasant travel anecdote, "My Turkish Grandmother," concludes the volume. This potpourri of feminism, book and film reviews, and travel sketches forms a diverse group of articles that have virtually nothing in common except that they owe their authorship to Nin, who is at her most articulate stylistically in many of them.

The first section, "Women and Men," opens with "Eroticism in Women," an essay in which Nin objects to the new style of bluejeans, "which make her body seem like those of [a man's] cronies, seemingly with only one aperture of penetration [.] If it is true that woman's eroticism is spread all over her body, then her way of dressing today is an absolute denial of this factor" (*Sensitive Man*, p. 9). For Nin, the true liberation of eroticism lies in accepting it in all its forms, rejecting the guilt imposed by past cultures, remaining "open to its surprises, varied expressions" (ibid., p. 11) and, to add her own particular formula for full enjoyment, fusing "it with individual love and passion for a particular human being," and mingling it with "dreams, fantasies, and emotion for it to attain its highest potency" (ibid.). In "The New Woman," Nin describes (in a lecture, originally) the joys of creation, of self-growth and discovery, of the new, creative woman's freedom from guilt. She foresees the day when men can recognize their feminine qualities and women their masculine aspects so that people can fulfill themselves completely. The new woman: she is a woman who can "be courageous, can be adventurous, she can be all these things. And this new woman who is coming up is very inspiring, very wonderful. And I love her" (ibid., p. 19). In the other articles from the feminist section, Nin reiterates many of the ideas presented in ampler detail in *A Woman Speaks*. She notes, for example, that the nature of her contribution to women's liberation has been psychological, not political, and she explains the value of her approach. She notes, with some vigor, that practical problems are often solved by psychological liberation; the group does not always give strength, slogans can fail to liberate effectively, but liberation from within can allow women to know their obstacles and problems. The model Nin approves is that of Ralph Nader, the consumer advocate, for he demonstrates what a single inspired person can do for others. In the title essay, Nin indicates that her talks with women across the country have shown her that the traditional macho physical masculine type won't do for everyone any longer; these intelligent and gifted women "seem to have transcended the attraction for the conventional definition of a man" (ibid., p. 46). The sensitive man they seek is one who is aware of women's needs, who gives her freedom to grow and develop, who allows her to be what she is. The new women play no roles. "The new man is helping by his willingness to change too, from rigidities to suppleness, from tightness to openness, from uncomfortable roles to the relaxation of no roles" (ibid., pp. 51–52). Sensitivity that might once have been regarded as weakness (especially in men) is now regarded as constructive awareness to the needs of others. "Let us," urges Nin, "start the new regime of honesty, of trust, abolishment of false roles in our personal relationships, and it will eventually affect the world's history as well as women's development" (ibid., p. 54).

The second section, "Writing, Music, and Films," is an assortment that includes not only a number of book reviews, but Nin's short description of how she began printing on her own press and an essay in praise of Dr. Otto Rank. This section tells us what Nin's tastes are, perhaps, and what some of her literary energies were directed toward when she was not editing new portions of the *Diary*. It shows us Nin adept at writing about music and films, as well as literature. The third section, "Enchanted Places," will be more familiar, in tone at least, to those who have read in Nin's novels and *Diary* the rich descriptions of places such as Mexico and Fez. The South Seas and other tropical areas seem to have had a special attraction to her, as one can sense by reading the selections included here. All of them allow Nin's articulateness and verbal richness to reach their height; her vocabulary is as splendid and colorful as the places she describes.

It is difficult to arrive at a just critical estimate of this volume. There may be something for almost everyone, and yet it, more than any other book of hers to appear so far, may stand as an example of a book that will attract a readership first because of its author and only second because of its content.

19

Conclusion

For Nin, perhaps more so than with most writers, the significance of her achievement in twentieth-century literature is linked closely to her literary career. As a fiction writer she tried consistently to keep before her the same principles that she later sustained so effectively in the *Diary*, but the nature of her attempt to describe and simulate psychological reality was often not apparent to her readers during the late 1930s through the early 1960s and in fact was not made clear until she became one of her chief literary critics and analyzed her works in the *Diary* and in *The Novel of the Future*. The fiction and novels never gained a substantial readership until, ironically, her work was popularized and to some extent made intelligible by the huge success and gratifying reception of the *Diary*. Even *The Novel of the Future* probably was marketable because of the immense interest generated by volumes 1 and 2 of the *Diary*. These points are important, for it was Nin's chief aim for many years to be accepted and recognized as a special writer of fiction, one whose psychological penetrations into character and whose luxurious diction set her far apart from nearly all who were being published during these decades. Only after she perceived that the *Diary* would be her most acclaimed contribution to letters did Nin seem to recognize that her mode of autobiography was as effective a vehicle for her ideas as the novels. It is not the first time that a writer has tenaciously subscribed to a particular approach or genre, only to find later that acceptance and literary success lay in quite a different direction.

291

Nin's interest in writing literature was stimulated by her years in Paris and her association with a literary coterie that included Henry Miller and Lawrence Durrell. Her literary sensitivities already awakened by an appreciation of D. H. Lawrence, Nin began writing fiction of her own during the late 1930s with her friends serving as critics. *The House of Incest* (1936), her best work, is a surrealistic prose poem in which matter and manner are matched perfectly. *The Winter of Artifice* (1939), now a collection of three novelettes, was less successful but prefigured much of her later fiction. *Under a Glass Bell* (1944) is a collection of stories that vary in quality. Some of them were taken almost verbatim from the manuscript diaries; most of them are set in Paris; and all of them are characterized by Nin's unique style and diction, both of which many are tempted to label "exotic," a term about which Nin herself felt uneasy. In her subsequent works of fiction, the so-called continuous novel, Nin presented a series of female characters in all their psychological complexity. It was the unfavorable reception of these works to which Nin had devoted herself so assiduously that embittered her (at least for the time being) against the American readership, critics, and publishers. She was always able to find some group of supporters and admirers, however, who encouraged her. That she was driven to publish her works herself during the early 1940s is proof enough of her dedication and fortitude against what she perceived to be a hostile and crassly insensitive audience.

With the publication of the first volume of the *Diary* in 1966, Nin's career took a dramatic turning, and the legendary diary began to come to life. From the beginning it captured the imagination of important critics and large numbers of readers, although from its inception it was controversial, because it clearly was not an uninhibited account of her life during the years 1931 through 1934. That some people close to her had chosen to have their portraits excised from the *Diary* led certain readers to surmise what else might have been excluded, and from time to time Nin has been charged with presenting a *Diary* that conceals as much as it reveals (her husband of many years, for example, does not appear in the pages of the *Diary* as a developed character, although he is referred to both in the text and in introductory material). More important, perhaps, is the tone of the *Diary*, which simulates sincerity and authenticity but which necessarily is limited because at its most accurate it is likely to be a selected and stylized portrait of the diarist herself, a persona who functions as the chief character. It is this character who develops, whose complexities and nuances are explored, and who finally succeeds in her attempt to arrive at a point in life where she is both accepted and accepting. Many of the techniques that Nin used in the *Diary* are used in the novels, but through verisimilitude and editorial care, and because of the basic nature of the raw materials from the diary, the *Diary* is frequently as engaging in its intensity and richness as the fiction is not. Initially Nin endured charges of narcissism and self-aggrandizement when the *Diary* was published. Whatever the reasons might be, the later *Diary* deals much more than early volumes with others in Nin's life and also more openly with her human weaknesses and difficulties in coping with problems. Through the editing of the original manuscript diaries by Nin and Gunther Stuhlmann, the published versions must be seen as carefully constructed works of literature, even if the construction (especially in some of the later volumes) lacks coherence and unity. This fragmentation, natural to a manuscript diary, came to be seen as a weakness in volumes 3, 4, and 5, chiefly because volumes 1 and 2 are well sustained and unified in many aspects of their presentation. Those who are uncertain about the nature of the persona usually reserve judgment until the manuscript diaries can be consulted, admitting nonetheless that the characterization of the diarist is her own conception of herself. Many questions concerning the essence of the manuscript diary remain unanswered.

The *Diary* has gathered to itself an enthusiastic readership, often among the young and among women. Nin's popularity was never so high as in the early 1970s, when she lectured frequently and was able to publish her credo more directly than before in magazine articles, and later in the books *A Woman Speaks* and *In Favor of the Sensitive Man*. She was never an indiscriminate or uncritical supporter of the women's liberation movement, but she advocated liberation for all people with psychological understanding and psychoanalysis as the basis for her point of view. She held the mysteries of the mind, represented by psychoanalysis in science and by surrealism and the subconscious in literature, in high esteem. One of her chief tenets for self-fulfillment was to encourage her readers or listeners to achieve selfhood by discovering and honoring the true nature of their wishes and dreams, an idea inherited in part from D. H. Lawrence in her young womanhood, but which was reinforced by psychoanalysis and the apprenticeship she served under Dr. Otto Rank. By the mid 1970s Nin became regarded as a celebrity, an important speaker for the point of view of women, and as one of the most important diarists of the twentieth century. Her fiction, although kept in print, is, regrettably, generally not given great attention. Nin was too long neglected, and she has been praised to excess recently for the wrong reasons. Her greatest value is as a legitimate cicerone through the feminine psyche, as an author who shows both women and men that the pursuit of one's completeness is a difficult task that must be undertaken, even though it is unpleasant to do so and even though it might not be successful in the end. She was nonetheless an optimist in a landscape of psychological despair, and her vision was augmented by her dedication to moderation and understanding.

Notes

NOTES TO CHAPTER 1

1. Anaïs Nin was born in Neuilly, France, on 21 February 1903. Anaïs, her mother (Rosa Culmell), and two brothers (Thorvald and Joaquin) were deserted by her father (Joaquin, the musician) in about 1912. The four of them moved to New York City where young Anaïs enrolled in P. S. No. 9. She did not complete her formal schooling, and in her teenaged years she was a model and a dancer. She was married at about the age of eighteen and returned to Paris, presumably with her husband, in the 1920s.

2. Published as *The House of Incest* (Paris: Siana Editions, 1936), no edition after the first includes the definite article in the title. In the first edition, the 1947 Gemor edition (New York), and in the text included in *Under a Glass Bell* (London: Editions Poetry, 1947), Sabina is Alraune and Jeanne is Isolina. The text to which we refer throughout our book is the Swallow printing of the paperback edition that Nin had published herself in 1958 with photomontages by Val Telberg (Chicago: Swallow, n.d. [1961]).

3. *D. H. Lawrence: An Unprofessional Study* (Denver: Swallow, 1964), p. 18.

4. *On Writing* (Yonkers, N.Y.: Alicat Book Shop, 1947), pp. 20-21.

NOTES TO CHAPTER 2

1. Obviously an inauspicious time for a book to appear, 1939 also saw the publication of *The Grapes of Wrath, The Day of the Locust, The Web and the Rock*, and *Finnegans Wake*, to name but a few notable works.

2. For a comment on the different contents of *Winter of Artifice*, see Benjamin Franklin V, "Anaïs Nin: A Bibliographical Essay," in *A Casebook on Anaïs Nin*, ed. Robert Zaller (New York: New American Library, 1974), pp. 25-33. Throughout this chapter we refer to the text of *Winter of Artifice: Three Novelettes* (Chicago: Swallow, n.d. [1961]).

3. Nathaniel Hawthorne, "The Birth-Mark," *Mosses from an Old Manse*, The Centenary Edition of the Works of Nathaniel Hawthorne, Vol. X (Columbus: Ohio State University Press, 1974), pp. 38-39.

4. The first quotation is from "Lilith," in *The Winter of Artifice* (Paris: Obelisk Press, 1939), p. 111. The second is from "Winter of Artifice," in *Winter of Artifice: Three Novelettes* (Chicago: Swallow, n.d. [1961]), p. 55.

NOTES TO CHAPTER 3

1.   *New Yorker*, 1 April 1944, pp. 73-4. Wilson's review is the one of any of Nin's works that is most frequently cited. It should be noted that the book he reviewed consists of the first eight stories and not of all thirteen that constitute the present *Under a Glass Bell*.

2.   The first edition (February 1944) was printed in a run of 300 copies; the second edition (June 1944) consisted of 800 copies. The two books are significant not only for the stories they contain, but also because they are handsomely made books, enhanced by the engravings of Ian Hugo. Both are rare books. Our textual references are to the easily accessible Swallow edition (Chicago: Swallow, n.d. [1958]).

3.   *Under a Glass Bell* (New York: Gemor, 1944), p. viii.

4.   Leo Tolstoy, *Anna Karenina*, trans. Louise and Alymer Maude, World Classics Series (London: Oxford Univ. Press, 1939), 2: 32.

5.   A version of the first part of the story (pp. 11-16, l. 3, in the Swallow edition) was published as "Life on the Seine," in *Matrix* 3, no. 2 (May-June 1941): 13-16. The last section (pp. 21-25 in the Swallow edition) originally appeared as "I Shall Never Forgive the King of England," in *Matrix* 3, no. 3 (1941): 28-33.

6.   *Under a Glass Bell* (New York: Gemor, 1944), ibid.

7.   Nin wrote two other stories that are not included in *Under a Glass Bell*. "Woman in the Myth" appeared in *Twice a Year* 5-6 (Fall-Winter 1940-Spring-Summer 1941): 413-22, and was revised for inclusion in *Ladders to Fire*. "Sabina," published in *The Chicago Review* 15, No. 3 (Winter-Spring 1962): 45-60, will be discussed in chapter 8.

NOTES TO CHAPTER 4

1.   *Ladders to Fire* (London: Peter Owen, 1963), p. 5.

2.   *Ladders to Fire* (New York: Dutton, 1946).

3.   The prologue is a slightly revised version of the prologue to *This Hunger* (New York: Gemor, 1945). It is difficult to determine why Nin dropped it from later editions when it had appeared in each of the first two editions. It may be that it tells too much about her intentions in the work, part of the art of which is in showing and not telling the inner workings of the characters. All subsequent references to *Ladders to Fire* will be to the Swallow edition (Chicago, n.d. [1966]). The date on the copyright page, 1959, is not the date of this edition.

4.   *Ladders to Fire* (New York: Dutton, 1946), p. [7].

5.   Djuna's understanding of Larry's actions (or lack of actions) is just that, an understanding. She does not applaud him or think that Lillian should not try to order her chaotic life (cf. *Ladders*, p. 33).

6.   This opportunistic illness foreshadows Zora's in *The Four-Chambered Heart*.

7.   This story of Lillian and Helen was published as "Woman in the Myth," in *Twice a Year* 5 & 6 (Fall-Winter 1940-Spring-Summer 1941): 413-22.

8.   Anaïs Nin, *The Novel of the Future* (New York: Macmillan, 1970), p. 134.

9.   Ibid., p. 135.

NOTES TO CHAPTER 5

1.   The edition to which we refer throughout is the Swallow (Chicago) paper edition that has been in print since 1966.

2.   We are told on p. 130 that Lillian and Jay are married, but there is no evidence that her marriage with Larry has been terminated or that the one with Jay is legally binding. Because it is difficult to believe that the hedonistic Jay would consider participating in such a relationship, their marriage may be either an unofficial understanding between them or a common law arrangement.

NOTES TO CHAPTER 6

1.   Originally published in 1950, we refer throughout to the Swallow edition (Chicago) that has been in print since 1966.

2.   New York: Duell, Sloan and Pearce, 1950, p. [137], and London: Peter Owen, 1959, p. [137]. The second part of the novel begins on p. 138 in the Swallow edition.

NOTES TO CHAPTER 7

1.   Paris and New York: British Book Centre, 1954; London: Neville Spearman, 1955; New York: Avon, [1957]; Denver: Alan Swallow, 1966; New York: Bantam, 1968 (rpt. 1974, 1977); London: Peter Owen, 1971; Harmondsworth, England: Penguin, 1973. Throughout this chapter we refer to the text of the Swallow edition (now published in Chicago).

2.   We soon learn that Sabina has felt for years that an eye, a person, has been observing her. The lie detector is the physical embodiment of that feeling and therefore functions, at least partially, as her superego.

3.   The idiosyncrasies of the short first section of this novel (pp. 5–10) lead to the structural trickery in *Collages*. In the opening pages Nin includes passages that appear toward the end of the book (pp. 118–25), as well as some that she used before in *Ladders to Fire* (p. 108) and *The Four-Chambered Heart* (p. 166). Other previously used passages occur throughout the novel: *Spy*, p. 46, *The Four-Chambered Heart*, p. 178; *Spy*, p. 47, *The Four-Chambered Heart*, p. 161; *Spy*, p. 109, *Children of the Albatross*, p. 119; *Spy*, p. 124, *Children of the Albatross*, p. 123, and *The Four-Chambered Heart*, p. 167. The effect of this technique is to unify the whole of the continuous novel.

4.   One may argue that because she is not her real self with Alan she is therefore not unfaithful to him in her various sexual encounters. There is likewise some confusion over the fidelity of the classical Sabina to Hadrian, and it is possible, but unlikely, that she is the prototype for Nin's character. See *The Oxford Classical Dictionary*, ed.M. Cary, et al. (Oxford: Oxford Univ. Press, 1961), p. 785, for a brief comment on the classical Sabina.

5.   This is another example of Alan's insensitivity to his wife's individuality. He wants her to be as she was when they were first married, and he wants her to like what he likes.

6.   In his desire to make women into something they are not, Philip is as odious as Alan (or as Molnar in "Hejda"). His fantasy of an armless woman suggests the dancer in *House of Incest* who loses her arms because she has been too possessive and then regains them and escapes, alone, from the sterile house. Her natural state is as a whole woman. In denying them arms, if only in his fantasies, Philip is making women crippled and subservient to him.

7.   Nin read her own works to drumming and chanting accompaniment by Josephine Premice (*Let Me Read You My Own Stories as the Story Tellers of Old*, Sound Portraits: Collectors' Series, first folio, 1948).

8.   *Chicago Review* 15; no. 3 (Winter-Spring 1962): 45-60. The quotation is from the recto of the lower cover.

NOTES TO CHAPTER 8

1.   For a further discussion of this and other textual problems in Nin's work, see Benjamin Franklin V, "Anais Nin: A Bibliographical Essay," in *A Casebook on Anaïs Nin,* ed. Robert Zaller (New York: New American Library, 1974), pp. 25-33. Nin discusses the problems of the continuous novel in her preface to *Cities of the Interior* (Chicago: Swallow, 1974). We refer throughout this chapter to the Swallow text (Chicago) of *Seduction of the Minotaur* that has been in print since 1961.

NOTES TO CHAPTER 9

1.   *Collages* (Chicago: Swallow, 1964). All references to this book are to this edition.

2.   The original dust jacket (as well as the cover on the first two paperback printings) consists of a reproduction of a collage, tinted orange (the novel's dominant color), by Jean Varda, one of the characters in the book. An American hardcover edition is no longer in print, and the paperback printing regrettably no longer includes that original cover.

3.   See also Henry James's "The Real Thing" for an analogous situation.

4.   It is verbatim except p. 7, l. 2; and p. 122, l. 27.

NOTES TO CHAPTER 10

1.   Leon Edel, "Life Without Father," *Saturday Review,* 7 May 1966, p. 91.

2.   Ibid.

3.   Henry Miller, "Un Etre Etoilique," *Criterion* 17 (October 1937): 33.

4.   *The Booster,* the journal of the Miller-Durrell-Nin group, edited in Paris, 1937-38.

5.   Edmund Wilson, "Doubts and Dreams: 'Dangling Man' and 'Under a Glass Bell,' " *New Yorker,* 1 April 1944, p. 73.

6.   Duane Schneider, *An Interview with Anaïs Nin* (Athens, Ohio: Duane Schneider, 1970), p. 10.

7.   Gunther Stuhlmann, "Preface," in Anaïs Nin, *The Diary of Anaïs Nin 1931-1934,* ed. Gunther Stuhlmann, 6 vols. (New York: The Swallow Press and Harcourt, Brace & World, 1966-76), Vol. 1, 1931-1934, p. xi (hereafter cited as *Diary*).

8.   Anaïs Nin, *The Novel of the Future* (New York: Macmillan; London: Collier-Macmillan, 1968), p. 85.

9.   See Schneider, *Interview,* p. 7.

10.   Ibid., p. 4.

11.   Ibid.

12.   *Thucydides: The History of the Peloponnesian War,* ed. Sir Richard Livingston (New York: Oxford Univ. Press, 1960), p. 44.

13.   Schneider, *Interview,* p. 30.

NOTES TO CHAPTER 12

1. *The Works of Lord Byron: Letters and Journals*, ed. Rowland E. Prothero (London: John Murray; New York: Charles Scribner's Sons, 1904), 4:342.

NOTES TO CHAPTER 14

1. Gunther Stuhlmann, "Preface," in ibid., 4: ix.

2. Matthew Arnold, "Wordsworth," in *Essays in Criticism: Second Series* (London: Macmillan, 1911), pp. 143-44.

3. It was not always easy for Nin to convince people of what she was and what she believed in. Miller's excessive praise and faith in her led one person, Harry Herkovitz, to see her as a myth created partly through Miller's eyes. "In our first talk," she wrote, "he saw me as a composite of June, myself, and the women in *House of Incest*. I realized he did not see me as I am, that he was seeking a myth. He was calling on an Anaïs as described by Henry, which bears no resemblance to reality" (*Diary*, 4: 18). Herkovitz tried to plunge Nin back into a past from which she was liberated.

4. Lynn Sukenick, "The *Diaries* of Anaïs Nin," *Shenandoah* 27, no. 3 (Spring 1976): 101.

NOTES TO CHAPTER 15

1. Gunther Stuhlmann, "Preface," in *Diary*, 5:vii.

2. Strangely enough, even the preface to volume 5 is very short, comprising fewer than three full printed pages.

3. Nin wrote, "When *A Spy in the House of Love* came out, Mary Green was employed by the British Book Center to help with publicity. The only thing she did for me was to accept a malicious review in the magazine she edited and to take me for an interview with Barry Gray. This took place late at night, about 11:30, and I was to be thankful for that. She admired him because he had once been beaten severely in a fight for the unions. As if this equipped him for discussing a literary book!" (*Diary*, 5:163).

NOTES TO CHAPTER 16

1. The authors include themselves in this group.

2. *Diary*, 6:376.

3. For example, did the word *Xerox* exist in 1954? (see *Diary*, 5:203).

4. *Diary*, 6:35. See 6:55-56 for a list of other titles that Nin wished to use sometime, such as *Archipelago of Guilt, The Burning Prisoner, On a Bed of Lime*, and *Hit by an Asteroid*. Other titles for manuscript volumes of the diary include *Disintegration, The Woman Who Died* (1931), *Journal of a Possessed* (1932), *Flagellation* (1933), *Incest* (1933), *Schizoid and Paranoiac; The Triumph of Magic, Black and White* (1933), *Vive la Dynamite* (1936), *The Only Way to Conquer the World Is to Make It Transparent. Ne Touchant a la Terre que par le Sexe* (1939), and *House of Death and Escape* (1940). Many others are listed.

NOTES TO CHAPTER 17

1. *On Writing* (Hanover, N.H.: Daniel Oliver Associates, 1947); *Realism and Reality* (Yonkers, N.Y.: Alicat Book Shop, 1946).

2. In *The Canadian Forum* XIII, no. 121 (October 1930): 15–17.

3. Published in Paris by E. W. Titus in 1932 in an edition of 550 copies. All references to this title are to *D. H. Lawrence: An Unprofessional Study* (Denver: Swallow, 1964).

4. *Diary*, 1:5.

5. Letter from Nin to the authors, 30 March 1967.

6. New York: Macmillan; London: Collier-Macmillan, 1968.

7. See Duane Schneider, "Thomas Wolfe and the Quest for Language," *Ohio University Review* 11 (1969): 5–18.

8. The actual method of Nin's composing the diary is difficult for an outsider to understand; there is some evidence in the *Diary* that revisions and rearranging of passages occurred. Nin stated on one occasion in 1969 that she reserved the evening hours for writing the diary (*An Interview with Anaïs Nin* [Athens, Ohio: Duane Schneider, 1970], p. 17). Also, see *Diary*, vol. 6, passim, for more details on the composition of the diary.

NOTES TO CHAPTER 18

1. *A Woman Speaks: The Lectures, Seminars, and Interviews of Anaïs Nin*, ed. Evelyn Hinz (Chicago: Swallow Press, 1975).

2. *In Favor of the Sensitive Man* (New York: Harcourt Brace Jovanovich).

Selected Bibliography

Primary Sources

D. H. Lawrence: An Unprofessional Study, 1932.

The House of Incest, 1936.

The Winter of Artifice (novelettes), 1939; revised, 1942; enlarged, 1961.

Under a Glass Bell (stories), 1944; enlarged, 1947; enlarged, 1948.

This Hunger (novelettes), 1945.

Ladders to Fire, 1946; shortened version, 1963.

Realism and Reality, 1946.

Children of the Albatross, 1947.

On Writing, 1947.

The Four-Chambered Heart, 1950.

A Spy in the House of Love, 1954.

Solar Barque, 1958; enlarged as Seduction of the Minotaur, 1961.

Cities of the Interior (collection of five previously published novels), 1959;
    enlarged, 1974.

Collages, 1964.

The Diary of Anaïs Nin 1931–1934, 1966.

The Diary of Anaïs Nin 1934–1939, 1967.

The Novel of the Future, 1968.

Unpublished Selections from the Diary, 1968.

The Diary of Anaïs Nin 1939-1944, 1969.

An Interview with Anaïs Nin, 1970.

Nuances (excerpts from previously published works), 1970.

The Diary of Anaïs Nin 1944-1947, 1971.

Paris Revisited, 1972.

Anaïs Nin Reader (collection of previously published material), ed. Philip
K. Jason, 1973.

The Diary of Anaïs Nin 1947–1955, 1974.

A Photographic Supplement to the Diary of Anaïs Nin, 1974.

A Woman Speaks: The Lectures, Seminars, and Interviews of Anaïs Nin, ed.
Evelyn J. Hinz, 1975.

The Diary of Anaïs Nin 1955–1966, 1976.

In Favor of the Sensitive Man and Other Essays, 1976.

Delta of Venus Erotica, 1977.

Waste of Timelessness and Other Early Stories, 1977.

Linotte: The Early Diary of Anaïs Nin 1914–1920, 1978.

SECONDARY SOURCES

A.   *Bibliographical:*

Franklin, Benjamin, V. "Anais Nin and the Rare Book Trade," *Under the
Sign of Pisces: Anaïs Nin and Her Circle*, 3:1 (Winter 1972), 11–16.
———. *Anaïs Nin A Bibliography*. Kent, Ohio: Kent State University
Press, 1973.
———. "Anaïs Nin: A Bibliographical Essay," *A Casebook on Anaïs Nin*,
ed. Robert Zaller. New York & Scarborough: New American
Library, 1974, pp. 25–33.

B.   *Critical:*

I.   Books:

Evans, Oliver. *Anaïs Nin*. Carbondale & Edwardsville: Southern Illinois
University Press, 1968. The first and best study of Nin's works,
exclusive of the *Diary*.

Hinz, Evelyn J. *The Mirror and the Garden: Realism and Reality in the Writings
of Anaïs Nin*. New York: Harcourt Brace Jovanovich, 1973
(originally published in 1971). The first book to deal with the
criticism and the *Diary* along with the novels.

Zaller, Robert, ed. *A Casebook on Anaïs Nin*. New York & Scarborough: New American Library, 1974. A substantial collection of essays, many not previously published.

Spencer, Sharon. *Collage of Dreams: The Writings of Anaïs Nin*. Chicago: Swallow, 1977. Argues that Nin's artistic achievement was based on her ability to transform mundane materials into beautiful entities.

Mosaic, 11:2 (Winter 1978). Special Nin issue edited by Evelyn J. Hinz.

II.   Articles (This list is highly selective. Many of the articles written on Nin are either excessively adulatory or harshly critical; we have not listed those, but instead have included ones that in our judgment present a balanced view of her art or are historically significant in her literary career.):

Evans, Oliver. "Anaïs Nin and the Discovery of Inner Space," *The Prairie Schooner*, 36:3 (Fall 1962), 217-31. The best short introduction to Nin's fiction.

Kuntz, Paul G. "Art as Public Dream: The Practice and Theory of Anaïs Nin," *The Journal of Aesthetics and Art Criticism*, 32:4 (Summer 1974), 525-37. Also included in *A Casebook on Anaïs Nin*, pp. 77-99. An analysis of the different meanings of "proceed from the dream outward."

Miller, Henry. "Un Etre Etoilique," *Criterion*, 17.66 (October 1937), 33-52. Also included in *A Casebook on Anaïs Nin*, pp. 5-23, and in several collections of Miller's works. Perhaps the article that has introduced the most readers to Nin.

Schneider, Duane B. "The Art of Anaïs Nin," *The Southern Review*, 6: 2 (Spring 1970), 506-14. Also included in *A Casebook on Anaïs Nin*, pp. 43-50. Discusses the unity in Nin's work.

Spencer, Sharon. "Anaïs Nin's 'Continuous Novel' *Cities of the Interior*," *A Casebook on Anaïs Nin*, pp. 65-76. A good introduction to Nin's fiction.

Stern, Daniel. "The Diary of Anaïs Nin," *Studies in the Twentieth Century*, 2 (Fall 1968), 39-43. Considers Nin's modernity.

Stone, Laurie. "Anaïs Nin: Is the Bloom off the Pose?" *The Village Voice*, 26 July 1976, pp. 43-44. A fairly critical examination of the first six volumes of the *Diary*.

Sukenick, Lynn. "The *Diaries* of Anaïs Nin," *Shenandoah*, 27:3 (Spring 1976), 96–103. A perceptive essay on Nin's honesty as an author.

Wilson, Edmund. Review of *Under a Glass Bell*, *New Yorker*, 1 April 1944, pp. 73–74. Also included in *A Casebook on Anaïs Nin*, pp. 3–4. Because it represents the first acceptance of her work by an established literary figure, this is Nin's most important review.

Zinnes, Harriet. "Anaïs Nin's Works Reissued," *Books Abroad*, 37: 3 (Summer 1963), 283–86. A good summary of Nin's fiction.

Index

Albertine: 190, 199
Allendy, Dr. René: 177, 180–85, 189, 210
Amherst College: 229
Aristotle: 180
Arnold, Matthew: 223, 231
Artaud, Antonin: 51, 177, 183–84, 190, 210
Austen, Jane: 233
Avon Books: 260

Bach, Johann Sebastian: 256
Barker, George: 208
Barnes, Djuna: 4, 280
Beach, Sylvia: 202
Beckett, Samuel: 13, 253, 261
Beethoven, Ludwig van: 128
Bekins Storage: 255
Bel Geddes, Norman: 192
Bergman, Ingmar: 288
Black Sun Press: 211
Blake, William: 14, 173, 286
Bloom, Roger: 262, 263–64
Bogner, Dr. Inge: 238–39, 242, 244, 253, 254, 259
Booster, The: 169, 196
Booth, John Wilkes: 159
Breit, Harvey: 220
British Book Centre (publisher): 246
Brown, Frances: 203, 211, 214–15, 231, 235, 255, 256
Brussels World Fair: 263
Byron, George Gordon, Lord: 189

Calderón de la Barca, Pedro: 264
Capote, Truman: 280
Carteret, Jean: 190, 199
Chekhov, Anton: 198
Chirico, Giorgio di: 138
Christ: 234
Circle: 229
Coleridge, Samuel T.: 73, 167
Collier's: 204, 218
Conrad, Joseph: 178

Cooney, Blanche: 202, 213, 214
Cooney, James: 202, 213, 214, 220
Crosby, Caresse: 202, 203, 209, 211, 218
Crosby, Harry: 211

Dali, Mrs.: 211
Dali, Salvador: 211
Dante Alighieri: 206
Dartmouth College: 229
Debussy, Claude: 117
Demosthenes: 115
De Quincey, Thomas: 167
Deren, Maya: 235
Dostoevsky, Feodor: 219
Doubleday & Co. (publisher): 205, 247
Dreiser, Theodore: 191, 218, 219, 231
Druks, Renate: 261
Duchamp, Marcel: 110, 124, 126, 157
Dudley, Flo: 211
Dudley, John: 211
Duell, Sloan and Pearce (publisher): 246
Duncan, Robert: 202, 203, 211, 212–14, 216
Duras, Marguerite: 263
Durrell, Claude: 262
Durrell, Lawrence: 187, 193, 194–96, 200, 201, 210, 217, 249, 253, 262, 263, 292
Durrell, Nancy: 195
Dutton, E. P. (publisher): 83, 223, 226, 228, 246, 247

Edel, Leon: 168
Eliot, T. S.: 231
Emerson, Ralph Waldo: 77
Evans, Oliver: 262, 265
Eve: 262

Fanchette, Jean: 262, 263
Farrar and Straus (publisher): 247
Feinstein, Harold: 262
Field, Frances: see Frances Brown

305